Data-Centric Systems and Applications

Sven Casteleyn • Florian Daniel
Peter Dolog • Maristella Matera

Engineering
Web Applications

 Springer

Sven Casteleyn
Vrije Universiteit Brussel
Department of Computer Science
Web and Information Systems
Engineering Lab
Pleinlaan 2
1050 Brussels
Belgium
Sven.Casteleyn@vub.ac.be

Peter Dolog
Aalborg University
Intelligent Web and Information Systems
Department of Computer Science
Selma Lagerlöfs Vej 300
9220 Aalborg
Denmark
dolog@cs.aau.dk

Florian Daniel
Università di Trento
Dipartimento di Ingegneria e Scienza
dell'Informazione
Via Sommarive, 14
38100 Povo (TN)
Italy
daniel@disi.unitn.it

Maristella Matera
Politecnico di Milano
Dipartimento di Elettronica
e Informazione (DEI)
Piazza Leonardo da Vinci, 32
20133 Milano
Italy
matera@elet.polimi.it

ISBN 978-3-642-26919-6   e-ISBN 978-3-540-92201-8
DOI 10.1007/978-3-540-92201-8
Springer Dordrecht Heidelberg London New York

ACM Computing Classification (1998): D.2, H.3.5, K.6, J.1

Cover design: KünkelLopka GmbH

Printed on acid-free paper

Springer is part of Springer Science+Business Media (www.springer.com)

To our families and partners

Preface

The Web is nowadays omnipresent: we use it at home for private reasons, and we use it at work for professional reasons; we use it for fun (e.g., gaming) and for serious interactions (e.g., home banking), via fixed stations and via mobile devices, and these are just few of the motivations for and the contexts in which we exploit such a powerful medium. The Web has indeed probably become the number one reason for private PCs at home, and the most important kind of "business card" for companies and institutions. Very likely, each of us has already tried at least once online applications such as `Amazon.com` for buying books or CDs, `Ikea.com` for buying furniture, and, of course, `Google.com` for searching Web sites. Similarly, most of us can no longer imagine a travel planning without the flight booking and hotel reservation systems that are accessible over the Web. We could cite many other examples where the Web is playing a major role, but we believe there is no need for further convincing the reader that the Web has become an indispensable instrument to the most of us.

While the potential, contents, and features offered via the Web are fascinating and attracting an ever growing number of people, there is also a steadily increasing number of people who are interested in developing applications for the Web. If one likes the Web, there is nothing better than developing an own Web site or Web application. Yet, depending on the result one aims to achieve, writing a good application for the Web might be an intricate and complex endeavor that typically requires profound knowledge of the way the Web works.

This book is about engineering Web applications, that is, about developing Web applications according to sound principles, models, and methods. There are many books about Web development available on the market. Most of them focus on specific programming aspects (e.g., data design, presentation design, or Web services), programming languages (e.g., PHP, Java, .NET, JavaScript) or on HTML/XML development. Then, there are many so-called edited books, which assemble independent contributions by multiple authors that, together, cover some aspects of Web development. With this book, we aim to provide a comprehensive book that covers the whole development life cycle of Web applications, that does not focus too much on specific technologies, and that offers an integrated view on all the addressed topics, also thanks to the adoption of models providing high-level abstractions.

Writing such a book was not an easy task. Bringing together the ideas, knowledge, and personal believes of four authors with different backgrounds and experiences was indeed challenging. Uncountable discussions via email and lots of Skype phone conferences were necessary to reach this final version of the book, while we could still go on (and actually do) with new discussions on additional topics and ideas. However, in order to come to a conclusion, writing a book also means taking decisions and keeping deadlines. We sincerely tried to stick to our internal calendar, but only seldom we succeeded. The tones in emails and on the phone were sometimes even harsh, yet fair, but eventually we could always come to an agreement on how to improve what had been written so far and to proceed. Writing a book is also this, arguing and defending ideas, but we are convinced the book benefited from each discussion and, hence, that it was worth to spend the energy we invested into each discussion.

The present version of the book represents the result of about two years of work. Though integrated, the book reflects the characteristics of each author, either because one gave more emphasis to details and technical aspects and another paid more attention to modeling aspects, or simply because some parts have influences from software engineering and others from data engineering or model-driven development. We however think this book provides a good balance between our respective backgrounds and "cultures" and – as outlined in the introduction of this book – we think that it provides a variety of readers with interesting and stimulating contents.

As for the acknowledgments, we would like to stress that many people contributed to the publication of this book. We want to thank them all.

Special thanks go to Stefano Ceri and Mike Carey, who gave us the possibility to publish the book in the renowned series "Data Centric Systems and Applications". Many thanks go to Ralph Gerstner by Springer for assisting and guiding us during the whole production process. We are also deeply indebted to the reviewers and the manuscript copy editor; their comments and annotations effectively helped us improve the book in both language and content.

Finally, we would like to thank our families, partners, and friends for encouraging (and also tolerating!) us during the writing of this book.

Brussels, Trento, Aalborg, Milan
May 2009

Sven Casteleyn
Florian Daniel
Peter Dolog
Maristella Matera

Contents

1

Introduction

The first Web site, created by Tim Berners-Lee and Robert Cailliau at CERN (European Nuclear Research Center), consisted of a collection of documents with static content, encoded in the HyperText Markup Language (HTML). Since then, the Web has evolved from an environment hosting simple and static hypermedia documents to an infrastructure for the execution of complex applications. Several technologies have enriched the scenario and the Web has progressively become a multi-domain platform, offering support not only for information delivery, but also for application execution. Nowadays, complex Web applications, such as eCommerce systems, large-scale corporate platforms, collaborative distributed environments, social networks, and mobile services, are almost omnipresent.

There are some features that characterize Web applications and distinguish them from traditional software systems:

- *Higher accessibility of information and services*: compared to closed intranets or desktop systems, the World Wide Web enables access to information and services for far more users simultaneously. Different modalities and views on data and services need to be designed to support different user needs.
- *Document-centric hypertext interface*: the offered information and services have to be mapped onto a hypertext document. Interconnections between various views on information and pages require peculiar design abstractions to understand and represent the resulting hypertext structures and their traversals.
- *Variable technologies for data management*: data is distributed on the Web in various formats, schemas, and technologies, such as XML, RDF, and traditional databases. Designers need to pay attention to the design of data structures, of the access to external data sources, and of the mapping between them.

S. Casteleyn et al., Engineering Web Applications: *Data-Centric Systems and Applications.*
DOI: 10.1007/978-3-540-92201-8_1, © Springer-Verlag Berlin Heidelberg 2009

- *Variable presentation technologies and engines*: different presentation formats must be addressed to accommodate the characteristics and display capabilities of different browsers and different devices.
- *Architecture complexity*: the higher level of accessibility and the lighter nature of clients (the Web browsers) require distributed, multi-tier architectures for the access to information and services.

Developing Web applications therefore involves several intrinsic challenges, which imply the adoption of adequate technologies and methodologies. Sound methodologies, forming the baseline for rigorous and repeatable development processes, are especially needed to cope with the complexity of current Web applications and to ensure their quality.

In this book we discuss the most prominent issues of Web application development in the context of well-established engineering processes that cover the whole product life cycle. We especially stress the importance of models as a means for: (i) addressing the complexity of Web applications at some level of generalization, abstracting from low-level details, and (ii) shaping up rigorous and systematic development processes, possibly complemented with automatic tools. This is the philosophy that also drives *Web engineering*, a recent discipline focusing on the adoption of models, systematic methodologies, and tools for the design, development and evaluation of high-quality Web applications. This book aims at showing how Web engineering methods can provide effective solutions for addressing the major issues posed by Web application development.

1.1 The Web Engineering Scenario

Nowadays, there is a huge variety of Web products, ranging from simple collections of static HTML pages to full-fledged, distributed applications using the Web as execution platform. The average *Web user* is not really able to infer the actual complexity of a Web application by just looking at its front end rendered through the Web browser. The HTML markup defining the presentation of Web pages is nothing but the surface of an application, while the actual application logic is running on a remote Web server or, in some cases, on multiple distributed remote servers. What the user directly perceives is the look and feel of the application, its usability, its accessibility, response times, and similar.

Behind the scenes, that is, below the surface, there is the *Web developer* who constructs the application trying to satisfy the user's needs and expectations. Typically, this is a non-trivial task because developing good Web applications requires a profound knowledge of principles driving the Web, architectural patterns, communication techniques, design methods, and so on.

Figure 1.1 illustrates the described scenario and provides some more insights into the design decisions that a developer must be able to take during

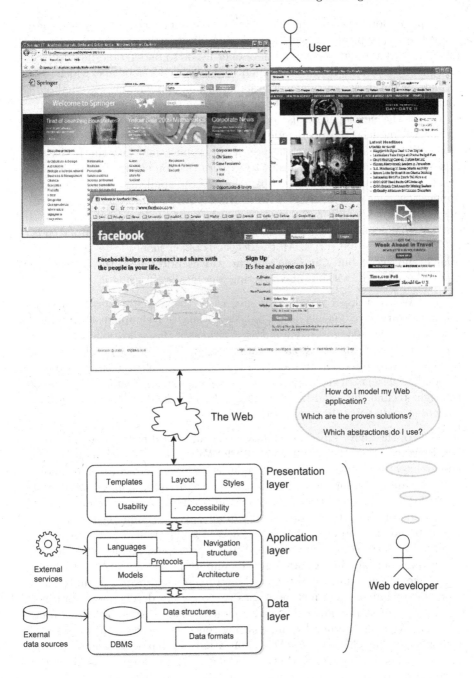

Fig. 1.1. The Web engineering scenario: developers are confronted with a variety of choices and challenges, while users only know about an application's front-end

Web application development. Commonly, Web applications are divided into several layers, typically a data layer, an application layer, and a presentation layer. At the *data layer*, the developer needs to understand how to best structure the data underlying the application under development, which data formats or database management systems to use, and whether external data sources might be used as well. At the *application layer*, things get more complex, and the developer needs to decide on the programming and markup languages, models, protocols, and application architectures to be used. He also defines the navigation structure of the application, i.e., the paths the user can follow (navigate) in order to explore the content of the application and to enact or use implemented operations. If the application also integrates application logic that is sourced from third parties, remote (Web) services might be used as well. Finally, at the *presentation layer* the developer focuses on "external" concerns, such as the layout of the the application front ends, HTML templates and styles. All the decisions taken should foster appeal, usability, and accessibility, in order for the end users to "like" the application and to be satisfied, without encountering any hurdles in using it.

The Web developer is not only subject to these architectural concerns. As in software development in general, developing a Web application implies following methodologies or *development processes* that allow one to master the overall complexity of Web application design. That is, the developer must be able to properly elicit and analyze *requirements*, translate them into corresponding *designs* of the application, *implement* the application by choosing the right technologies and instruments, *test and validate* the result, *operate*, *maintain*, and *evolve* the application as needed.

Most of the above problems and tasks are addressed by software engineering. However, given the peculiarities of the Web, the underlying assumptions and architectural conventions, the standards, and the characteristic technologies, we think Web engineering is peculiar in its nature. While developing a standalone application in general allows the developer to operate more freely (e.g., normally a customer does not impose any programming language or layout paradigm), properly developing a Web application requires being acquainted with the conventions of the Web, its principles, and its technologies.

In this book we aim at conveying the important aspects that a developer must take into account, the conceptual instruments addressing them, and the modeling techniques and methodologies that may aid development. In other words, we aim at providing the reader with the necessary knowledge to understand Web engineering, by emphasizing concepts, methods, processes and instruments that characterize Web application development, while focusing less on specific technologies, which we think are adequately covered by the huge variety of specific books already available on the market.

1.2 Structure of the Book

The book is structured into different parts, each one providing the reader with a different level of insight into the development process. As graphically represented in Figure 1.2, we distinguish three parts: *Understanding Web engineering*, *Engineering Web applications*, and *Looking forward*.

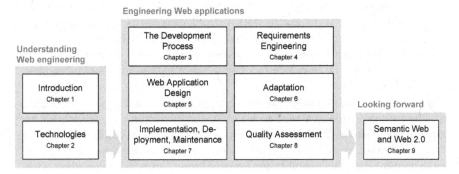

Fig. 1.2. The structure of the book

This introduction is already a piece of the first part of the book, along with the next chapter, which focuses on the technologies that are typical of the Web and that the reader should know in order to understand the discussions of the subsequent chapters. The second part is the central one and comprises six chapters that discuss the Web application development process and its main activities. The final part of the book focuses on the latest trends and the challenges that characterize future Web applications.

Chapter 2 discusses the set of technologies, components, and architectural patterns that characterize Web applications. In chronological order, the chapter reviews technologies like HTML for static pages, XML and relatives, client-side application logic (e.g., in JavaScript), server-side application logic (e.g., in Java), n-tier architectures, and Web services. The aim of the chapter is not to teach the reader how to use each of the described technologies, but rather to convey which are the peculiarities of each technology, why they are used, and what is their specific benefit.

Chapter 3 reviews some of the traditional software development processes, also called software life cycles. It then provides our own considerations on the development process of modern Web applications and slightly adapts the traditional models to the pace of the Web and of the new emerging practices. The chapter also discusses three Web-specific development processes by looking at three of the most prominent Web engineering methods, i.e., WebML, WSDM, and OOHDM. The chapter serves as guideline for chapters 4-8.

Chapter 4 discusses the first activity of each software development process: requirements engineering. It introduces the necessary concepts, describes the typical requirements engineering process, and introduces techniques for the analysis of organizational requirements, of the application domain, and of navigation and interaction requirements. A set of examples facilitate the understanding of how to apply the techniques in practice.

Chapter 5 is the most important chapter of this book; it discusses the design of Web applications. The aspects addressed by the chapter are workflow design, data design, navigation design, presentation design, and architecture design. Special focus is put on state-of-the-art Web engineering methods, such as WebML, WSDM, and OOHDM, that abstract design concerns and aid the development. These methods are particularly valuable instruments in the hands of Web developers (and the readers of this book) because they contribute a large body of knowledge and experience packed into concise models and formalisms.

Chapter 6 extends Chapter 5 with a design concern that has characterized the recent years of research in the area of Web engineering, i.e., adaptation to individual user needs. The chapter provides insights into four different aspects of the adaptation problem: localization and internationalization, personalization and adaptation, accessibility for impaired users, and design for adaptation with product line engineering.

Chapter 7 focuses on the implementation, deployment, and maintenance of Web applications. The chapter does not aim at providing complete implementation techniques or instruments (because this is not the main focus of the book). Rather, it discusses some typical implementation decisions that need to be taken after the design of the application has been completed. It also shows some of the current Web application frameworks and engineering tools that might facilitate the implementation task. The chapter concludes with some considerations on the deployment of applications and on their maintenance and evolution.

Chapter 8 describes the state of the art in quality assessment methods and techniques for Web applications, taking into account a variety of different perspectives. The chapter then discusses testing techniques for Web applications and usability evaluation practices. The chapter further provides insights into the relationship among Web engineering methods and quality assessment techniques and discusses some prominent assessment tools that automate the quality assessment task.

Chapter 9, finally, concludes the book with a brief discussion of some advanced topics that provide a flavor of the current and future trends in Web application development. Specifically, the chapter provides a high-level view on the Semantic Web and on Web 2.0/3.0, with special attention to Web engineering methods and principles.

1.3 Intended Audience

In the writing of this book, we did not target any specific kind of reader and instead aimed at providing valuable information and knowledge to a variety of different audiences with sometimes also diverging needs or expectations:

- *Researchers* in the area of Web engineering will find in this book a comprehensive overview of the current state of the art and of the most prominent research approaches that characterize Web engineering. The level of detail and the technicalities are kept at a level that provides them with the necessary context and understanding, while for the details the researcher will find references to the original works and the authors of the contributions.
- *Teachers and professors* alike will find in the book a balanced discussion of the typical design concerns in Web application development, highlighting which are the main lessons to be learned and pointing to those references (e.g., design methods and abstractions) that we think can facilitate the understanding of the topic by students.
- *Students* will find in the book a complete overview on Web development, telling them *why* specific solutions have been adopted or *when* they are appropriate. With this book, students will not learn how to program a Web application. Our intent is rather to provide them with the necessary awareness of which problems a Web developer must face and how they can be solved. The practical details, e.g., teaching how to use a specific programming language, how to work with XML, how to design layouts and styles, are already extensively covered by other books.
- Finally, *Web developers* will find in the book an academic (yet easily understandable) view on the problem of Web engineering, providing them with the abstractions, methods, models, and assessment techniques that are discussed in the context of international conferences and workshops or published in scientific journals. This book therefore allows them to confront the practical knowledge they have earned in their everyday work with the aspects and issues that instead fascinate academic research.

Although we overview the typical technologies used in Web engineering, in this book we do not provide explanations of the technologies that would allow the reader to straightforwardly implement a Web application. The intention is rather to explain the underlying concepts and benefits and to ease the understanding of the book. While this should allow also the inexperienced user to follow the discussions and to appreciate the contributions by the various works introduced throughout the book, the reader would definitely benefit from some background knowledge on Web engineering (also practical!), especially regarding topics like HTML, Web architectures, and dynamic Web pages.

According to the structure of the book described in the previous section and to the above considerations, the reader already familiar with Web technologies and Web architectures can easily skip Chapter 2. The chapters in the central part of the book are chronologically organized according to the typical development process. The concepts and ideas described in each of these chapters are incremental, in that each chapter builds on its direct predecessors. Yet, all chapters are sufficiently independent in their explanations, so as to allow the more skilled reader to read just the chapter he is interested in, without impacting the understandability of the chapter.

2

Technologies

Since the creation of the first Web site by Tim Berners-Lee and Robert Cailliau at CERN, the Web has evolved from an environment hosting simple and static hypermedia documents to a platform for the execution of complex applications. The first Web sites consisted of collections of documents encoded in the HyperText Markup Language (HTML). The displayed contents (both text and graphics) were static, meaning that they were explicitly specified in the HTML document and formatted by means of special HTML elements defining presentation properties. Since then, several new technologies have progressively enriched the Web scenario.

The very first evolution step aimed at extending the presentation capability of HTML through a better separation of content and presentation and through the inclusion of client-side scripting and pluggable components. This improved the page interactivity and enabled the client to execute business logic (e.g., the validation of data inserted through forms).

The emergence of the eXtensible Markup Language (XML) and of server-side scripting solutions further changed the way of building Web pages, driving the shift from Web sites to Web applications. Web pages became dynamic, meaning that they could be composed at runtime by dynamically extracting content from a data source and dynamically composing the final page rendition, thanks to parameterized page templates. Also, some extended architectures for Web servers (such as Java2EE or Microsoft .NET) enabled the development of large-scale, data-intensive Web applications, ensuring a high level of availability, security, and scalability.

More recently, Web services standards and the so-called Service-Oriented Architecture (SOA) have been proposed with the aim of enabling Web applications to invoke operations exposed by self-contained and self-describing software components.

This chapter illustrates the different technologies at the basis of this evolution by highlighting the driving factors and the consequent progression of proposals that during the last few years have made simple Web sites evolve into very complex Web applications.

S. Casteleyn et al., Engineering Web Applications: *Data-Centric Systems and Applications.*
DOI: 10.1007/978-3-540-92201-8_2, © Springer-Verlag Berlin Heidelberg 2009

2.1 The HyperText Transfer Protocol (HTTP)

The *HyperText Transfer Protocol* (HTTP) is the very basic ingredient on which the Web is founded. It is a client-server application protocol that defines a standard format for specifying the request of resources on the Web. The protocol was invented in the early 1990s with the aim of creating a distributed hypermedia system, enabling access to interconnected multimedia documents stored in servers communicating through a TCP/IP network.

Through HTTP a user using a client application (e.g., a *browser*) can request resources available on a remote server (the *Web server*). Typical resources exchanged through HTTP are HTML pages, i.e., multimedia documents including hypertextual links to other HTML documents. More generally, a request may be related to a file of any format stored on the Web server or to the invocation of a program to be executed on the server side. Since such resources are distributed over the Internet, they need an identification mechanism to be located and accessed. The identifier for referencing resources is a string, called the *Uniform Resource Locator* (URL), which specifies the protocol used for the resource transfer (e.g., HTTP for Web page exchange, or other protocols, such as FTP, supported by the browser), the name or the IP address of the machine hosting the resource, an optional port number denoting the access to a specific server port, and the document name and location in the Web server's file system. For example, the URL `http://home.dei.polimi.it/matera/index.html` denotes the file named `index.html` stored in the directory named `matera/` in the file system managed by the Web server installed on the host named `home.dei.polimi.it`. Additionally, parameters (the so-called "query string") can follow to enable, for example, the transfer of processing instructions or simple data provided by users through forms.

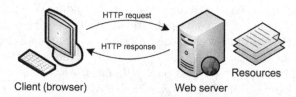

Fig. 2.1. Request-response cycle of HTTP

How does HTTP work? As illustrated in Figure 2.1, when the user types a URL into the browser address line or when the user clicks on an anchor within a page representing a URL for a given resource, the browser issues an *HTTP request*, in which a *request line* specifies an *HTTP method*, the *URL of the requested resource*, and the *protocol version*. The most important HTTP methods are *GET* and *POST*. The GET method submits a plain request for a resource to the Web server, and allows the user to submit simple inputs via the *query string*. The POST method submits a request that allows the user to submit complex inputs (for example, a long text or a file) to be processed by the server. With the POST method, the user input is packaged as an attachment to the request, and constitutes the so-called *request body*.

When receiving the request, a server locates the resource and sends a response to the client. The response message includes a *status line*, which includes information about the protocol version and a numeric status code with its associated message (for example, *HTTP/1.1 404 Not found*), and a *message body* carrying the actual resource to be exchanged.

In order to enable the exchange of additional information, further fields (called *headers*) can be added to both the request and the response. More details on such headers, and in general on the HTTP protocol, can be found on the W3C Web site at the address `http://www.w3.org/Protocols/`.

2.2 The HyperText Markup Language (HTML)

Besides managing the request and transfer of resources through the HTTP protocol, a Web browser also handles the visual presentation of the resources. The *HyperText Markup Language* (HTML) is used to express the content and the visual formatting of Web pages.

HTML is a "markup" language. An HTML page consists of a mix of texts and images (the content to be displayed by the browser) and special elements, called *tags*, which delimit portions of content to tell the browser how they must be displayed or to define links to other Web pages. The document presentation is then managed by a processor embedded in the Web browser, which receives as input the marked-up content and transforms it into a rendered document by interpreting the meaning of the tags.

As can be seen in Figure 2.2, HTML tags are symbols enclosed within angle brackets. Most tags are used in pairs, because they must delimit portions of content; therefore HTML markup is constructed with:

1. A *start tag* marking the beginning of an element;
2. A number of *attributes*, which are label-value pairs defining desired behaviors or additional element properties, and which are included in the start tag. For example, the <FONT> tag in Figure 2.2 specifies the attributes `face` and `size` to define font type and size for the delimited text.
3. Some *content* (text, graphical elements, and in general objects to be displayed on the page). In Figure 2.2, the content "A simple HTML page" is marked as heading (<H1>); other contents are the text below the title and the image.
4. An *end tag*, which has the same name as the start tag, but is preceded by the special character "/". This tag is optional for some elements. For example, there are some empty elements, which do not delimit content and therefore do not require end tags. The <IMG> tag used to specify the image in Figure 2.2 is an example of an empty tag.

```
<HTML>
 <HEAD>
  <TITLE>Inserting an image and an anchor </TITLE>
  <META name="keywords" content="HTML, example">
 </HEAD>
 <BODY>
  <H1>A simple HTML page</H1>
  <P>With an embedded image:</P>
  <P align="left">
   <IMG src="http://www.dei.polimi.it/images/logo.gif">
  </P>
  <P align="left">And with a link to an external resource: </P>
  <P align="left"><FONT face="Arial" size="+1">
    <A href="http://www.polimi.it">Click here</A>
    to open the home page of Politecnico di Milano...
   </FONT></P>
 </BODY>
</HTML>
```

Fig. 2.2. A simple HTML page with an embedded image and a clickable hyperlink

The whole HTML document is delimited by the <HTML> tag and consists of two main sections:

- The *header*, delimited by the <HEAD> tag, includes general information about the document, for example, the document title (delimited by the <TITLE> tag), or the keywords used by search engines for document indexing (delimited by the <META> tag).
- The *body*, delimited by the <BODY> tag, includes the actual content and the markup specifying its presentation properties.

Besides tags for text formatting, two basic and very peculiar HTML elements are the tags for link definition and image inclusion, which respond to the need for defining hypertextual multimedia documents on the Web:

- As illustrated in Figure 2.2, the anchor tag <A> defines the starting point (i.e., the *anchor*) of a hypertextual link (with content "Click here"). The delimited text is therefore rendered in a special way (for example, under-lined and in a different color); a click on it generates an HTTP request for a corresponding resource to be displayed. The URL of the new resource, which is the *target* of the hypertext reference, is specified in the href attribute of the tag.

- The <IMG> tag specifies the insertion into the document of an image, whose URL is specified using the src attribute (see Figure 2.2). When the browser renders the HTML page and encounters the <IMG> tag, it sends an additional HTTP request to the Web server for the file specified in the src attribute. Once the image is received the browser displays it inside the HTML page.

Other common HTML tags are:

- *Block elements*: used to define the structure of a document. Examples are tags for delimiting paragraphs (<P>) and for marking headings at different levels (e.g., <H1> for the highest-level title).
- *List elements*: support the definition of lists. Examples are tags for ordered lists (tag <OL>) and bulleted lists (<UL>).
- *Table elements*: support the definition of tables for multidimensional data arranged in rows and columns. The tag <TABLE> contains a number of el-ements to provide a rich table structure. The <TBODY> element groups the table's rows. The tag <TR> specifies individual rows; each <TR> contains <TH> or <TD> elements for header cells or data cells, respectively. Some other optional elements then enable the definition of the table caption (<CAPTION>) or of header and footer rows (<THEAD> and <TFOOT>).
- *Form elements*: used for the definition of forms for the gathering of user input. The element <FORM> typically contains some nested elements spec-ifying form controls (such as <INPUT> for input insertion, <SELECT> for option selection, <TEXTAREA> for a multi-line text input, and <BUTTON> for including submit, reset, or push buttons) through which the user inputs data or interacts with the Web page.

It is worth noting that, in order to enhance the HTML potential for the creation of rich and interactive Web pages, the use of tags expressing graphic and formatting properties (such as <FONT> or <TABLE>), as proposed by the initial HTML versions, is now deprecated. The following section illustrates the evolution of HTML to support better rendition capabilities and a broader range of interactive features.

2.2.1 Cascading Style Sheets (CSSs)

The first HTML pages were characterized by low presentation and interaction capabilities. However, with the expansion and diffusion of the Web, such sim-ple documents soon became inadequate, and new presentation requirements started to emerge. In December 1997, the W3C Consortium[1] issued a stable version of HTML, HTML 4, and started an evolution process based on new technologies and languages to be combined with HTML to overcome its observed shortcomings.

One of the most innovative features introduced by HTML 4 is the separation of content and presentation, achieved through the introduction of the *Cascading Style Sheets* (CSSs). CSSs allow page designers to define the look-and-feel of Web pages separately from the page markup and content written in HTML.

A *style sheet* is a set of rules that tell the browser how to present a document. A rule is made of two parts: a *selector*, which specifies the HTML tag to which the style rule applies, and a *style declaration*, which expresses the style property to be attached to the HTML tag mentioned in the selector. As an example, the following code fragment defines the color and font size properties for the <H1> tag:

```
<HEAD>
 <TITLE> CSS Example </TITLE>
 <STYLE type="text/css">
   H1 { font-size: 20pt; color: red }
 </STYLE>
</HEAD>
```

Style rules can be embedded in the document they apply to by means of the <STYLE> tag. Alternatively, especially when multiple documents must share the same presentation style, the style rules can be written in a separate file linked to the HTML documents. In the following example, the <LINK> tag, placed in the head section of the HTML document, specifies a reference to a style sheet named style.css:

```
<HEAD>
  <TITLE>CSS Example</TITLE>
  <LINK rel="StyleSheet" href="style.css" type="text/css">
</HEAD>
```

2.3 The eXtensible Markup Language (XML)

As shown in the previous sections, some technologies have been combined with HTML in order to make Web clients more dynamic and able to support a richer set of presentation and interactivity features in Web pages. However, HTML still shows some limitations, which prevent designers from matching the broad and varying range of requirements that characterize specific application domains. First of all, HTML is not extensible, and therefore cannot be

---

[1] W3C is a governing body which regulates the definition of Web standards.

customized for special needs (for example, the specification and presentation of mathematical and chemical formulas). Also, although HTML 4 and CSS enforce the separation of content and presentation, HTML remains weak in its ability to describe the structure and the meaning of a document's content.

The *eXtensible Markup Language* (XML) addresses the previous lacks. It is used to create new markup languages since it enables the definition of arbitrary sets of tags to describe the structure of documents. With this respect, XML is not merely a mark-up language, rather it is a *meta-language* that standardizes the syntactic rules through which users can define their collections of custom tags that are best suited to the needs and semantics of a specific application domain. It was indeed proposed with the aim of producing a simplified version of SGML, a language that supports the definition of new markup languages.

XML-based documents are generally used for describing and exchanging data. XML tags are used to delimit pieces of content; the interpretation of such content is completely left to the applications that process them. The uses of XML therefore cover a variety of applications, including electronic data exchange, document storage and transformation, document exchange in e-commerce and B2B transactions, and more.

Another advantage of XML is that it provides a way to express the page content, without interweaving content and presentation properties. Presentation for XML data is defined in a separate document, a CSS, as introduced in Section 2.2.1, or a file written with the Extensible Stylesheet Language (XSL), as will be shown in Section 2.3.4. This allows one to define several presentations for one and the same data set, a very important characteristic in the current context of use where multiple client devices with different display capabilities are used to access Web applications.

The rest of this section introduces the most salient ingredients of XML and the related technologies that make it possible to exploit XML for the production of Web applications.

2.3.1 Well-Formed XML Documents

In order to be processed correctly, each XML document must be *well-formed*, that is, it must obey to some structural rules:

- It must begin with a line, declaring the language version.
- Each element must be delimited by an opening and a closing tag. The content between the two tags is the value of the element, which can be text or other tags. Some elements, the so-called *empty tags*, may not have the closing tag, but they have the "/" symbol at the end of the tag name (e.g., <emptytag/>).
- The document must have one root element, and all the other elements must be properly nested, that is, any element containing an inner element must not be closed before the inner element is closed.

- Elements may have attributes with values that must be delimited by quotes (" ").

```
<?xml version="1.0" ?>
<article>
   <title> Mashing up Context-Aware Web Applications </title>
   <author> Florian Daniel </author>
   <author> Maristella Matera </author>
   <publishing category="conference" year="2008">
      <publication>
         Proceedings of WISE 2008
      </publication>
   </publishing>
   <section title="Introduction">
      <text>
         Text for the section Introduction
      </text>
      <figure file="figure-sec1.jpg"/>
   </section>
   <section title="Rationale and Background">
      <text>
         Text for the section Rationale and Background
      </text>
      <codeExample>
         Code Example
      </codeExample>
    ... ...
    ... ...
   <section title="References" type="bibliography">
      <text>
         Text for the section References
      </text>
   </section>
</article>
```

Fig. 2.3. An example of a well-formed XML-based document representing data about a scientific article

Figure 2.3 shows a well-formed XML document representing data about a scientific article. The document starts with the declaration of the XML version. The root element, <article>, then includes some elements describing the title, the authors, the publication, and the article sections. It is worth noting that some elements have *attributes*, such as type and year for the element <publishing>. Also, the <figure> element is *empty*, since it does not delimit content.

2.3.2 Valid XML Documents

If on the one hand an advantage offered by XML is the flexibility in the definition of custom tags, on the other hand it should be possible to define some validity constraints over the structure of a document to avoid the use of invalid tags, and to guarantee accurate processing by the programs in charge of manipulating XML data.

Document Type Definition (DTD)

In order to address the validity concern, XML documents may be associated with a *Document Type Definition* (DTD), which defines the format of a class of XML documents by describing the elements that can be used in the documents, as well as the admissible values and attributes for each element. Figure 2.4 shows the DTD for the XML document shown in Figure 2.3.

```
<!ELEMENT article (title,author+,publishing?,section+)>
<!ELEMENT title (#PCDATA)>
<!ELEMENT author (#PCDATA)>
<!ELEMENT publishing (publication)>
<!ELEMENT publication (#PCDATA)>
<!ELEMENT section (text+,figure*,codeExample*)>
<!ELEMENT text (#PCDATA)>
<!ELEMENT figure EMPTY>
<!ELEMENT codeExample (#PCDATA)>
<!ATTLIST publishing
          year CDATA #REQUIRED
          category (conference|journal|book) #IMPLIED>
<!ATTLIST section
          title CDATA #REQUIRED
          type (abstract|bodySection|bibliography)#IMPLIED>
<!ATTLIST figure
          file CDATA #REQUIRED>
```

Fig. 2.4. A DTD for the scientific article document represented in Figure 2.3

The DTD defines `<article>` as a complex element, consisting of a set of subelements: one subelement of type `title`, one or more (denoted by the "`+`") subelements of type `author`, zero or one (denoted by the "`?`" symbol) subelement of type `publishing`, and one or more elements of type `section`. The elements `<publishing>` and `<section>` are in turn complex. For example, `<section>` is composed of one or more subelements of type `<text>`, zero or more (as denoted by the "`*`" symbol) subelements of type `<figure>`, and zero or more subelements of type `<codeExample>`. With the exception of `<figure>`, which is an empty element, all the elements have textual content (`#PCDATA`).

The `ATTLIST` clause is then used to define some constraints on attribute values. For example, the DTD declares that the element `<publishing>` has the attributes `year`, which consists of character data (`CDATA`) and is mandatory (`#REQUIRED`), and the attribute `category`, which may have one of the specified values (`conference`, `journal`, or `book`) and is optional (`#IMPLIED`).

A DTD can either be embedded into the XML document or be an external file referenced in the document, as shown in the following example, where the line `<!DOCTYPE article SYSTEM "article.dtd">` imports the DTD file `article.dtd`.

```
<?xml version="1.0"?>
```

```
<!DOCTYPE article SYSTEM "article.dtd">
<article> ... </article>
```

XML Schema Definition (XSD)

Despite their utility in defining the syntax and structure of XML documents, DTDs present some shortcomings. First of all, a DTD only allows the definition of textual content for XML elements (#PCDATA); it does not support the declaration of data types. This prevents XML parsers from controlling accurately the element contents and the attribute values. A DTD does not allow the specification of how many times elements may appear in a document, i.e., whether a given element may be used zero, one, or multiple times in a same document. Similarly, is is not possible to define the exact order of elements in a document. Also, it is not possible to define XML documents referencing more than one DTD, and therefore it is not possible to merge documents to create new ones. An additional weakness is that the DTD syntax is different from the XML syntax, and therefore developers are required to become familiar with a language that is different from XML.

XML Schema Definitions (XSDs) solve these problems. Like a DTD, an XSD defines the structure of a family of XML documents. However, differently from a DTD, an XSD is a valid XML document itself that uses a standard set of tags for element declaration, defined by the XSD specification [W3Cb].

Figure 2.5 shows the example of an XSD specifying the syntax of the XML document illustrated in Figure 2.3. More details on the XSD syntax can be found on the W3C site [W3Cb].

2.3.3 Namespaces

One of the advantages of the definition of XML-based documents is the possibility to reuse elements deriving from different schema definitions. It should be possible, for example, to integrate documents describing technical articles with documents describing bibliographic sources. Such integration, however, is not without problems: ambiguity problems can occur, since the names of elements and attributes in different documents can collide. For example, an address element belonging to a document representing personal data could have the name of the email address element defined in a document representing email messages. Parsers analyzing such "hybrid" documents should know which schema must be considered for validation. A mechanism for schema identification is therefore needed.

Namespaces provide a solution to such a problem. A namespace identifies a set of names for elements and attributes, and provides an identifier for univocally referencing such names. The role of the identifier is to prevent the names belonging to a given set from possibly colliding with names belonging to another set. That is, if a document uses elements deriving from different

```
<?xml version="1.0" encoding="UTF-8"?>
<xs:schema xmlns:xs="http://www.w3.org/2001/XMLSchema">
  <xs:element name="article">
    <xs:complexType>
      <xs:sequence>
        <xs:element ref="title"/>
        <xs:element ref="author" maxOccurs="unbounded"/>
        <xs:element ref="publishing" minOccurs="0"/>
        <xs:element ref="section" maxOccurs="unbounded"/>
      </xs:sequence>
    </xs:complexType>
  </xs:element>
  <xs:element name="title" type="xs:string"/>
  <xs:element name="author" type="xs:string"/>
  <xs:element name="publishing">
    <xs:complexType>
      <xs:sequence>
        <xs:element name="publication" type="xs:string"/>
      </xs:sequence>
      <xs:attribute name="category" type="xs:NCName"/>
      <xs:attribute name="year" use="required" type="xs:integer"/>
    </xs:complexType>
  </xs:element>
  <xs:element name="section">
    <xs:complexType>
      <xs:sequence>
        <xs:element name="text" type="xs:string"/>
        <xs:choice minOccurs="0">
          <xs:element name="codeExample" type="xs:string"/>
          <xs:element name="figure">
            <xs:complexType>
              <xs:attribute name="file" use="required" type="xs:NCName"/>
            </xs:complexType>
          </xs:element>
        </xs:choice>
      </xs:sequence>
      <xs:attribute name="title" use="required"/>
      <xs:attribute name="type" type="xs:NCName"/>
    </xs:complexType>
  </xs:element>
</xs:schema>
```

Fig. 2.5. An XML Schema Definition for the article XML document defined in Figure 2.3

schemas, it should be possible to reference each namespace and the schema that defines it.

The first code lines in Figure 2.6 show how to include references to namespaces and their corresponding XML schemas within the XML document describing articles. The `xmlns:xsi` attribute imports the definition of the XSD tags, while the attributes `xmlns:art` and `xmlns:biblio` specify the namespaces the document refers to and two prefixes, `art` and `biblio`, to be used within the document as namespace identifiers. The two attributes of type `xsi:schemaLocation` then specify a reference to the namespaces and their corresponding XSD files.

```
<article
 xmlns:xsi="http://www.w3.org/2001/XMLSchema-instance"
 xmlns:art="http://www.mysite.com/article-xml/article"
 xmlns:biblio="http://www.mysite.com/article-xml/bibliography"
 xsi:schemaLocation="http://www.dominio.it/xml/article/article.xsd"
 xsi:schemaLocation="http://www.dominio.it/xml/bibliography/biblio.xsd">
 ... ...
 ... ...
  <art:section title="References" type ="bibliography">
    <biblio:bibliography>
       <biblio:author>
         Florian Daniel
       </biblio:author>
       <biblio:author>
       / Maristella Matera
       </biblio:author>
       <biblio:title>
         Mashing Up Context-Aware Web Applications
       </biblio:title>
       <biblio:year>
         2008
       </biblio:year>
    </biblio:bibliography>
  </art:section>
</article>
```

Fig. 2.6. Referencing and using a namespace in the article XML document

The following code lines in the example then represent an article section of type **bibliography** by using the two namespaces previously imported: the **art** namespace provides tags for the definition of a generic section, while the **biblio** namespace provides tags for the structuring of bibliography sections.

2.3.4 Presenting XML Documents

As already highlighted in the previous sections, the intended use of XML is to describe the strcture of data and not how data must be displayed on a Web page. However, presentation of XML data can be managed by means of separate style sheets defining presentation and formatting properties.

For example, similarly to what happens with HTML pages, CSS rules can be associated with XML elements to define their presentation properties. However, the intended use of CSS is mainly for the presentation of HTML pages, and therefore they lack some useful features, such as the possibility to extract and display the value of element attributes. Additionally, very often XML documents describe data in a format that cannot be "directly" displayed in a browser – they require some transformation. In these and other cases, CSSs are not able to properly manage the presentation of XML data.

The eXtensible Stylesheet Language (XSL) has been therefore introduced to flexibly manage the transformation and presentation of XML documents. It supports three main activities: (i) the *retrieval* of the data to be transformed and presented, (ii) the *transformation* of such data, and (iii) the specification of *formatting properties* to be applied when data are presented. Each of these activities is supported by a specific language:

- *XPath* : a language for writing expressions that allow the retrieval of elements and attributes within an XML document on which transformations (for example, those necessary for generating the document presentation) are applied.
- *XSL Transformations* (XSLT) : a language for specifying transformations of XML documents.
- *XSL Formatting Objects* (XSL-FO) : a language for defining the rendition of a document.

Given the three languages, XSL supports the specification of pattern-matching rules, called *templates*, that are similar to the rules of HTML CSS. More specifically, an XSL rule contains a *matching part*, selecting the target XML elements, and an *action part*, specifying how the retrieved elements must be transformed or formatted.

It is worth noting that the three languages are not strictly connected to each other. For example, depending on the requirements of the specific application to be built, XPath can be replaced by another language, for example, XQuery [W3Ca], without requiring any modification in the formatting rules specified with XSL-FO. Also, one can decide to avoid the use of XSL-FO for data formatting, while defining an XSLT transformation to directly produce (X)HTML code (see the next section). This is actually the most common approach for generating the presentation of XML documents. For this transformation, it is enough to use XPath for the matching part of the XSL rule, which is in charge of retrieving the elements in the source document that are affected by the rule, and XSLT for the action part, which is in charge of transforming the retrieved elements into (X)HTML code.

The presentation of XML documents therefore needs two main ingredients:

- *An XSL style sheet*: a template describing how data must be processed and transformed into a presentation format.
- *An XSLT processor*: takes as input the source document and the XSL style sheet and performs the transformations to generate a new file specifying the data presentation according to a selected presentation format (XSL-FO, XHTML, WML, etc.)

In general, an XSL style sheet has the following structure:

```
<?xml version="1.0"?>
<xsl:stylesheet version="1.0"
     xmlns:xsl="http://www.w3.org/1999/XSL/transform">
  ...
  transformation templates
  ...
</xsl:stylesheet>
```

The root element `<xsl:stylesheet>` encloses the transformation templates to be applied to the source XML document. Each template identifies some elements in the document by means of an XPath expression, and processes the elements to obtain a result in a given format. For example, with reference to the XML document describing articles, the following template generates the title of the second section of the article:

```
<xsl:template match="/article/section[position()=2]">
  <xsl:value-of select="@title"/>
</xsl:template>
```

In particular, the element `<xsl:value-of>` retrieves the value of an element or an attribute and produces it as output. Besides transforming elements, templates can also be used to add new elements or to discard elements from the source document, to sort elements, to process elements on the basis of the evaluation of some conditions, and so on.

2.3.5 An XML Application: XHTML

XHTML is a redefinition of HTML 4.0 based on XML. It is a response to the plethora of proprietary extensions that were generated to enhance HTML. Instead of issuing a new HTML version collecting all the acknowledged extensions, the W3C consortium redefined the language: the XHTML elements are the same as those defined in HTML 4.0, but the syntactic rules are different. Therefore, XHTML answers to two fundamental needs: on the one hand it makes HTML evolve into an XML-based language, thus achieving all the benefits of language extensibility and precise syntax for document structuring; on the other hand it preserves compatibility with all the tools and software platforms supporting HTML 4.0.

The most notable difference introduced by XHTML is that, due to the XML-based definition of the language, documents must be well-formed. This basically implies that:

- XHTML elements must be properly nested. For example, while HTML admits the following nesting of tags:

  ```
  <b><i>This text is bold and italic</b></i>
  ```

  in XHTML all the elements must be properly nested within each other, as in the following:

  ```
  <b><i>This text is bold and italic</i></b>
  ```

- XHTML elements must always be closed. Therefore, nonempty elements must have an end tag, while empty elements either must have an end tag or their start tag must end with "/>".
- XHTML elements must be in lowercase. This is needed because XML is case-sensitive.

- XHTML documents must have one root element. Therefore, all the XHTML elements must be nested within the <html> root element. All the other elements can have subelements, which must be in pairs and correctly nested within their parent element.

Such new features are important, especially if we consider that XHTML pages can be more effectively processed by programs that are now spreading in the Web context, such as search engine spiders, tools for speech synthesis, and browsers running on portable devices.

Three XHTML versions are currently available and are published as W3C recommendations. Issued in 2000, *XHTML 1.0* consists of an XML-based rewriting of HTML 4.0. *XHTML Basic* is instead a "limited" version of the language, specifically conceived for mobile devices (e.g., PDAs and cellular phones). It includes only those elements that are suitable with respect to the rendering capabilities of such devices. For example, it does not support frames, which are not used in this context. It is gradually replacing WML (Wireless Markup Language), the language so far used for coding WAP (Wireless Application Protocol) applications. *XHTML 1.1* represents the first attempt to introduce modularity. The fundamental elements (that is, the set of tags that define the document structure) are grouped into independent modules, which can be implemented or excluded depending on the peculiar needs. According to the W3C, this is the basis for the possibility to extend XHTML with other (personalized) modules.

2.4 Dynamic HTML and Client-Side Business Logic

Up to now, we have discussed the protocols and document types that characterize the Web domain. In Section 2.2.1, we said that HTML 4 introduced CSS as a way to address novel presentation requirements. Along with the recognition of new *presentation requirements*, HTML 4 also recognized the need for new and more complex *interactivity features*. Such features encompass the capability both to dynamically change a Web page's presentation properties inside the browser (i.e., the client) and to execute pieces of business logic at the client side (via dedicated *scripting languages*), for example, to validate data inserted into form fields. The answers to this demand are *dynamic HTML* and *AJAX*, and also *embedded applications* and *embedded multimedia objects*; we discuss the different approaches next.

2.4.1 Common Scripting Languages

Client-side scripts are programs interpreted and executed by the browser when the page is loaded or when the user invokes some events over the HTML elements of the page. When included in the HTML code of a page, scripts are delimited by the <SCRIPT> tag, placed either in the head section of the HTML document or in its body. Scripts in the head section are executed when they are explicitly called, or when an event declared as an attribute of an HTML element triggers them. Scripts in the body section are instead executed when the HTML page is loaded. It is also possible to reference external script files in the head section of the HTML code.

JavaScript and JScript are two different dialects of the standardized ECMAScript[2] language. JavaScript is Netscape's implementation of the language, and JScript is Microsoft's implementation; VBScript is another scripting solution proposed by Microsoft that is inspired by Visual Basic's programming language. While JavaScript is nowadays adequately supported by most of the Web browsers on the market (although not all of them implement the latest version or all the programming features), JScript is supported only by Microsoft's Internet Explorer. As a consequence, over the last few years JavaScript has become the de facto standard for client-side scripting. However, the sometimes not fully standard-compliant implementation of JavaScript in the different browsers (and versions thereof) still requires the developer to take browser-specific peculiarities into account when designing JavaScript application logic. That is, although JavaScript is the most widely adopted client-side scripting solution, its cross-browser portability is not yet fully guaranteed.

2.4.2 Dynamic HTML

Client-side scripting languages are the enabling factor for *dynamic HTML*. Scripting languages represent the *active* part in the dynamic HTML approach, while the HTML markup language represents the *static* part, which is subject to dynamic modifications by the scripting logic. Modifications or accesses to the HTML document are performed by leveraging the Document Object Model (DOM), a platform and language independent model to represent HTML or XML documents. DOM is an interface providing methods and properties through which scripts can dynamically access and update the content, structure and style of documents [W3C09]. More specifically, the DOM supplies a standard set of objects for representing HTML and XML documents, a standard model of how these objects can be combined, and a standard interface for accessing and manipulating them. A Web browser does not require the DOM to display an HTML document. However, the DOM is required by scripts to inspect or modify a Web page dynamically. In other words, the DOM is the way a script sees the state of its containing HTML page and of the browser.

The combination of client-side scripting, HTML, and DOM represents a powerful solution for implementing dynamic behaviors (e.g., interactive and highly responsive features) in the browser. Figure 2.7 shows a page in which a JavaScript function opens an alert box displaying the message "HELLO

---

[2] More details on the language and its precise specification can be found at http://www.ecma-international.org/publications/standards/Ecma-262.htm.

```
<HTML>
<HEAD>
  <TITLE> JavaScript Example </TITLE>
  <SCRIPT type="text/javascript">
     function hello_message() {
        alert("HELLO WORLD")
     }
  </SCRIPT>
</HEAD>
<BODY>
  <FORM>
     <input type="button" onClick="hello_message()" value="Display message">
  </FORM>
</BODY>
</HTML>
```

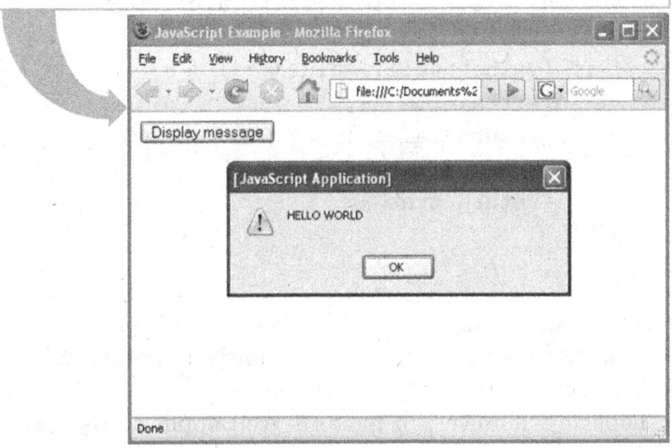

Fig. 2.7. Example of a script included in the head section of an HTML page

WORLD" when the user clicks on the button "Display message". The HTML code of the page defines the button within the <FORM> block. An onClick event is attached to this button; therefore, pushing on the button triggers the onClick event, which in turn triggers the JavaScript function hello_message, defined within the <SCRIPT> tag placed in the head section of the document. The function opens the alert box.

2.4.3 Client-Side Business Logic and AJAX

Modern Web applications are increasingly leveraging client-side application logic, thus shifting the strict client-server paradigm of the early Web applications toward a distributed paradigm where the traditional distinction of client and server is increasingly blurred.[3] Hence, the client-side application logic is no longer simply used to enrich the application's presentation layer with dynamic user interface features, but instead is a part of the overall business logic

---

[3] See, for example, Section 9.2 on Web 2.0/3.0, a technology where advanced client-side logic has been gaining momentum over the last years.

of the application. In the former case, the application may typically also be
used without the client-side presentation features; if, instead, the application's
business logic is distributed over the client and the server, the application cannot work properly without the client-side logic.

The following JavaScript code provides a very simple example of client-
side business logic, i.e., the validation of user input: events can be attached
to form fields to trigger a function that validates the input that has been
provided to the field to ensure that only correctly formatted input is sent to
the Web server. Specifically, the example below checks whether a required
field (declared as a function parameter) has been left empty:

```
function validate_field(field,alertmsg) {
  with (field) {
    if (value==null||value=="") {
      alert(alertmsg);
        return false }
      else {
        return true }
  }
}
```

If the required field is blank, an alert box displays a message (also declared
as a function parameter), and the function returns false. Alternatively, if a
value is entered, the function returns true.

Typically, however, in modern Web applications it is not enough to just
validate user inputs at the client side. The client-side scripting languages allow
developers to implement even complex programming logic running inside the
client browser, but up to a few years ago such logic was restricted to dynamic
HTML, form validation, and alert messages, as there was no possibility to
communicate with the world outside the currently viewed page (the so-called
sandbox protection mechanism).

Only recently the implementation of the XMLHttpRequest API inside the
most common client browsers has finally enabled client-side scripts to also
perform HTTP requests to a Web server, transparently in the background
and independently of the user interaction. In the case of JavaScript, the con-
junctive use of JavaScript, XMLHttpRequest, XML, and DOM is commonly
known as AJAX (Asynchronous JavaScript and XML), by now almost a synonym for Web applications that are distributed over client and server. AJAX
finally enables developers to make the most of dynamic HTML, as now it is
possible to load content from the Web server and add it dynamically to the
viewed page, without requiring the Web browser to refresh or reload the entire
page. This finally leads to more responsive and ergonomic applications.

2.4.4 Embedded Applications

While the scripting languages are seamlessly integrated with the browser and the HTML markup, there are also Java applets and ActiveX controls, which enable the implementation of business logic that runs at the client side. They are not as integrated into the browser as the scripting languages and, hence, do not allow dynamic HTML. They rather represent small "standalone" applications that are embedded in the HTML markup of a Web page, downloaded when accessing the page, and locally executed while viewing the page. As standalone applications, they are executed in a completely independent fashion and need to provide their own user interface, but they may leverage existing code libraries (e.g., for the design of the graphical user interface). While this means that a developer may need to implement from scratch the interface of the applet or ActiveX control, it also means that he can program full-fledged applications, starting from powerful programming languages such as Java or C#.

The embedding of applets or ActiveX controls into the HTML markup of a Web page relies on the `<object>` tag. The following code snippet shows, for example, how to embed a Java applet into HTML (ActiveX controls are embedded similarly):

```
<object classid="java:myapplet.class"
        codetype="application/java-vm"
        width="600" height="400"></object>
```

The attribute `classid` instructs the browser to load the `myapplet.class` Java class; the `codetype` attribute tells the browser that the object is a Java application; and the two attributes `width` and `height` set the applet's dimensions. According to where the `<object>` tag is placed in the layout of the Web page, the browser will arrange a placeholder for the applet that is filled when executing the applet, which thus becomes an integral part of the overall layout of the page.

The execution of Java applets requires the installation of the Java Virtual Machine on the client PC, a cross-browser application that guarantees the executability of applets independently of the adopted client browser or operating system. Unfortunately, the same is not true for ActiveX controls, supported only by Microsoft's Internet Explorer, which heavily hinders a wide adoption of ActiveX controls on the Web.

In the beginning (before the introduction of AJAX), only embedded standalone applications like Java applets or ActiveX controls were able to establish proper communication channels between the piece of code running in the client browser and the application's Web server, as those technologies could rely on the availability of suitable, ready-to-use code libraries. This was one of the strong features of applets and ActiveX controls, which heavily determined their success.

2.4.5 Embedded Multimedia Objects

While the scripting approach might be too restrictive in certain situations, the development of effective standalone applications to be embedded into a Web page might be too time consuming in other situations. Due to the fact that more and more Web applications aim at interactivity and multimedia features (e.g., applications that make heavy use of sound, music, animations, or videos), there is a growing emphasis on effective multimedia interfaces. To overcome the shortcomings of the previous two approaches to the design of such kinds of user interfaces, Adobe Flash,[4] Microsoft Silverlight,[5] and JavaFX[6] provide programming environments and client-side execution platforms for the development of highly interactive multimedia applications or presentations.

Adobe Flash leverages *ActionScript*, a proprietary scripting language based on ECMAScript, similar to JavaScript and JScript (which are thus very similar in their syntax to ActionScript). Silverlight may be programmed in any of the *.NET languages* supported by the client environment. JavaFX, Sun's answer to the development of RIA applications, is programmed in *JavaFX Script*, a declarative scripting language inspired by Java that can be run on any platform with an installed Java platform (the JavaFX interpreter generates conventional Java bytecode).

The languages and their execution platforms are tailored to the design of interactive multimedia applications that, just like Java applets, can be embedded into the HTML markup code of a Web page through the `<object>` tag. All three approaches require the installation of a so-called browser plug-in in order for the browser to be able to run the embedded objects. The required plug-ins can be downloaded for free from the platforms' Web sites and are typically easy to install, even by inexperienced users; if supported by the browser, the installation may also be performed automatically.

As for the communication with the Web server to enable real distributed applications, Adobe Flash is equipped with a powerful communication mechanism called *Flash Remoting*, which facilitates the communication between the client-side ActionScript and server-side resources (e.g., Java classes or beans running on the server). Flash Remoting leverages a proprietary message format, the *Action Message Format* (AMF), that is used to serialize or deserialize ActionScript objects for transmission via HTTP, and a Java servlet[7] that runs on the Web server and acts as a *gateway* between the client-side ActionScript and the server-side Java classes. JavaFX supports client-server communication via two standard Java communication mechanisms: (i) the

---

[4] http://www.adobe.com/it/products/flash/

[5] http://silverlight.net/

[6] http://www.sun.com/software/javafx/index.jsp

[7] There are also implementations of the Flash Remoting gateway in other languages; on http://www.amfphp.org/ you can find, for example, an implementation for PHP.

Remote Method Invocation (RMI) technology, or (ii) the *Java API for XML Web Services* (JAX-WS). Similar communication features are also supported by Microsoft Silverlight. A detailed discussion of the various communication features is however out of the scope of this book.

2.5 Dynamic Web Pages and Server-Side Business Logic

Since its creation, the Web has evolved from an environment hosting static hypermedia documents to a platform able to support the execution of complex applications. E-commerce applications are a prominent example: their pages need to be updated daily, to show, for example, the offers of the day or the new available products; they must also support operations, such as the purchase of a product. The establishment of XML technologies and some extensions to the traditional client-server architecture paved the road for the development of *dynamic Web pages*, composed at runtime by dynamically extracting content from a data source and by building the final page rendition "on the fly".

2.5.1 Common Gateway Interface (CGI)

The simplest way to dynamically build a Web page in response to an HTTP request is to let the HTTP server delegate the retrieval of dynamic data and the construction of the page to an external program, which receives some input parameters and generates an output page. The invocation of the external program occurs when the HTTP request coming from the browser includes a URL pointing to a CGI program instead of to a static document.

To make the server communicate with the external program it is necessary to use a standard interface, called *Common Gateway Interface* (CGI). CGI allows the Web server to invoke programs, called *CGI programs*, that are executed "on the fly" to dynamically construct the page. A CGI program can issue queries over a database to extract data which it then uses to assemble an HTML page, or it can store user inputs in the database by inserting or updating data in it.

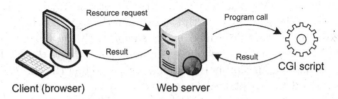

Fig. 2.8. Dynamic construction of a Web page in response to an HTTP request

Figure 2.8 illustrates the computation steps that characterize the dynamic generation of a page through CGI:

1. The client issues an HTTP request to the server for the execution of a CGI program. The request may also include some input data; for example, a request for a search program will transport the search keyword.
2. Using the CGI interface, the HTTP server invokes the external program (i.e., the CGI script), passing the input data and parameters coming with the HTTP request.
3. The external program constructs the result page and sends it back to the HTTP server.
4. The HTTP server assembles the HTTP response, which embeds the page constructed by the external program, and sends it back to the client.

The location of the CGI script in the server's file system is specified as a URL in the HTTP request, the same way the location of an HTML page is specified. In order to undertake the appropriate action, the HTTP server is configured to distinguish between the requests referring to static resources and those referring to CGI scripts: while the former are served by sending the resource (e.g., an HTTP page) back to the client, the latter imply the execution of the script before the response can be assembled and sent back. To instruct the server about where in the file system to locate the HTML pages and the CGI scripts, a mapping of the different directories on the HTTP server can be specified in a configuration file. In this way, the server knows that if the URL of an HTTP request points to a specific directory (for example, the directory named `cgi-bin`), then the requested file is a program to be executed.

The Web server and the CGI programs communicate by means of system variables, initialized by the HTTP server upon receipt of the HTTP request. These variables describe the parameters of the HTTP request (such as the HTTP method used, the number of bytes attached to the request, etc.), and are useful for the execution of the CGI program.

The Web server also communicates to the CGI scripts possible user input, which is collected through the client (by means of forms) and transported with the HTTP request by means of the GET and POST methods (which we already introduced in Section 2.1):

- *The GET method*: communicates the user input as label/value pairs appended to the requested URL. For example, when the URL `http://www.mydomain.org/cgi-bin/search?Key=search_key` is received, the server invokes the search CGI script, located in the `cgi-bin` directory, and initializes a CGI variable, called *query string*, with the label/value pair (`Key=search_key` in the pervious example). In this way, the CGI script can get the user input simply by fetching and decoding the content of this variable. The CGI script is then invoked by passing to a system shell a command line, whose length can be at most 256 characters. Due to this limitation, the GET method is used when the client needs to communicate to the server only few simple parameters.
- *The POST method*: attaches the user input to the HTTP request using the message body. Therefore, differently from the GET method, the POST

method is able to support the transmission of large amounts of data from the browser to the Web server. More specifically, the browser packages the user's input in the body of the HTTP request and sends it to the Web server. The Web server then extracts the user's input from the message body, and sends it to the standard input of the CGI script, which can then use it for performing a business action and generating the response.

The user input is collected through forms. Figure 2.9 shows the HTML code and the corresponding Web rendition of a simple form that uses the GET method to communicate keywords to a search CGI program. The form is delimited by the <FORM> tag and is composed of two <INPUT> elements: a text field, for entering the search keys, and a button, for submitting the keys to the Web server. The *action* attribute of the <FORM> element specifies the URL of the program to be called when the "Search" button is pressed. The *method* attribute then specifies the HTTP method to use for sending the input.

```
<HTML>
<HEAD>
<TITLE>Form example</TITLE>
</HEAD>
<BODY>
  <H1>Search</H1>
  <P>Please enter search key: </P>
  <FORM name="form1" method="post" action="search">
      <INPUT type="text" name="textfield">
      <INPUT type="button" name="Search" value="Search">
  </FORM>
</BODY>
</HTML>
```

Fig. 2.9. A simple form that allows users to enter search keywords

CGI extensions

CGI is the simplest way of dynamically publishing or updating content on the Web, but its architecture has some significant drawbacks, which make it impractical in most situations. The leading problem is performance: for each HTTP request for a CGI script, the Web server initiates a new process, which is only terminated at the end of the execution of the script. Process creation and termination are very costly activities, which may quickly become the performance bottleneck, also because the different active processes must compete for system resources such as the main memory.

Additionally, terminating the process after the CGI script is executed after each request prevents information about the user interaction from being retained between consecutive user requests, unless such information is stored in a database, which again impacts performance. Terminating the process also prevents the management of shared resources, such as a database, used by multiple users across multiple HTTP requests. Finally, CGI programs cannot link to other stages of Web server request processing, such as authorization and logging.

To overcome such limits and to cope with applications that demand a high level of performance and the retention of user session data, more complex communication infrastructures have been proposed. For example, several vendors developed proprietary APIs for their servers, which, however, sacrificed the simplicity of CGI.

FastCGI was introduced as a language-independent, open extension of CGI, improving performance while overcoming the limitations of server-specific APIs. FastCGI is a Web server interface that is conceptually very similar to CGI, with the major difference that FastCGI processes are *persistent*: after processing a request, they wait for a new request instead of terminating.

Request processing in a FastCGI application proceeds as follows:

1. The Web server creates FastCGI processes to handle requests. The processes may be created at startup or on demand.
2. Each FastCGI process initializes itself and waits for a new connection from the Web server.
3. When the client sends a request, the Web server opens a connection to the FastCGI process. The server transports the CGI environment variables and the input over the connection.
4. The FastCGI process sends the output back to the server over the same connection.
5. When the FastCGI process closes the connection, the request is complete. The FastCGI process then waits for another connection from the Web server.

An alternative to CGI: Server Side Includes (SSIs)

Other solutions comparable to CGI can be used to build dynamic pages. For example, *Server Side Includes* (SSIs) are *directives* placed inside the HTML code and evaluated on the server while the pages are being served. This allows the Web server to add dynamically generated content to an existing page, without having to serve the entire page via a CGI program or other dynamic technologies.

SSI directives have the following syntax:

```
<!--#directive parameter=value parameter=value ... -->
```

As can be observed, they are formatted like *HTML comments*. Therefore, if the Web server is not SSI-enabled, the directive will not be processed, and the browser will simply ignore them; otherwise, the directive will be replaced with its results.

To call SSI from a Web page, the Web server must be enabled and configured to interpret SSI commands, and the Web page must be named with the `.shtml` extension, instead of with the usual `.html` or `.htm`. The server is therefore able to parse the Web page looking for comments that, in the case of SSI directives, tell the server which operations must be performed before sending back the Web page to the client.

Several SSI directives can be used. The most commonly used are shortly illustrated in Table 2.1. Beyond the basic set of directives, which are mainly used to generate contents, some advanced commands can also be used to set variables and to use variables in comparisons and conditions.

It is worth noting that the decision of when to use SSI and when to have pages entirely generated by an external program usually depends on the amount of content that needs to be regenerated every time the page is served. SSI is a way to add small pieces of information, such as the current date and time. However, if the majority of the Web page is being generated when it is served, other solutions have to be adopted.

2.5.2 Web Server Extensions

The limitations of the CGI/FastCGI architecture and the SSI solution previously described can be overcome by extending the capabilities of the Web server with an application execution engine (see Figure 2.10), where the programs for computing the HTTP response can be processed in an efficient way, without being terminated after each request, and shared resources can be associated with one or more applications and concurrently accessed by multiple users. Such an extended architecture typically also offers a main memory environment for storing session data whose duration goes across multiple HTTP requests.

Table 2.1. Some common SSI directives

Directive	Description
echo	It displays the value of some HTTP environment variables. For example, the directive `<!--#echo var="DATE_LOCAL" -->` displays the today's date.
include	It is used to include the content of one file (HTML page, text file, script, etc.) into another. A typical example is the inclusion of files coding parts of pages that are persistent throughout the whole Web site, such as navigation bars, headers and footers. For example, the directive `<!--#include virtual="/navigationBar.html" -->` includes the file `navigationBar.html`, coding a persistent navigation bar. The parameter `virtual` specifies the path of the file to be included. In alternative, the parameter `file` can be used to specify a file path relative to the directory of the document being served.
fsize and flastmod	They return the size and last modification date of some files on the server. For example, the directive `<!--#flastmod virtual="home.html"-->` returns the last modification date of the file `home.html`, whose path is specified trough the `virtual` attribute.
exec	It executes a program, script, or shell command on the server. The `cmd` parameter is used to specify a server-side command, while the `cgi` parameter is used for expressing the path to a CGI script.

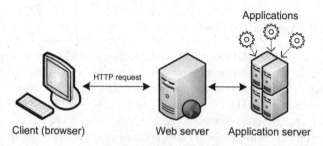

Fig. 2.10. The extended Web server architecture

Servlets

An example of extended Web server architecture is *Javasoft's Servlet API* (illustrated in Figure 2.11), which associates the Web server with a Java Virtual Machine (JVM). The JVM supports the execution of a special Java program, the *servlet container*, which in turn is in charge of managing session data and executing *Java servlets*.

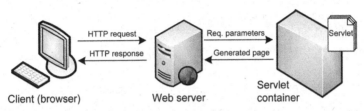

Fig. 2.11. Java servlet architecture

Java servlets are Java programs that can be invoked by HTTP requests to dynamically construct pages. The servlet container is responsible for receiving the HTTP request for the servlet execution from the Web server, creating a user session when needed, invoking the servlet associated with the HTTP request, and passing to the servlet the parameters transported by the HTTP request, wrapped in the form of a Java object. In general, the servlet container is in charge of optimizing the life cycle of servlets, by sharing them with all the clients that require their services. In this way, it is possible to reduce the operations for the creation and elimination of the servlet objects and for establishing the connections with data sources.

There are different types of servlet, each one implementing the `javax.servlet.Servlet` interface, included in the servlet API specification, which supports the management of the servlet life cycle through the following steps:

- The servlet class is loaded by the servlet container during start-up by means of the `init()` method. This method initializes the servlet before it can serve any request.
- After initialization, every time a servlet service is required, the container calls the `service()` method, which determines the kind of request and dispatches it to an appropriate servlet method.
- Before shutting down, the container calls the `destroy()` method to remove the servlet instance, releasing all its resources.

In the case of HTTP-specific services, servlets extend the class `HTTPServlet`, a standard implementation of the `Servlet` interface for the HTTP protocol that offers basic primitives for interacting with the servlet container, such as the functions for inspecting the HTTP request and the session data, and for writing the output (i.e., the generated page markup) to the HTTP response. Figure 2.12 gives an example of a simple servlet generating an HTML page.

```
import java.io.*;
import javax.servlet.*;
import javax.servlet.http.*;

public class SimpleServlet extends HttpServlet {
 public void doGet(HttpServletRequest request, HttpServletResponse response)
  throws ServletException, IOException {
    response.setContentType("text/html");
    response.setHeader("Pragma", "no-cache");
    PrintWriter out = response.getWriter();
    out.println("<HTML>");
    out.println("<HEAD>");
    out.println("<TITLE>Servlet Example</TITLE>");
    out.println("</HEAD>");
    out.println("<BODY>");
    out.println("<H1>This is a simple page generated through a servlet</H1>");
    out.println("</BODY>");
    out.println("</HTML>");
  }
}
```

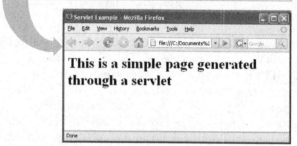

Fig. 2.12. An example of a Java servlet that generates an HTML page

The servlet, called SimpleServlet, extends the HttpServlet class and overrides the doGet method, which is invoked by the servlet container when an HTTP request based on the GET method is received. The method produces an HTML page, which is then sent back to the client. The two parameters of the method represent the request to be processed and the response to be produced. Some methods enable their manipulation. For example, the method setContentType is used to define the type of the response (in this case, an HTML page), while the method setHeader controls some parameters of the page to be sent back to the client. For example, the attribute "Pragma no-cache" sets an HTTP header that prevents the browser from caching the page.

The method getWriter allows the servlet to return data back to the client. More specifically, the method returns an output stream (the out object) through which the resulting page is sent back to the client. Every data printed on this output stream is sent back to the client. In the example, all the invocations of the println method print some HTML markup and some textual content, incrementally constructing the page sent back to the client.

Server-side scripting

Server-side scripting is a technique for building dynamic pages, which consists of inserting into HTML *page templates* programming instructions to be executed by a server program to determine the dynamic parts of the pages. The programmer thus may add the necessary scripting instructions to the HTML template that, as shown in Figure 2.13, must then be deployed in an extended Web server equipped with a *scripting engine* capable of interpreting the server-side scripting instructions.

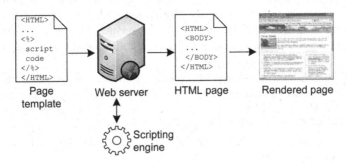

Fig. 2.13. The execution of a server-side scripting page template

When an incoming HTTP request refers to a page template, the Web server forwards the page template to the scripting engine, which processes the embedded programming instructions to determine the dynamic parts of the page and includes them in the page template. The generated output is a plain HTML page that is sent back to the Web server, which in turn forwards it to the client. For the browser receiving the result page, the server-side processing is completely invisible, and the HTML code received is perfectly identical to that of a manually produced, static page.

Despite the similarity, the coding style of server-side scripts is completely different from that of servlets. A servlet contains programming instructions for printing the entire page, whereas a page template contains regular HTML, with programming instructions limited to the computation of the variable part of the page. Thanks to this separation between static and dynamic content, server-side scripting page templates are typically easier to write and maintain.

Today, a broad variety of server-side scripting languages is available on the market. Factors influencing the choice of the most appropriate language include the availability of the technology on the target platform, the support for the scripting language by the Web server, the cost (free or not), and the complexity of the required functionality. In the following, we summarize three of the most prominent representatives of scripting languages (we will next focus on the JSP language):

- *PHP*: PHP ("PHP: Hypertext Preprocessor") is one of the most popular server-side scripting languages today. It draws its popularity from the fact that it is free, open source (with a huge supporting community), available on all major platforms, and is supported by all popular Web servers. It is in essence an imperative dynamically typed language, enhanced with object-oriented programming constructs.
- *ASP*: ASP, an acronym for Active Server Pages, is Microsoft's closed-source solution technology for server-side scripting. It was originally designed for and only supported by Internet Information Server (IIS). Although some solutions have become available to run ASP script on other Web servers, it is still most reliable combined with ISS. Furthermore, unlike PHP, it is not tied to one particular scripting language. ASP uses Microsoft Visual Basic Scripting Edition (VBScript) as the default scripting language, but others can be used.
- *Perl*: Perl, originally designed as a string manipulation language, grew to be one of the most popular server-side scripting languages today. It stems from the early days of the Web, when it was used for CGI scripting. Now, it is a dynamically typed multi-paradigm programming language, freely available on most platforms. Like PHP, it is open source, and enjoys the support of a large community.

Java Server Pages (JSP)

JSP is a simple but powerful technology that extends Java servlets. A JSP page is composed of blocks of static code (HTML, JavaScript, CSS, etc.), mixed with dynamic blocks, i.e., portions of Java code executed by the scripting engine.

As illustrated in Figure 2.14, the first time that the Web server (a *JSP container*) receives the request for a JSP page, the JSP template is translated into a servlet, which is then compiled, stored in the main memory, and executed to generate the page, with the static HTML simply being printed to the output stream associated with the servlet's `service` method. Such output is then sent to the client, which interprets and renders it in the same way as a simple HTML page.

Each time the Web server receives a request for the same JSP page, it verifies whether changes to its code occurred since its creation by checking the content of the `Last_Modified` HTTP header. If not, the servlet stored in memory is recalled; otherwise, the JSP page is recompiled and a new servlet instance is created and stored in memory. For this reason, the first access to a JSP page requires a longer time (the so-called *first-person penalty*), while the following requests are faster.

As illustrated in Figure 2.15, a JSP page is composed of the following elements:

- *Directives*: are used to communicate information about the page to the JSP container and to specify options about the translation of the page

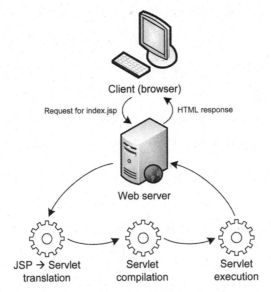

Fig. 2.14. The translation of JSP pages into servlets

to a servlet. The **page** directives relate to page properties, such as the language used for the expression of scripts within the page, the URL of the error page, session tracking instructions. Besides page directives, the **include** directive can be used for importing files to be combined with the JSP page, while the **taglib** directive declares libraries of personalized tags used within the page to code the invocation of some actions (see the next paragraph on server-side executable tags for details).

- *Scripting elements*: enable the inclusion of code written in the language declared through the directives (generally Java). They can specify *declarations* of variables and methods, *expressions* returning strings to be displayed in the final HTML page, or arbitrarily complex portions of code, called *scriptlets*.
- *Actions*: are tags that invoke the execution of actions. The JSP specification offers a set of standard actions to include resources (both static or dynamic) in the JSP page (<jsp:include>), to forward the processing of the current resource to another static resource, a servlet, or a JSP page (<jsp:forward>), and to invoke the execution of Java components (see Table 2.2). An extension of this set is provided by the Java Standard Tag Library (JSTL). Libraries of *custom tags* can also be defined and used within JSP pages to invoke functions not covered by the standard actions and JSTL (see the next paragraph on server-side executable tags for details).

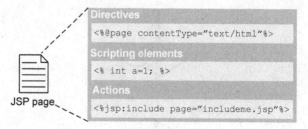

Fig. 2.15. The structure of JSP pages

```
1   <%@page language="java"%>
2   <%@page contentType="text/htlm"%>
3   <%@page import="java.util.*"%>
4   <html>
5    <head>
6     <title>An example of Java Server Pages </title>
7    </head>
8    <body>
9     <% out.println("A simple JSP example."); %>
10    <%= new Date() %>
11   </body>
12  </html>
```

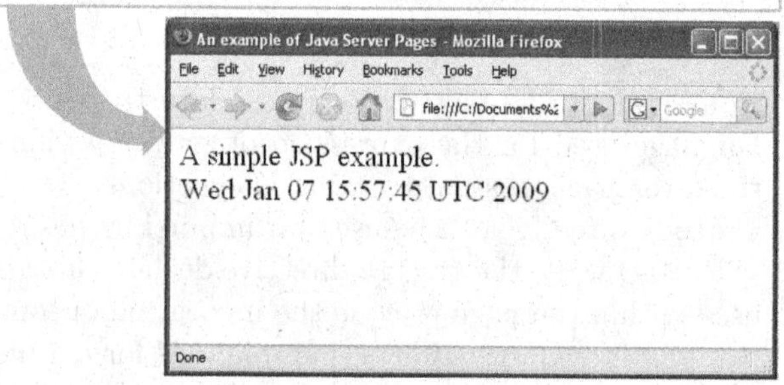

Fig. 2.16. An example of a JSP page

Figure 2.16 reports a very simple example of a JSP page. The HTML markup (lines 4-8 and 11-12) constitutes the *page template*. The other lines are JSP elements:

- Lines 1-3 correspond to *page directives*: the first line specifies the language used within the page (Java), the second one the type of the document to be generated (**text/html**, according to the MIME standard), and the third one imports a Java package (**util**).
- Lines 9 and 10 are examples of *scripting elements*. Line 9 is a *scriptlet*, that is, a portion of Java code displaying a message in the final rendered page. Line 10 is an *expression*, whose result (the current date) is transformed into a string displayed on the final rendered page.

It is worth noting that scripting elements can access some *implicit objects*, i.e., objects that the JSP container makes directly available to the JSP pages, without any need for the JSP pages to instantiate them. The most important objects are:

- `request`: it is an instance of a class implementing the `ServletRequest` interface, included in the package `javax.servlet`. It stores the HTTP request received by the client, and its methods allow access to information related to the request, such as possible parameters (`getParameters()` and `getParameterValues()`); or to the client issuing the request (`getRemote-Addr()` and `getRemoteHost()`).
- `response`: it is an instance of the class implementing the `ServletResponse` interface, which can be used to manage the response to be sent back to the client. It enables in particular access to the output stream, to set properties of the generated HTTP response, such as an error or a cookie to be sent back to the client.
- `out`: it is an instance of the class `JSPwriter`. By means of methods such as `print()` and `println()`, it allows us to write on the output stream corresponding to the response to be delivered to the client.
- `session`: it allows us to associate an identifier of the user requesting a page with a parameter whose value can be maintained by the JSP container and retrieved when serving any subsequent request by the same user. In this way, it is possible to keep track of the selections made by a user during navigation using one or more session variables. Details on session management are reported in in the following.

Server-side executable tags

Although server-side scripting facilitates the development of dynamic Web applications, it does not eliminate the need for mixing programming with content and markup. The need remains for the programmer and the graphic designer to work jointly on the same source file, which limits a full "separation of concerns" between the various aspects of Web development: the static content, the look and feel, and the programming logic. The so-called *server-side tag libraries* take a further step in the direction of separating content and markup from the programming of a dynamic page template.

Tag libraries are available both in the Java world, starting from Version 1.1 of the JSP specification, and in the Microsoft .NET platform, as part of the ASP.NET language. The key idea behind them is to mask the programming code necessary for dynamic content production through tags, which can be inserted in the page as regular markup elements, but are executed by a runtime interpreter. With a tag library, content and programming are not mixed up in the page template markup. The template consists of only content and markup; the markup includes special XML tags that are executed by a server-side program to produce further content and/or HTML markup.

In JSP, custom tags are used to invoke *JavaBeans*, reusable Java software components (Java classes), that can be used for building different types of

Table 2.2. JSP standard actions for the inclusion of JavaBeans.

Tag	Description

`<jsp:useBean>`	It invokes the execution of a JavaBean, that is a Java Component that runs in any Java Virtual Machine. In particular, it associates an instance of the corresponding Java class with an identifier, also defining the scope of the created object. For example, the following code
	
	 `<jsp:useBean id="myBean" scope="session"`
	 `class="JavaClass" />`
	
	 creates an instance of the class `JavaClass`, and associates it to the identifier `myBean` that can thus be used for accessing class methods and variables. The scope of the created instance is the `session`, meaning that the object will be visible to all the pages requested within a same session. Other possible scopes are `page` (the page where the instance is created), `request` (all the pages computed within a same request), and `application` (all the pages within a given application).

`<jsp:setProperty>`	It is a sub-action of `<jsp:useBean>`, used to set some properties of a JavaBean.
`<jsp:getProperty>`	It is a sub-action of `<jsp:useBean>`, used to get the values of some properties of a JavaBean.

Java applications (applets, or even more complex standalone applications) in any application domain. Whether JavaBeans are used to develop simple applets or more sophisticated applications, they can be easily integrated into JSP pages: the JavaBean code will be hidden to the developer of the JSP page, who will only need to invoke the methods exposed by the corresponding Java class.

The integration of JavaBeans into JSP pages is possible thanks to some JSP standard actions, illustrated in Table 2.2.

Stateful Web applications

The Web server extensions previously described offer an efficient way of implementing stateful Web applications, that is, HTTP-based applications capable of retaining the state of the user interaction. State information can be stored at the client side, in the form of *cookies*, or at the server side, in the form of *session data*.

A cookie is an object created by a server-side program and stored at the client (typically, in the disk cache of the browser), which can be used by the server-side program to store and retrieve state information associated with the client. For example, a typical use of cookies in the context of e-commerce applications is to store user preferences, which are transparently communicated to the server whenever the user accesses the application, so that the Web server is able to personalize the application to the user's preferences.

A cookie is created at the client side when the HTTP response sent by the server includes a `Set-Cookie` HTTP header, filled with the piece of information to be stored at the client. The cookie may include a description of the range of URLs for which some associated state information is valid. Any future HTTP requests made by the client that fall in that range of URLs will transmit the content of the cookie back to the server. The duration of the state information associated with a cookie is independent of the duration of a server-side session, and is decided by the client, who may explicitly delete his cookies.

State maintenance at the server side requires the server to identify and distinguish the HTTP requests of the various clients, and to associate each piece of state information with the user it belongs to. This requirement is fulfilled by creating a *session identifier* upon the arrival of the first HTTP request of a new client, and by making the browser communicate the identifier to the server in all the subsequent HTTP requests, so that the server can treat such requests as belonging to the same user session. For example, in the servlet architecture, the servlet container creates a new session identifier for each HTTP request coming from a client not already associated with a valid session identifier, and exploits cookies to force the browser to communicate the session ID at each HTTP request. A disadvantage of cookies is that the user can disable their support in the browser. To overcome this problem, the same data that would be stored in the cookie, for instance, the session identifier, can be preserved for the duration of a session using a technique called *URL rewriting*, which appends the state information as extra parameters in the URLs embedded in the page sent to the client. In this way, the client communicates the needed information to the server even in absence of cookies, but the server-side application code must take care of appending to URLs embedded inside the dynamically generated pages the extra information to be maintained. In the servlet environment, URL rewriting for the communication of the session identifier is facilitated by a utility function, which automatically appends the session identifier to a dynamically produced URL.

When a session is active, the server-side execution engine can associate state information with it. Typically, such information is temporary, and resides in some main-memory data structures whose duration is the same as that of the user's session. In the servlet environment, session data are wrapped inside the *session* object that offers to servlets functions for retrieving and updating information pertaining to a user session.

The duration of sessions managed at the server side depends on some server settings (typically a timeout after the last user's request is defined). In some cases the session can be terminated through suitable instructions whereby a server-side program can explicitly invalidate the session. When explicit invalidation or timeout occurs, the next request from the client causes the server to create a new session identifier.

2.5.3 Multitiered Architectures

Large-scale Web applications, such as portals, e-commerce applications, and community sites, are typically exposed to a very large number of concurrent requests. For this reason, they must ensure a high level of availability. A modular, multitiered architecture can fulfill such requirement, offering an environment where the different application components can be easily replicated to increase performance and to avoid single points of failure.

Architectures of large enterprise Web applications are commonly organized into three layers:

- The *presentation layer*: the most "superficial" layer, in charge of processing requests coming from the client and constructing the HTML page. It is managed by means of the Web server extensions already described in Section 2.10 (containers and script engines), which are able to dynamically construct the HTML pages to be sent back to the client, based on the data produced by the execution of some business components in the underlying application logic layer.
- The *application logic layer*: the intermediate layer, in charge of executing components realizing the application's business logic. It is the most relevant layer, since it offers the set of application functions that can be executed by users by means of the application pages. The presentation layer exploits such components to obtain the data required for the dynamic construction of Web pages. To produce such data, the business components communicate with the underlying resource management layer to access persistent data sources or legacy enterprise systems, or to invoke external services.
- The *resource management layer*: represents the ensemble of services offered by different systems, such as those supporting the access to databases and transaction processing systems, or to enterprise information systems, or, in general, to external Web services (see Section 2.6).

In order to be realized, three-tiered architectures need an execution environment supporting interlayer communication. *Application servers* provide such an environment. By providing an intermediate layer between the Web server and the backend for resource management, they enable the efficient execution of business components in the application logic layer, thus supporting the construction of dynamic pages according to the execution flow depicted in Figure 2.17.

The Web server accepts the HTTP request coming from the client and transforms it into a request to the scripting engine. The scripting engine executes the program associated with the requested URL, which may also include calls to business components hosted in the application server. Typically, such calls involve the retrieval and elaboration of data from one or more data sources, such as corporate databases or legacy systems. The components

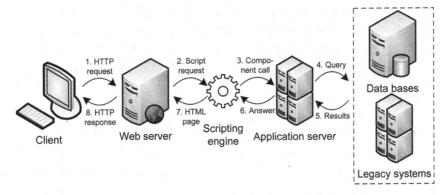

Fig. 2.17. An application server architecture

managed by the application server dispatch the query to the data source, collect the query results, possibly elaborate them, and send them back to the scripting engine. Query results are then integrated into the HTTP response by the scripts executed in the scripting engine to obtain a result HTML page to be sent back to the client by the Web server.

The application server architecture represented in Figure 2.17 has many commercial implementations, which vary especially for the supported programming languages and the communication protocols. The two most comprehensive solutions are *Java Enterprise Edition* (Java EE) and *Microsoft .NET*. The two frameworks have several characteristics in common: both are software platforms conceived for multitier, object-oriented, distributed applications. However, Java EE emphasizes application portability with respect to operating systems, but restricts the programming language to Java. Conversely, Microsoft .NET has a multi-language development environment, but is limited to the Microsoft operating systems.

Figure 2.18 shows the typical layered organization of Java EE applications. Several components realize different business logic functions distributed over client machines, the Java EE server machine, and the database or legacy machines at the back end. Applets and Dynamic HTML pages run on the client machine. Servlets and JSP pages are Web components running on the Java EE server. The Java EE server also hosts *Enterprise JavaBeans* (EJBs), which are components implementing the application business logic.

The core of the platform indeed consists of the EJB API, which dictates the rules for defining object-oriented components in distributed, multitiered enterprise applications. Like JavaBeans, EJBs are Java classes. However, differently from JavaBeans, they provide an object-oriented transactional environment that is specifically conceived for building distributed, multitier enterprise components. In particular, EJBs alleviate the role of the application developer, allowing him to concentrate on the programming of the business logic only, while eliminating (or at least reducing) the need for handling typ-

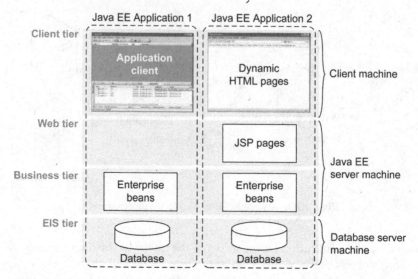

Fig. 2.18. A typical organization of a Java EE Web application [JBC$^+$07]

ical issues of enterprise applications, such as transactional behavior, security, and threading. Such issues are managed by the application server.

Three types of EJBs allow developers to cope with the different needs arising in the development of enterprise Web applications:

- *Session Beans*: manage the application's business logic, being in charge of performing operations implementing the application functions.
- *Entity Beans*: are used to represent data to support operations, such as reading data from and writing data on persistent data sources (databases or legacy information systems).
- *Message-Driven Beans*: support the development of asynchronous applications, such as systems for posting emails or SMSs.

It is worth noting that if in a Web application EJBs are invoked by the servlets and the JSP pages in the Web tier to compute the dynamic contents of pages, EJBs have been conceived for reusability, allowing different technologies (possibly in a distributed execution context) to use the same application logic layer. Therefore, potentially other EJBs, applets, or external services or systems can invoke an EJB. This feature greatly facilitates the development and the maintenance of the business logic layer, since it supports the decoupling of the constituent components from any specific use of the component in a specific domain or application.

2.5.4 How to Access Data

As discussed in the previous sections, a Web application must be able to connect to a data source. This takes place through database APIs, which offer a set of utility objects that hide the details of the database interaction, thus facilitating the programming of database-aware applications.

Relational databases are the most adopted products for storing Web application contents, and SQL is the most popular language to extract and manipulate the data stored in relational databases. The most diffused libraries for relational databases are *Microsoft ODBC* and *Javasoft JDBC*.

ODBC and JDBC

A standard way to connect to databases is using the Open DataBase Connectivity (ODBC) standard, which is implemented by various server-side scripting languages (including PHP, as previously discussed). ODBC was developed by Microsoft in 1991, and offers a set of DBMS-independent function to connect to, access, and manage a database. The ODBC architecture consists of four components:

- *Application*: calls ODBC functions to submit SQL statements to the database, and retrieves results, if applicable. SQL queries can be executed to retrieve information, add or delete information, or manipulate the database structure. In a Web environment, the application is the Web application itself, performing the calls throught the server-side technology.
- *Driver Manager*: loads and unloads drivers on behalf of the application. The Driver Manager processes ODBC function calls or passes them to a specific driver.
- *Drivers*: process ODBC function calls, submit SQL requests to a specific data source, and return results to the application. If necessary, a driver modifies an application request so that the request conforms to syntax supported by the associated DBMS.
- *Data Source*: consists of the data the user wants to access and its associated operating system, DBMS, and network platform (if any).

An ODBC implementation thus provides support for the various ODBC functions and (database) drivers, allowing us to connect to the DBMS of our choice. ODBC allows connecting to a nonrelational data source as long as an appropriate driver is available.[8] Once a data source has been set up, ODBC allows easy connection and handling of it. The ODBC architecture was devised in such a way as to abstract the specific data source used for the user (the programmer). In principle, it allows the use of multiple, heterogeneous data sources, and changing the underlying DBMS without touching the application code.

JDBC, sometimes dubbed the "Java ODBC equivalent," is a Java API developed by Sun Microsystems to connect to and manage a database. JDBC is very similar to ODBC in design, and essentially allows us to connect to

---

[8] ODBC drivers exists for example to connect to XML files or spreadsheets.

a database, and to send queries and process the results. JDBC provides native database drivers, and also allows ODBC connections through the JDBC-ODBC bridge.

Other DBMS connectivity solutions

As already mentioned, some programming languages, including server-side scripting languages, provide a proprietary solution for database access. Sun Microsystems provides JDBC as a solution for database access in Java. Perl prescribes DataBase Interface (DBI) as a database interface. Microsoft offers ActiveX Data Objects (ADO), and on a lower level, Object Linking and Embedding DataBase (OLE DB), as a general-purpose interface to access (not necessarily relational) data sources. All these solutions aim to abstract from the specificities of the underlying database, and provide the developer with higher-level solutions to access the data source. It should be noted that most proprietary solutions allow bridging to ODBC, whereby the application gains access to existing ODBC drivers.

Choice of DBMS

Various Data Base Management Systems (DBMSs) are available on the market today. Typical commercial systems include Oracle, Sybase Adaptive Server Enterprise, Microsoft SQL Server, and Microsoft Access. The most popular free DBMSs today are PostgreSQL and MySQL. Choosing a DBMS is not an easy task and generally depends on the particular needs of the Web application. MySQL is the preferred choice of many Web developers, simply because it is a fast and free open-source solution supported on the most common platforms. Important features it lacked (such as transactions and nested queries) have been added in later releases. Yet, for more demanding use, a commercial DBMS might be a better choice.

Object-Relational Mapping frameworks

An approach often used in object-oriented programming languages is Object-Relational Mapping (ORM) frameworks. These frameworks allow the programmer to handle and manipulate data in the system as if they were regular objects in the application code, while the actual data in fact reside in a (relational) database. The objects are then called *persistent*. In essence, the programmer handles and manipulates the objects; the ORM framework makes sure that, upon request, the correct object instances are generated (retrieving the necessary data from the database) and, in case operations are performed on the objects, the changes are correctly reflected in the underlying database. This requires a mapping between the object-oriented object structures (basically classes with their properties and relationships) and the relational structure of relational databases, and the creation and execution of correct database queries to retrieve data and handle any update operations performed on the persistent objects.

The ORM framework thus handles many jobs a developer otherwise needs to perform manually, and generally makes life easier for (Web) developers. Programmers, especially those familiar with object-orientation but not yet familiar with (relational) databases, often prefer ORM frameworks compared to "manual" data access and manipulation. However, ORM frameworks introduce an additional software layer, and typically do not fully take advantage of the underlying DBMS's functionality, slowing down data access and manipulation in the Web application. In particular for large data-intensive Web applications, this might be a factor to consider.

Both free and commercial ORM frameworks are available for most programming languages (including the ones previously covered: PHP, Perl, ASP). Web Application Frameworks (see Section 7.2.1) typically incorporate an ORM framework as basic support for Web developers.

2.6 Web Services and Remote Business Logic

Today, modern Web application architectures go beyond distributing the presentation layer, application logic layer, and resource management layer over multiple tiers. So-called Web services allow an application to seamlessly integrate and reuse application logic that runs on remote servers, independently of the application interacting with it. That is, just like Web users invoke a Web application that runs on a remote Web server, Web applications (or also Web services) can invoke a Web service that runs on a remote Web server. While the invocation of a Web application typically returns HTML markup that is rendered by the Web user's browser, Web services typically return data (e.g., text, a list of products, pictures) or application control information (e.g., a payment confirmation) in XML. In practice, a Web service may also wrap, i.e., provide a programming interface to, an entire, remote application, comprising its own presentation, application logic, and resource management layers. As a result, an application that integrates multiple Web services implements a distributed architecture in which parts of the application run locally and other parts run remotely, effectively transforming the Web into an application platform.

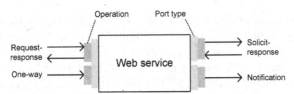

Fig. 2.19. External interfaces of a Web service

Web services are self-describing, self-contained software modules that are accessed via a network, such as the Internet, complete tasks, solve problems, or conduct transactions on behalf of a user or application [Pap08]. Figure 2.19 illustrates the interface features that characterize Web services. A Web service may support four types of operations: (i) the *request-response* operation invokes the service and expects an answer back; (ii) the *one-way* operation invokes the service and does not expect any answer back; (iii) the *solicit-response* operation.is initiated by the service (e.g., the service calling another service) and expects an answer back; (iv) the *notification* operation is initiated by the service and does not expect any answer back. Request-response and solicit-response operations can be used for the implementation of *synchronous* communication patterns, one-way and notification operations allow the implementation of *asynchronous* communication patterns. The operations of a service can be grouped into so-called *port types*, which represent the interfaces of the service, which, in turn, are associated with the *interaction protocol* the interfaces support. A service may therefore have multiple interfaces accessed via multiple interaction protocols.

2.6.1 The Web Service Description Language (WSDL)

Web services are published on and accessed over the Web. In order to tell the users of a service how the service looks like and how it can be invoked, Web services are described in the so-called Web Service Description Language (WSDL) [CCMW01]. WSDL is an XML language that allows the *abstract* description of services in terms of data types, messages, operations, port types, bindings, and a service endpoint. Specifically, data types, messages, operations, and port types describe the structure of a service's interfaces, the bindings describe which interaction protocols (e.g., SOAP over HTTP or SOAP over SMTP) the service supports via its port types, and the service endpoint describes where to physically access the service (i.e., its URL). WSDL is abstract in that it is independent of the implementation of a service, the platform, and the Web server the service runs on. WSDL descriptions can typically be both understood by human developers and automatically interpreted via software.

2.6.2 The Simple Object Access Protocol (SOAP)

Once an application or developer knows the WSDL description of a service, they can easily set up a communication channel with the service and invoke its operations. In order to use a Web service, it is not necessary to know the internals of the service, that is, for the user of a service it is irrelevant whether the service is implemented in Java, .NET, PHP, Perl, or similar. Interactions are indeed coded as XML messages, which are sent via the Simple Object Access Protocol (SOAP) [BEK+07], a standard communication protocol for XML over HTTP or SMTP that is supported by almost all of today's programming languages. SOAP too is platform-independent.

SOAP encapsulates service interactions (messages) in a so-called *envelop*, which is composed of an optional header and a mandatory body:

```
<soap:Envelope xmlns:soap="http://schemas.xmlsoap.org/soap/
envelope/">
  <soap:Header>
    //here go the header instructions
  </soap:Header>
  <soap:Body>
    //here goes the message payload or operation invocation
  </soap:Body>
</soap:Envelope>
```

The *header* allows the extension of the SOAP message format with additional features. For instance, the header might contain message routing or control information, such as encryption, correlation, transaction parameters, that are important for endpoints or intermediate routing nodes. The *body* carries the actual service-specific payload, i.e., the data sent to or received from a service. Typically, the payload is encoded in XML; other formats (e.g., binary files or images) can be embedded as well. SOAP supports the four operation types described above and can be used for the implementation of both synchronous (RPC-style) and asynchronous (message-style) communications.

2.6.3 The Service-Oriented Architecture (SOA)

The application of Web services, however, goes far beyond remote modules for applications. The use of standard communication protocols like SOAP and HTTP and of abstract WSDL descriptions and the fact that Web services are distributed over the Internet and possibly accessed by a multitude of different users or applications facilitates the so-called *loose coupling* of services with its users. That is, Web services have a neutral interface definition and can be used by any application supporting the SOAP protocol.

In order for a potential user of a service to find the WSDL descriptions of the service and to inspect the features of the service, Web services can be registered in dedicated *registries* that can be queried by users. The Universal Description, Discovery, and Integration (UDDI) specification specifically serves this purpose and provides a standard for the organization of and interaction with Web service registries. The role of UDDI for Web services is similar to the one of a phone book for telephone numbers.

The availability of registries and the capability of loose coupling of Web services enable a new paradigm of interoperability among software modules. Specifically, Web services implement a so-called *Service-Oriented Architecture* (SOA), which puts into communication service providers with service consumers via registries.

Figure 2.20 graphically depicts the typical SOA: A service *provider* (e.g., an airline carrier) implements a Web service (e.g., a flight search service) and

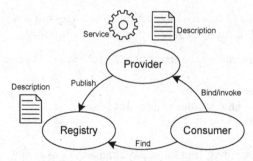

Fig. 2.20. The Service-Oriented Architecture

describes it via WSDL. The description is *published* in a *registry*, which can be searched by the service *consumer* (e.g., the developer of a travel agency application). If he *finds* a service with the functionality he is searching for, he can *bind* to the service and *invoke* (i.e., use) its operations. If adequately instructed, not only the developer of the travel agency's Web application (at development-time), but also the Web application itself (at runtime) might browse the registry in order to identify services to connect to.

As this example shows, the SOA is a natural enabler of business inter-actions over the Web, such as Business-to-Business (B2B) or Business-to-Consumer (B2C) relationships. The SOA fosters the use of standard protocols, maximizes flexibility, and lowers interoperability hurdles.

2.6.4 Service Orchestration and Choreography

Web services can be combined in a variety of different ways, possibly imple-menting a logic that provides the user of the composite solution with features that add value compared to the value of the same services used individually. Services might be integrated as modules into applications, as described ear-lier in this section, or they might be used for the development of composite services or distributed interaction patterns. A composite service is called an orchestration, while a distributed interaction specification is called a choreog-raphy [ACKM03].

An *orchestration* is an executable specification of a business process that interacts with Web services. The specification is typically interpreted by a so-called business process or service orchestration engine, which is in charge of invoking the services in the right order, mediate data formats, and keep track of the state of the process progress. The engine therefore acts as the (central) coordinator of the orchestration. The most important language for the specification of service orchestrations is the Web Services Business Process Execution Language (BPEL) [JE07], an XML language with workflow-like modeling constructs.

A *choreography* is an interaction protocol agreed on by multiple interact-ing parties, i.e., services. A choreography cannot be executed by an engine;

rather, it describes the interaction patterns of each partner participating in the conversation. In order to achieve the common goal (i.e., the successful completion of the choreography), each partner commits to abide by the protocol; control is distributed over all partners. The most representative choreography language is the Web Services Choreography Description Language (WS-CDL) [KBR+04].

In order to enhance the features of standard SOAP services, a set of advanced specifications and standards have been defined, which are commonly known under the name of WS-* specifications and extend the information carried in the header of SOAP messages. For instance, WS-Coordination allows the definition of correlation information for a set of messages (in order to uniquely identify the conversation), WS-Transaction allows the definition of transactional scopes over orchestrations, WS-Security provides means for the encryption of SOAP messages, an so on.

2.6.5 RESTful Services

The use of the above technologies in the development of Web services has become a de facto standard in many application areas, especially in enterprise and business environments. Indeed, SOAP/WSDL services in combination with the WS-* specifications provide all the necessary instruments for the development of complex, distributed applications. However, it is important to recognize that Web services not mandatorily need to be implemented using those technologies, only. For instance, during the last few years we have witnessed the emergence of so-called *RESTful services*, i.e., of Web services that are based on the REpresentational State Transfer (REST) architectural principles [Fie07]. The four main principles are:

1. Operations are based on standard *HTTP methods* (GET, POST, PUT, DELETE) performed on resources identified by URIs. The common semantics is: a GET on a URI retrieves a resource; a POST on a URI creates a new resource; a PUT on a URI updates a resource; and a DELETE on a URI deletes the resource.
2. Services are rigorously *stateless*. Services do not keep any session data at the server side.
3. State information is encoded in *URIs*. When a client performs an operation, in the answer he gets one or more URIs back that allow him to progress in the interaction with the service. That is, URIs are used to represent state information and to interact with the service.
4. Data is transferred directly *over HTTP*, e.g., via XML or JSON (JavaScript Object Notation). The payload of the message is added to the body of the HTTP operation, and MIME types can be used to identify the type of payload.

RESTful service are particularly suitable for simple interactions and uses. Especially AJAX Web applications foster the adoption of RESTful services,

as they alleviate the client from parsing SOAP and guarantee better performance. Complex, SOAP-style services might be implemented as well the
REST way, yet advanced features like reliability, coordination, transactions,
and similar are not yet adequately supported in REST.

2.7 Summary

This chapter illustrated the most prominent technologies, standards, and specifications that constitute the foundations for developing Web applications. We
started from the basic protocols and languages, such as HTTP, HTML, and
XML. Then, we discussed how a combination of technologies (HTML, DOM,
and JavaScript), collectively known as Dynamic HTML, extended the capabilities of HTML as a document markup language, allowing for sophisticated
interactive features and client-side business logic.

We then outlined the important approaches for building pages dynamically, ranging from CGI to server-side technologies (such as servlets, server-
side scripting (JSP), and tag libraries). The organization of the different application components into multitier architectures was also illustrated.

The last section introduced Web services as one of the current trends in
software development for the Web. We introduced the concepts of orchestration and choreography, the so-called WS-* specifications, and RESTful services. In this book, we will further investigate the role of Web services in the
development of Web applications, while the actual development of services is
out of the scope of this book. The interested reader is referred to books like
[ACKM03] and [Pap08].

2.8 Further Readings

A starting point for understanding the Web is the specification of HTTP 1.0
[BLFF96], which marks marks the foundation of the Web. Other historical
documents on the birth of the Web are available at the Web site of the W3C
Consortium (http://www.w3.org/History.html).

HTML [BLC95, Rag97] has been the subject of a large number of textbooks and documents. A complete and easy to use online reference manual of
all HTML 4 tags can be found at [Gro]. Also, XML textbooks abound. We
mention the books [Lau01] and [Har01], which offer an extended coverage of
XML and of all the most important related standards, including XSL.

For developers needing materials on dynamic page generation with Java
servlets and server-side scripting with JSP, Sun's Web site offers the official
reference guides and technical documentation [Mic09a, Mic09b]. The reference source for the Java Enterprise Edition platform is the Web site by Sun
[JBC+07], which contains the platform specifications and a number of tutorials and developers' guides on the different extension APIs.

The official reference for application development with the Microsoft .NET architecture is the section of the Microsoft Developer Network devoted to it, reachable from the home page at `http://msdn.microsoft.com`. Various books have appeared on the subject since Microsoft's first announcement of the .NET platform; among the available titles, [MS01] provides an effective tutorial on the integration of .NET server-side controls and databases. An online source of materials on everything related to the .NET world is [Car], which contains tutorials, articles, and links on all aspects of .NET development.

The Web site of the W3C Consortium certainly offers a wealth of resources on Web standards [RHJ99, Rag98, BPSM$^+$08, W3C98, FGM$^+$98] and should be continuously monitored by the reader interested in the technological evolution. The Web site of the W3 Schools [Sch] is also a very valuable source of information about Web standards and technologies. The site offers step-by-step tutorials on several Web-related technologies, including HTML, CSS, JavaScript, XML, XSL, Server-side scripting, Web services, and more. The W3C Consortium also organizes a yearly conference (called the WWW Conference), where the research and industrial communities meet to discuss the future of the Web.

3

The Development Process

The Web technologies discussed in the previous chapter enable the development of Web applications ranging from small, ad hoc solutions to complex Web information systems. Before focusing on the actual development of such kinds of applications, i.e., the *products*, we would like to focus on the *process* that leads to the creation of a Web application. Understanding software development processes (in general, not only for Web applications), the main development activities that need to be performed, their interconnections, and their temporal order are of fundamental importance for the success of a software product. In this book we follow a top-down approach to the organization of the contents and discuss first the way (Web) application development is organized, so as to discuss then the single activities that we will identify in this chapter.

Note that if we shift our point of view from that of the developer or project manager to that of the software product, what was before a *software development process* can now be seen as *software life cycle*, that is, a model that describes the life of an application, from its inception to its dismissal. *Software development process* and *software life cycle* are thus synonyms used in the literature depending on which view one prefers to highlight. As this is a book about Web engineering, we will use more the term *software development process*, though *software life cycle* may be used as well.

In this chapter, we will first discuss software development and its processes that are generally executed for any software product, in order to introduce the reader to the basic concepts and activities. We will then describe a possible development process more specific to Web applications and discuss its differences with more traditional development processes. We will also introduce some examples of concrete Web development processes, in order to introduce the reader with the peculiarities of the Web. The rest of the book will then be structured according to a typical process model.

S. Casteleyn et al., Engineering Web Applications: *Data-Centric Systems and Applications.*   57
DOI: 10.1007/978-3-540-92201-8_3, © Springer-Verlag Berlin Heidelberg 2009

3.1 Decomposing the Software Development Process

In today's software industry it is hard to find products that are planned, implemented, and tested by a single developer, as the complexity of modern (Web) applications typically requires the involvement of several different experts who are able to address specific development requirements more precisely. Depending on the size of the application and the actors involved in the development process, building an application may be an intricate undertaking, exposed to a variety of risks that might compromise the success of the final application. In order to control the software development process, it is thus of fundamental importance to understand its constituent activities, its actors, and their interconnections.

3.1.1 Activities in Software Development

Software development is a creative process leading to an innovative software product or system. Usually, this process is not just one monolithic block of work that takes as input some ideas about the application to be developed and produces as output a perfectly fitting solution; the process can be decomposed into a set of basic activities with well-defined boundaries and meanings. Such activities aim at *understanding* the problem, *planning* a solution, *carrying out* the plan, *examining* the result for accuracy, and *resolving* possible errors or inaccuracies. Traditionally, the software development process is organized into the following basic activities:

- *Requirements engineering*: aims at understanding the problem.
- *Design*: aims at planning a solution to the problem.
- *Implementation*: translates the plan into running application code.
- *Testing and evaluation*: aims at identifying coding errors or inconsistencies between the collected requirements and their implementation.
- *Deployment*: brings the solution to the customers.
- *Maintenance*: aims at monitoring a running system and keeping it healthy and running.
- *Evolution*: aims at improving the developed solution over time, providing new input to the development process in the form of new requirements.

More precisely, *requirements engineering* aims at understanding a product's needed capabilities and attributes. The analysis concentrates on *functional requirements*, referring to the functions that the system must be able to support, as well as on *nonfunctional requirements*, referring mainly to the quality of the offered solution. This implies identifying the general idea behind the system, as well as the stakeholders that require the new solution, the motivations for the production of a new system and the final usage environment. The collected requirements are elaborated with the aim of producing some high-level models of the system that abstract from irrelevant details of the problem domain.

After a subset of the application's requirements has been understood, the *design* can follow. The design activity aims at specifying a solution, which must meet functional and efficiency requirements, as well as possible constraints derived from the target environment. Requirements previously collected are therefore refined, restricted, and enhanced to satisfy possible technological constraints.

There are different views characterizing software design. For example, Pressman [Pre05] describes software design as a system of activities for data/class design, component design, interface design, and architectural design. Considering different separate views helps us shape better the specific aspects of the system, such as structure, behavior, interoperability, data, and control flow. It also enforces *separation of concerns*, a basic software engineering principle stating that approaching a problem by separating the different involved concerns may help us cope with complexity and achieve some required engineering quality factors such as adaptability, maintainability, extendibility, and reusability.

During *implementation*, the different design views are transformed either manually or with the help of automatic generation tools into corresponding program code (structured into modules and/or files), database tables, and configuration files. Implementation may require the use of existing code libraries, a variety of different programming languages and communication protocols, and different hardware devices.

The *testing and evaluation* activity is typically conducted in parallel with the previous activities, because the correctness and reliability of intermediate results – not only of the final product – is of fundamental importance to guarantee the quality of an application. The most relevant quality concerns addressed by this activity are related to *functionality* (i.e., the correctness of the application behavior with respect to specified functional requirements), *performance* (i.e., the throughput and response times of the application in average and peak workload conditions), and *usability* (i.e., ease of use, communication effectiveness, and adherence to consolidated usage standards).

The *deployment* of a ready application delivers the developed application to its users. Depending on the nature of the application, this activity may imply the installation of the software on client PCs, the setup of central application and database servers, the configuration of communication middleware, and so on. Closely related with the deployment of a new software solution is the instruction and training of the future users of the application, especially in cases where the delivered solution represents a radical change rather than an incremental one.

Maintaining a deployed and running application means keeping the application in a healthy state, so as to guarantee high availability and to reduce failures. This may imply periodical checks of log files, bug reporting, and the cleaning up of temporary files, as well as the application of bug fixes or security patches, in order to keep the application always up to date.

Finally, *evolution* of an application aims at addressing new requirements that typically only emerge once the application has been used for a certain amount of time, and users start providing their feedback and comments. Evolving an existing application is more than bug or error fixing, and addressing the new requirements may require the whole development process to start anew in order to apply the required changes to the application. In addition – despite the rigorous application of software engineering techniques – oftentimes only after the deployment of the application does it become clear that certain requirements have not been met, and the application needs to be adjusted accordingly.

3.1.2 Actors in Software Development

As already hinted at in the introductory paragraph of this section, usually the above activities are not performed by one and the same person. Instead, the software engineering experience has led to the definition of a set of professional profiles, each of which dedicated to specific problems or activities in the software development process:

- During requirements engineering, the *application analyst* collects the motivations that trigger the development of the application and turns them into a specification of the application requirements. In doing so, he interprets the long-term strategic business goals and constraints and transforms them into short-term, concrete, application requirements.
- In application design, the *data architect* focuses on those application requirements that deal with content and domain data. He produces a conceptual data model that organizes the data into a structure and a representation that can be accessed and used by the application.
- The *application architect* focuses on those application requirements that deal with the functions and services that are to be delivered. He develops a conceptual solution of the application logic (expressed by means of models, figures, or specification languages) that builds on top of the data model.
- Based on the specifications produced, the *programmer* or *developer* implements the solutions sketched by the data and application architects and tests and evaluates the implemented solutions. In most cases, the programmer also manages the deployment of the application.
- The application *administrator* is then the main actor in the deployment and evolution activities, being in charge of maintaining the application, providing for periodical backups, managing the community of users, and collecting feedback from the users.

Of course, the overall development process also involves the actual *users* of the application, especially in the evaluation of the usability of the application and its evolution over time. But users themselves are not actively involved in the production of the software artifact, the reason we do not list them as main actors in the development process.

3.2 Structuring the Software Development Process

The decomposition of the software development process into its basic activities and the identification of its main actors is a first step toward the successful management of the development process. A successful management, however, also demands some additional knowledge, i.e., the *order* of the activities and possible *transition criteria* [Boe88]. It is the structuring of the software development process into well-formalized *process models*, starting from the previously identified activities, which enables the easy definition of a suitable order and of intermediate results and milestones [GJM02].

3.2.1 The Waterfall Model

One of the first explicit formalizations of a development process is the so-called *Waterfall model*. The Waterfall model suggests a sequential organization of the development activities. Only completing one activity allows starting its successor activity. The completion of an activity is typically associated with the delivery of a product, e.g., documentation or program code; therefore, the Waterfall model is oftentimes regarded as a *document-driven* process model [Boe88].

The Waterfall model was probably the first popular process model, and it is still widely adopted in may development situations today. Its main shortcoming is its inflexibility in adapting already completed activities in response to changing requirements or knowledge emerging in later stages of the development process. Also, bad design decisions that are taken early in the process are propagated unchanged to subsequent activities, i.e., in a strict Waterfall model it is difficult to undertake retroactive actions to fix errors made in already completed activities.

A variance of the Waterfall model, which has been introduced to address this shortcoming, is the Waterfall model *with feedback*. It keeps the sequential order of activities, but also allows backward communication (e.g., from the implementation activity to the design activity) in order to accommodate changes that impact previous activities.

3.2.2 The Spiral Model

As time passed, it became increasingly more evident that the simple sequential order of the Waterfall model does not suffice to describe the real situation of many large software projects. Indeed, in most cases several of the constituent activities of the process model may need to be repeated two or more times, which is in clear contrast with the sequence imposed by the Waterfall model.

As an answer to the growing practice to iterate several times over the same activities, in 1988 Boehm [Boe88] proposed the so-called *Spiral model*, an incremental development process model that pays special attention to *risk management*. The Spiral model is graphically shown in Figure 3.1. The model

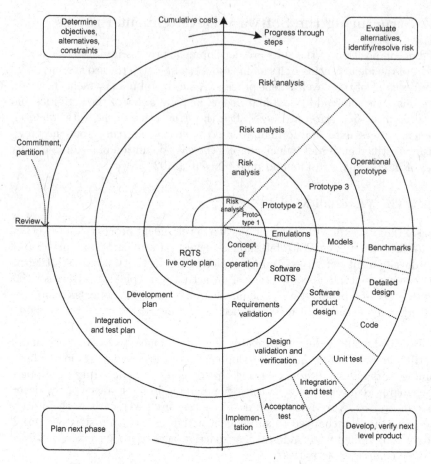

Fig. 3.1. The spiral model according to Boehm [Boe88]

explicitly suggests developing a software project in an incremental and iterative fashion by means of four convolutions, each one aimed at solving a specific development subproblem. Each convolution results in a prototype documenting the achievements of the respective convolution, accompanied by a risk analysis. The risk analysis considers various alternatives for achieving the project objectives, highlighting possible risks and their relevance, and suggesting solutions for preventing or eliminating such risks. The model is based on the idea that the incremental development of different versions of prototype applications implicitly reduces risk.

The Spiral model may also be interpreted as a *metamodel* that is able to accommodate different development models, adding risk as new dimension to the management problem [GJM02].

3.2.3 The Unified Model

Over time, the incremental or iterative practice of the Spiral model has inspired several other process models. One prominent example is the *Unified Software Development Process* (Unified process [JBR99]) and its adaptation to the development of Web applications [Con99] and Catalysis [DW98].

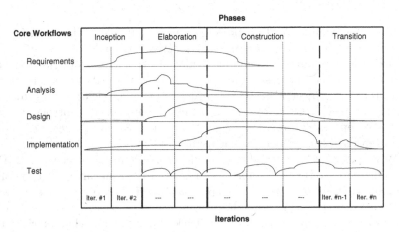

Fig. 3.2. Phases, workflows, and iterations in the Unified Process Model [JBR99]

According to the Unified process [JBR99], a software product is built along several cycles; Figure 3.2 shows a high-level view of the process. Each of the cycles ends with a product release and is executed in four separate phases:

- *Inception*: in this phase, the general idea of the system along with a tentative architecture and a set of critical use cases is developed.
- *Elaboration*: in this phase, several architectural views of requirements and design models are created and the most critical use cases are realized. At the end of the phase the project manager should be able to justify the resources to be allocated for the software project and to claim that the project is feasible under the identified risks and the granted budget and human resources.
- *Construction*: in this phase, the complete product is developed, and all the requested use cases are realized. Minor changes to the architecture are allowed if developers uncover better solutions. At the end of the phase, a product is transferable to the users.
- *Transition*: in this phase, a small group of experienced users tests the product and suggests improvements and discovers defects and shortcomings. The phase also involves personnel training and support. Finally, the product is exposed to the full user community.

Each phase is further divided into several iterations. The phases are executed according to known workflows: requirements, analysis, design, implementation, and test. Each workflow produces several artifacts. The adopted analysis and modeling techniques are those suggested by the Unified Modeling Language (UML) [Gro00].

3.2.4 Other Models

Recent practices influenced by agile development approaches, like extreme programming [Bec00], do not prescribe which activities should be executed and in which order. Organizations and particular projects may adopt just some of the above-mentioned processes, activities, phases, or workflows according to the needs of the projects. However, in order to be able to learn from projects, the adopted processes should be well defined. Well-defined, controlled, measured, and repeatable processes help organizations to continuously evaluate and improve software project management.

CMM and SPICE are reference models for organizing processes. CMM defines five levels of organizations with respect to the maturity of their software processes: *initial, repeatable, defined, managed, optimized*. The levels are characterized by the way in which software processes are defined, measured, controlled, and improved based on feedback. They are also characterized by the software development processes that are considered and standardized in the organization. The processes then are based on the activities described above. In addition, some other product management activities, like planning, risk identification, configuration management, contract management, project tracking, and process management (including peer reviews, training, quality management, process change management, and defect prevention), may also be involved. For further details on these, the reader is referred to books such as [Hum89, IPW+95, FC99] and reports such as [PCCW93, EG96].

3.3 Web-Specific Software Development Processes

Web applications are a special instance of generic software applications, and, hence, Web engineering can be seen as special instance of software engineering. Developing applications for the Web implies adhering to a few well-defined rules or conventions, which provide for a stable, robust, and scalable development and execution framework. Taking into account such Web-specific peculiarities allows a better tailoring of development process models. In the following, we introduce a characteristic process model, the so-called *online evolution model*, which stems from our experience in the development of Web applications and from the simple observation of the life cycle of modern Web applications that are available on the Web.

3.3.1 The Online Evolution Model

Figure 3.3 graphically shows the structure of the online evolution model. The model consists of five main activities, i.e., *requirements analysis, design, implementation, testing and evaluation*, and *maintenance and evolution*, and of seven transitions among the activities. The coarse activities in the online evolution model very much resemble the traditional activities in the software development process. A main difference is the interpretation of the *deployment* as transition, and not as a first-class activity. In the domain of the Web, deploying an application to its users is indeed not a big deal, as the centralized architecture typical of Web applications, the absence of independent client-side application code, and the browser as execution environment greatly facilitate and speed up the deployment activity.

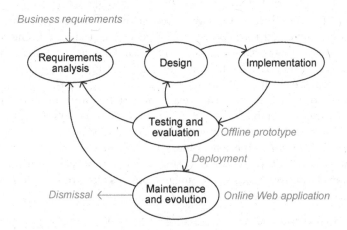

Fig. 3.3. The online evolution model for modern Web applications.

As for the transitions, the model proposes an explicit connection from the maintenance and evolution activity to the requirements analysis activity. It is this transition that characterizes the model: Connecting the maintenance and evolution activity to the requirements analysis activity closes a second cycle in the model that involves the requirements analysis activity; we call this the *evolution cycle*. The first cycle is the one that spans the design, implementation, and testing and evaluation activities; we call this the *build and test cycle*. The two cycles correspond to two phases that are peculiar to modern Web applications: offline development and online evolution. Indeed, as highlighted in Figure 3.3, the build and test cycle refers to the incremental development of the application that will go online, while the evolution cycle refers to the incremental evolution which the application undergoes over time once it is online.

In general, the two cycles are characterized by different cycling times: the former faster, the latter slower. The two iterative and incremental cycles appear particularly appropriate in the context of the Web, where applications must be deployed quickly (in "Internet time"), and requirements are likely to change during the development phase. As a matter of fact, increasingly the common practice in Web development is to substitute documentation artifacts (as heavily adopted in the Waterfall model) with real application prototypes, and to involve end users as early as possible for testing and evaluation. Also, while in traditional software engineering an application is released only once all the requirements have been met, for Web applications it is more and more common practice (and desirable) to publish online applications, even though not all the requirements have been met yet. Early user feedback is becoming more important, and evolution is finally being seen as a real opportunity for improvement and less as an annoying adaptation of a functioning application. The evolution cycle is thus increasingly gaining importance.

As an example of this trend, consider the Google search engine's Web site. Although users might not always be conscious of simple changes, Google' is continuously evolving the features and interface of the search engine. According to Adam Bosworth's (Vice President at Google) keynote speech at the 2007 International Conference on Web Engineering, Google is constantly adding new features to its Web applications, measuring whether the expected improvements or user behaviors can be accommodated, and consolidating features that prove their viability. Think, for instance, of the Web site thumbnails accompanying the single search results that were added some time ago to enrich the user's browsing experience, but then dropped because of little value to users who were not yet familiar with those sites. A successful evolution, instead, was the introduction of the suggestion to switch to Google Maps for user inquiries that contain location data.

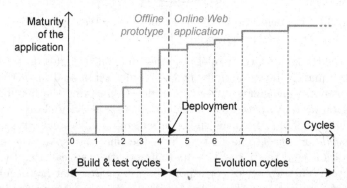

Fig. 3.4. The maturity of the Web application increases as a result of the combination of incremental development and continuous evolution

The effect of the two development cycles in the online evolution model on the maturity of the actual Web application under development is schematically represented in Figure 3.4. The incremental releases of the offline prototype in the build and test cycle occur rapidly, and the maturity of the application increases in big steps. After the deployment of the application, the incremental upgrades of the online application occur less frequently (evolution cycles), and they add less value to the application. However, they to add value, continuously, and are an integral part of the application's life cycle.

The online evolution model discussed here is not intended to prescribe any rigid development process for Web applications. Rather, it describes the product life cycle of modern Web applications, as can be determined by observing the online dynamics of such kinds of applications. As such, the online evolution model may also be the result of the application of, for example, the Unified process to Web applications. In that case, however, each instance of the evolution cycle would result in a new instantiation of the development process.

It is worth noting that taking into account the peculiarities of the Web also allows us to further refine the core development activities of Web applications, adding a second layer of detail to the development process model. Web applications share some architectural, technological, and usage characteristics that allow us to further separate the previously discussed development activities into smaller concerns. For instance, the design activity of Web applications can typically be separated into *data design*, *navigation design*, and *presentation design*.

At this stage, we will not deepen the structuring of the above-described Web development activities into their subactivities. The following chapters, however, will discuss the single activities of the development process by providing some more insight into Web-specific peculiarities.

3.3.2 Web-Specific Actors

Independently of the previous analysis of the main development activities, we can say that Web application development involves the actors already discussed in Section 3.1.2, with two additional roles that are integer to the Web: the *graphic designer* and the *webmaster*.

Graphic designers are in charge of presentation design. The graphical appearance of Web applications is very important for both usability considerations and the attractiveness of the application. Graphic designers conceive the graphical appearance of the application, structure contents and images into layouts, and select suitable style properties (e.g., fonts, colors, and the size of images) based on the nonfunctional requirements dealing with the customer's graphical corporate identity and with acknowledged communication standards. The strong separation of concerns applied to the design activity demands only little, if any, programming skills from graphic designers,[1] which fully enables them to work with the software and design tools they are used

---

[1] We will came back to this consideration in Section 7.1 when discussing some presentation implementation issues.

to and to integrate their sketches with little effort. Especially, the use of so-called *mock-ups* (graphical interface prototypes that do not yet support any real application feature) is very popular for discussing appearance character-istics with the customer and to get early user feedback.

Webmasters are in charge of the maintenance and partly also the evolution of a Web application. Typically, each Web application that is online offers somewhere (e.g., in the contacts page or in the footer of the pages) the possibility to contact a person (the webmaster) to communicate, for example, broken links or other problems with the application. The role of the webmaster is common practice today, and it is new in the software development scenario, as there is no such role in traditional software development processes.

Considering that a large part of the applications developed for the Web can be categorized as content management systems or data-intensive Web applications, we can distinguish two more actors, not directly involved in the development of the application itself but rather focusing on the contents of the application: the *content author* and the *content manager*. The content author creates new content (e.g., news articles, documentations, photos, blog entries, etc.) to be added to and published by the application. The content manager is responsible for content aggregation, content evaluation, quality assurance, and the final publishing.

3.4 Examples of Web-Specific Development Processes

The previous discussion introduced the reader to the online evolution model. In this section, we describe a few Web-specific application development models that can to some extent be accommodated by the online evolution model. The models refer to three well-known conceptual Web application development methods, i.e., WebML [CFB+02], WSDM [TL98], and OOHDM [SR98]. They will be explained in more detail in Chapter 5 when discussing the design phase in the development process.

3.4.1 The WebML Model

The Web Modeling Language (WebML) [CFB+02] is a visual language and development method for specifying the content structure of a Web application and the organization and presentation of contents in the form of hypertexts. The WebML method was proposed in 2000 [CFB00a] and then refined until it ensured a complete coverage of the development process [BCC+03], thanks to the availability of generative techniques supporting the automatic production of the application code.

The main contribution of WebML is the proposal of a mix of concepts, notations, and techniques for the construction of data-intensive Web applications, which can be used by Web development teams to support all the activities of the application life cycle, from analysis to deployment and evolution. The proposed mix blends traditional ingredients well known to developers, such as Use Case specification with UML and conceptual data design with the Entity-Relationship model, with new concepts and methods for the design of hypertexts, which are central to Web development. Therefore, the value of the proposed approach is not in the individual ingredients, but in the definition of a systematic framework in which the activities of Web application development can be organized according to the fundamental principles of software engineering, and all tasks, including the more Web-centric ones, find adequate support in appropriate concepts, notations, and techniques.

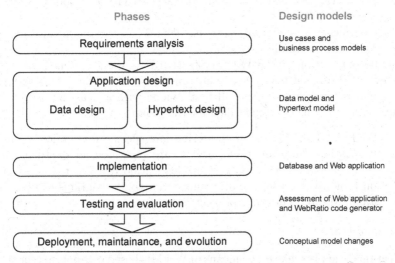

Fig. 3.5. Phases in the WebML development process [CFB⁺02]

Figure 3.5 shows the WebML approach to the development of Web applications. Inspired by Boehm's Spiral model, and in line with modern methods for Web and software application development [Con99, JBR99], the WebML process is applied in an iterative and incremental manner, in which the various phases are repeated and refined until results meet the application requirements. The product life cycle therefore undergoes several iterations, each one producing a prototype or a partial version of the application. At each iteration, the current version of the application is tested and evaluated, and then extended or modified to cope with the already collected requirements, as well as with newly emerged requirements.

Out of the entire process illustrated in Figure 3.5, the "upper" phases of analysis and design are those most influenced by the adoption of a conceptual model. The WebML method therefore focuses on them. However, as shown in the rest of this section, the adoption of a model also benefits the other phases.

Requirements analysis

In WebML, the requirements analysis phase aims at producing the following results:

- The identification of the *groups of users* addressed by the application. Each group represents users having the same profile, or performing the same activities with the same access rights over the same information classes.
- The specification of *functional requirements* that address the functions to be provided to users. For each group of users, the relevant activities to be performed are identified and specified; each activity is a cohesive set of elementary tasks.
- The identification of *core information objects*, i.e., the main information assets to be accessed and/or manipulated by users.
- The decomposition of the Web application into *site views*, i.e., different hypertexts designed to meet a well-defined set of functional and user requirements. Each user group will be provided with at least one site view supporting the functions identified for the group.

The WebML method does not prescribe any specific format for requirements specification. However, table formats are suggested for capturing the informal requirements (such as the group description table or the site views description table). UML use case diagrams and activity diagrams can be also used as standard representations of usage scenarios.

Application design

Application design is achieved by means of WebML-based conceptual schemas, which express the organization of the application domain and navigation components at a high level of abstraction, independently of implementation details. According to Figure 3.5, application design involves two activities:

- *Data Design*: corresponds to organizing core information objects identified during requirements analysis into a comprehensive and coherent data schema.
- *Hypertext Design*: produces site view schemas on top of the data schema previously defined. The distinguishing feature of the WebML approach is the emphasis on conceptual modeling for hypertext specification.

The models provided by the WebML language for data and hypertext design will be better described in Chapter 5.

Implementation

The WebRatio CASE tool [CFB+02, Web07b] largely assists designers in the implementation of the database and of the Web application. First of all, it offers a visual environment for drawing the data and hypertext conceptual schemas. Such visual specifications are then stored as XML documents, and these are the inputs for the WebML code generator, which supports data and hypertext implementation. In Section 7.2.2 of this book we will come back to the WebRatio CASE tool and provide a brief discussion of its features.

Testing and evaluation

The WebML model-driven approach benefits the systematic testing of applications, thanks to the availability of the conceptual model and the model transformation approach to code generation [BFTM05]. With respect to the traditional testing of applications, the focus shifts from verifying individual Web applications to assessing the *correctness of the code generator*. The intuition is that if one could ensure that the code generator produces a correct implementation for all legal and meaningful conceptual schemas (i.e., combinations of modeling constructs), then testing Web applications would reduce to the more treatable problem of validating the conceptual schema.

WebML development also fosters innovative techniques for quality evaluation. The research in this area has led to a framework for the model-driven and automatic evaluation of Web application quality [FLMM04, LMM04, MLME04]. The framework supports the *static* (i.e., compile-time) analysis of conceptual schemas, and the *dynamic* (i.e., runtime) collection of Web usage data to be automatically analyzed and compared with the navigation dictated by the conceptual schema. The static analysis is based on the discovery in the conceptual schema of design patterns, and on their automatic evaluation against quality attributes encoded as rules. Conversely, usage analysis consists of the automatic examination and mining of enriched Web logs, called conceptual logs [FMM03], which correlate common HTTP logs with additional data about i) the units and link paths accessed by the users, and ii) the database objects published within the viewed pages.

Maintenance and evolution

In the WebML model-driven process maintenance and evolution also benefit from the existence of a conceptual model of the application. Requests for changes can in fact be turned into changes at the conceptual level, either to the data model or to the hypertext model. Then, changes at the conceptual level are propagated to the implementation. This approach smoothly incorporates change management into the mainstream production life cycle and greatly reduces the risk of breaking the software engineering process due to the application of changes solely at the implementation level.

3.4.2 WSDM

The Web Site Design Method[2] was initiated by De Troyer and Leune [TL98] in 1998, and therefore was one of the first Web design methods.

---

[2] Later re-baptized as Web Semantics Design Methods.

Although WSDM was originally aimed at creating kiosk Web sites, it steadily evolved to a complete (semantic) Web design method supporting both functionality and a wide range of additional design concerns (localization, accessibility, semantic annotations, adaptivity, etc.). Some of these issues will be discussed in more detail later in this book.[3]

WSDM is a multi-phase Web design method, where each phase focuses on one particular design concern. It possesses the following characteristic features:

- *Methodology*: more than other methods, WSDM is a methodology. In addition to offering explicitly defined design primitives and models to describe a Web application at different levels of abstraction, WSDM also offers the designer aid on how to obtain the instantiations of these different models in order to obtain a well-structured, consistent, and usable Web application. WSDM thus offers the designer guidelines and techniques, thereby providing an explicit and systematic way to define Web applications.
- *Audience-driven*: consistent with knowledge established from user interface design and usability research, WSDM recognizes the importance of the users and thus takes as an explicit starting point an analysis of the different kinds of users (called audiences) and their (different) requirements and characteristics. This analysis will subsequently steer the impending design. Such an approach, where the users are taken as a starting point for the further design, is called an *audience-driven* approach.
- *Semantic Web technology*: with the rise of the Semantic Web, WSDM has been transformed to take advantage of Semantic Web technology. This was done in two ways. First of all, the Semantic Web Ontology Language OWL was used internally to define the different WSDM design models and for describing the information and functionality present in the Web application. Secondly, WSDM was also extended to generate semantic annotations alongside the (traditional) Web application, thereby effectively enabling the Semantic Web.

Figure 3.6 shows the different WSDM phases, along with the design models each gives rise to. As already explained, all these models are expressed in the Semantic Web Ontology Language OWL. Together they form the WSDM Ontology.

The next paragraphs explain in more detail each of WSDM's design phases:

Mission statement

The specification of the mission statement is the first phase of the WSDM design process. The intention is to clearly set the boundaries for the design by identifying the purpose of the Web site, the topics, and the target users. The mission statement is used during the design to ensure all required information

---

[3] Interested readers can read all about WSDM on http://wsdm.vub.ac.be/.

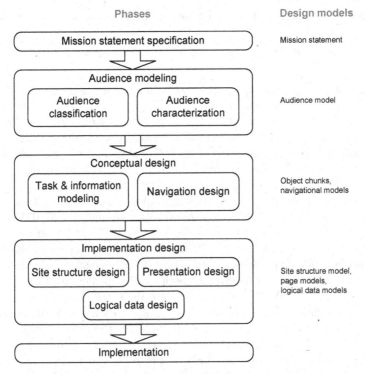

Fig. 3.6. Overview of the WSDM design method

and functionality are present, and all targeted users are supported. After the design process it is used to verify whether the formulated goals set for the Web application have been fulfilled. The mission statement is formulated in natural language.

Audience modeling

During the audience modeling phase, WSDM takes into account the fact that different visitors may have different needs and goals, and thus require particular support more specifically tailored to their needs. During the *audience classification* subphase, the targeted visitors, who were informally identified in the mission statement, are refined and classified into audience classes. An audience class is a group of visitors that has the same information and functional requirements. Any audience class that has (the same or) some additional requirements compared to another audience class is called an audience subclass. This partial order relationship gives rise to a hierarchical structure, called the audience class hierarchy. The "visitor" audience class is always the top of this hierarchy. It represents the requirements that all visitors have in common. During the *audience characterization* subphase, for each audience class, the characteristics, navigation, and usability requirements for their members are also formulated. These will be taken into account in the subsequent design phases.

Conceptual design

The conceptual design phase is split into two subphases: *task and information modeling* and *navigation design.*

During task and information modeling, the designer models the tasks that need to be performed by the different audience classes, along with the required content and functionality. For each requirement that was formulated during audience modeling, a task model is defined. Each task model consists of a decomposition of the task needed to fulfill the particular requirement into elementary tasks, along with the temporal relations between them (e.g., sequential, order-independent). To perform this task analysis, WSDM uses a slightly modified version of Concurrent Task Trees (CTTs) ([Pat00] for CTTs, [TC03] for WSDM modifications to CTTs). Subsequently, for each elementary task a so-called object chunk is created, which describes exactly what information and/or functionality is required to perform this elementary task. WSDM uses OWL (see e.g. [CPT06]) to formally describe these object chunks.

During navigation design, the (conceptual) navigation structure is modeled in an implementation-independent way. It indicates the general organization structure of the Web application, i.e., how the different visitors will be able to navigate through the site. In WSDM, the basic navigation structure is based on the audience class hierarchy: for each audience class, a navigation track is constructed. Such a navigation track can be considered as a sub-site, containing all and only information and functionality needed for this audience class. The internal navigation structure within a navigation track is based on the (temporal relations in the) task models. The navigation model consists of three basic modeling elements: conceptual navigation nodes indicating units of navigation, links between these navigation nodes, and the object chunks which are connected to the navigation nodes.

Implementation design

During the implementation design, the conceptual models are complemented with all necessary details to prepare for the actual implementation, which can be generated automatically. In the first subphase, the site structure design, the conceptual navigation structure is mapped onto actual pages. Several site structures are possible, depending on device, context, and platform (e.g., different screen sizes may give rise to different site structures). During the presentation design, the general look and feel for the Web site is defined. For the different kinds of pages (e.g., home page, leaf page) templates may be defined that will serve as a base when designing the actual pages. During page design, the designer decides for each actual page the concrete interface elements (e.g., a dropdown list or radio buttons to represent a single-choice list), how to position these elements and the information and functionality described in the object chunks, and the general look and feel of the page. This results in so-called page models. In the case of a data-intensive Web site, a database or CMS (Content Management System) can be used to store the data. In this case, the actual data source, and a mapping between the conceptual data model (i.e., the object chunks) and the data source, are specified during the *(logical) data design* subphase.

Implementation

Given the relevant (instantiated) design models (i.e., the object chunks, navigation model, site structure model, page models), and, in the case of a data-intensive Web site, the data source and the (logical) data design, the actual Web site can be generated automatically. Literature describes two prototype implementation performing this code generation process: an XSLT-based transformation pipeline [PCY+05] and a Java-based servlet [Cas05]. For more information on implementation of Web applications in the context of Web site design methods, see Section 7.2.2.

3.4.3 The OOHDM Model

Object-Oriented Hypermedia Design Method (OOHDM) [SR98] is one of the first methods adopted for Web application development projects. It has its roots in the hypermedia domain and focuses on helping the development of applications that involve hypertext/hypermedia paradigm features explore distributed heterogeneous information. The OOHDM method features object-oriented abstractions for analysis and design of information-intensive Web applications. Besides the modeling abstractions, and similarly to WSDM and WebML, it also provides a methodology which guides a developer through different activities in the Web application development. The main features of OOHDM are [SR98]:

- *Navigation views*: OOHDM adopts a notion of navigation views for specifying how information objects should be grouped when explored by a user in a navigation session.
- *Navigation contexts*: OOHDM proposes navigation contexts as grouping abstractions to organize the navigation space.
- *Separation of concerns*: OOHDM features separation of concerns. The domain conceptual issues are separated from navigation issues and both of them are separated from presentation issues. Query language is used to connect models from different viewpoints.

Figure 3.7 depicts the OOHDM phases together with the design models that result from them. Here we briefly describe these phases. We will concentrate on the details of some of the models and modeling techniques provided by OOHDM later, in Chapter 5.

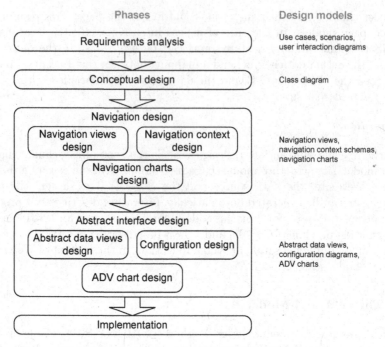

Fig. 3.7. Overview of the OOHDM design method

Requirements analysis

The primary goal of this phase in OOHDM is to capture and understand functional and nonfunctional requirements of the Web application. The requirements analysis, sometimes also called requirements capture, is use case driven. This means that the functional requirements are elicited with a help of use cases, actors, and stakeholders of a Web application. The use cases are further refined to scenarios which reflect use tasks. OOHDM features so called user interaction diagrams [VSdS00], which capture how a user should interact with the application when fulfilling certain use cases.

Conceptual design

OOHDM conceptual design is concerned with the design of information structures for representing the content provided in Web application. Well-known object-oriented principles are applied during this phase. The result is a class diagram extended with special constructs to attribute multiple values and perspectives. This feature is especially important for multi-modal Web applications and Web applications with semi structured content. The classes with relationships can be grouped into subsystems. Conceptual design is separated from other activities and deals only with application domain classes without a connection to any further application solution for viewing and organizing the content.

Navigation design

OOHDM navigation design is concerned with navigation structures supporting a user exploring information provided in a Web application. Cognitive issues are taken into account to reduce the information overload and to support the user in getting oriented in the information hyperspace. The navigation design produces views of the information structures, which can be different for different audiences. This is reflected in navigation context schemas where common views are grouped under one context. Navigation design may be also extended with behavioral specifications through navigation charts specifying some reactive behavior. Navigation models are connected to conceptual models. They use underlying concepts from the conceptual models to derive right perspective on information structure either by restricting it, projecting it, or transforming and combining it with other concepts. Different navigation views and schemas can be built for different purposes or users from a single conceptual model.

Abstract interface design

Abstract interface design follows object-oriented design principles and focuses on perceivable objects defining how navigation views should be displayed and augmented with further interaction elements, such as buttons and links. Abstract data view charts may be used to specify the behavior of presentation objects. The abstract data views follow the same principle as the navigation views. They can be seen as façade abstractions, representing different appearances of the navigation nodes to different users in different contexts. They feature also a behavioral and interactive aspect and are therefore very suitable for describing also modern interactive Web applications.

Implementation

OOHDM does not use any specific implementation framework. It is up to the development team to decide how to transform the results of the aforementioned phases into implementation. The development team makes a decision on architecture such as client-server, database management system to store information structures and data, application and web server to compute navigation and presentation views and handle user interaction events. Refer to [JSR02] for details on mapping to an architecture based on J2EE and the Model-View-Controller model.

3.5 Summary

Summing up the lessons learned in this chapter and the considerations that led to the definition of the online evolution model, we can say that Web-specific development processes in general distinguish themselves from traditional software development processes because of the following general characteristics:

- *Continuous* and *fast* development and release times are paramount.
- Web development processes are less documentation-based and, rather, put high emphasis on *prototypes* (prototypes are much more expressive than technical documents, especially to unskilled customers).
- High *user involvement* and early feedback is desirable.
- A new actor enters the development process: the *graphic designer*.

If we look at the activities in the development process, we can also identify the following activity-specific characteristics:

- The *requirements analysis, design,* and *implementation* activities can be further detailed into typical Web-specific subactivities. This allows for the conception of specific processes, instruments, models, and tools, assisting developers and lowering risks.
- The *implementation* activity is highly standards-based. This contributes to the fast adaptation of developers to new projects, to higher interoperability of the conceived solutions, and to elevated robustness.
- The *deployment* of Web applications is typically fast. There is no need for client-side code that requires manual installation procedures, and, hence, there is no need for complicated installation and deployment processes. Installation and deployment come almost for free, and consistency among clients is implicitly guaranteed.
- The continuous (online) *evolution* of Web applications is an integral part of the development process. The development cycle continues even after the deployment of the application. This may be indispensable if we want to keep the attractiveness of the Web application high and enlarge the application's audience.

The organization of the following chapters is based on the online evolution model depicted in Figure 3.3.

3.6 Further Readings

Web engineering processes have been described from several points of view in a number of publications. The development of hypermedia-oriented Web application was discussed in [NN95, NN99]. They concentrate mostly on the design process, which is characterized as a motion in a four-dimensional space of guidelines for *hypermedia application, hypermedia design and development, hypermedia system,* and *human factors*. The readings are recommended as a general introduction to Web process guidelines frameworks. Similarly, [DB02b] concentrates on the design organization framework as a five-dimensional space of hypermedia application, notation, development process, aspect, and degree of formality. The design process is then considered as a chain of instances over the dimensions.

Another Web application development model, inspired by Software Engineering Institute's Capability Maturity Model (CMM) framework [PCCW93] and the SPICE architecture of process assessment [EG96], the IMPACT-A method [LBW99], is based on a three-dimensional space formed by following dimensions: *process entities*, *hypermedia entities*, and *time*. The process dimension is characterized by entities such as `Resource`, `Activity`, and `Artifact`. The `Resource` can be a `tool`, a `skill`, or a `person`. Hypermedia high-level entities are `structure`, `navigation`, `behavior`, and `interaction`. The method contains two high-level phases: preparatory phase and execution phase. The preparatory phase is concerned with choosing a model, the quality attributes for assessment, the measuring methods for those attributes. The execution phase is carried out for each development project. The model serves as a guide for developers to understand development. Attributes assist developers identify particular aspects that are important for assessment. Tasks are guides for attribute assessment.

The Hypertext Design Model HDM [GP93], W2000 [BGP01], the Relationship Management Methodology (RMM) [ISB95], UML-based Web Engineering (UWE) [HK00], and Scenario-Based Object-Oriented Hypermedia Design Methodology (SOHDM) [LLY99] are examples of other development methods with slightly different views on the organization of activities and processes.

Proceedings from the World Wide Web conference and the Web engineering conference, collections such as [MD01, KPRR03], and books such as [DLWZ03, PJC98, Pre05, CFB+02, Con00] are sources for further valuable insights into Web application development processes.

4

Requirements Engineering

The primary goal of this chapter is to facilitate the understanding of the main principles behind requirements engineering for present day Web applications. Web applications live in a certain organizational context where they serve specific purposes and where they provide services. The organizational context might be closed, as with Web applications serving particular organizations, or open, as with Web applications serving a wide range of users (e.g., Amazon. com).

The requirements usually reflect the needs of users and stakeholders in the organizational context and the constraints that are posed on the Web application services. Requirements engineering can therefore be seen as a set of activities that lead to the specification of these needs and constraints. Several researches [Low03b, Ove00, Low03a] pointed out that Web applications distinguish themselves from regular software systems in a number of ways. The differences, which affect the requirements the most, are:

- They are characterized by a document-centric hypertext interface.
- They focus on information publishing rather than on services, i.e., contents changes and evolves very frequently;
- the user's and the stakeholder's contexts are often not known in advance.
- Even when the stakeholders are known, they do not know how the Web application is going to affect their business model.

As pointed out in [Ove00], the document-centric interface and evolving character rather stress publishing requirements, and require an editor rather than a requirements engineer. In this chapter, we will not go into further detail on this issue. We will, however, look at the methods which focus on the functional side of information editing, emerging from the viewpoint that assumes that Web applications are a subclass of information systems. Examples of such methods include OOHDM [SR98], WebML [CFB00a], WSDM [TL98], or Relationship Management Methodology (RMM) [YB00].

This chapter is mostly devoted to the traditional requirements engineering view on Web application development, with emphasis on the techniques

S. Casteleyn et al., Engineering Web Applications: *Data-Centric Systems and Applications.*
DOI: 10.1007/978-3-540-92201-8_4, © Springer-Verlag Berlin Heidelberg 2009

used for the analysis of functional requirements from different perspectives, including the application content, the organizational context, the navigation, and the user interface.

This chapter uses the following convention to describe the requirements engineering techniques. It first defines each technique, describes which concepts each technique provides, how it is used on an example, and discusses various suggestions when to use it and in which combination with other techniques. Please note, that the combinations presented in this chapter are not total.

4.1 Web Requirements Engineering Concepts

Web applications can be considered as a special class of software applications. The web applications can serve as a part of a larger system: information, organizational, control, etc. It is important to understand the system, how such applications fulfil their role in the system, and which constraints are posed on the application by the system. The purpose, role, context, and constraints for a Web application are defined by requirements.

Software requirements in earlier software methodologies have been seen as a specification which provides a contract to be fulfilled by the software application being developed [Roy87]. In those methodologies, software application design and implementation immediately follow requirements specification, i.e., they begin after the requirements engineering phase is fully complete. With advances in agile methods [Lar03], however, requirements changes have been accepted as a general principle during software development and deployment, especially when the system is deployed in iterations and increments. Thus, requirements engineering is usually interleaved with early stages of design and implementation. Both approaches are applied in Web development projects.

4.1.1 Software Requirements with Relevance to the Web

Before we start introducing the relevant techniques for Web application requirements engineering, we summarize basic terminology in requirements engineering and its relevance to Web applications. We distinguish between *functional* and *nonfunctional* requirements for software applications [Som04].

Functional requirements

Generally speaking, the functional requirements are those stating what the system should do, which services it should provide, and to which input data it should react.

Functional requirements in Web application development usually map to what an application propagates to a Web site user interface, which input dialogs, such as forms, or even more interactive multimedia plug-ins should be available at a particular Web page, which functionalities they invoke, which links they influence, and how certain information service pages link to each other. Functional requirements for Web applications incorporate:

- *Organization Requirements*: representing different viewpoints on the organization or environment where a Web application will be applied.
- *Application Domain Requirements*: representing different requirements for content which is required in a Web application.
- *Navigation Requirements*: representing requirements on how to organize the navigation between different pieces of information or services provided in a Web application.
- *Interaction Requirements*: representing requirements concerning interaction with and user interfaces to information and services in a Web application.

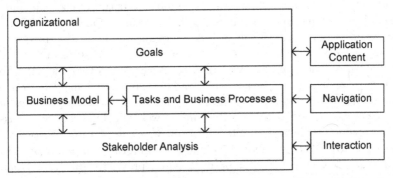

Fig. 4.1. Usual options for activities in requirements analysis and their dependencies

The Web application functional requirements engineering activities are depicted in Figure 4.1. As pointed out at the beginning of this chapter, the main differences of Web applications compared to traditional software systems are in the impact the Web application will have on the business model of an organization. This is why we emphasize the techniques which are related to organizational aspects, starting with goals analysis, business model and value analysis, business processes and tasks analysis, as well as stakeholder analysis model. These models provide a context for subsequent application domain, navigation, and interaction requirements analysis. The result of such analysis is documented as *organization requirements*.

The *application domain requirements* are very important, especially for information-intensive applications. Very often, Web applications deal with data: they collect, transform, process, and present them to users. This is especially the case for Web applications dealing with a lot of content or data, such as online product catalogs and virtual museum collections. There are three distinctively different views on information studied in information analysis:

- *Information content*: refers to collections of and relationships between (pieces of) content.
- *Information flow*: refers to how content changes as it goes through different parts of the system.
- *Information structure*: refers to an internal representation of content.

The information domain analysis and requirements coming from the domain are a significant part of requirements analysis for Web applications as nowadays most Web applications are content- or information-driven.

It is quite common for Web applications that their users and organization are not known in advance. This is especially the case for some classes of Web applications such as eCommerce Web sites (e.g., `Amazon.com`) or Web applications provided through application service provider portals. The initial requirements for such applications are derived directly from the application domain. The *domain requirements* [Som04] sometimes also supplement functional or nonfunctional requirements for software applications which are elicited from a user. Most of the Web development methods described in the literature or used in practice refer to application domain analysis or to the domain analysis and design activity as an integral part of a development method. This usually involves typical stakeholder and user stereotype analysis, or information entity analysis based on a literature review or common practices in a domain. For example, a domain of accounting would include concepts/classes or entities which refer to accounts, their subtypes, accounting practices and transactions. If a Web site should communicate information about products, the domain analysis will look at product types, product items, and product features, as well as navigation requirements between them.

The unique feature of web application is to explore provided information and services by performing act of navigating. The *navigation requirements* usually comprise how the underlying data and services should be grouped when user navigates through them, how they are associated to each other for navigation purposes and what are other required dependencies between different navigation requirements.

The act of navigation is a result of user interaction. The *interaction requirements* specify which are the constraints and conditions for user interaction, which navigation concepts and underlying data will be provided to the user and when and which interaction possibilities a user will have to be able to use, process, update, and navigate in information and services the web application provides.

The order in which the activities should be performed is not given. The first activity, as well as the focus of requirements analysis depends usually on which role is leading the requirements [Ove00]. For example, a user interface design expert will very likely start with task models and how the application is going to be used and will follow with interaction spaces. A business analyst will likely start by analyzing business goals and values, followed by business process analysis. An information engineer will very likely start by looking at the information structure without considering the organizational requirements explicitly.

Nonfunctional requirements

The nonfunctional requirements are those stating constraints on the functionality the system should provide, such as timing constraints, development process constraints, constraints on standards, and so on. The nonfunctional requirements can be further classified into [Som04]:

- *Product Requirements*: specifying product behavior, such as how much memory is needed, what performance should be achieved in execution, i.e., what requirements are put on the Web infrastructure and the Web application that it runs.
- *Project Organizational Requirements*: posed by the customer's and developer's organizations, process standards, programming language, and so on.
- *External requirements*: devoted to all requirements which are derived from or imposed by factors external to the system, such as interoperability requirements with systems already running at the customer site.

Nonfunctional requirements for Web applications include, but are not limited to, the performance of a Web server, the choice of application server, the constraints on links in general, the requirements for Web page resolutions, external information services to be integrated, the requirements for distribution of Web application server functionalities to different locations, and so on.

Product, project organizational, and external requirements for Web applications are similar to those of any other kind of software system. If a Web application should be a portal integrating information flow of different business processes of an organization, these should be analyzed and perhaps documented in a kind of process model. Product requirements refer to a distribution of the functionality among clients, various servers and a Web server, including a database management system and other distributed database engines, if needed. External requirements involve requirements posed by an external Web site's Web service interface, data format, and so on.

The requirements are usually documented in a so-called *requirements document* [Som04].

4.1.2 Requirements Engineering Processes

Basic requirements engineering processes involve a feasibility study [Som04], elicitation and analysis [Som04, Pre05], elaboration and specification [Pre05], requirements negotiation [Som04, Pre05], requirements validation [Som04, Pre05], and requirements management [Som04]. We will briefly elaborate on each of these processes in the following:

Feasibility study

For completely new systems, a feasibility study is recommended: a process which should identify stakeholders, affected business processes or domains, schedule and cost constraints, and integration requirements with existing systems, and could also involve an early prototyping. The feasibility study should also identify how the system contributes to overall business objectives, how the situation could look without the system, whether the planned technology was already used within the organization, and so on. By early prototyping, the risk of misunderstanding the goal of the Web application in the organization could be decreased.

Requirements elicitation and analysis

The main goal for this stage is to *discover* what the system should do. This stage can be envisioned both when the customer is known and unknown. In the first case, requirements elicitation is performed with the customers or stakeholders involved mostly through *interviews* or *ethnography*. In the latter case, a domain expert can be involved to help specify generic requirements. Literature and domain knowledge is another source for requirements discovery.

Interviews

Where stakeholders are available, informal or formal interviews are one of the main techniques used in requirements engineering. By interviewing stakeholders and users, the main viewpoints to requirements are discovered. Interviews may be closed to answer specific prescribed questions or open where no predefined agenda is prepared. A key point in the interviews is to have a basic common terminology. Otherwise, the interviews analysis may lead to improper or misunderstood requirements.

Ethnography

Ethnography is an important technique used to discover requirements connected to the whole context of the system. Ethnography is an observational technique which studies social phenomena in organizational settings. It can be used to discover requirements which are implicit and not articulated by stakeholders. Besides consulting software engineering literature (see for example [MS04, Som04]), the Web engineering community recognizes the importance of ethnography as one of the interpretative techniques in research or practice.

Requirements elaboration and specification

Requirements elicitation and analysis may already involve requirements elaboration, such as requirements *classification*, requirements *prioritization* and *negotiation*, and requirements *documentation*, also called *specification*. Note that in some literature, these phases may be treated separately. In the following sections we will concentrate on how to structure requirements by using particular modeling techniques used mostly in Web development projects.

Modeling

Modeling is an important part of requirement analysis and specification. It helps us to structure the requirements from different viewpoints, to understand them, and to focus on those most relevant for the application. Modeling can focus on the functional aspect of the system to accomplish a view on input, output, and transformation functions, or it can focus on behavioral aspects to accomplish a view on the internal and external events, and how they affect a system's behavior.

Viewpoints

Viewpoint-oriented requirements analysis explicitly recognizes the different perspectives the different stakeholders may have. Different approaches and frameworks proposed for viewpoint-based analysis provide explicit organizational support for representing, identifying, and resolving conflicts between requirements stated by different stakeholders. The conflicts can be further prioritized and resolved by requirements negotiation. In this chapter we recognize this principle, and the following sections are structured according to viewpoints relevant for Web application requirements engineering.

Requirements negotiation

Requirements negotiation aims at agreeing on the scope of the system to be built and the consistency of analyzed requirements. It may be performed in iterations as part of requirements elicitation and analysis or after requirements are specified in order to prioritize them and to agree upon which part of the requirements will be implemented.

Requirements validation

Requirements validation should confirm that the requirements produced in the phases described above actually specify the desired system. The requirements are checked for validity, consistency, completeness, and verifiability. The requirements validation might be performed in interviews, by prototyping, and by test-case generation [Som04].

Requirements management

As requirements may change over time and can come from different stakeholders, it is important to establish practices to identify, control and track requirements. Requirements management deals with those activities. It involves a number of activities related to traceability of requirements in the design, to the stakeholders and to different versions of the system. It also involves procedures for identification and application of changes to requirements.

Difficulties

The difficulty with requirements engineering processes is in people (users, stakeholders) who are usually not experienced enough, are not able to elicit or externalize usually tacit knowledge about the requirements adequately enough, and are not able to specify their requirements in sufficient detail. Additionally, they often do not know precisely what the scope of the system should be. Another problem is that the stakeholders in software processes provide conflicting requirements views. Also, volatility of requirements might be very high, and, furthermore, requirements can change due to the environment, organizational, or domain changes or simply as the understanding of them evolves. As pointed out above, in the case of unknown users or unknown business model implications of a Web application to be introduced in the organization, the danger exists to misunderstand the business the system should support, or the knowledge of the domain which serves as a source for the generic requirements for the system.

4.2 Organization Requirements Analysis

Organization requirements analysis focuses on analysis of the context in which a Web application will reside and serve its purpose. The context is described by one of the following requirements viewpoints:

- *Business Value Model*: describes requirements on which values will be exchanged between actors that will use the Web application.
- *Business Information Flow Model*: refines values from the business value model to requirements information flows to effectively exchange the business values envisioned.
- *Goals Model*: describes what goals (and relationships between them) stakeholders have in pursuing the Web application development project.
- *Business Process Model*: describes processes that lead to fulfillment of the business values.
- *Task Model*: describes requirements for tasks a user needs to perform at the Web application user interface realizing the business process model.
- *Audience Model*: describes clustering of functional requirements according to audience classes (users/persons) that will use the system.

In the following subsections we will look at the abstractions used to model and understand the aforementioned viewpoints.

4.2.1 Value-Based Requirements Analysis

Value-based requirements engineering [GA01, GA03] has emerged as a reaction to a problem with e-Commerce applications. The e-commerce applications usually change company business model as they introduce additional sales and marketing channels for the companies. The value-based requirements engineering therefore looks at how such application influences the business model. The method features the e^3-value technique, which facilitates understanding and structuring an organization business model in terms of its values and in terms of how they should be supported by a Web application or an information technology system.

The e^3-value technique helps us to capture how business values are exchanged in a network of enterprises grouped in different market segments and represented by different actors distributing and consuming things of business value [GYvdR06].

A Business Value Model is a model which describes how actors in networked businesses grouped in different market segments exchange business values [GA01].

The e^3-value technique provides the following constructs to capture the business value model:

- *Actor*: an independent entity in business value exchange which consumes or creates a business value.
- *Value object*: an object (anything such as goods, money, information) which carries on could create an economic (business) benefit or a value for any actor in the model.
- *Value port*: a port through which actors exchange values, either requesting them or providing them to other actors.
- *Value interface*: groups value ports according to the economic reciprocity that one value must be exchanged or traded for other values.
- *Value exchange*: connects two value ports and represents an instance of one or more trades.
- *Market segment*: groups actors who value economic objects equally, such as a group of consumers.
- *Value activity*: an activity which creates a profit and is performed by an actor (an actor can have activities).
- *Dependency path*: the whole path of value exchange connecting a consumer need, actors, connection elements, connectors between various value interfaces (AND, OR), and dependency boundaries.

Figure 4.2 depicts an example of a business value model for selling furnished apartments. Apartment Buyer can choose from various apartments

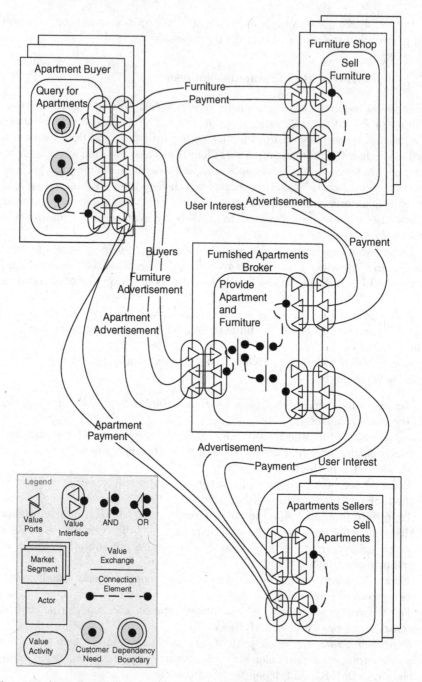

Fig. 4.2. An example of the business value exchange model for a Web application mediating services of agencies selling apartments and accompanying furniture

provided on the market by various `Apartment Sellers` through the `Furnished Apartments` broker. He is performing `Query for Apartments` value activity for retrieving the apartments. The buyer can further configure his furniture for the apartment he chooses and can buy it from the `Furniture Shop`. He can utilize the `Sell Furniture` value activity. `Apartment Buyer`, `Apartment Sellers`, `Furnished Apartments Broker`, and `Furniture Shop` are therefore actors in the model. As buyers and sellers respectively in this case represent a set of similar actors with the same business values, they are also modeled as market segments for the brokerage business. The actors in the model exchange different values through value interfaces. For example, `Apartment Buyer` needs advertisements for apartments and furniture from the `Furnished Apartments` broker. The advertisements represent a business value exchanged for an increased number of buyers. Therefore, the broker will continuously develop its credibility and as a result increase the number of buyers who buy the apartments through the broker. Similarly, the `Furnished Apartments` broker lives from payments of `Furniture Shops` and `Apartment Sellers` advertising through him (as payment for published advertisements as business value). In return, the `Furniture Shops` and `Apartment Sellers` increase their revenues through successful trades and continuously provide new advertisements so that the customers can notice their products. Therefore, the `Furnished Apartment` gets connected through advertisements for apartments and furniture, which are related to user interests, advertisements, payments for advertisements, apartment and furniture sales. These create the dependency path in the model.

The above example shows how a Web application, provided through a broker, changes the business model of three different actors or segments. It helps us to analyze the impacts the application development team should focus on in the development. The e^3-value technique is not only useful in profit-making networked organizations. It can be used to model value exchange that could be based on intangible benefits, as in library systems, knowledge management or transfer systems, research support information exchange, and so on. The technique can also be used to clarify values for even simpler information-serving Web sites. When applied, it encourages value-oriented thinking, i.e., what the Web site should actually provide to be as attractive as possible and what the external targeted audience is.

In the enterprise environment, the business value analysis is usually focused on top management, customers, and marketers, i.e., those who are usually deciding on the business value. For other domains, these roles have to be mapped to appropriate counterparts. For the universities and research institutions, university management which includes for example deans and rector have to be addressed. For libraries, the library managers need to be addressed together with library users. For information and marketing Web sites, company CEOs together with marketing managers need to be addressed, and representatives of he target audience need to be considered.

4.2.2 Business Information Flow Analysis

The high level business value exchange modeled in the previous section with the e³-value technique needs to be decomposed into finer information exchange between the actors. WebML+ [TL03] incorporates the business value exchange modeling as an input to the subsequent information flows analysis.

An Information Flow Model is a requirements analysis model which defines, at a high level of abstraction, the flow of information between the system, the organization, and the external entities [TL03].

The information flow model of WebML+ adopts actors from the e³-value model. It decomposes the business values into a number of information flows that carry on information from the various types of information units. The following elements are used within the information flow model:

- *Actors*: the roles users play in the system annotated with actions they usually perform.
- *Supplied Information Units*: persistent or transient information which is directly supplied by a system or an actor without any change.
- *Derived Information Units*: persistent or transient information which is computed and composed out of various pieces of information supplied.
- *Processing Units*: used in conjunction with derived information units. They model an abstraction of a process or procedure which computes or derives composite information structures needed by actors.
- *Information Flows*: represent how information flows from one actor to another through various processing and information units.

Figure 4.3 depicts an example of an information flow schema for the furnished apartment buyers scenario used in the previous section. It models just a fragment of the information flow related to the Query for Apartments, one of the buyer's actions. The Query is represented as a supplied information unit (supplied by the buyer) and it is connected to the CreateRoomWithFurniture processing unit for composing rooms with existing furniture. The Room with Furniture derived information unit is one of the information structures the system under construction needs to supply. The derived information unit is composed out of the four supplied information units, namely Query, Room, Price, and Furniture. All of these supplied information units are transient, i.e., they are supplied dynamically when a request from a buyer is being issued. Furthermore, the Furnished Apartments actor provides Apart. Info (abbreviated from Apartments Information), which represents information flow of stored advertisements on apartments. Similarly, other business values depicted in Figure 4.2 and actors can be refined into information flows.

As can be seen from the example, the information flow models an overall view on the requirements posed on an organization system, including Web applications supporting a fragment of them. This technique provides a viewpoint which helps to clarify which of the business value exchanges will be realized by a Web application. The technique remains abstract and does not

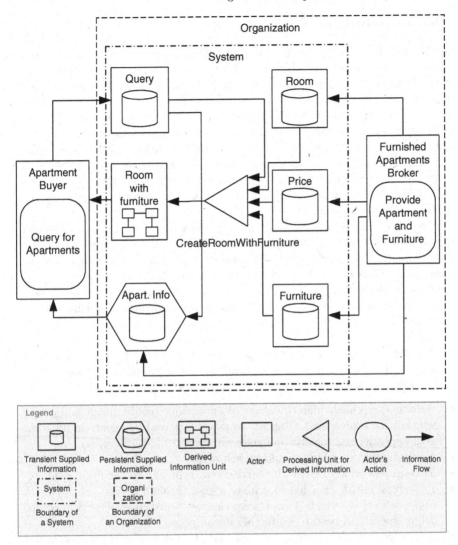

Fig. 4.3. An excerpt of a WebML+ fragment on apartment information with rooms and furniture. The WebML+ schema refines the eValue model from Figure 4.2

bind the analysts to any architectural or implementation issues. It also serves as a good input for other Web design methods which can decompose the information flows and units into Web site schemas, hypertext schemas, or other models which are closer to the architecture of the application or implementation environment.

4.2.3 Goals Analysis

Goal-based requirements analysis is another technique for early requirements engineering and is very suitable for Web application requirements engineering as they uncover the goals which are behind the new business values and business models a web application is introducing. The goals analysis focuses on strategic incentives for particular requirements. It covers the gap between requirements which specify what a system should do and incentives based upon which certain requirements have been stated. This information is very valuable as it can help us to identify and resolve conflicting requirements as well as the strategic values within an organization. Goals, similar to the business values described above, are very important for the success of a system in an organization or environment.

The i* [Yu97] is one of the modeling frameworks for goals analysis in requirements engineering. It is abbreviated as *i* because of the distributed intentionality of actors who interact between each other not through tasks or information flows but rather through goals or intentions [GYvdR06].

A Goal Model is a network of dependencies between a set of actors, goals, tasks, and resources. It models dependencies between the actors through the goals and intentions they have and considers how they can eventually be achieved.

The i* framework supports the elicitation of distributed intentionality and tries to facilitate an improved understanding of it by capturing the dependencies (explicit knowledge) between various entities:

- *Actors*: the stakeholders involved in expressing requirements and goals, who can be represented as agents or as roles played by agents in different goal dependencies (agents and roles are special kinds of actors).
- *Goals*: intentions which should be achieved.
- *Tasks*: tasks which need to be carried out, typically to achieve a goal.
- *Resources*: entities needed to achieve a goal through a task.
- *Soft goals*: goals which do not have clearly identified explicit criteria for achievement and need to be further decomposed.
- *Dependencies*: connect instances of the above-mentioned entities into a dependency network showing how different actors relate to each other through goals, tasks, resources, and soft goals.

Further relationships, such as *decomposition* or *role indication*, are used in the goal models . Decomposition is used when certain goals need to be decomposed into a subnetwork of goal dependencies. Role indication is used when an agent plays several roles within the goal network of dependencies. Refer to [Yu97] for further relationships and elements of the i* framework. The i* framework is also supported by a so-called Organization Modeling Environment (OME).[1]

---

[1] http://www.cs.toronto.edu/km/ome/

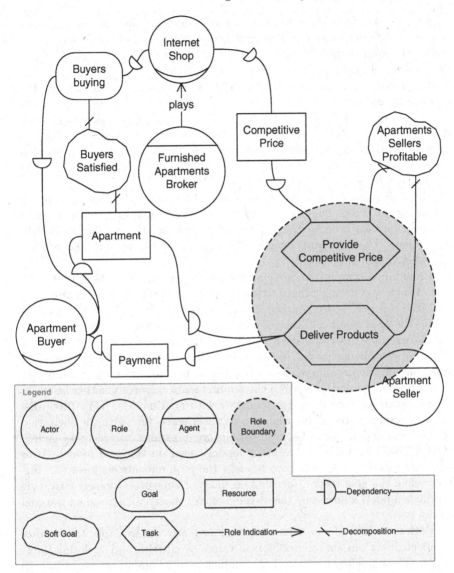

Fig. 4.4. An example of a goal model according to the i* method derived which corresponts to parts of eValue model depicted in figure 4.2

Figure 4.4 depicts an example of a goal model for our apartment buyers scenario as discussed above. The goal model provides another viewpoint on the early requirements for such a system with the three actors identified in the analysis of business value exchange. Here we show just a fragment of the model. Satisfaction (`Buyers Satisfied` soft goal) is the main goal for the `Apartment Buyers` (represented here as a role played by users). It is a soft goal because it is difficult to predict common criteria of success for this goal. It depends on an `Apartment` delivered from an `Apartment Seller`. This is modeled by dependency links directed from the buyer to seller. The direction of this dependency (i.e., from buyer to seller) is denoted by half circles on the dependency lines.

One indication that the buyers are satisfied is that they are buying through the `Internet Shop`. `Buyers buying` is therefore a goal of `Internet Shop`. This can be measured by the number of buyers and the number of bought apartments. The `Internet Shop` is a role played on behalf of the `Furnished Apartments Broker` agent.

Providing a competitive price and delivering the apartments at that price and of high quality contribute to the `Apartment Sellers Profitable` soft goal (the soft goal is decomposed into two activities). Both activities are also within the `Apartment Seller` role boundary (i.e., belong to the role).

The example described above shows that the goal model is complementary to the value exchange model. In fact, it provides a different and very important viewpoint on early requirements and incentives behind the exchanged business values. In our opinion, it is up to the requirements engineer whether he starts with a business value exchange model or with goal models. [GYvdR06] discusses a combined technique where an engineer starts first with the elicitation of goals and dependencies between various organizations (strategic dependencies) followed by the e^3-value actor model based on the goal model. After achieving consistency of the two models, the requirements engineer can further refine the goal model, focusing on internal enterprise interest (strategic rationale model) followed by the e^3-value model of activities based on the goal model.

Both models can be used for reasoning purposes. For example, the requirements engineer can analyze conflicts in values by eliciting and exploring the i* model. The modeling can reveal the conflicts and inconsistency and can help an organization align strategic goals as well as learn about different incentives. This exploration helps the requirements engineer understand which goals are the main drivers for a Web application being developed.

The e^3-value model can be used for profitability analysis by exploring different valuations of the business value. The results of profitability analysis can be associated with an i* model as attributes of its elements. These attributes can be used to analyze whether various goals are achieved by propagating goal dependencies and goals analysis. Refer to [vdRGY05] for more details on reasoning with i* and e^3-value models.

4.2.4 Business Process and Task Analysis

Business process models and task models usually share a common notation. Both of them usually reference some processes or activities connected by control flow relationships. However, they usually look at the model from different viewpoints. While business process models describe how an organization operates to achieve a business value through connected sets of activities, task models describe how a system is being used through a set of connected activities. They also come from two different domains. Task models come from the human-computer interaction field and are usually used by user interface designers. Business process models come from the business information systems area and are usually used by business analysts to capture, analyze, and optimize business procedures leading to economic value. In both cases, various slightly different techniques have been proposed, leading more or less to the same result. For example, various Integrated Definition methods (IDEF)[2] have been introduced for business process modeling. IDEF0 provides a simple language to model flows of activities an organization performs. IDEF3 provides means to model sequences of events or activities describing how a system works. [BVGH00] compares the IDEF techniques with Petri Nets, place transition nets also used for modeling workflows in organizations. [DFHS04] compares some formalisms used for task models. Business Process Modeling Notation (BPMN) [OMG09] and UML activity diagrams [Gro00] have recently been adopted the most, both focusing on modeling business activities, events which trigger and control them, messages, and control flows between them. Here, we focus on the UML activity diagrams to illustrate the concepts. Refer to [OMG09, Gro00] for details.

The UML activity diagrams provide the following main elements to capture activities or processes:

- *Activity*: a unit of work performed by an organization, or a task a user will perform at a user interface of a Web application.
- *Control flow link*: a link which connects different dependent activities, stating their causal dependencies, such as one activity being performed after another.
- *Initial state*: a state where a business process or a task sequence begins.
- *Final state*: a state where a business process or a task sequence ends.
- *Fork*: a place where a control in a business or a task sequence splits into several concurrent processes or tasks.
- *Join*: a place where control from various business activities or tasks performed concurrently merges into a single flow.
- *Decision point*: a place where a decision on which following activity or task the control will be moved needs to be made.

---

[2] http://www.idef.com/

- *Swim lane*: a partition of a business process model or a task model which is dedicated to activities or tasks of an actor if more than one actor is being modeled.

Business process analysis

Business process analysis focuses on the exploration of the tasks an organization performs to achieve a profit. The business process analysis is the next abstraction level below the business value exchange analysis, the business information flow analysis, and goals analysis. It looks at how the connection between different business value interfaces depicted in the e^3-value models is internally decomposed into work processes. It also looks at how the goals, resources, and tasks from the i* models are connected by control flow relationships. A business process model can be created in iterations. Starting with the i* and the e^3-value models is one option for the requirements engineer, but not the only one. A requirements engineer does not have to start with any of the previously described models. He can start first by capturing the current state of business processes in an enterprise and derive the business value exchanged, and the value interfaces from current process models. Later, by analyzing the i* and e^3-value , he can propose alternative business processes (business process reengineering).

A process is a set of activities performed to produce a product [Rol98]. The business process model describes a route to be followed to reach a product [OHM$^+$88] or a service.

Figure 4.5 depicts an example of a business process model for our apartment buyers scenario. The three actors are taken directly from the e^3-value model and mapped onto three swim lanes of activities: Apartment Buyer, Apartment Broker, Apartment Seller. Note, that there could be more complex relationship between market segments from e^3-value technique and swim lanes in general. Here we illustrate only the simplest possible mapping between them.

The fourth swim lane for the furniture seller is omitted. Each role or actor has its own activities performed or triggered by a flow control shift. The whole process starts with the Query for Apartments activity performed by an apartment buyer. The apartment broker needs to analyze advertisements which suit the query (Analyzing Advertisement activity). He may contact other apartment sellers not only in his database (Contacting Sellers). Note that here we could use a decision point where the apartment broker may analyze whether he will first provide a buyer with advertisements he has and contact the sellers only when the buyer issues such a request. We omitted this complication here so as to describe just the concept. In real situations such decision points in business processes are very common and necessary.

The business process continues with activities at various apartment sellers to create an offer (Offering an Apartment activity). The apartment broker

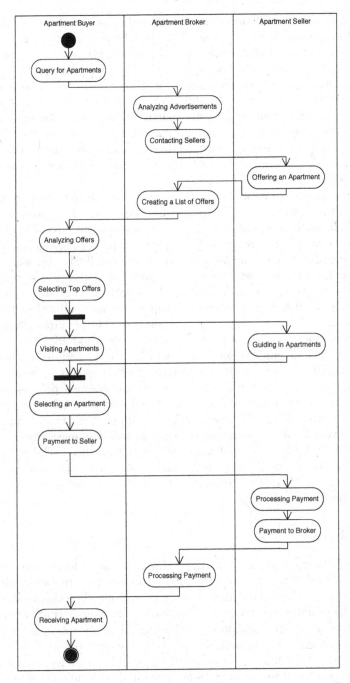

Fig. 4.5. An excerpt of a business process model for our business application example from figure 4.2

waits until he receives all the offers and after that he creates a list of offers matching the buyer query and sends it to the buyer (**Creating a List of Offers** activity). Note that here we could also model this process by additional activities such as sending the list, receiving the list, and so on.

The apartment buyer continues with analyzing offers, selecting a subset of the offers he wants to personally check by visiting the apartments together with an agent representing the apartment seller (fork for two concurrent activities, **Visiting Apartments** by apartment buyer and **Guiding in Apartments** by apartment seller), selecting an apartment, paying the seller for the apartment and broker for advertisements, and receiving an apartment from the seller.

The example above shows how activity models can help to capture a business process in organizations. The resulting process model is abstract, i.e., does not tell anything about how the activities are performed. They can be performed manually, electronically (e.g., payment processing can be done by an Enterprise Resource Planning system), or are candidates for support by a Web application being developed. It also shows that the values exchanged between the actors are embedded within the activities. This can be modeled by attaching object flows to the activity graphs. We have omitted this to keep the model simpler, but in some cases it might help. The activities can be also derived from goal models and extended, with further activities necessary to achieve a goal. Goals can also serve as annotations to the activities. The UML provides tagged values for that. The activity models usually serve as inputs for decision making about which activities in the business process need to be re-engineered and which activities can be optimized by introducing automated procedures of an IT system or a Web application. For example, the triggering event for a new advertisement can be sent automatically by a Web portal if the portal is integrated with the apartment seller back-end system. Payment can be realized electronically and processing posted automatically by integrating the ERP (Enterprise Resource Planning) back-end system with an online bank of the buyer.

Task analysis

Task models have emerged due to the widespread use of interactive systems and a need to cover requirements for such systems in a more systematic way. The task analysis shows how users will use the system. The task analysis belongs to the usability requirements analysis, which extends traditional functional requirements specification with additional requirements concerning the ease of use of the (Web) application, i.e., on how (easily) the user will be able to use the system, which tasks he needs to be able to perform, and which functionalities should be available to facilitate him performing these tasks. It is believed that in this way the increasing complexity of user interface design of interactive Web or software applications can be better managed; eases the implementation phase and produces better and easier to use user interfaces.

The importance of this technique is emphasized in those applications where a user needs to interact with several open dialogs or pages (even concurrently) to accomplish his task [PMM97]. Again, the task model helps in analyzing and understanding those tasks. As stated above, we will concentrate on the UML activity diagrams to explain the concept of task models. We adopt the task model notation adopted for Rich Internet Applications (RIAs) in the Abstract Design for Rich Internet Application (ADRIA) method [DS07]. However, other notations exist and have been adopted in Web application development, such as concurrent task trees [dTC03]. For the purpose of this book, the task model is intended as set of activities related to each other by control flow relationships. It models a task route a user has to go through in the system (by following the dialogs which implement the task model specification) if he wants to accomplish his goal.

In UML activity diagrams , typical user activities are placed in the model and a control flow is drawn between them. They may be grouped into swim lanes for each stakeholder. They can be structured into subtasks as well. Typically, a task model is assigned to each representative use case. We do not deal with use cases in this book as they are commonly known and used in Web application requirements analysis.

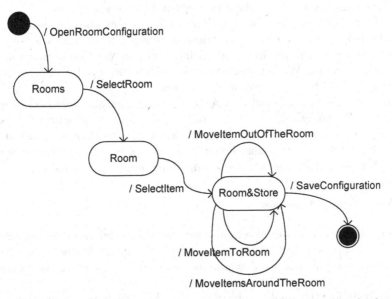

Fig. 4.6. An example of a task model excerpt in a Web application for buying furniture [DS07]

A simplified task model for the furniture shop (see [DS07]) is shown in Figure 4.6. It shows three main activities a user can do in the furniture online shop (apartment broker Web application): browsing a room list (Rooms state), exploring a room (`Room` state), and configuring the room with furniture from the store (`Room&Store` state).

As can be seen from the above example, the task models are clearly different from business process models even though they can be described by the same notation. They reside on a different level of abstraction. While the task models focus on requirements on the system's use, or, in other words, requirements stated in tasks users will perform when interacting with it, the business process models address higher-level activities which focus on how certain products or services will be created without considering Web application support.

In fact, one business process activity can be decomposed and realized by one or more alternative task models. Figure 4.6 can be, for example, a decomposition of the `Analyzing Offers` activity of the `Apartment Buyer` actor from Figure 4.5. When task models are created depends strongly on the requirements engineer's preference. He can start exploring task models and how a particular, innovative Web application can be developed for a specific domain. This may occur when there is no explicit customer yet. However, if there is an explicit customer, usually there is at least a prioritized list of business actions available before specific task models are created.

Very innovative engineers can start exploring various alternative user interface designs and task models after goals and values are known.

Different sketches and prototypical user interfaces can be created together with the help of task models even without knowing the details on how activities are performed and in which business process they are involved in an enterprise where the Web application is going to be deployed. Such creativity can actually lead to completely new processes.

Task models can also reflect information flow analysis discussed in section 4.2.2. By analyzing Figure 4.6 one can intuitively recognize that the depicted task model refines the `Room with furniture` derived information unit in Figure 4.3 and explains the requirements on how an apartment buyer should browse, explore, select, and change furniture in such a room.

4.2.5 Audience Analysis

Audience analysis is a useful technique for classifying and decomposing actors identified in previous techniques. It is used as an input for further structuring of information and functional requirements according to whom they belong to.

The technique is usually applied in Web development with existing customers but can also be useful when there is no explicit customer, such as in the case of the development of an open Web application for generic information access. The audience analysis can serve in that case as a tool for reasoning on potential user types and requirements which may be posed by them. In this case, an audience analysis can be performed with an external expert. The

expert can be asked to play the role of a customer or a potential user for eliciting the requirements. The Web Semantics Design Method (WSDM) features
a technique for such an audience analysis [CT01].

In WSDM the targeted visitors are classified into *audience classes*. An audience class groups (targeted) users with similar requirements. Using the subtype partial-order relation, the audience classes are organized in a hierarchy,
where each subtype defines an audience class that has additional requirements
associated compared to its superclass. Other relations, such as the possible
transition (of a user) from one audience class to another, may also be specified.
The result of the audience analysis is an Audience Model, which consists of a
hierarchy of audience classes, called the Audience Class Hierarchy. It denotes
how different user types relate to each other as subtypes. The Audience Class
Hierarchy is complemented with a specification of the possible transitions of
one audience class to another.

To derive this model, the audience analysis of WSDM prescribes to model
the activities of the organization, and people involved in it. The resulting
model is an activity diagram, where the people involved are actors, and potential audience classes. The audience analysis thus provide a viewpoint on
how the audience classes relate to activities identified either by a business
process model or a task model, and how the relate to each other.

The audience analysis technique thus describes two models: an activity
model, identifying potential audience classes and relating them with their activities, and an Audience Model, hierarchically presenting the audience classes
based on subset relations among their associated sets of information and functional requirements. Transitions among audience classes transformation from
members of one audience class to another.

The audience analysis technique thus provides the following elements:

- *Audience class*: a group of potential Web application visitors that belong to
  the target audience of the Web application, and have the same information
  and functional requirements. This element is used in both the activity
  diagram and the Audience Model.
- *Generalization/Specialization relationship*: relates one or more audience
  classes which share a subset of functional or information requirements.
  This element is used in the Audience Model.
- *Transition*: relates audience classes where instances of one audience class
  can be transformed to instances of another. This element is used in the
  Audience Model.
- *Association*: relates audience classes if there is a functional or information
  relation between them (for example, a request for transfer of information
  from one user type to another). This element is used in the activity diagram.
- *Activity*: can be taken from a business process or task model if they are
  used, or defined independently, and identifies which activity should be

performed by one or more audience classes. This element is used in the activity diagram.
- *Dependency*: relates one or more audience classes to activities (functional requirements) which are posed on them. This element is used in the activity diagram.

Different audience class hierarchies may exist for different viewpoints of functional requirements (e.g., authorization requirements). WSDM describes a formal method, based on a set of simple questions, to automatically derive the audience class hierarchy. The algorithm is based on the construction of a matrix of boolean values, allowing us to derive audience classes and subtype relations between them. The interested reader is referred to [CT01] for more information on the algorithm.

Let us illustrate the use of the WSDM audience analysis technique on the apartment buyer scenario we use throughout this chapter. By considering the different activities that users need to perform, we obtain the (simplified) activity diagram shown in Figure 4.7. We notice the activities Buying an Apartment, Offering an Apartment and Analyzing Offers (i.e., possibly identified using the business process model depicted in Figure 4.5). Buying an apartment is done by Apartment Buyers, offering an apartment by Apartment Sellers. Analyzing offers can be realized by any kind of visitor to the Web site: Apartment Buyer as he wants to buy the best suited apartment, Apartment Seller as he wants to make a competitive offer, and Visitors (i.e., passers-by of the Web site) simply out of curiosity.

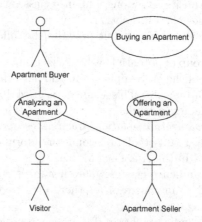

Fig. 4.7. Activity diagram for apartment buyer and seller scenario

Based on this activity diagram, we derive the audience class hierarchy depicted in Figure 4.8 (a). The requirement "Analyze Offers" is a common requirement by all audience classes, and is thus associated with Visitors. Apartment Buyers and Apartment Sellers each have additional requirements, respectively "Buying an Apartment" and "Selling an Apartment", and are therefore depicted as subclasses of the Visitor audience class.

Figure 4.8 (b) shows an additional audience class hierarchy for our example, based on the authorization requirements of the visitors. It can be obtained by an activity diagram similar to the one depicted in Figure 4.7. It shows Not-Registered users, whose authorization requirement is "registering", Registered users whose authorization requirement is "logging in", and Pre-registered users, whose authorization requirements are "logging in" and "confirming registration" [3].

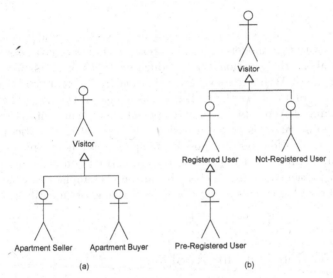

(a)   (b)

Fig. 4.8. Audience Class Hierarchy for apartment buyer and seller scenario: a) Apartment Buyer and Apartment Seller as subclasses of Visitor; b) Registered and Not-Registered User as subclasses of Visitor, Pre-registered User as subclass of Registered User

For some Audience Class Hierarchies, Audience Class Transitions can be specified. In the example of the Authorization Class Hierarchy, a Pre-registered User may become a Registered User by confirming his registration. A Not-registered User may become a Registered Users by registering. Registered users may become either Apartment Buyers or Apartment Sellers, by logging in. These Audience Class transitions are depicted in Figure 4.9. For a formal method to derive audience class hierarchies, and merging different hierarchies, representing different viewpoints, into one single audience class hierarchy, we refer the interested reader to [CT01].

---

[3] Pre-registering could for example be required for apartment sellers, by physically passing by an office of the brokerage service, to avoid fraud.

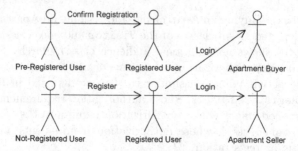

Fig. 4.9. Transition Diagrams for the Authorization Class Hierarchy

The above examples show that the audience analysis technique is useful in combination with task models or business process models to further structure and reason about the functionalities of different types of users. It is a first step in identifying Web site views or navigation tracks. It may also help in prioritizing requirements as the audience classes may be taken as the source for the planning of Web application development or subsequent iterations. The audience class hierarchy is probably easier to identify when activities or tasks are already known. However, it is possible to apply it as a next refinement step after information flow modeling, where certain information flows and entities belong to a particular audience class. It can be also applied as a next step after i* and e³-value models as a refinement of the actors identified by those techniques.

4.3 Application Domain Analysis

Application domain analysis is a commonly used technique to identify requirements for content or information structures which will be served by a Web application. The application domain analysis can be a refinement step of the information flow analysis discussed earlier in this chapter (Section 4.2.2).

The information units and information flows which are identified in such an information flow model are extended with structural relationships, entities, and attributes necessary to carry on the information flows and preserve the required information. Another option is to derive an application domain model by analyzing the domain literature and exploring concepts identified by a domain expert for other requirements engineering activities.

Later, the application domain model can be aligned with other models discussed earlier. Many Web design methods start with this technique to understand the vocabulary of the business or environment where a Web application will operate. The application domain model is created as a result of the application domain analysis.

The application domain model defines a set of concepts or entities and their respective attributes which specify the content required in a Web application.

The concepts are linked together by different types of relationships, such as generalization/specialization, association, composition, and so on.

The application domain model resulting from the application domain analysis comprises abstract concepts, which are provided as information in a Web application. Moreover, the application domain model could serve as a model for indexing content items. The content items can be considered as instances of particular concepts, or as sets of structural features of concepts describing them.

Some Web application design methods for data-intensive Web applications employ traditional object-oriented principles to analyze content requirements. The Object-Oriented Hypermedia Design Method (OOHDM) [SR98] or UML-based Web Engineering (UWE) [KBHM00] are examples of methods where object-oriented application domain analysis plays a central role. Similarly, during its data modeling phase WebML employs entity-relationship models to analyze the data [CFM02] to be published on the Web, and Web Semantics Design Method (WSDM) first used Object-Role Modeling (ORM) [TCP05] , and later adopted Ontology Web Language (OWL) [CPT06] for the same purpose. Other Web design methods use other or custom requirements analysis techniques.

The application domain model typically provides the following elements:

- *Concepts or classes*: represent structural entities relevant for a Web application content.
- *Attributes*: represent slots for content or content metadata values to be maintained about content concepts or classes.
- *Relationships*: represent structural relationships between the entities stating either composition semantics, specialization/generalization semantics, or association.

Let us continue with the apartment buyer scenario, and look at the Room with Furniture information unit identified in Figure 4.3. The information unit is derived from the supplied information on rooms, price, and furniture. To further analyze data structures necessary for preservation of content about rooms and furniture, a model similar to the one exemplified in Figure 4.10 is needed. We use UML Class Diagram notation.

The Apartment class consists of Room, Suggest List, and Furniture List information classes. The Suggest List maintains records identifying suitable furniture for a given apartment. Various criteria can be used to classify such furniture and rank it. We list just OfferId and timestamp attributes and omit further details on the other criteria here.

The Furniture List contains the furniture placed in the apartment already. Room Item-s are placed in the room either on the Floor or on the Wall. The Placement class generalizes them and is used to connect the Room Item to the Apartment and the Room.

Also, there are shared attributes between Room Item and Shop Item for recommended furniture. They are listed in the Item class. A user can explore

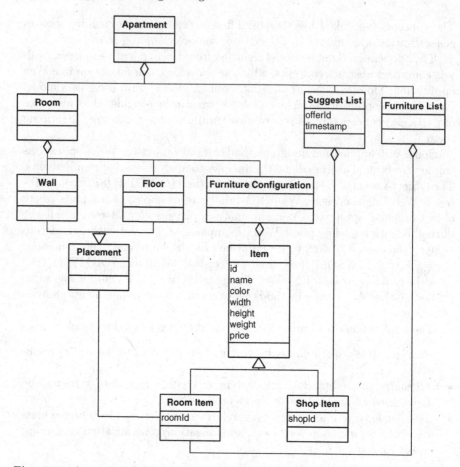

Fig. 4.10. An excerpt of the UML class diagram for the apartment room configuration domain adapted from [DS07]

these information structures when interacting with the already mentioned Room with Furniture information unit.

The above example shows how the domain analysis model can look like. It also shows how it links to the information flow analysis model. The application domain analysis can also be created concurrently with the other activities mentioned above. For example, exchanged business values from the e^3-value and resources and goals from the i* goals models can serve as preliminary inputs for the classes of the application domain model.

4.4 Navigation and Interaction Analysis

Navigation analysis is concerned with requirements for navigation and related information needed to fulfill certain user tasks. There are two main classes of applications with two different perspectives on navigation analysis: *business applications* and *general purpose applications*.

Business applications are intended to support certain organizational tasks. Therefore, navigation analysis is derived from workflow and business models in the organizations, and is usually represented by activity graphs.

General purpose applications such as publicly available Web sites and online shops are not bound to a particular business organization and may be embedded in many contexts. Therefore, business or workflow models are less used for the analysis of such applications. They rather employ task models reflecting predictions on what a user can do with such applications without bindings to any business entity.

4.4.1 Navigation Relationships

Navigation and linking between information fragments or pages is fundamental to Web applications. In navigation analysis, it is important to understand which information fragments and features of the Web application to link. In order to better understand conceptual relationships based on domain analysis, Relationship Navigation Analysis (RNA) [YB00] has been introduced. RNA is rooted in hypertext research and provides a taxonomy of relationship types and attributes to be used to reason about the classification of relationships in a domain. These relationships will later be implemented as links between pages. RNA furthermore prescribes a process on how to conduct such a relationship analysis. Information flow analysis is another model which can serve as an input for navigation requirements analysis.

The RNA method consists of five high-level activities:

- *Stakeholder Analysis*: this step concerns an analysis of the people who will use an application in order to classify them into standard user types.
- *Element Analysis*: this step results in concepts which represent information fragments to be linked.
- *Relationship Analysis*: this step concerns the analysis of relationships between elements by using a generic relationship taxonomy and domain-dependent and independent categories.
- *Navigation Analysis*: this step concerns the analysis of possible navigation structures to access the analyzed elements based on different tasks.
- *Evaluation Analysis*: this step concerns the analysis of benefits and costs associated with the analyzed and identified elements, relationships, and navigation structures.

RNA provides a knowledge elicitation framework and serves as a generic questionnaire when analyzing information fragments or concepts for Web applications. The information fragments concern information objects from a domain, people, commands, meta-information, or complex activities provided with a set of commands. The provided generic relationship taxonomy consists of the following relationship types taken from [YB00]:

- *Generalization relationship*: describes relationships between information items where concepts of an information item are subsumed under concepts of another information item which participates in such a relationship.
- *Characteristic relationship*: describes relationships between information items where concepts of an information item are attributes, parameters, metadata, or other background information of concepts indexing another information item participating in such a relationship.
- *Descriptive relationship*: describes relationships between information items where concepts of an information item are definitions, illustrations, explanations, and other descriptive information of concepts indexing another information fragment participating in such relationship.
- *Occurrence relationship*: describes relationships between information items which describe occurrences of the same concepts.
- *Configuration/aggregation relationship*: describes relationships between information items which together form a whole both structurally and functionally.
- *Membership/grouping relationship*: connects an information item to other members of a collection or a collection as a whole.
- *Classification relationship*: connects an information item to its instance or a class.
- *Equivalence relationship*: connects information items with instances of exactly the same concept.
- *Similar/dissimilar relationship*: connects information items which share some degree of positive or negative similarity.
- *Ordering relationship*: connects information items in a sequence.
- *Activity relationship*: connects information items related by an activity they support or describe.
- *Influence relationship*: connects information items where one item participating in the relationship instantiates a concept that has influence on a concept instantiated in another information item participating in the relationship.
- *Intentional relationship*: connects an information item to another one describing goals, issues, decisions, opinions, and comments associated with the item.
- *Socio-organizational relationship*: connects an information item to another one with a position, authority, alliance, role, and communication according to social settings or an organizational structure.

- *Temporal relationship*: connects information items to temporarily related items.
- *Spatial relationship*: connects information items related in spatial dimensions.

The relationship types mentioned above are further categorized. Composition, aggregation, membership, and grouping are grouped under the whole-part/composition category. Descriptive, occurrence, and characteristic relationship types are grouped under self-relationships. Together with generalization/specialization and classification they form an internal category of generic relationships. External relationships contain comparison and association/dependency categories. The comparison relationship types are equivalence and similar/dissimilar types. The rest of the relationships belong to the association/dependency category.

Relationship types can be further associated with attributes. The attributes are used to identify whether it is a structural relationship, an implemented/operation relationship such as a menu item, a schema relationship such as the relationship between schema elements, a statistical relationship such as the one generated from underlying data, a process relationship such as a relationship between tasks, a coordinated relationship such as when an item always occurs concurrently with another, or a coupling relationship such as relationship between consistency-dependent items.

The methodology provides further domain-independent categories, for example, for an ordering relationship where several options are provided to encode series, rank, and adjacency, or a descriptive relationship such as explanation, illustration, or definition.

4.4.2 High-Level Interaction and Navigation Units

Navigation relationships are usually analyzed in connection to higher-level interaction or navigation units. Several works on navigation units, navigation views [SR98], and interactions spaces [NeC00] have emerged which share a common ground: user interaction, navigation structure at a higher level, or relation to tasks. Here, we will focus on interaction spaces to explain the idea. We will employ the notation from the Abstract Design for Rich Internet Applications (ADRIA) method [DS07].

Interaction space models are conceptual models which define how a particular task from a task model is going to be supported by a user interface [NOP+06, DS07].

The main purpose of interaction space analysis is to analyze how information from the problem domain will be grouped for different stakeholders and users and how it will be supplemented with additional actions which support the identified tasks. The grouped navigation or interaction units are interconnected with the relationships. The main elements of the interaction space models are:

- *Interaction Spaces*: conceptual elements modeling requirements for user interaction at a user interface to fulfill a task modeled by a task model (see Section 4.2.4).
- *Relationships to Application Domain Classes*: they link, associate, aggregate, or generalize content classes as needed for the user interface.
- *Relationships between Interaction Spaces*: they associate, navigate, aggregate, and generalize interaction spaces with the other interaction spaces to form a navigation space.

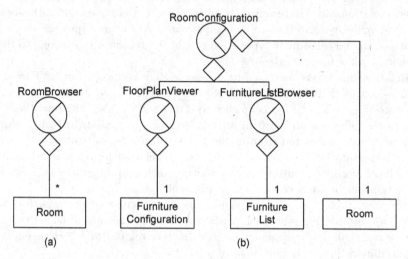

Fig. 4.11. An example of the UML class diagram for interaction spaces in a Web application for buying furniture [DS07]

A simplified interaction model from [DS07] (navigation relationships as well as details of interaction spaces are suppressed) is depicted in Figure 4.11. It follows the same scenario of an apartment buyer and refines the task model from Figure 4.6. The example shows a browser and a view of an application domain class. Each interaction space is further connected to the data classes it uses. For each transition and state in the task model, we consider relevant interaction spaces. For example, we need a Room Browser that shows the rooms. A selection is made by pointing out one object in the list. We need a FloorPlanViewer and a FurnitureListBrowser to show the contents of the room. In this list, an object can be selected by pointing to it. Moving it around should be a drag and drop function. These two interaction spaces are parts of an overall interaction space that we call RoomConfiguration. Finally, we need an interaction space for saving the furniture configuration.

The above example shows how a structural model of interaction spaces can be used as a refinement of application domain model. The model is useful whenever a composite collection of information or a view on information is required to be interactive. Besides connection to application domain, task models can be combined with interaction spaces as it is done in ADRIA method . This way, a designer has two complementing viewpoints: task models representing behavioral aspects of human activity with a system, and extended class diagrams as interaction space models representing structural aspects of human activity with the same system.

4.5 Summary

This chapter provided an overview on the requirements engineering process for Web applications and various techniques used to better understand various requirements viewpoints. First, we looked at the main differences of Web application requirements as compared to those of generic software systems. Second, we elaborated on the different types of requirements for Web applications and explained their dependencies. Third, we discussed various techniques used in the requirements engineering process for Web applications.

The chapter dealt with value-based requirements engineering, exploring business values and business models a new Web application can introduce when deployed at a customer site. The chapter discussed the refinement of the business value exchange model into information flows between the actors who will use a Web application. It further discussed the goal-oriented requirements analysis of Web applications as well as its use together with business value models.

Business processes and task models, which look at internal processes and user tasks within an organization or a system being developed, provide a next level of abstraction in requirements engineering for Web applications. Audience class analysis is discussed as a techniques used to structure requirements according to user types. The user types are refinements of the actors identified in business value and goal models.

Application domain analysis is provided as a technique which helps explore content requirements for a Web application. Navigation requirements analysis and interaction spaces are two techniques described in this chapter to give a reader an idea on structural requirements for navigation as well as user interaction in connection with business process and task models. The chapter also provided some examples on how to combine various techniques and explained that not all of them are necessary in every project. Note that there are other possibilities for combining them beyond the ones described in this chapter.

4.6 Further Readings

There are various other sources for further readings which expand on the aspects explained in detail in this chapter. A comprehensive review with extensive references to current state of the art of requirements engineering for Web applications can be found in [CK04]. Further details on reasoning on business values can be found in [KGT04]. Further details on using and reasoning on goal models in Web application engineering can be found in [MESP02, BP04]. Business process modeling is explored by various methodologies such as UWE [KKZH04] or WebML [BCFM06]. Further comparison of different requirements engineering for Web application content and navigation, as well as meta-modeling for requirements, is explored in [CK07]. Last but not least, World Wide Web (see [HCH+08] for 2008 edition), Web Engineering (see [SCD08] for 2008 edition), and Requirements Engineering (see [TF08] for 2008 edition) conference series are a good source for additional information on requirements for Web applications.

5

Web Application Design

The main goal of Web application design is to facilitate the understanding of the solution that is going to be developed (i.e., the Web application), as opposed to the understanding of the users and the context in which the solution is deployed, which is addressed by requirements engineering. Web application design can be regarded as the set of activities that refine the abstractions identified during requirements analysis with the aim of specifying the organization of the application data, navigation, presentation, and architecture.

Note that not necessarily all the requirements need to be collected and analyzed before the design starts. In case of incomplete requirements, the development cycle can proceed by addressing those requirements that are already well understood. The uncovered requirements will be elaborated in follow-up iterations.

As pointed out already in Chapter 4, Web applications distinguish themselves from regular software systems. Naturally, this distinction equally applies to Web application design. The most important peculiarities of the Web application domain that require specific design approaches are:

- *Higher accessibility of information and services*: the World Wide Web enables access to information and services for far more users simultaneously than closed intranets or desktop applications. Different modalities and views on data and services need to be designed to support the varying user needs.
- *Document-centric hypertext interface*: as with the requirements, this influences the Web application design as well. The information and services have to be mapped onto hypertext documents. Additionally, interconnections between various dialogs, views on information, and pages make the design of Web applications different, and require specific abstractions to understand and represent the composition of the different hypertext elements and their traversals.
- *Different data management, data access, and processing technologies*: data are distributed on the Web in various formats and technologies, from tra-

S. Casteleyn et al., Engineering Web Applications: *Data-Centric Systems and Applications.*
DOI: 10.1007/978-3-540-92201-8_5, © Springer-Verlag Berlin Heidelberg 2009

ditional relational databases to more recent technologies, such as those based on XML and RDF. This requires that a designer pays attention not only to the organization and processing of local databases, but also to the access to (possibly heterogeneous) external data sources.

- *Variable presentation technologies and engines*: differences in Web browsers and access devices need particular attention in presentation design, to address issues such as the different presentation styles required by the different devices, the content density, i.e., the number of content items that can actually be displayed on the screen of a specific device, and so on.
- *More complex architectures*: the architecture of a Web application resembles the architecture of distributed information systems, with application components residing on different tiers. However, the front end of Web applications makes things more complex. For example, Web pages are client-side elements that can embed objects and scripts requiring interactions with server-side resources. This and other issues need the definition of *ad-hoc* architectural patterns and adequate modeling techniques.

The main purpose of Web application design is to communicate the logical organization of a Web application along its different perspectives (data, hypertext, presentation, architecture), and to facilitate decision making on implementation alternatives, especially with respect to the peculiarities discussed above. Model-driven approaches [MCF03] are proposed as a way to facilitate the specification of Web application design thanks to the abstractions provided by the models. In some cases, models also serve the purpose of "executable programs", written in high-level languages that abstract from implementation details, being however still amenable to the automatic translation into models that are close to execution platforms.

This chapter will discuss the main design abstractions for Web application design, as proposed in the most notable Web engineering methods. The aim is to show how design models can facilitate the understanding and structuring of a Web application. The principles of model-driven Web engineering will be also shortly introduced (further details on the model-driven architecture paradigm will be provided later in Chapter 7).

5.1 Design Concepts

While the implications of the Web environment on Web application design require new design abstractions to capture various perspectives, different from those adopted for traditional software systems, general principles and concepts stay valid. Before introducing the relevant techniques for Web application design, we summarize the basic terminology in software design, and its relevance to Web applications. We also shortly comment on the design process.

5.1.1 Design Principles

Three fundamental design principles known from software engineering are *abstraction, refinement*, and *modularity*. In Chapter 4 we touched upon the abstraction already. In this section we will further expand on that, and relate the main Web application design abstractions to the ones discussed in the software engineering literature. We also touched upon refinement as an activity that maps the abstractions used to explore, reason about, and communicate the requirements onto the abstractions used in design. Refinements can be further applied to go back and forth between different design abstractions along different design viewpoints. Modularity, is another important feature in Web application design, which requires identifying well defined modules facilitating the management of complexity.

Abstraction

Abstraction is one of the main design principles to manage the complexity of software (and Web) applications. Abstraction allows us to concentrate on a problem at some level of generalization, independently of low-level implementation details. There are many ways to take advantage of abstractions in the development of software projects. For example, *domain-oriented abstraction* promotes the use of application domain terminology, as also commonly done in requirements engineering, to facilitate the interactions with the user or the customer. *Solution-oriented abstraction*, on the other hand, exploits objects, classes or procedures, as used by the target programming language, to facilitate the discussion of the software organization within the development team. The *procedural abstraction*, looking at named sequences of instructions, *data abstraction*, looking at named collections of data, and *control abstraction*, looking at program control mechanisms, are other kinds of abstraction that allow the development team to reason on the application software organization, without requiring the detailed inspection of the application code.

Let us now look at some of the abstractions commonly used in Web application design. Chapter 3 identified workflow design, data design, navigation design, presentation design, and architecture design as the main activities in the design of Web applications. As illustrated in Figure 5.1, these activities produce design abstractions that, as commonly agreed upon among members of the Web engineering community, show mutual dependencies. Such dependencies do not have a temporal ordering semantics. They represent that certain design models might depend on each other in terms of the employed concepts. For example, workflow design influences data and navigation design, because the identification of data entities and the organization of the application hypertext strongly depend on the tasks identified during the initial workflow analysis. Data and navigation design then influence presentation design, while the architecture specification refines data, navigation, and presentation into application subsystems or components and provides an overall view on the organization of the Web application.

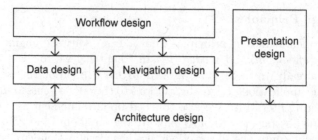

Fig. 5.1. The activities in Web application design and their dependencies

The decision on how to sequence the modeling activities depends on the priority that a development team assigns to a particular perspective. For example, in the Web engineering community two main approaches have emerged depending on whether the application development is approached from an information or a user perspective:

- *Information-centric design processes* start with activities related to the back-end of an information system. Usually they start with the domain or data design and proceed with navigation design. Form the produced design artifacts, a workflow design can be derived. Presentation design is performed as the next step. The last step is usually architecture design to structure the application into components or modules.
- *User-centric design processes* start from the analysis of the users' activities. Workflow design is thus the first step, and the resulting workflow serves as an input for navigation design where workflows are transformed into sequences of navigation steps. For each navigation step a presentation design is performed. Concurrently, the data design is performed to specify data needed for user activities.

This chapter will discuss the different design activities and the most common techniques that lead to the production of the aforementioned design abstractions. Some hints about the design processes underlying the main Web engineering methods will be also provided.

Refinement

Refinement goes hand in hand with abstraction. As a design process continues, stepwise refinement of the abstractions is employed to clarify the details of the designs and its transformations to the models closer to the implementation environment. Refinement plays a crucial role in Web application design as well. Depending on the chosen approach, the navigation models refine either data models or workflow models. Similarly, presentation models are refinements of the navigation models. The data, navigation, and presentation models are mapped onto the architecture that describes the overall organization of the Web application.

Structural partitioning is a common approach to structure a system for follow-up refinements. The partitioning can be horizontal or vertical. The horizontal decomposition identifies modules on the basis of the main program functions. In Web application design, horizontal partitioning is used to allocate Web pages and business logic operations to different site views. This approach is for example used in the WebML method to allocate pages and operations to different hypertext modules, each one addressing the needs and functionality of a specific user segment. Vertical partitioning is based on a top-down principle of work allocation, i.e., upper modules are control modules, while lower modules are the ones performing the task without separating input, transformation, and output functions. For example, in WebML pages play the role of controllers that allocate work to their embedded data units and operations, which are the modules actually accessing and operating on data.

Modularity

Modularity is a principle of software system design that enables the software to be manageable. The software is decomposed into a set of modules that are integrated to satisfy the collected requirements. Modularity contributes to better understandability of the subproblems the software is supposed to solve, to better integrability, and to easier introduction of changes that do not affect the whole system; it also reduces the impact of failures to specific submodules. One largely adopted modularization technique is *information hiding*, according to which the implementation details of an object, module, package or class, are hidden and only the information that is needed for using and integrating the module is disclosed through a proper *interface*.

Modularization is adopted in all Web application design methods. Object-oriented Web design methods employ classes and objects that enforce information-hiding. Web sites, pages, navigation views, and other conceptual structures help modularize and encapsulate information and operations. Similarly, architectural modeling techniques feature subsystems, modules, components, and parts as modularization elements.

5.1.2 Design Process

It is difficult to prescribe a common design process for Web applications. The adoption of a design process depends on many factors, including the selected modeling language and approach. For example, in a plan-driven process the models are central artifacts created in the design activity, whereas in an agile process the models are used mostly as sketches that designers use for a better understanding of the system before they start coding and testing. We can, however, agree at least on a definition and on a few goals a design process should adhere to.

The design process is a creative activity where the main goal is to transform and map high-level requirements onto an implementation programming environment. The driving principles are abstraction and continuous refinement into more detailed models, that step by step become closer to the formalization required by the programming environment (i.e., the application code).

Borrowing the concepts underlying the well-known Unified Process [JBR99], the goals of Web application design can be summarized as follows:

- Understand the issues related to the technical environment on which the software will operate, such as programming languages, user interface technologies, database technologies, concurrency, and so on. As we will see later in this chapter, this plays a crucial role in data design for Web applications. On the other hand, this is less of an issue with some of the abstract conceptual design methods coming with a default technology, therefore relieving the designer from decision making about the choice of technology.
- Understand and create a model of requirements for individual modules and subsystems. Requirements and design are very closely interrelated. We have already discussed the major abstractions for requirements modeling in Chapter 4; in this chapter, we will devote space to the main Web application design abstractions.
- Use a design for planning and decomposing the implementation work into smaller, more manageable pieces.
- Capture the major interfaces between subsystems. As we will see, in some design methods these are captured in a so-called Web software architecture.
- Use as much as possible a common notation for the design within a team. Some of the design methods cover a complete Web application design cycle. In this chapter we have chosen a different approach: to discuss various design notations provided by different methods so that a designer can understand them and decide which one suits him best.
- Decide on an appropriate design abstraction so that the implementation is a more or less straightforward refinement of the design without significant change of structure. This can be achieved by employing either a design abstraction coming with an appropriate transformation technology and engine able to interpret it (for example WebML, which will be discussed in various places of this chapter), or UML and a model-driven approach to create transformations from various abstractions into particular implementation environments (as, for example, in the case of WebSA – see Section 5.6).

5.2 Workflow Design

The workflow design is a follow-up refinement of a business process model described from an organizational perspective during requirements analysis.

In Section 4.2.4, we have described a business process analysis. Based on it, workflow design extends and enacts those parts of the business process model that need to be automated by a Web application. In fact, a workflow is a special kind of business process that is case- and order-based [vdAvH02]. This characteristics allow us to define the exact work product of such a business process (a *case*) and also where such a business process starts and how it proceeds (the *activity order*). This restriction on business processes provides us with a possibility to formalize an execution of the workflow activities by a model close to an execution environment. This is also in line with the definition given in [Dei00], where a workflow is defined as a business process that can be supported by a workflow management system, an electronic system that can execute workflows. In our case, the workflow should be embedded in the Web application being developed. In this chapter we therefore focus on models that describe a business process that can be supported by a Web application in partial or full execution.

The first step in a workflow design is to determine which of the activities in the business process will be implemented by the Web application. Of course, this is only possible when we have a business process model in advance. In this case, the workflow design model is explicit and represents an orthogonal perspective in Web application design focusing on activities and tasks that will be performed by a system in connection with the business activities performed by humans. However, as it is argued in [BCFM06], an alternative approach is to extend hypertext modeling with explicit workflow concepts. As hypertext models will be extensively discussed later in this chapter, in this section we will discuss only the first approach: the workflow design model as an explicit design model in Web application design. We also refer the reader to [BCFM06] for a discussion on the workflow concepts that extend a hypertext model.

We adopt UML activity diagrams to illustrate the workflow design. Other notations exist and are used, such as the Business Process Modeling Notation (BPMN [Gro06]) and Petri Nets [vdAvH02]. It is up to the designer, and depends on his background, which notation he prefers. We will use here as example an online magazine Web application and expand on it in the following sections. Our scenario is based on a simplified workflow for ordering magazines, where the application supports the retrieval and selection of articles.

Figure 5.2 illustrates the workflow. It starts with an event triggered by somebody who would like to order articles. Based on the event, a librarian accesses the application, where the Home Page displays the list of articles sorted in chronological order (Display the list of Articles (chronological order) activity). The librarian can either browse that list (Browse Articles) activity) or switch the viewpoint such that the results are grouped by Author or by Highlights. When the librarian finally finds appropriate articles, he issues an order (Select and Order Magazine activity). Based on the order, the application prepares an invoice (PrepareInvoice activity) and packages it together with the selected magazines (Package activity). As a follow up, the magazines together with the invoice are sent to the librarian (Send activ-

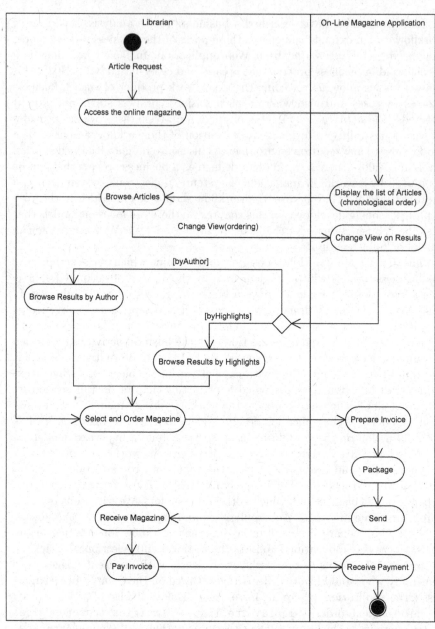

Fig. 5.2. The workflow model for ordering articles through an online magazine

ity). When the librarian receives the package (`Receive Magazine` activity), he pays the invoice (`Pay Invoice` activity), which ends his workflow. The online Web application workflow ends after receipt of the payment (`Receive Payment` activity).

As can be seen from the above example, the workflow design models are good at mapping user activities, tasks, and processes to the tasks that a Web application must perform. They are good at describing a procedural knowledge, i.e., how the application will react and align to the user activities. They are very powerful for describing routine and administrative processes. They are not as good at describing processes that cannot be formalized as control flows. As can also be intuitively seen, the workflow design can be combined with business process analysis and task analysis used in requirements engineering. Usually, transitions and activities from business and task models are decomposed into Web application tasks and activities.

5.3 Data Design

Data design is a well-established activity that is fundamental especially for those Web applications that need to manage a huge amount of data. Data design produces a refinement of the application domain model identified during requirements engineering, with the purpose of outlining how content will be stored and processed by the Web application. The result is a *data model* that specifies the structures used to store the data underlying the entities and the relationships previously identified in the application domain model.

The data model may differ depending on the data base management system (DBMS) that is chosen for storing and processing data. If a relational DBMS is used, a relational data model must be derived from the application domain model. This can be done by following the traditional rules for transforming content entities and relationships into relational tables [Ull88]. Other DBMSs based on different theories can be chosen as well. For example, in case of an XML database, such as ORACLE XML DB,[1] an XML tree structure will result from the transformation of the application domain model into the data model. If a triple store is selected, such as SESAME,[2] the data model will describe classes and relations used to annotate instances.

In this section we will concentrate on the relational data model, which is the leading solution for the development of Web applications. Its main elements are:

- *Relation*: a set of *tuples*, each one representing a "fact" about a given concept (an entity or a relationship of the application domain). A relation can be also seen as a table structure definition (a set of column definitions) along with the data appearing in that structure (the table rows).

---

[1] http://www.oracle.com/technology/tech/xml/xmldb/index.html
[2] http://www.openrdf.org/

- *Attribute*: the ordered pair <*attribute name, type name*>. It corresponds to a column of a relation table. An attribute value is a specific value for the type of the attribute (i.e., the entry in a specific column and row), which can be either scalar, multi-value, or an item of a complex type.
- *Constraints*: properties that must be satisfied for data items to be correct and consistent. The most important constraints refer to the definition of primary key and foreign key. A *primary key* is an attribute whose values uniquely identify the tuples within a relation. A *foreign key* identifies a set of attributes in one (referencing) relation, whose values are the ones of a set of attributes that are primary key in another (referenced) table. Foreign keys are used to represent dependencies between relations that correspond to one-to-one or one-to-many relationships between entities in the application domain model.

The above-mentioned elements are those supported by every relational DBMS. Some high-level abstractions, generally adopted in the application domain model, such as generalization/specialization relationships, many-to-many relationship cardinality, and multi-value attributes, are not directly supported. Hence, the application domain model must be restructured before it can be translated into a relational data model. For example, the generalization/specialization relationship in an Entity-Relationship schema can be transformed into two one-to-one relationships between the sub-entity and the super-entity.[3] Each many-to-many relationship is split into two one-to-many relationships between the two original entities and a new entity is placed between them. Composite attributes are transformed into the set of their simple component attributes. Multi-value attributes instead require the addition of new separate entities, associated with the original entity through one-to-many relationships. Once such a restructuring is applied, the application domain model can be transformed into a relational data model.

Let us now illustrate the data model in the online magazine scenario described above. We start from the application domain model and show how it can be transformed in a data model representing the organization of data. We adopt the online magazine example described in [SR98] and represent its application domain model as a UML class diagram.

Figure 5.3 depicts the resulting schema. It describes how Story, the main content class in the online magazine Web application, relates to one or more Authors. Each author in turn can be associated with one or more stories. Story can be specialized into further concepts, namely Essay, Translation (if one or more translations of the original story exist), or Interview. Essays and interviews may use illustrations in the form of Media (either Video or Photo). Interviews are granted by authors.

Figure 5.4 depicts the relational data model derived from the previous model. The relations Story and Author derive from the corresponding entities

---

[3] Other transformations for a generalization/specialization relationship are possible. For more details on this topic see [Ull88].

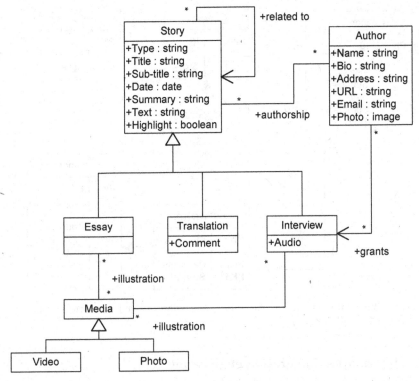

Fig. 5.3. A UML class diagram for the domain model of the online magazine application [SR98]

in the domain model. The generalization/specialization relationship between Story and Essay is refined into a one-to-one relationship between the Story and Essay relations and the association between the two relations is expressed by means of foreign keys. The other subclasses of the Story class can be similarly translated (they are not depicted in Figure 5.4 for sake of simplicity). The Authorship and the EssayMedia relations represent two many-to-many relationships of the application domain model, namely the relationship between Story and Author and the relationship between Essay and Media. The generalization/specialization relationship between Media and the two subclasses Video and Photo is translated by keeping the superclass Media and by adding the selector attribute Type that enables the distinction between the two media types.

It is worth noting that the resulting data model can support the execution of the workflow model depicted in Figure 5.2 if the workflow model is created in advance. Otherwise, the workflow model can also be created as a follow-up model describing the way the online magazine data can be used.

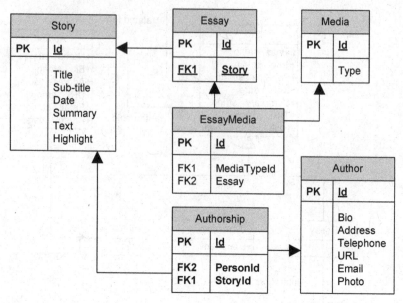

Fig. 5.4. The data model for the online magazine derived from the application domain model in Figure 5.3

5.3.1 Information integration engineering

Sometimes, a Web application needs to extract information from distributed external sources. To enable this, components for mapping representation schemas and semantics have to be developed. The HERA methodology [HBFV03, VH05] deals with information at the analysis and design levels by introducing so-called integration modeling. Subsequently, the integration model further drives the development activities. We will not go into further detail here, but find it important to mention at least the typical activities involved in this process. We refer the reader for details on notation and for guidelines for integration modeling to [HBFV03, VH05].

Typical activities involved in information integration engineering are:

- *External application domain model analysis*: this activity is concerned with the analysis of the conceptual model of external information relevant for the Web application to be developed. It also comprises an analysis of the conceptual model of the environment where the information has to be delivered.
- *Analysis of possible interconnections between Web application and external application domain analysis*: the application domain model of the Web application to be developed and the external conceptual models are compared, and possible interconnections and mappings are sketched.

- *Analysis of the mechanisms to access external information*: access mechanisms and query languages supported by the external sources are analyzed and possible scenarios for querying the external information are sketched.
- *Design of mediating infrastructure*: an architecture for information integration or mediator components is designed. A mechanism for information source mediation is selected (e.g., global-as-view [FLM98] or local-as-view [Hal01]). In addition, a strategy for exchanging information between the Web application and the external sources is designed (e.g., publish-subscribe, online access on demand, replication, and so on).
- *Implementation of the mediating infrastructure*: the mediating infrastructure is implemented as a subsystem or layer of the Web application or as a stand alone Web service.
- *Mediating infrastructure testing*: the infrastructure is tested for reliability, performance, and scalability, and against functional and data requirements.

5.4 Navigation Design

Navigation design is concerned with the structure of the navigation paths through information and services provided by the Web application. This is an essential activity in Web applications engineering, especially when navigation structures go beyond simple hierarchies and the Web application features a complex navigation behavior.

Two aspects must be addressed by navigation design: the *site structure*, focusing on how different navigation nodes must be defined and linked together to form a hypertext interface, and *navigation behavior*, focusing on the user navigation actions and on the events that they generate and that trigger changes in the traversed hypertext structures. In the following, we will discuss the principal design abstractions that different Web engineering methods propose to address these issues.

5.4.1 Site Structure Design

A number of navigation abstractions in Web application design are used to describe the organization of the hypertext interface, with specific emphasis on the identification of information chunks displayed in the hypertext nodes and the navigation mechanisms that allow users to move across different chunks. Different Web engineering methods refer to this phase with a different terminology, for example calling it *navigation design*, *site structure design*, or *hypertext design*. However, all of them share a common focus on the following concepts:

- *Atomic navigation items*: represent single information chunks composed of (attributes of) data entity instances. An example of an atomic navigation item could be the description of a book displayed in a Web page at *Amazon.com*. Usually, for each atomic navigation item the connection with the underlying data entity is specified.

- *Composite navigation items*: represent composite structures composed of atomic navigation items (or recursively of other composite structures). An example of a composite navigation item could be a book information fragment together with a list of recommended books at *Amazon.com*.
- *Contextual navigation structures*: represent navigation structures used to access atomic or composite navigation items. Examples of such structures are menus, guided tours, indexes, and so on.

Navigation views and navigation contexts

One technique for site structure design, supported in OOHDM [SRB96] and in UML-based Web Engineering (UWE) [Koc98], is *navigation view design*. Navigation views represent navigation items, both atomic and composite, which are derived as projections over the data entities of the application data model. They are defined as object-oriented views, by means of a query language similar to SQL. Specification of a navigation view includes view name, base data entity or class, and other classes inherited from the base class. Besides that, the view specifies projections of attributes from the base class as well as from the inherited classes. Selection conditions further constrain the information that can be navigated through such views.

Figure 5.5 depicts an example of navigation view derived from the domain model of Figure 5.3. As can be seen, navigation views are modeled similarly to object-oriented classes. The main navigation view is derived from the `Story` content class, and is characterized by the attributes `Type`, `Title`, `Sub-title`, `Date`, `Summary`, and `Text` – these data will be displayed in the corresponding navigation node. Note that the `Author` class does not appear in this schema, and that the `Author` and `Author_bio` attributes are derived from `Author` through a select statement that traverses the association between the `Story` and `Author` classes. `Essay`, `Translation` and `Interview` views are derived from the corresponding classes. Similarly to the `Author` and `Author_bio` attributes in `Story`, the `Interviewee` attribute in `Interview` is defined through a select statement that traverses the `grants` association.

Once navigation views have been defined, they can be grouped, indexed, and linked into the so-called navigation contexts. A *Navigation Context* describes the navigation mechanisms and structures that can be used to access navigation views. It organizes the navigation space into consistent collections that can be traversed following a particular order so that the user is enabled to perform his intended tasks [SR98].

There are different elements that can be used for the definition of a navigation context [SdAPM99]:

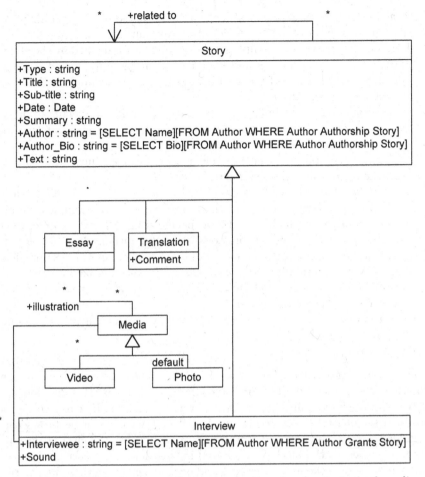

Fig. 5.5. An OOHDM schema specifying a navigation view for stories in the online magazine Web application [SR98]

- *Simple class-derived*: represents a context composed of those objects of a class that satisfy a given property.[4] A common example is given by all the instances of a class, e.g., all stories in our Web magazine example.
- *Class-derived group*: a set of simple class-derived contexts, selected by means of a parameterized property. For example, *Story by type* is a class-derived group; its elements are simple class-derived contexts, one for each possible value of the **Type** attribute.
- *Context delimiter*: delimits subgroups of contexts that are mutually accessible (and separates them from those not accessible.)

---

[4] OOHDM provides a language similar to SQL for specifying the selection properties for context construction, but the designers can use their own preferred language, especially when not using any case tool for further processing.

- *Simple link-derived*: represents all the objects related to a given object. An example is the set of all the stories of a given author.
- *Link-derived group*: a set of link-derived contexts. It is defined by specifying a one-to-many relationship and defining the simple link-derived contexts for each possible value of the relationship source. An example is the *Story by Author* context group.
- *Arbitrary*: describes enumerated sets, where elements can belong to different classes, as it happens, for example, when heterogeneous information items are presented in a guided tour collection.
- *Dynamic*: describes sets where the elements can change during navigation, e.g., the history or a shopping cart.
- *InContext classes*: special classes that decorate contexts, enriching them with variable attributes and methods (behavior). For example, the author's bio might not be included in a specific situation, for example, when traversing all the stories of a previously selected author. They also specify traversal behavior, such as behavioral features for computing the previous and next information items in the context. Traversal behavior can be sequential, circular sequential, index, or index sequential depending on how the in class behavior is defined.
- *Indexes*: describe access structures for contexts, such as menus, additional indexes, and guided tours.

Figure 5.6 depicts an example of navigation context schema derived from the story navigation view illustrated in Figure 5.5. A user can choose how to access the stories from the main menu, a general index. He can choose to access stories through an `Author Index` or a `Type Index`. He can also choose to see a set of `Highlights`, that, as described later on, can be browsed as a guided tour. `ByAuthor` and `ByType` are examples of class-derived groups. As represented by the black boxes placed in their left upper corner, there are indexes defined on them, for accessing and navigating among their information items. The definition of the context itself, by means of an InContext class, will specify the types of navigation allowed inside the context. Typical modalities are "sequential", "circular sequential", "index" (i.e., it is possible to navigate only from an index to an element and back), or "index sequential".

`Highlights` is an example of simple class-derived. It does not have any index associated with it because, as shown in Figure 5.7, navigation through its elements is defined as a guided tour. More specifically, the figure illustrates the InContext class that defines the inner structure and the navigation modality for the `Highlights` context.[5] The `Story` view is the main source for its content items. The `Author_bio` attribute is derived form the `Author` content class. The `next` and `previous` traversal links define a guided tour traversing of the content items in the context.

---

[5] Each context in the navigation context schema needs to be annotated with an InContext class. For sake of brevity, we do not report here the full specification. For more details the reader is referred to [SR98, SdAPM99].

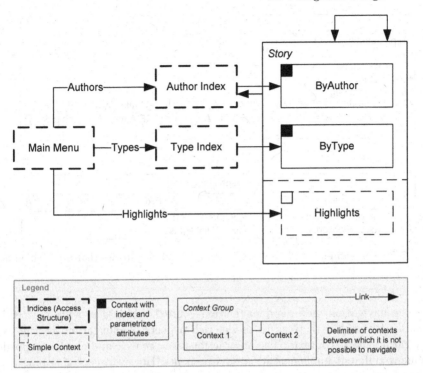

Fig. 5.6. An OOHDM navigation context schema for the stories accessed through the online magazine (adapted from [SR98])

As represented by the cyclic link on Story in Figure 5.6, the user can navigate between related stories. The arrow from Story to Author Index specifies that from any context the user can go back to the index of authors. The dashed line represents a context delimiter. The user can therefore switch between browsing stories by authors to browsing stories by type, and back. This means that the user looking at a story accessed though the Author Index is allowed to navigate to either the next story by the same author or to the next story of the same type. Instead, he is not allowed to navigate to the next highlight because the Highlights context is outside the context delimitation.

UML-based Web Engineering (UWE) supports similar concepts, though represented in UML. Several stereotypes, i.e., UML extension mechanisms, are proposed such as «navigation class» and «direct navigability» for the *navigation space model*, which is the counterpart of the navigation context schema in OOHDM. Other stereotypes are defined for the *navigation structure model* to represent concepts similar to the elements of the OOHDM navigation context schema, such as indexes, contexts, guided tours, menus, and selector queries [KBHM00].

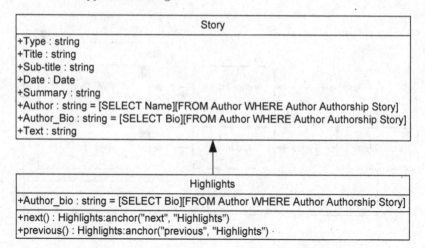

Fig. 5.7. An example of an "InContext class", grouping stories that are highlights (adapted from [SR98])

The navigation views and navigation context schemas provide powerful object-oriented abstractions to model rich aspects of navigation as well as navigation access contexts. The abstractions stay generic and can be mapped to many different implementation environments. However, each mapping requires further efforts, either to develop generators implementing the mappings, or to implement the abstract navigation specification in a particular programming environment. In the following we will show how alternative abstractions provided by the WebML model can be easily mapped to an implementation model.

Hypertext schema

The Web Modeling Language (WebML) [CFB00b, CFB00a] adopts the notion of *hypertext schema* to specify the structure of the hypertext, both in terms of content unit composition within pages and link definition. It shares with OOHDM the notion of contextual elements providing access to the application content. It differs from OOHDM because it provides explicit modeling primitives for representing different ways of projecting and selecting data from content entities and of displaying them within navigation nodes. Furthermore, the WebML hypertext schema integrates the OOHDM navigation view schema, identifying the composition of contents into specific hypertext nodes, and the OOHDM navigation context schema, identifying access mechanisms.

A WebML hypertext schema enables the definition of hypertext *pages* and their internal organization in terms of components, the so called *content units*, each one displaying the extracted content in a different modality. It also supports the specification of *links* between pages and content units.

The modular structure of a hypertext front end is defined in terms of *site views*, *areas*, *pages*, and *content units*. A site view is a particular hypertext, designed to address a specific set of requirements. Several site views can be defined on top of the same data, to serve the needs of different user communities, or for arranging contents as required by different access devices, such as PDAs, smart phones and similar appliances. Each site view may consist of areas, which are the main sections of the hypertext and comprise recursively other sub-areas or pages.

Page composition

Pages are the actual containers of information delivered to the user. The content units they are composed of represent the publishing of one or more instances of content entities, typically selected by means of queries over the relational tables deriving from the entities and relationships of the application domain model:

- *Data units* represent some of the attributes of a given entity instance.
- *Multidata units* represent some of the attributes of a set of entity instances.
- *Index units* represent a list of descriptive keys of a set of entity instances and enable the selection of one of them.
- *Scroller units* enable the browsing of an ordered set of objects.
- *Entry units* do not draw content from content entities, but publish a form for collecting input values from the user.

Data, multidata, index, and scroller units require the specification of a *source* and a *selector*. The source is the name of the content entity from which the unit content is retrieved. The selector is a predicate, used for selecting the actual objects of the content entity that contribute to the unit's content.

The previous collection of units is sufficient to logically represent arbitrary content on a Web interface. However, some extensions are also available, for example, the *multichoice index* and the *hierarchical index*, which are two variants of the index unit that respectively represent the selection by users of multiple objects and organize hierarchically a list of index entries defined over multiple entities. For more details on the complete set of WebML units the reader is referred to [CFB$^+$02].

Link definition

Units and pages in the hypertext schema are interconnected by *links* to form a hypertext structure. Links between units are called *contextual*, because they carry some information from the source unit to the destination unit, such as parameters needed for the computation of parametric selectors in the destination unit. In contrast, links between pages are called *noncontextual*.

In some cases, it may be necessary to differentiate a specific link behavior, whereby the content of some units is displayed as soon as the page is accessed, even if the user has not navigated its incoming link. This effect can be achieved by using *automatic links*, i.e., links that are "navigated" in the absence of a user's interaction as soon as the page that contains the source unit of the link is accessed. Also, there are cases in which a link is used only for passing contextual information from one unit to another and does not need to be rendered as an anchor. This type of link is called *transport link*, to highlight that it enables only parameter passing and not user interaction.

Global parameters

In some circumstances, contextual information is not transferred point to point during navigation, but can be set as globally available to all the pages of a site view. This is possible through *global parameters*, which abstract the implementation-level notion of session-persistent data. Parameters can be set through the *Set unit* and consumed within a page through a *Get unit*.

Operations

In addition to the specification of read-only Web sites, where user interaction is limited to information browsing, WebML also supports the specification of services and content management operations requiring write access over the information hosted in a site (e.g., the filling of a shopping cart or an update of the user's personal information). Some primitives express built-in *content management operations*, such as creating, deleting, and modifying an instance of an entity, and adding and dropping a relationship between two instances. The specification of *generic operations*, wrapping services outside the context of the Web application, such as the charging of a credit card by means of an external service, is also possible.

Figure 5.8 depicts a WebML hypertext schema for our online magazine example. Menus in WebML are generated from landmark pages (marked by the L label) in the form of navigation bars visible and accessible from any page of the hypertext. For simplicity, we here suppose that our online magazine includes three landmark pages:

- The Home Page (also marked by the H label), which displays a search form (Entry Search Key unit) that allows the user to enter a keyword to retrieve those stories that have a text including that keyword. The keyword is used by the selector of the Retrieved Stories unit to select relevant stories from the Story content entity. The unit displays a short description (a subset of Story attributes, e.g., the title and the summary) for all the retrieved stories, and allows the user to select a specific story and to navigate to the Story page, where the full description of the story is displayed.
- The page Authors, which displays the list of the story authors (Authors Index unit) from which the user can select a specific author. Given this selection, the Author's Stories multidata unit retrieves and displays a

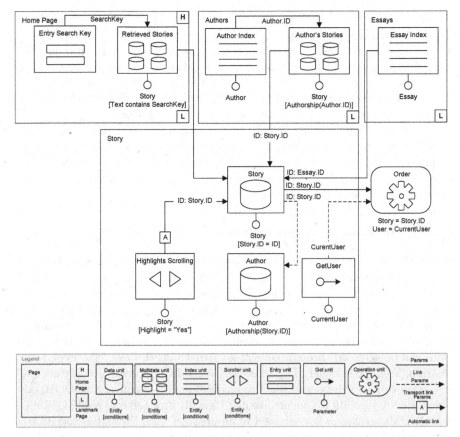

Fig. 5.8. An excerpt of the WebML specification of the hypertext interface for the news application

short description of all the stories written by the author,[6] and allows the user to select a story and to navigate to the **Story** page.

- The page **Essays**, which displays the list of the essay stories (**Essay Index** unit) from which the user can select a specific essay and navigate to the **Story** page.

Similarly to the previous pages, other landmark pages can be defined, for example to display the list of interviews and translations. We do not report them in this example for the sake of simplicity.

Selecting an item from the indexes in the pages **Authors** and **Essays**, or entering a keyword in the **Home Page**, leads the user to the **Story** page, where

---

[6] Note that the unit selector is defined on the relationship **Authorship** that in the application domain model associates an author with his stories (see Figure 5.3). In the data model, this relationship is represented by the table Authorship (see Figure 5.4).

the details of a selected story are published. The Story data unit displays the full description of a single story (title, sub-title, date, summary, text), retrieved by means of the ID parameter transported by the links entering the unit. The page also includes a scroller unit (Highlights Scrolling unit), that retrieves some highlighted stories (Highlight = "Yes") and organizes them in an ordered set that can be scrolled through *next* and *previous* links.

From the Story page, the user can finally order a story he is interested in. A link departing from the Story data unit activates the Order operation, a service running outside the online magazine Web application, which is in charge of wrapping the user and the story data and issuing the order. The user identifier, i.e., the global parameter identifying the current session, is retrieved by means of the GetUser unit.

Comparison of the two approaches

Both OOHDM and WebML provide generic modeling abstractions, which can be mapped onto any implementation model. WebML hypertext schemas integrate two separate aspects – composition and navigation model. The former is very similar to the views designed in OOHDM because it determines the composition of atomic or composite navigation nodes. The latter resembles the OOHDM navigation context schema because it defines how navigation items can be accessed through navigation structures. However, the hypertext design in WebML is richer. The composition model addresses how certain information chunks will be published in physical pages, in contrast to OOHDM where the information fragments are just logically grouped and related. While in OOHDM navigation is expressed in an abstract way, through associations between context classes, in WebML the navigation model specifies links between units and pages that in most cases corresponds to the anchors that the user can select in concrete Web pages.

All the previous differences are justified by one of the driving principles of WebML, the model implementability. WebML is indeed a platform-independent model, which however makes use of a standard way of describing navigation items, their interconnection and passing of parameters, their exposition in a user interface, so that a set of rules can be defined for automatically translating the platform-independent model into running code. We will show in the next chapter how implementability is achieved in a commercial tool, WebRatio [Web07b], supporting the automatic translation of WebML models into running application code.

5.4.2 Navigation Behavior Design

Navigation behavior design looks at navigation from a user interaction perspective. It aims at specifying what happens when the user performs an act of navigating or invokes any functionality offered by a navigation item. Here the assumption is that we have the contents already grouped as needed in navigation items, and we need to look at how to traverse navigation items and how navigation items change when the user navigates through them and performs any allowed interaction. We can therefore say that navigation behavior complements navigation design by offering a trail perspective: navigation is indeed modeled as a succession of states.

In a sense, navigation behavior design serves a similar purpose as the WebML hypertext design described in the previous section, because it provides a high-level view on how, and by executing which action, certain data can be accessed along different navigation items. Navigation behavior design however can be useful to specify with a major precision the semantics of navigation, i.e., which are the possible navigation states, which interaction and navigation actions can be performed in each state, and how navigation states change in response to the execution of such actions. For this reason, this technique has also been employed to describe the behavioral semantics of navigation modeling languages, such as WebML itself [CF01].

There are usually several *navigation trails* in a Web application. Each navigation trail is a path that a user can follow within a navigation space and that consists of *states* and *transitions*. A navigation state corresponds to an information chunk observed by a user in a hypertext node at a given time. A transition enables moving from one state to another. Transitions are usually caused by a user interaction event or by other events, such as time events or any other system-generated event. When a transition is fired it leads to the production of a new hypertext node – a new navigation state.

Several formalisms have been employed to represent navigation trails, such as State Charts [PTdOM98, DN03] or Petri Nets [SF89, FS94]. To give the reader an idea of navigation trail specification, we here illustrate the UML state diagram technique, as adopted within the UML-guide design method [DN03], which makes use of the following elements:

- *Atomic States*: represent the simplest displayable information chunk observed by a user at a given time. Each diagram must have a *starting pseudostate*, denoting the trail initial point.
- *Events*: trigger transitions in a state machine; they include user-generated or system-generated events, and the latter include time events.
- *Transitions*: represent active interconnections between information chunks, and usually correspond to associations in the application domain model. For each transition it is possible to specify the *event* that fires it, possible *guard expressions* conditioning its activation, and possible *actions* to be performed as soon as the transition is fired.
- *Superstates*: represent groups of atomic states, which may be arranged in an alternating or parallel fashion.
- *Parallel substates*: represent information chunks to be presented simultaneously. *Fork* and *join* pseudostates are used respectively for splitting and joining computations and enabling parallelism. The *SyncState* pseudostate

is used for synchronizing substates of parallel regions. It means that a navigation state as the product of information chunks can be composite, i.e., the navigation state can present an information chunk using several content fragments of different media types presented simultaneously.

Each state can have *side-effect actions*, which can be performed when a state is entered (*entry actions*), left (*exit actions*), or continuously until in the state (*do actions*). A side effect action is, for example, the initialization and rendering of content in a Web page, or the choice of presentation styles for a given information chunk. Actions can also process parameters.

The variability in navigation trails is modeled through *alternate (OR) states* and by decision symbols that can split a transition into several alternative transitions. In this way, navigation trails can specify alternative navigation paths and information chunks whose access is constrained by conditions referring to a specific user, content, device, or environment features.

Tagged values can be used to extend the semantics of elements in UML state diagrams. These are domain-specific properties that can refer to conceptual entities of the application domain model, or to specific terms specifying additional navigation requirements, and that can be used by generators for translating the state machine specifications into application code.

Navigation Trails for the Online Magazine

Figure 5.9 gives an example of navigation trail specification for our online magazine example. The diagram illustrates the alternative paths through which the user can reach the story navigation node (**Story** state), where he can access the data of a selected story and navigate through a collection of stories in a context determined by the navigation path previously followed.

As also specified in the OOHDM navigation context schema illustrated in Figure 5.6, the navigation starts from the main menu (**Main Menu** state), which in this case is modeled as a simple state accessible from the starting pseudostate. From this menu, the user can choose to go either to an **Essay Index** (**EssaysSelected** transition), to an **Author Index** (**AuthorsSelected** transition), or to a **Type Index** (**TypesSelected** transition). Each index is computed by means of an entry action in the corresponding state. The user can select an index item, and this selection fires a transition to the **Story** state that sets the value of the **groupby** parameter, thus determining a specific context for story browsing within the **Story** state. For example, the **EssaySelected** transition starting from **Essay Index** sets the **groupby** parameter to **Essay**, and this implies that, if reached through this transition, the **Story** state will allow the user to browse among essay stories.

Besides setting the value of the **groupby** parameter, the three transitions departing from the index states transport other parameters and execute some actions, all aimed at setting the navigation context in the **Story** state:

- The `EssaySelected` transition transports the identifier of the story selected in the essay index (`essayId` parameter), which is used to create a
  new story object (`Story:= new Story(essayId)`) to be displayed in the
  `Story` state. This object will be the starting point for browsing the essay
  collection within the `Story` state.
- The `AuthorSelected` transition transports the identifier of the selected author (`authorId`), which is used to create a new object for the selected author (`AuthorObj:=new Author(authorId)`). The action `AuthorObj.get
  Stories(groupby).getFirst()` then retrieves the collection of the au-
  thor's stories, and returns the identifier of the first story, which will be the
  starting point for browsing the collection in the `Story` state.
- The `TypeSelected` transition transports the identifier of the selected
  story type (`typeId` parameter); it is used to create a story collection
  (`Stories:= new Stories(typeId)`) that groups all the stories of that
  type. The `getFirst` method retrieves the first story in the type-based
  collection, which will be the navigation starting point within the `Story`
  state.

From the main menu, another transition, fired by the event (`Highlights
Selected`), allows the user to access some highlighted stories. It transports
the parameter `highlighted`, which represents the choice of the user to browse
a collection of highlighted stories. The parameter is used to build such a collection (`Stories:= new Stories(highlighted)`). The identifier of the first
story in the collection is then retrieved and passed to the `Story` state by
means of the `Story` parameter (`Story:=Stories.getfirst()`). Similarly to
the other transitions described above, the transition also sets the value of the
`groupby` parameter (`groupby:= Highlights`).

Once the `Story` state is reached by means of one of the above navigation
trails, the user can go back to the `Main Menu` (`BackToMenu` transition), or can
scroll a story collection (`Navigate` transition). The `direction` parameter in
the `Navigate` transition indicates the scrolling direction (previous or next)
selected by the user. The `Story.scroll(direction)` method retrieves the
story to be displayed (the previous or the next in the collection).

The constraints on how a user can switch among different story contexts,
as already discussed for the OOHDM example, are preserved as well. Recall
that in the OOHDM context schema these constraints are represented by
a dashed line delimiting the contexts among which the user is allowed to
switch. In state charts, we can use guard expressions to enable the activation
of transitions only in certain contexts. For example, while in the `Story` state,
the transition fired by the `byType` event is enabled only when the user is
in an author-based context (`groupby == Author`). This allows a user who
is browsing an author-based collection to switch to a type-based collection.
Viceversa, the `byAuthors` transition is enabled only when the user is in a
type-based context (`groupby == Type`).

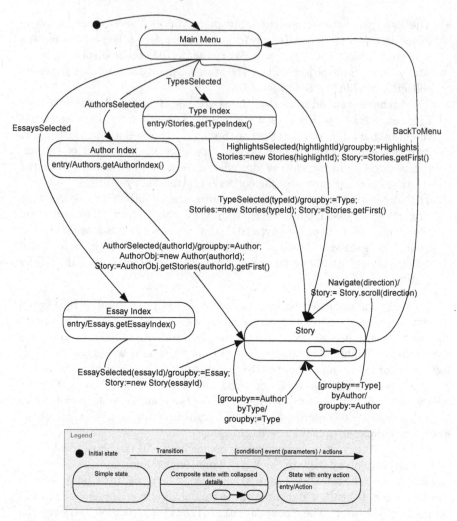

Fig. 5.9. A state diagram representing navigation trails in the online magazine example

Let us now look in detail at the Story state. As denoted by the two small connected ellipses, Story is a composite state. Figure 5.10 depicts a diagram that specifies its unfolded details. The state is composed of two concurrent navigation substates, each one representing a view on a content entity. The concurrent computation starts with the initialization of the main substate, Story Detail. Its entry action retrieves and displays the Story object passed through the traversed transition.[7] When the details of the master substate

---

[7] The groupby parameter in the entry action is used to determine the story collection the user can browse through in a given context.

are known, the synchronization with the other concurrently presented region can proceed. Two transitions are fired in parallel: a transition leading to the AuthorDetail substate, which activates the initialization of the state with content about the author of the story, and a back transition, which represents that the Story Detail substate remains active, and therefore its computation continues even after the transition to the AuthorDetail substate is fired.

Note that two kinds of synchronization are used, the traditional split into concurrent computations, rendered as a filled black rectangle, and the synchronization between regions separated by dashed lines. For this second synchronization type, the circle represents a possible queue that can be in place when separate computation threads are executed, and some threads waiting could be needed. Restrictions can be applied to the number of waiting synchronization requests in the queue. In that case, instead of the star, a positive number will be used.

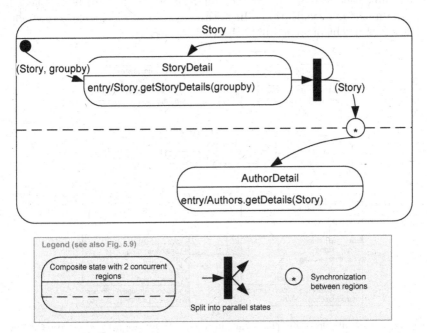

Fig. 5.10. Unfolded details of the Story composite navigation state. Two information fragments, generated from different entities, are rendered in parallel

Interfaces and data collections

So far we have illustrated navigation trail design, without discussing where and how data collections and methods used within actions must be defined. From this perspective, navigation trail design can be approached in two ways.

One possibility is to start with a high-level view on navigation states, as a refinement of task models from the requirements analysis phase. Stepwise refinements can be applied to decompose higher-level states into substates. However, detailed design of navigation trails is also concerned with the specification of rendering operations, to identify the methods that will be called and the objects that will be instantiated when a particular state is entered, left, or manipulated internally. Therefore, an integral part of navigation trail design is the enactment of the conceptual models defined during requirement analysis with collections, interfaces, and methods expressing more details on the application business logic [DS07].

Another approach is to build up the navigation trail model on top of navigation views, as the last activity in navigation design, similarly to what is done in the OOHDM navigation context schema. To be able to do that, for example with OOHDM abstractions, the navigation design needs to be refined and enacted as well with the definition of methods to be invoked in the state machine specifications. In both cases, we would arrive to a model that is a refinement of some kinds of structural models.

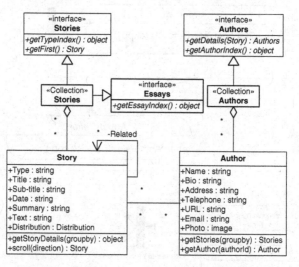

Fig. 5.11. An example of interface and data collection design for the online magazine application

Figure 5.11 depicts an object-oriented model that is a refinement of the conceptual model from Figure 5.3. The model is built in a traditional object-oriented design fashion, which slightly differs from the OOHDM navigation design discussed in the previous sections. The reason for doing this is to give the reader another, slightly different approach to data access design. The new model enriches the definition of the Story and Author classes with the methods that are used in the specification of the navigation trails illustrated in Figure 5.9. It also includes interfaces, defined on top of classes, to support the definition and management of data collections.

For example, the `Stories` interface provides a collection of stories plus some methods to manipulate it. The method `getTypeIndex` is used in the `Type Index` state in Figure 5.9 to compute an index of all the story types, while the `getFirst()` method is used in several transitions to retrieve the first object in a story collection. Similarly, the `Authors` and the `Essays` interfaces are used to build and manipulate the respective collections.

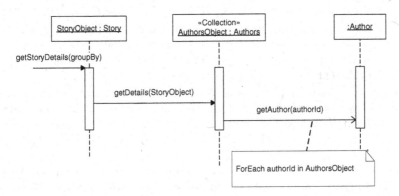

Fig. 5.12. A sequence chart showing the sequence of object interactions for the `StoryDetail` state

Especially in the case of complex state machines, composed of several layers of substates, it is also necessary to represent the life cycle of objects participating in the computation of navigation states, to understand the sequence of operations needed to instantiate certain objects, and the way such objects cooperate among each other. Figure 5.12 depicts a UML sequence chart that illustrates such an instantiation and collaboration sequence for the `Story` composite state. First of all, the `StoryObject` is instantiated according to the context transferred though the `groupby` parameter. When the story identifier is known, the `AuthorsObject` can be instantiated to create the collection of story's authors. For each author in the collection, an object of type `Author` is finally created to manage the display of data for each single author.

Such an interaction scheme is very useful to specify complex interactions of objects intervening in the computation of navigation nodes, and also supplies additional behavioral details that complete the state machine specification [DN03, Dol08]. State machines indeed nicely show an abstraction of navigation trails, but are less intuitive for object interactions.

Note that, in WebML for example, there is no necessity to draw such additional models, as there is one default behavioral semantics exactly specified through state machines and implemented by the WebRatio engine [CF01]. However, for those methods that do not adopt such a systematic approach for the definition of the model semantics, these additional specifications are useful to deeply understand a solution to a particular design problem, especially in highly interactive applications with complex object collaborations.

5.4.3 Web Service Interaction

Web services are an essential ingredient in the development of modern Web applications. As already introduced in Chapter 2, much emphasis has been devoted to technological, architectural, and implementation issues. However, if we especially consider the situation in which the interaction with Web services is *driven by users*, i.e., the users provide the necessary input and take the necessary decisions to guide the execution of the overall process supported by Web services, then we can easily realize that Web services interaction just provides a different facet of navigation design.

To describe the main elements of Web service interaction to be considered at the conceptual level, we will illustrate the modeling abstractions introduced by WebML, which has been extended with some "Web service units" [MBC+05] that implement the WSDL operations of SOAP/WSDL Web services.

WSDL operations are the basic units of interaction with a service, hence WebML supports all the four categories of operations, namely: *one-way*, *request-response*, *notification*, and *solicit-response* operations. A distinction is made between the operations initiated by the client (one-way and request-response), and those initiated by the service (notification and solicit-response): while the former are used in the specification of a Web application hypertext consuming a service, the latter – representing a way for publishing Web services – are specified within so-called *service views* that contain the definition of a service to be published.

Web Service Invocation

The specification of Web service invocation within a Web application exploits the request-response and the one-way operations.

Figure 5.13 shows an example of request-response operation. Suppose to extend the online magazine Web application with the possibility to retrieve the stories written by an author from a remote Web service (like, e.g., the Google Scholar Web service). According to the schema, the user can navigate to the **Search Story** page, where an entry unit allows him to enter a search keyword for the stories of a selected author. The unit **SearchStories** models the WSDL request-response operation for the interaction with the remote Web service. As represented by the two arrows, the operation involves the exchange of two messages: the request sent to the service and the response received from the service. More specifically, the operation is triggered when the user navigates its input link (e.g., he clicks on the search button in the **Search Story** page). Given the parameters transferred by this link (i.e., the author

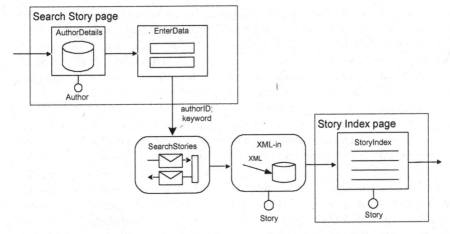

Fig. 5.13. Specifying a request-response operation

identifier generated by the **AuthorDetails** data unit and the search keyword entered by the user through the **EnterData** entry unit), a request message is composed and sent to the **SearchStories** operation exposed by the Web service. The response message generated by the Web service and sent back to the Web application contains a list of stories satisfying the search criteria. From this list, a set of instances of the **Story** entity are created[8] through the **XML-in** operation unit (which receives in input XML data and transforms them into relational data), and displayed to the user in the **StoryIndex** page.

One-way operations are modeled similarly to the request-response operations, with the main difference that the service will not provide any response. Therefore, once the message is sent to the service, the user proceeds with his navigation without waiting for any response.

Web Services Development

WebML also supports the development of Web services that can be invoked by third party applications. From the application point of view, developing and publishing a Web service does not require the specification of the interaction by users. The actions to be performed when the notification or the solicit-response operations are triggered are not specified through pages, but as a chain of operations (e.g., for storing or retrieving data, or for executing generic operations, such as sending e-mails). Therefore, Web service publishing can be specified separately from the site view describing the hypertext interface of the Web application, in a dedicated *service view* that collects the ports that expose the functionality of a Web service through WSDL operations.

---

[8] Further details about both data transformations and the storage of data retrieved from Web services can be found in [MBC+05]

Within the service view, a *port* represents the individual service, composed by a set of WSDL operations, while each individual WSDL operation is modeled through a chain of WebML operations starting with a solicit-response or notification operation. The business logic of a WSDL operation is described by a chain of WebML operations, specifying the actions to be performed as a consequence of the invocation of the service and possibly building the response message to be sent back to the invoker.

Each WSDL operation starts with a `Solicit unit` triggering the service, and ends with the `Response unit`, which sends a message back to the service. As an example of solicit-response operation, suppose to extend the online magazine application with the publication of a service providing the list of stories satisfying some search criteria. As illustrated in Figure 5.14, the WSDL operation is modeled through a chain of WebML operations starting with the `SearchSolicit` unit. The solicit unit receives the SOAP message of the requester, decodes the search keywords, and passes them as parameters to the next WebML operation in the chain. This is a so-called `XML-out` operation unit [MBC+05], which extracts from the application data source the list of stories that match the specified conditions, and formats it as an XML document. After the execution of the `XML-out` operation, the response unit (`SearchResponse`) composes the final response message.

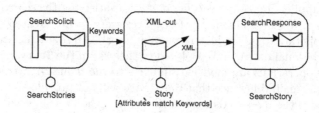

Fig. 5.14. Specifying a solicit-response operation

5.5 Presentation Design

Presentation design for Web applications aims at producing a model for the definition of presentation structures supporting the display of information and the invocation of services within the dialogs provided by the Web application. This means identifying the spatial placement of simple and composite presentation structures and the visual characteristics that decorate them. The browser display capabilities must be taken into account. The document-centric hypertext interface of current Web browsers, indeed, does not provide easy means to deal with complex interactive features. Also, the coherent positioning of interface elements, within interactive spaces dedicated to different classes of contents and services, must be carefully designed. Improperly composed user interfaces may indeed cause a cognitive overload, and lead to the well-known problem of users being lost in the information and service hyperspace.

Presentation design may consist of two main activities, at two different levels of abstraction. The first one, the *abstract presentation design*, is a refinement of navigation design aimed at specifying the composition of abstract elements into Web pages. These abstract elements mainly correspond to the content items and the functions previously identified during navigation design. The second one, the *concrete presentation design*, then identifies the concrete presentation elements (e.g., buttons, text paragraphs, images, and so on) that are used for rendering the abstract elements into Web pages, and combines them in a model that can be directly translated into a concrete technical representation of Web pages, such as HTML.

5.5.1 Abstract Presentation Design

Abstract presentation design describes the composition of elements for information display and functions invocation in Web user interfaces. Three main design techniques can be adopted for this purpose: *Abstract Widgets Design*, *Interaction Spaces Design*, and *Abstract Data Views Design*.

Abstract widgets design

Abstract widget design [dMS04] describes a user interface as a composition of widgets that represent classes of presentation elements playing the same "abstract" role within a Web user interface:

- *SimpleActivators*: react to external events, such as mouse clicks.
- *ElementExhibitors*: display some type of content.
- *VariableCapturers*: capture values of one or more variables; can be text boxes, drop-down lists, check boxes, and so on;
- *IndefiniteVariables*: capture untyped values entered by users.
- *PredefinedVariables*: allow the selection of a subset of values from a set of predefined values.
- *CompositeInterfaceElements*: represent compositions of any widget above.

Figure 5.15 illustrates the user interface of the Amazon.com entry page. The rounded rectangle boxes surround composite user interface elements, which consist of different concrete widgets, such as menu items, links, text paragraphs, buttons, and images. Figure 5.16 depicts a presentation model for the same page, which represents the structure, in terms of abstract widgets, of the four user interface elements highlighted in Figure 5.15. The Departments Menu element contains several simple activators that correspond to the links to navigate to the department menus. The figure explicitly represents the Books, Music, Movies & Games, and Electronics & Computers simple activators; the other simple activators in the menu can be modeled similarly.

Top Menu   Search&Buy

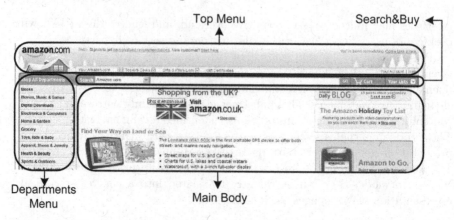

Departments
Menu   Main Body

Fig. 5.15. The user interface of the `Amazon.com` entry page. Rounded rectangles highlight composite user interface objects

The structure of the `Top Menu` and the `Search&Buy` elements is not represented in the figure. The `Top Menu` would be composed of simple activators, one for each link embedded in the navigation bar. The `Search&Buy` element would be composed of simple activators (one for the link to the shopping cart, and one for the link to the personal list), and variable capturers (one for the text box for entering the search key, and one for the drop-down list for selecting a search sub-domain).

Modeling the `Main Body` element is a bit more complex. On top of this element there is a link to the local Amazon service provider. We model it through the Local Amazon composite interface element. Its components are not detailed, but they would be a simple activator, representing the link anchor, and an element exhibitor, representing the logo of the local Amazon provider.

`Amazon Daily Blog` is a simple activator pointing to the blog content object. All the other elements are advertisements for different highlights. As shown for the `Highlight1` element, the inner structure of each highlight is made of the simple exhibitors `Title`, plus the `Image` and `Description` composite elements, both made of a simple exhibitor (displaying the image and the description text, respectively) and a simple activator, representing an anchor for the link to a more detailed description. The content of the advertisements is highly dynamic, since it changes based on the season, user preferences, marketing strategy, and so on. Therefore, the model simply enumerates them, without assigning them with a concrete name.

To specify how many highlights can be presented simultaneously in one page, one can explicitly represent all the corresponding presentation elements, but, since they all have the same structure, this would be redundant. Alternatively, the abstract widget model could represent the structure of a generic highlight only; this structure can then be mapped onto a navigation view

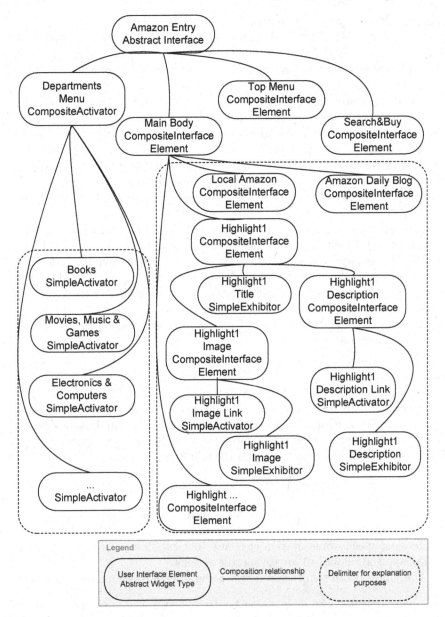

Fig. 5.16. An example of abstract widgets design for the Amazon entry page in Figure 5.15

(similar to the `Highlights` context depicted in the OOHDM example in Figure 5.7), onto a composition of content units specifying highlight navigation (similar to the WebML hypertext units in Figure 5.8), or simply onto a content class, to represent that presentation element actually corresponds to a multiplicity of content items. The number of highlights per navigation node, and the conditions specifying which content should be generated when rendering the Web page is therefore inherited from the navigation design.

As can be noted from the previous example, the abstract widgets design provides means to specify which type of widget can represent contents and functions identified during navigation design, and how they are clustered into Web pages. This technique abstracts from the navigation and content composition logics and focuses more on the pure composition of presentation elements within pages. As such, it can be fruitfully used if the abstract widgets are mapped onto elements of navigation design. In particular, while it can be redundant when used in combination with techniques that already enable the specification of page composition (for example, the WebML hypertext design), it can be very useful when coupled with techniques that do not address the grouping of content elements and functions within the final Web pages (for example, the OOHDM navigation view design). In this case, abstract widgets are used as facades or decorators of navigation views, enriching them with presentation characteristics.

Interaction spaces

In Section 4.4.2, we have defined and shown how to derive abstract interaction spaces from task models, and how to connect them to application domain classes. In the design phase, the specification of interaction spaces can be further refined and extended through the following elements [NOP+06]:

- *Input elements*: specify presentation elements that enable users to enter some input.
- *Output elements*: specify presentation elements that render some output of a system.
- *Actions*: specify presentation elements that enable users to interact with the application and to invoke specific actions.
- *Navigation relationships*: specify the navigation between interaction spaces.

Inputs, outputs, and actions can be derived from the task model defined during requirements engineering. Actions represent tasks; input elements represent the input parameters processed by actions; output elements represent the data displayed to and used by users to produce an input. Actions are usually represented at a high level of abstraction, in form of user understandable labels, without any reference to the methods of the application objects they correspond to. Additional refinements are therefore needed to get a presentation model closer to the implementation. To this purpose, interaction spaces can be, for example, combined with navigation trails (see section 5.7.2 for an example), where state and transition actions are precisely bound to object methods.

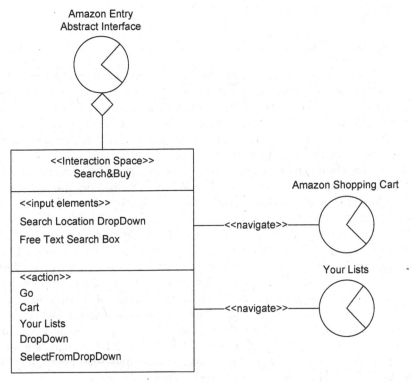

Fig. 5.17. An example of interaction space design, representing the *Sarch&Buy* object at the entry page of Amazon.com (see Figure 5.15)

Figure 5.17 depicts an example of interaction space design. It specifies the different elements for the Search&Buy interaction space in the Amazon.com entry page. The element Search Location DropDown models the drop-down list that allows the user to select an Amazon department in which to search for a product. The action SelectFromDropDown represents the possibility for the user to select a department from the list. The input element Free Text Search Box represents the text box for entering free search text. The Go action is used to submit the search query. The two actions Cart and Your Lists enable the navigation to the respective interaction spaces (represented in figure as collapsed objects). The DropDown action finally represents the possibility to unfold the user's personal lists directly in the entry page.

As can be seen from this example, interaction spaces provide a means to express the composition of input and output presentation elements within pages, the actions that a user can perform, and the navigation among different interaction spaces. They can be used as a stand alone technique, to represent the whole abstract presentation design, or they can be used in combination with the abstract widgets design, introduced in the previous section, to enrich this technique with the specification of actions.

Abstract Data Views

Abstract Data Views (ADVs) [CdL95] are extensions of object-oriented software models, introduced to specify user interface objects and their relationships with application objects. ADVs "observe" the application objects, called *ADV owners*, that manage the application data and business logics. In other words, ADVs are views over those states of the owners that the users can see, interact with, and manipulate [SRB96].

A user interface can be represented by combining different ADVs. Each ADV can be composed of lower level ADVs. Generalization/specialization relationships can be also used for ADV composition, thus fostering the reuse of some recurrent interface objects, such as global navigation bars.

The relationships between the ADVs and their owners are specified in composition diagrams similar to UML class diagrams. These relationships not only model that an ADV provides the user interface for the owner, but also that the ADV can trigger some of its methods. Each relationship implies the exchange of messages representing both the request of services from an ADV to its owners and the provision of services from an owner to its ADVs.

ADVs have been adopted for the specification of Web user interfaces in the context of the OOHDM methodology [SRB96]. The adopted notation uses boxes to represent an ADV or an ADV owner, dashed lines to represent service requests, and solid lines to represent service provisions.

Figure 5.18 depicts an ADV configuration diagram that models the structure of the highlights in the Amazon page reported in Figure 5.15. The composition of the ADV Highlight reflects exactly the structure of the highlight already specified in Figure 5.16. What is interesting in this example is the definition of the relationships between the ADV Highlight and its owner object, Product, to represent the invocation of owner methods to retrieve the data to be displayed by the interface elements.

Besides specifying the structural aspects, as in the example above, ADVs also address behavioral aspects, to model how user interfaces change their state in reaction to user actions. An example is when a user clicks on a highlight in the Amazon entry page (both its picture or an anchor embedded in its description) to get a more detailed description of the product. State charts can be used to model state transitions. For sake of simplicity, we use a textual annotation to specify the effect of clicking on the highlight (Event:Click). A click on the picture or on the description anchor (Pre-Cond:Focus(Picture) or Focus(Description)) generates additional events to close the highlight view and open the product details view (Post-Cond: OpenProductDetails;

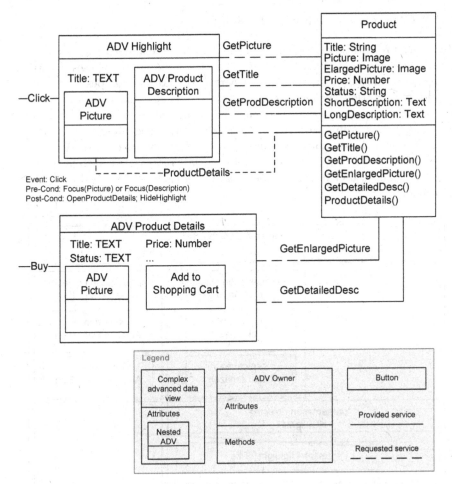

Fig. 5.18. An example of ADV specification for the Amazon.com entry page from Figure 5.15

HideHighlight). As a side effect, the ProductDetails() method is invoked to manage the change of the user interface view.

The new view for the display of the detailed description is modeled trough an additional ADV, (ADV Product Details), representing the interface where further information about the product, such as Price and Status, are displayed. Such product details, together with an enlarged picture, are requested to the Product object by means of the methods GetDetailedDesc and GetEnlargedPicture. Note that the ADV Product Details features another event, Buy, that triggers some methods over other owner objects to manage the insertion of the product into a shopping cart.

5.5.2 Concrete Presentation Design

Concrete presentation design is concerned with the composition of concrete interface elements within Web pages. The UWE method proposes a UML-based presentation model [BKM99], where some class stereotypes are used to model presentation elements, such as text fragments, images, audio, video, anchors, buttons, and forms, that can also be nested to model the hierarchical structure of Web pages. A composite element, called *presentation object*, is used to model any arbitrary composition of the previous objects. A presentation class that is not contained in another class represents a Web page. The behavior of each user interface object can in addition be described by a state machine.

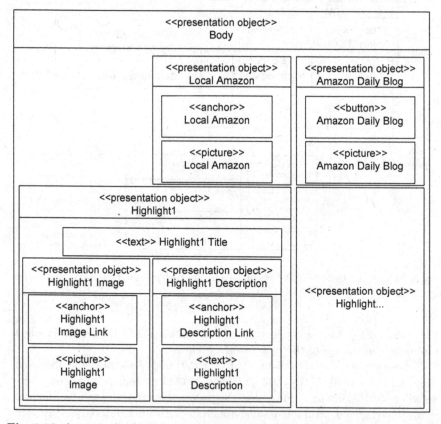

Fig. 5.19. An example of UWE presentation design for the entry page of Amazon.com from Figure 5.15

Figure 5.19 depicts the UWE presentation design of the Amazon entry page from Figure 5.15. It reflects the abstract presentation design already illustrated in Figure 5.16, but it uses presentation stereotypes, as defined in the UWE presentation model, to represent major details about the final rendering of the page.

Note that a similar mapping from abstract to concrete presentation design is suggested in the context of the OOHDM method [dMS04]. Concrete presentation elements, similar to those proposed by the UWE model, are defined in an ontology. The abstract widget design discussed in Section 5.5.1 is refined and mapped on that ontology by specifying a set of statements that express mapsTo properties and restrictions on mapping sources and targets. The result is an OWL-based user interface description, which annotates the abstract widgets with labels from the concrete widget ontology.

5.6 Architecture Design

Architecture design aims at capturing the significant decisions about the organization of a software system, to highlight the constituent subsystems, components and interactions. In a Web application, this implies addressing some choices about the application business logic, to establish a reference model for the implementation activities. A commonly used approach is to define a decomposition of the application software, to represent the distribution of components at the different application tiers (e.g., static and dynamic pages, forms, applets, and any other kinds of software component enriching the Web pages at client side or executed at server side), and the relationships defined among them (e.g., links connecting pages).

In this section, we will give an overview of the main issues architecture design deals with, by reviewing two well-known methods. We start with the design technique proposed by Conallen in the context of the Web Application Extension for UML (WAE) [Con00]. We then illustrate the Web Software Architecture (WebSA) approach [MG06], also based on a set of UML extensions, whose main advantage is the provision of architectural models that can be easily integrated with pre-existing functional models defined, for example, through any of the design methods reviewed in this chapter.

5.6.1 Conallen's Web Application Extension for UML

In 2000 Jim Conallen proposed a technique for architecture design, which extends UML with additional semantics and constraints to model Web specific architectural elements [LC02]. According to this method, architecture design starts with the definition of a *component diagram*, representing the application components, their interfaces, their relationships, and the classes from the domain model that realize them. In addition to identifying classes and collaborations, the design activities also include the partitioning of components into objects residing at the different application tiers. The distribution of objects over the client and the server side is the main focus, but other application layers, if any, can be considered as well.

One of the main novelties of the method is the specification of Web pages as architectural elements. Being part of the application front-end, Web pages are fundamental elements in navigation and presentation design. Nevertheless, Web pages represent the liaison between the browser and all the other subsystems of a Web application; for this reason, they offer the opportunity to capture the main architectural elements and their collaboration. From the modeling perspective, Web pages can be considered objects and, as such, they could be specified, for example, through UML classes. However, the traditional UML notation would not capture some features that are specific to Web applications. For example, it would be difficult, or impossible, to model that, if a page includes a server-side script, then its HTML must be generated "dynamically" at the server, and this requires the interaction between the Web page (a client-side object) with server-side resources. Things become even more complex if we want to specify that a completely separated set of functions run exclusively at the client side, for example, because the page includes client-side scripts.

In Conallen's method, the previous concerns are addressed by stereotypes that purposely extend the traditional UML notation. In the *component view*, adopted to represent the physical modules and executables that make up the runtime system, the two stereotypes <<static page>> and <<dynamic page>> represent the two classes of Web pages. In the *logical view*, each of these objects is then partitioned along the different application tiers. Web pages in the application front end are therefore modeled by means of the <<client page>> stereotype. They can include forms (represented through the <<Web form>> stereotype), or any kind of embeddable component (represented through the <<object>> stereotype). The Web application business logic is instead modeled by the <<server page>> stereotype. Several other stereotypes, representing relationships among the previous stereotyped elements, are also provided, such as <<link>>, representing HTML anchors, <<submit>>, representing a request to a server page that transports form field attributes, <<build>>, representing the HTML output of the execution of a server page that is sent to a client page, and so on.

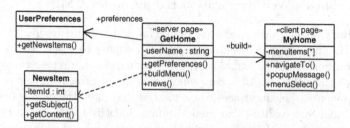

Fig. 5.20. The architectural design of a personalized Web page [LC02]

Figure 5.20 and 5.21 illustrate a modeling example based on Conallen's extensions, which represents the architectural elements intervening in the execution of the Home.jsp component, a JSP page that publishes news filtered according to user preferences [LC02].

In figure 5.20, the server page GetHome models the server-side aspect of the page. The class includes the attribute username, and the three operations getPreferences(), buildMenu(), and news(). It also has an association with the class UserPreferences, and a dependency on the class NewsItem.

The previous operations are used at the server side to build the HTML code of the client page. The HTML part of the page is modeled with the MyHome client page. In addition to having dynamic content embedded in the HTML, this class also specifies the use of client-side scripting, as it is evident from the defined variable and operations.

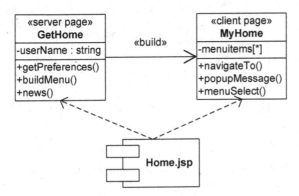

Fig. 5.21. The realization of the Home.jsp component through client and server pages [LC02]

As shown in Figure 5.21, each **server page** and **client page** is realized by components that represent the mapping to URLs. GetHome and MyHome, for example, are realized by the Home.JSP component. This component represents how the two logical pages are in practice managed through one source code component.

5.6.2 Web Software Architecture (WebSA)

The majority of Web engineering methods especially focuses on a functional perspective, providing elements for data, hypertext, and presentation design. Very few methods support the implementation activities by means of techniques and tools for the automatic generation of code. None of them, at least among those reviewed in this book, provides support for architectural design. The Web Software Architecture (WebSA) approach [MG06] aims at filling this gap. It introduces architectural modeling as an explicit and orthogonal design activity, which can be however fully integrated with the functional design models defined through any other Web engineering method. The adoption of the WebSA is especially fruitful in methodologies that also provide support for code generation (for example, WebML), since it empowers them with the possibility to specify explicitly the architectural model, reducing the need of adhering to predefined architectural choices, generally settled by the automatic generation engine.

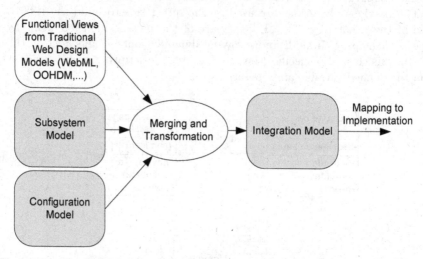

Fig. 5.22. The WebSA dependencies between architectural models adapted from [MG06]

WebSA features three architectural models:

- The *subsystem model* identifies the application subsystems and their distribution among layers, according to architectural patterns.
- The *configuration model* details the components and the connectors that make up the application.
- The *integration model* merges the architectural view, specified by the two previous models, with the functional view expressing data, hypertext, and presentation design.

Figure 5.22 depicts the relationships between the three models (shaded in gray). The functional view can be defined through any design method. The subsystem and the configuration model define the Web application architecture according to the WebSA primitives. WebSA is compliant with the MDE paradigm (see Section 5.8). Therefore, models are formalized by means of a MOF metamodel, and transformations are provided to generate the final implementation model. First the conceptual models (both functional[9] and architectural) are mapped to a platform independent model, the so-called *integration model*, that merges functional and architectural elements by defining mappings between them. The integration model is then amenable to transformations in any implementation model, fulfilling the requirements of any possible execution platform.

The WebSA configuration model best represents the architectural point of view. The remainder of this section will discuss it in more details, while we refer the reader to [MG06] for a deeper discussion of the other WebSA models and on model merging and transformations.

Configuration Model

The WebSA configuration model defines the architecture of a Web application by means of elements that represent the different software components and connectors. More specifically, each element in the model represents an abstraction of one or more software components concurring to the same functionality or role [MG06]:

- *WebComponent*: represents a class of software components sharing the same role in a Web application. An example of Web component is a server page as a generic container for some server-side functionality.
- *WebPart*: represents a class of software functionality that is part of a Web component and that needs to be represented explicitly within the Web component, since, for example, it expresses specific requirements for the communication to or from other components. An example of WebPart is a portion of a server page that serves the purpose of computing a menu.
- *WebConnector*: abstracts the communication between either Web components or Web parts. The connection is established through *WebPorts*, which are interaction points between a WebComponent, or a WebPart, and their environment.
- *WebPattern*: is an abstraction of an architectural pattern that can be used to express specific composition of architectural elements. An example of a WebPattern entity is the well-known Model-View-Controller pattern.

Figure 5.23 depicts an example of configuration model for an architecture similar to the one depicted in Figure 5.20.

The Client Page and Server Page components are depicted as generic templates. The Web Browser receives the user's request and renders the corresponding Client Page. Each client page is responsible for sending messages to the Client Handler WebPort of the MVC WebPattern (the structure of this pattern is collapsed here for brevity). The MVC component reacts to such messages by means of the Screen Data WebPort, which is in charge of fetching

---

[9] The Web engineering method adopted for the specification of the functional design has to be MDE-compliant as well.

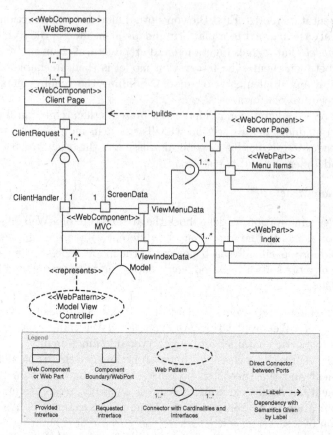

Fig. 5.23. An example of WebSA configuration model, for an architecture similar to the one illustrated in Figures 5.20 and 5.21

the data from the `Server Page`. More specifically, the `Server Page` builds the client page by instantiating two WebParts, `Menu Items` and `Index`. The two connectors, `ViewMenuData` and `ViewIndexData`, fetch data from such Web-Parts. The `MVC` component, furthermore, requests an interface from a `Model` that aggregates data needed for the user interface. Further patterns and components can be connected to the configuration model.

The configuration model represents an abstract design for a generic run-time engine able to interpret the functional models of a Web application. For example, the runtime structure of the WebML-based applications, as generated by the WebRatio tool (see Section 7.2.2 for more details), can be represented similarly to the example depicted in Figure 5.23. The WebRatio engine merges the functional view described through the WebML design model into an execution model that can be interpreted by the WebRatio engine. The WebSA approach opens up such transformation and merging process, and allows a designer to define his own transformation rules.

Integration Model

The WebSA integration model supplies the structural design of a Web application in a platform-independent way. It integrates the subsystem and configuration models with the application functional viewpoint [MG06]. Here we will show the principle of refining the configuration model into the integration model. A similar refinement, more focused on implementation structures, then applies to the derivation of a platform-specific implementation model.

The merging and transformation between functional and configuration views consists in annotating the configuration model components with labels from data, navigation, and presentation models, and mapping them onto the architectural patterns used in the configuration model. The integration model syntax is similar to the one of the configuration model. However, instead of WebParts and WebComponents, it uses concrete stereotypes, such as `server page`, `model`, `view`, and `controller`, that correspond to the elements defined in the configuration model. The integration model, indeed, instantiates the configuration model elements, and labels them with the names defined in the application functional models.

Figure 5.24 depicts an example of WebSA integration model that derives from the configuration model reported in Figure 5.23. The model specifies the structure of the `Server Page` WebComponent. The generic `Server Page` template, specified in the configuration model, is instantiated by the `:MyHome` server page and two embedded subpages: `:Menu Items` and `:News Items`. `:News Items` connects to the `:News Items` view through the `IViewNews` interface. Similarly, the user interaction is captured through the `:Main Controller` component. `:News Items` and `:Main Controller` are both connected to the `:News Items` model, which is in charge of feeding news data. The `:News Items` view is also connected to the `:User Preferences` view, which feeds data about user preferences, necessary for filtering and recommending news items. All such component instances are part of the Home module.

The connection towards the `Client Page` in the configuration model is represented by the connector `WebInterface`. The connectors to data components are omitted in this example, but they need to be modeled in the integration model if the Model-View-Controller pattern is adopted. The final step to fully complete the design cycle is the transformation of the integration model into an implementation model reflecting the concrete requirements of an implementation platform, such as Java Server Pages or Microsoft .NET technologies.

5.7 Extensions for Rich Internet Applications

So far we have looked at the design of traditional Web applications with thin clients and most of the application logic residing on the Web server.

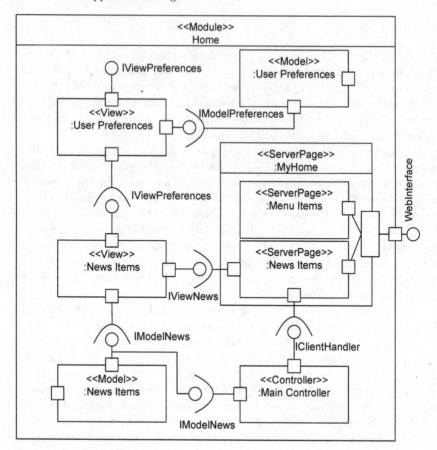

Fig. 5.24. A WebSA integration model deriving from the configuration model from Figure 5.23

Let us now look at a further class of more interactive and more responsive applications, commonly known as Rich Internet Applications (RIAs). RIAs have been first conceived by Adobe when introducing products for multimedia authoring, such as Flash. Recently, with the introduction of AJAX, most Web 2.0 applications, especially well-known social applications such as Facebook or Google Desktop, moved toward interactive functionalities, similar to those provided by desktop applications. The following features characterize RIAs [BCFT06]:

- Sophisticated interface behaviors, like drag&drop, animations, multimedia synchronization.
- Mechanisms to minimize client-server data transfers by moving the management of interaction and presentation layers from the server to the client.
- Data storage both at the client and server side.

- Data processing (e.g., the creation of new data items or data filtering) executed both at client and server side.

To address the previous features, the design methods for traditional Web applications required some extensions, to support especially the modeling of client and server side computations and their synchronization. Table 5.1 summarizes the new conceptual primitives introduced at different levels. Such new elements are also shortly described in the following.

Table 5.1. Summary of extensions for RIA design

Method	Model	Elements
WebML [BCFC06]	Hypertext and Data Model	**Hypertext Model:** client- and server-side units, pages, selectors, and operations
ADRIA [DS07]	Structural, Behavioral, and Data Model	**Structural Model:** interaction space, input, output, actions, associations, navigation
		Behavioral Model: state charts with actions calling client- or server-side methods, concurrent regions
		Data Model: client- and server-side entities, client, server, and inter-layer relationships
RUX [TPSF07]	Abstract and Concrete Presentation	**Abstract Presentation Model:** connectors, media, views, generalizations, associations and aggregations
		Concrete Presentation Model: controls, layouts, navigators, handlers, temporal presentation
OOH4RIA [MGPD08]	Presentation and Orchestration Model	**Presentation Model:** widgets, containers, other concrete presentation objects, such as text boxes and buttons
		Orchestration Model: stereotyped states, such as screenshots, orchestral widgets, concurrent regions, conditions and actions

5.7.1 WebML extensions

WebML introduces the distinction between client-side and server-side objects, both in the data model and in the hypertext model. Furthermore, it introduces the concept of data object persistence, which enables the distinction between permanent and temporary objects. The most significant extensions of the data model are related to the representation of temporary client-side objects and their association with persistent server-side objects. The extended hypertext model then offers new modeling elements to specify units and pages to be computed at the client side.

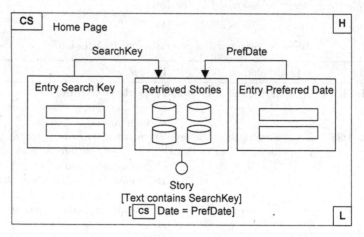

Fig. 5.25. The Home Page from Figure 5.8, extended with RIA features

Let us recall the example illustrated in Figure 5.8 and let us modify the Home Page by introducing some client-side objects. Figure 5.25 depicts the new page. As denoted by the CS label, the Home Page is now a client-side page.[10] It contains two entry units for specifying search criteria: Entry Search Key allows users to enter a keyword to be matched in the story text; Entry Preferred Date allows users to enter a specific publishing date. The parameters SearchKey and PrefDate are used by the parametric selectors of the Retrieved Stories multidata unit. More specifically, the selector condition "Text contains SearchKey" is executed at the server side, following the conventional WebML semantics already described in Section 5.4. The condition "Date = PrefDate" is evaluated at the client side, to further filter the story instances retrieved by means of the server side selector. Therefore, when the link exiting the Entry Search Key unit is navigated, a round-trip to the server is needed to re-compute the multidata unit's content. The navigation of the link from the Entry Preferred Date unit instead causes the client side evaluation of the selector condition on the story list previously computed at the server-side.

---

[10] In order to prevent conflicts with the discussion of context-aware applications in Section 6.2.3, we here use the label "CS" (for "client-side") instead of the label "C" used by the authors in [BCFC06].

For more details on the WebML extensions for RIAs, the interested reader is referred to [BCFC06].

5.7.2 ADRIA extensions

ADRIA proposes an extension of the object-oriented analysis design with task models and interaction spaces to model RIA features such as client-side computations and synchronization between client- and server-side objects.

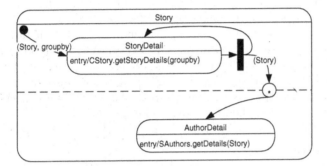

Fig. 5.26. The Story composite navigation state from Figure 5.10, refined with annotation of server-side and client-side computations

Let us recall the example from Figure 5.10, which describes how a story detail of the online magazine is computed step by step by synchronizing two concurrent presentation regions. The figure does not yet specify whether the invoked objects must be computed at the client or at the server side. Let us assume, for example, that the story details must be loaded and successively managed at the client side, while the author details need to be synchronized with the server at any time. To specify this behavior, ADRIA suggests a simple convention to annotate client-side computed methods with the "C" label and server-side computed methods with the "S" letter. The result of such a refinement is depicted in Figure 5.26.

The reader interested in more details about the ADRIA extensions for RIA is referred to [DS07] for more details.

5.7.3 The RUX method

RUX is a method that specifically addresses the design of multi-device and interactive multimedia Web interfaces. It has been conceived independently of the well known design methods for Web applications but, as proved by its integration with WebML [TPSF07] and with UWE [PTMC+08], it can be easily plugged into any other method modeling the application data and business logic.

RUX features a three step refinement process for the design of rich user interfaces. Similarly to other methods, the *abstract interface design* starts the process with a high-level specification that is independent of any kind of spatial, look and feel and behavior detail. This design step leverages elements such as *connectors* (establishing the relations between interface objects and data objects in the data model), *media* (denoting device-independent information chunks, which can be rendered through different types of media), and *views* (representing clusters of media), in a way that recalls the OOHDM ADV modeling. The *concrete interface design* is still platform independent but specific to a device or group of devices. It focuses on spatial, temporal, and interaction aspects of the interface objects. The *final interface design* contains all the necessary details to produce the user interface code targeting the selected implementation platform (e.g., FLEX, AJAX or Laszlo) and client devices. The method is conform to the MDA paradigm (see Section 5.8 for more details), because it uses transformation rules for transforming the initial abstract model into the concrete interface design, and for converting this intermediate model into the final interface design.

5.7.4 OOH4RIA

OOH4RIA [MGPD08] is an extension of the model-driven design method OO-H [GCP01], which aims at supporting the development of RIAs. It consists of two new models, the *presentation model* and the *orchestration model*, which complement the already existing OO-H models for the design of the application content (*domain model*) and navigation (*navigation access diagram*). The presentation model is specifically defined to target the Google Web Toolkit, capturing its different widgets. Widgets are either basic GUI elements (e.g., a button), or composite widgets (e.g., a grid). *Screenshots* can be used to specify the spatial arrangement of widgets that will be rendered together on the screen. A screenshot thus acts as a widget container. Once the presentation model has been defined, the orchestration model captures the interaction between the widgets and the rest of the system, the navigation between screenshots and the way widgets react to user actions. The OOH4RIA models, as well as any other OO-H model, are specified in UML by means of MOF meta-models. This feature supports the semi-automatic generation of the application code based on model transformations (see Section 5.8 for more details), both for client-side and server-side application components.

5.8 Model-Driven Engineering and Web Engineering

As mentioned at the beginning of this chapter, Web application design strongly relies on a clean separation of concerns and the rigid use of appropriate abstractions. Typically, Web engineers capture the different design concerns in different models specifically defined for their particular purpose:

requirement, data, navigation (also including functionality), and presentation models. By allowing the designer to concentrate on one particular design concern at a time, the complexity of designing a large Web application is effectively reduced.

In a more general context, this form of engineering, where models are specified and gradually refined, is known as *model-driven engineering*. Advantages of this approach are the rigorous separation of concerns, the fact that the modeling primitives lie closer to domain concepts (as opposed to implementation details) and thus are more intuitive for the designer to specify, the possibility to (partly) transform one model into another, be it automatically using model transformations, or manually. Finally and arguably most importantly, model-driven approaches provide a relative independence of the actual targeted implementation, because they allow different implementations to be generated from the specified models. All Web engineering methods described in this book and most of the methods known in literature rely to a large extent on the model-driven paradigm.

The best-known model-driven engineering initiative is the Model-Driven Architecture (MDA) [MM03], initiated by the Object Management Group (OMG). It is based on OMG's standards, mainly the Unified Modeling Language (UML) for modeling purposes, the MetaObject Facility (MOF) as a meta-modeling specification and Query/View/Transformation (QVT) for transformation purposes. MDA consists of three types of models, depending on the specific viewpoint on the system:

- *Computational-independent models (CIM)*, a vocabulary of the problem domain, that defines business terms, facts, and rules useful to specify the application domain and the system requirements.
- *Platform-independent models (PIM)*, used to specify the system without any bias to a concrete implementation.
- *Platform-specific models (PSM)*, used to add necessary implementation specific details targeting (different) implementation platforms.

Transformations defined between the different models allow to (partly) convert one model into another.[11] Going into further detail on MDA would lead us too far from the purpose of this book. However, to illustrate the model-driven paradigm in the context of Web applications engineering, we will illustrate the main ingredients of UWE [KKZB07], a Web engineering method that, being based on the OMG standards, adheres to the MDA paradigm.

The UWE development process consists of business, functional and architectural modeling, and a set of model transformations. As such, a set of models is created, each belonging to one of the MDA viewpoints:

- During *business process modeling*, the Web designer describes the content requirements, the functional requirements in terms of navigation needs

---

[11] An elaborate description on model transformation is reported in section 7.2.3

and business processes, and the interaction scenarios for different groups of users. To do so, UWE proposes the use of use case diagrams, possibly enhanced with UML activity diagrams. These models adhere to the MOF compliant WebRE metamodel [CK06], and correspond to the CIM in the MDA paradigm.

- During *functional modeling*, the Web designer describes content, functionality, navigation and presentation. UWE applies the same separation of concerns that has been abundantly discussed in this book, describing different models for functionality, content, navigation and presentation concerns. The first uses UML activity diagrams as modeling tool; all others use UML class diagrams, extended with some Web specific elements, such as navigation classes, that are defined in a *UWE profile*. For architectural modeling, UWE relies on WebSA [MKK05], described as a MOF compliant UML metamodel. Once these models have been created, UWE proposes an intermediate step to merge them in the so-called *big picture model*, typically achieved by applying model transformations. All the aforementioned models correspond to the PIM in the MDA paradigm.

- For *architectural modeling*, literature describes alternative approaches. One approach consists of adding (possibly multiple) architectural details as early as possible, complementing the functional models at PIM level. The architectural model could be integrated with the big picture model, obtaining the *integrated model*, also situated at the PIM level. A third proposal consists of incorporating the architectural details directly into the final generation process, obtaining the platform specific implementation. In this case, the architectural details are (implicitly) situated in between PIM and PSM level.

All UWE models are described in the UWE metamodel, defined using MOF as an extension of the UML metamodel. The UWE metamodel is also mapped to a domain specific UML profile, with proprietary notation for Web specific elements. In section 7.2.3, we go into detail on the model transformations.

5.9 Hypertext Models

Let us conclude this chapter by discussing a historical perspective on Web application engineering rooted in theoretical hypertext models. We believe that such perspective is worth to be mentioned because several design methods presented in this chapter are based directly or indirectly on it. The Web itself, as initially conceived by Tim Berners-Lee and Robert Cailliau, has taken inspiration from hypertext models.

Hypertext models were introduced in early 90's to provide unambiguous and systematic descriptions of the structure of off-line (i.e., not published on the Web) hypermedia systems. The aim was to investigate issues such as the interoperability among different systems, and the integration of hypertext functionality into desktop systems. Based on their main contribution, the proposed models can be divided into *hyperbase models* and *layered hypermedia models*, the former focusing on the organization of hyper-linked data, the latter providing a reference architecture for hypermedia systems.

5.9.1 Hyperbase Models

Grounded on the research on conceptual data models, hyperbase models were proposed to specify the structure of (hyper)linked data and the operations for manipulating and managing such data within hypertext networks. They rely on the idea of *nodes* representing information chunks and *links* representing interconnections between information.

A pioneer hyperbase model was HAM [CG88]. Using graphs to define a node-link structure, this model investigated and solved some key issues, such as the specification of histories, the use of filters based on direct queries (precursors of the search function very common in current Web applications) to complement the navigational access, and the implementation of access control. If on one hand this model was simple and intuitive, on the other hand the graph theory showed some limitations, for example in supporting sharing of information between different nodes, and the definition of composite objects. For this reason, alternatives models were proposed.

In 1989, Tompa introduced a new formalism based on hypergraphs [Tom89]. Its most relevant contribution was the distinction between *content* (the information) and *structure* (the nodes). It also introduced the definition of links where both the source and the target could be a group of nodes, not just single nodes as imposed by graph-based methods. Similarly, the *Trellis Model* [SF89, FS94] suggested the separation between the hypertext structure and the information content. It also introduced a modeling dimension related to information presentation. Its most relevant contribution was however the specification of the browsing semantics. Petri nets were used to model concurrent navigation paths through nodes, both atomic or composite.

These and other models inspired the early hypermedia models, such as the renowned *Hypertext Design Model* (HDM) [GP93], and its object-oriented version, OOHDM [SR95].

5.9.2 Layered Hypermedia Models

Layered hypermedia models have been proposed as reference models for the design of hypertext management systems. Layers in such models correspond to different modeling dimensions, namely storage, structure, and presentation. The *Dexter Reference Model* [HS94] is one of the best known examples, probably the most influential model. It proposed a reference architecture providing a common vocabulary for the comparison of different hypertext systems and models. It also aimed at setting the basis for the development of interoperability standards.

As represented in Figure 5.27, the model features three layers:

- The *Storage layer* is the central layer and the main focus of the Dexter model. It represents the node-link hypertext network as a "database" composed of a hierarchy of *components* (i.e., nodes in a hypertext network) interconnected by *links*.
- The *Runtime layer* is related to the dynamic aspects of components, i.e., the tools to access, view, and manipulate the network structure. The model covers only basic presentation mechanisms, capturing the essentials of the interaction.
- The *Within component layer* deals with the internal structure and content of each component. This layer is not elaborated within the Dexter model, and is left open to all the possible data types and structures that can be included in a hypertext node.

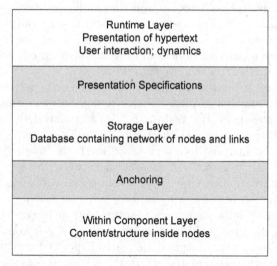

Fig. 5.27. The layered architecture proposed by the Dexter reference model [HS94].

The interface between the runtime layer and the storage layer is the *presentation specification*. The interface between the storage layer and the within component layer is the *anchoring specification* [HS94], related to the identification of source and target locations of links within node contents.

Other models were successively proposed to extend the Dexter model. For example, the *Amsterdam hypermedia model* [HBvR94] refined it with the ability to specify the presentation and composition of various (especially sequential) multimedia information types.

The *Adaptive Hypermedia Application Model (AHAM)* [BHW99] then extended the storage layer with the specification of the *teacher model* and the *user model.* The former serves as a base for adaptation and gives a mechanism for modeling the structure of user characteristics, such as knowledge, preferences, goals, and so on. The teacher model specifies the adaptation rules.

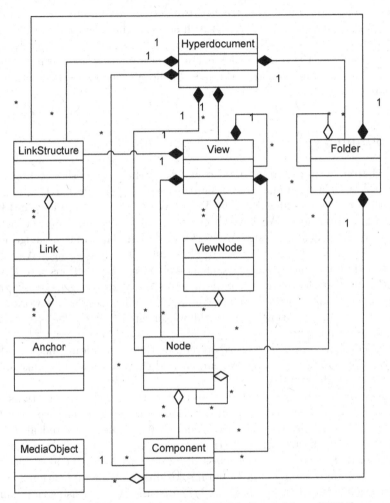

Fig. 5.28. The base model for DFHM adapted from [TD96].

Tochtermann and Dittrich [TD96] introduced the *Dortmund Family of Hypermedia Models (DFHM)*, which generalizes some architectural features that are common to several hypermedia models. The model aimed at flexibility, in particular supporting differing variations of data types. Therefore it could be regarded as a family of interrelated models, rather than one model with fixed data type specifications.

As illustrated in Figure 5.28, DFHM supports constructs for components, nodes, links, composite nodes, views, folders, and hyperdocuments. A *component* is an abstraction of concrete *media types*. A *node* is a self-contained information unit and encapsulates one or more components or nodes. *Links* connect several nodes and are attached to components by an *anchor*. Links can be grouped into *link structures*, which support the definition of different access contexts. *Views* group nodes, links, components and media objects, and identify specific access contexts, for example personalized for specific users. *Folders* have semantics similar to those of the file system. The aforementioned objects together form a *hyperdocument*.

5.10 Summary

In this chapter we have provided an overview of the main design techniques and issues that Web application design deals with. The design techniques reflect the needs stemming from the World Wide Web environment and its underlying technologies. We have discussed that the essential design viewpoints in Web application design are workflow design, data design, navigation design, presentation design, and Web application architecture design. We have also touched upon some extensions such as Web service interactions and RIAs.

With workflow design, we have discussed activity diagrams as one of the abstractions capturing workflows for Web applications. Besides the workflow model we have also mentioned the workflow concepts that can be integrated into navigation modeling.

In data design, we mostly focused on refining the application domain model into a relational data model, but we emphasized that this is not the only data management model suitable on the Web.

Navigation design distinguishes structural and behavioral abstractions. It also distinguishes object-oriented abstractions, and abstractions specific to the Web. We have discussed both of them. In the object-oriented abstraction we based our discussion on OOHDM, using navigation views, navigation contexts, and in class navigation class decorators as the main abstractions to facilitate understanding of navigation solutions for Web applications. Web domain-specific design viewpoints have been discussed mainly using the example of the WebML hypertext schema, which integrates navigation composition and context into one model. We have discussed navigation behavior design on the abstraction of navigation trails and user navigation steps. We have utilized the state machine approach to illustrate the abstraction concept. We have connected the navigation trail design to interfaces and data collections as the main access structures used to connect navigation trail abstractions to content. Furthermore, we have also discussed how to connect navigation models to Web service abstractions by using the WebML extension for Web services. We have also touched upon Web design patterns as an important aspect in Web application design.

Presentation design features abstract presentation design and concrete presentation design. Abstract presentation design was discussed on abstract data views as used by OOHDM, abstract widgets as commonly used in user interface design, and interaction spaces used for capturing interaction objects at a user interface level. Concrete presentation design refines abstract presentation design to a model closer to a user interface usually rendered by standard Web browsers.

Web application architecture design focuses on the overall structuring of the Web application into subsystems, parts, and components. We have discussed a UML extension for Web applications which supports server-side and client-side components, such as scripts, pages, and classes. We also illustrated the WebSA design technique, which is a model-driven technique, based on the idea of integration and transformation of traditional design views in Web application engineering with component configuration and integration views where different architectural patterns such as Model-View-Controllers can be directly utilized.

Rich Internet Applications present additional requirements for Web engineering methods. We discussed extensions to existing methods to cater specifically for RIAs.

In the last part of the chapter we have discussed a historical perspective on Web application design which is rooted in the hypermedia design community. We have touched upon two different approaches there: hyperbases and layered models.

5.11 Further Readings

Several other teams have focused on other aspects of Web application design. We refer the reader to the Subject-Oriented Hypermedia Design Method (SO-HDM) [LLY99], which combines object-oriented view access structure nodes (ASNs) as additional abstraction. RMM [ISB95] provides slices as elements for navigation context specification and HERA [HBFV03] extends it with a Semantic Web data model. HDM [GP93] provides perspectives for its components and entities. The Trellis model [SF89, FS94] for specification of browsing semantics with Petri Nets and colored Petri Nets could be another model used for navigation trail design. XHMBS (eXended Hyperdocument Model Based on Statecharts) [PTdOM98] is another state-chart-based model for navigation trail design. Web Composition Markup Language (WCML) [GG99] is another XML-based architecture design model utilizing abstractions of components for Web applications. We also refer the reader to the latest additions of WWW, Web Engineering as well as Web Information Systems Engineering conferences. Last but not least, we also refer the reader to a collection on Web engineering methods [RPSO08] for further details on Web application design methods and techniques.

6

Adaptation

The previous chapter explained how the main concerns in Web application development, i.e., data, hypertext, and presentation design, are addressed by modern Web application development methods and techniques. In this chapter we provide the reader with some more insight into how some typical functional requirements, peculiar to the domain of the Web, can be designed. More precisely, in this chapter we focus on the peculiarities of different kinds of *adaptation* in the design of Web applications, that is, on how Web applications can be tailored to a broad spectrum of different audiences, each with its very own requirements and expectations. Developing applications that can be adapted to different situations or needs is particularly important on the Web, where applications are accessible from all over the world and may be used via a variety of different client devices. The exact characteristics of an application's audience can typically no be fully predicted at development time, and applications need to put into practice some features that allow the users or the applications themselves to take those characteristics into account. We discuss here three of these features and conclude the chapter by discussing a design methodology that naturally puts adaptation at its center:

- *Localization and internationalization*: with the Web as a global communication medium, the ability to reach a global audience comes almost for free. However, the social, cultural, and historical backgrounds of communities from different parts of the world differ largely. Localization and globalization tackle exactly this issue. In this section, we will discuss the problems involved, the behavioral studies underlying internationalization and localization approaches, the impact of localization and globalization on the Web engineering process, and how the problems related to this subject are addressed in current practice.
- *Personalization and adaptation*: while localization focuses on how to gear a Web application to the needs of a broader spectrum of users, based on their demographic and cultural singularity, personalization and user-centric adaptation typically focus on the tailoring of a Web application

S. Casteleyn et al., *Engineering Web Applications*, Data-Centric Systems and Applications,
DOI: 10.1007/978-3-540-92201-8_6, © Springer-Verlag Berlin Heidelberg 2009

to the needs of the individual user. Personalization allows an application to provide customized services and content by taking into account the identity of the user, while adaptation and its particular cases – adaptivity, adaptability, and context-awareness – go beyond the user's identity and allow the application to take into account a much broader set of properties, possibly triggering an adaptive behavior. This is a hot research topic, and we will show some interesting concepts and methods.

- *Accessibility and users with disabilities*: most of us appreciate the current trend toward Web applications that are rich of features, comparable to what we know from traditional desktop applications. But there are also people with disabilities, such as blind or visually impaired users or users involved in disabling activities (e.g., driving a car), who encounter un-surmountable difficulties when navigating only simple Web sites. This is especially the case if applications have not been developed with accessibility for this kinds of users in mind. A discussion of the current efforts for accessible Web applications is thus not only interesting but also due.

- *Design for adaptation with product line engineering*: Web applications that can be localized, personalized, or made accessible for people with disabilities typically rely on a common engineering principle, i.e., the principle of separation of concerns. Separating those features of a Web application that are common across different cultures, users, or people with different disabilities from features that vary across the wide variety of users is key for clean and comprehensible development. Software product line engineering has been built around such a separation of concerns. The approach deals with the systematic identification and management of common and variable assets in a software product, which together form a product family. In this last section, we will show an application of product line engineering to the Web.

6.1 Localization and Internationalization

In contrast to information made available through classical media (i.e., newspaper, radio, television), information published on the Web is easily and instantly accessible from all over the world. While such a global communication medium offers tremendous opportunities, it also presents particular challenges to Web designers targeting this global public. After all, this global audience is extremely diverse, differing in language, education, culture, location, etc. Targeting all of them inevitably requires taking into account their particularities, in order to offer a Web site which is understandable, accessible, and acceptable to all these different communities. The research fields tackling these issues are those of localization and internationalization. In this section, we will discuss the particular problems involved, introduce standard terminology, review the anthropological research underpinning the work, and finally present recent work on Web engineering and localization and internationalization.

Before we continue, we explain how the terms localization and internationalization will be interpreted in this book.

6.1.1 Terminology

Although there are no standard definitions, the terms *internationalization* and *localization* are quite well understood. In this section, we will provide the reader with some working definitions. We start from the term *locale*, which refers to a geographical region in which people somehow share some common (e.g., historical, social, cultural) values and language.

The term *locality* is sometimes used as a synonym for locale. Identifying different locales is an important aspect for localization, as we will see later. Subsequently, *internationalization* is used to indicate the process of identifying and separating all locale-specific elements from the rest of the software product (Web site).

Internationalization is frequently abbreviated as "i18n[1]". Instead of internationalization, some prefer the term *culturization*, as i18n may give the impression that it is restricted to the borders of nations, where culturization (correctly) emphasizes that in fact the process considers different cultures. However, the term internationalization has become the standard terminology, and is most widely used. The goal of internationalization is thus to separate any locale-specific information, so that it can be easily customized when targeting a specific locale. This process of customization is called *localization*. More specifically, localization is the process of adapting a software product (Web site) to specifically target a certain locale.

The abbreviation "L10n"[2] is often used as a shorthand for the term "localization."

There is clear interplay between internationalization and localization: the purpose of i18n is to make subsequent localization easier, faster, of higher quality, and more cost-effective. Note however that internationalization is not a prerequisite for localization: indeed, often localization is a concern that only comes into play (long) after a Web site was developed and deployed. Although still possible, in this case the effort and cost for localization increases dramatically.

6.1.2 History and Problems Involved

Internationalization and localization are not new: tailoring a user interface to particular countries or cultures predates the World Wide Web. Historically,

---

[1] 18 refers to the number of letters that is omitted in the term "internationalization."

[2] Analogously to i18n, 10 refers to the number of letters omitted from the term "localization." Furthermore, the leading "L" is often capitalized to avoid confusion between uppercase "i" and lowercase "l" in certain fonts.

most commercial software originates from the US, where it initially targeted the Northern American market only. When exporting software products, at first a one-size-fits-all approach was used: the software is simply exported as it is. While this leads to a spread of typical North American icons and idioms, and a certain global understanding of these, it was quickly argued that it hinders the acceptance of user interfaces and software products. Localization was the answer, which primarily consisted of translating software for different linguistic markets. Soon, however, the realization came that translating alone was not sufficient: cultural and social considerations equally hinder acceptance of software products.

On the Web, where every Web site is accessible from all over the world, localization issues become even more important. If a Web site is truly targeting the global market, any cultural-, social- or language-specific references may pose a problem. In particular, the following non-exhaustive list may require alteration when targeting different locales:

- *Language*: the most obvious difference between locales, and also the one most commonly tackled by localization approaches, is language. Multilingual Web sites are common these days, as most Web sites targeting a global audience are available in different languages (e.g., Google, Hotmail, MSN) for different locales. Even for locales with the same language, different spelling or terminology may be used (e.g., UK versus US spelling).
- *Weights and measures*: measures of length and weight differ depending on locale (e.g., metric system in Europe versus US custom unitary system in the US, such as meters versus feet and inches).
- *Currency*: monetary units vary from locale to locale (e.g., Australian dollar versus US dollar, euro).
- *Formats*: many units are represented in different formats by different locales. As examples, consider time (e.g., 2 p.m. versus 1400 hours), date (e.g., 21-01-1977 versus 01-21-1977), numerical data (e.g., 3.14 versus 3,14), addresses (e.g., US addresses include a state, typically not needed for other locales), postal codes, telephone numbers, etc.
- *Metaphor*: some metaphors may be locale-specific, and could thus be wrongly or not at all understood by other locales. A typical example is the US mailbox: in the US, outgoing mail can be put in the mailbox, where it is collected to be sent. In many other cultures, this outbound mail function of a mailbox does not exist. Using the US mailbox metaphor will thus not be understood or understood incorrectly by different locales.
- *Colors*: colors are highly culture specific, and may have different meanings for different locales. For example, red symbolizes good luck or celebration in Chinese culture, while in Western culture it tyipcally denotes denotes "stop" or "danger".

- *Icons*: use of icons is often locale-specific, and might be hard to understand for other locales. For example, a modified Uncle Sam recruitment icon[3] might be well understood by Western culture as an icon for recruitment, yet be incomprehensible for other cultures.
- *Historical references*: for example, referring to the Sun King in European culture will generally be understood as a reference to the French king Louis XIV (and all the connotations that come along), but will be completely meaningless for other (e.g., Asian, Arabic) cultures.
- *Cultural aspects*: cultural aspects such as gestures [MCMO79], morality, ethics, humor, etc. will influence acceptance of a Web site for different locales. For example, the thumbs-up gesture is known as "O.K." or "good" in some cultures, but is an insult in other cultures.
- *Religious aspects*: obviously, different religions have different values, which need to be taken into account when targeting different locales. As an example, Islamic cultures may be offended by scarcely clothed women advertising products, while this is a well-known advertising technique in Western culture.

As already mentioned, this list is non-exhaustive, but clearly illustrates that a lot of issues need to be taken into account when localizing a Web site.

6.1.3 Hofstede's Cross-Cultural Theory

The principles and guidelines underlying internationalization and localization stem from anthropolical research, where cultures and cultural differences have been studied. Anthropologists have tried to divide and categorize the world, to find definitions for cultural values, which they call cultural dimensions. Ample research has been done to identify and categorize cultural values (e.g., Fons Trompenaars [THT97], David Victor [Vic97], Quincy Wright [Wri55]), but possibly the best known and most influential study is the one of Geert Hofstede [HH04]. This Dutch anthropologist carried out a large-scale study between 1967 and 1973 among IBM employees of 64 different countries (of which 40 were used at first, and later extended to 54). Subsequent studies validated his work and extended it to different fields (e.g., commercial airline students, students) and included more countries. These studies resulted in a model identifying five main dimensions for national cultural differences:

- *Power-distance*: the extent to which the less powerful members of organizations and institutions accept and expect that power is distributed unequally. This represents inequality (more versus less), but defined from below, not from above. It suggests that a society's level of inequality is endorsed by the followers as much as by the leaders.

---

[3] Popularly known in American culture by the 1917 US Army recruitment poster by J. M. Flagg

- *Collectivism vs. Individualism*: the degree to which individuals are integrated into groups. On the individualist side we find societies in which the ties between individuals are loose: everyone is expected to look after himself or herself and his or her immediate family. On the collectivist side, we find societies in which people from birth onwards are integrated into strong, cohesive in-groups, often extended families (with uncles, aunts and grandparents) which continue protecting them in exchange for unquestioning loyalty.
- *Femininity vs. Masculinity*: refers to the distribution of roles between the genders, another fundamental issue for any society, to which a range of solutions are found. Hofstede's studies revealed that women's values differ less among societies than men's values, and men's values from one country to another contain a dimension from very assertive and competitive and maximally different from women's values on the one hand, to modest and caring and similar to women's values on the other. The assertive pole has been called "masculine" and the modest, caring pole "feminine". The women in feminine countries have the same modest, caring values as the men; in the masculine countries they are somewhat assertive and competitive, but not as much as the men.
- *Uncertainty avoidance*: deals with a society's tolerance for uncertainty and ambiguity; it ultimately refers to man's search for Truth. It indicates to what extent a culture programs its members to feel either uncomfortable or comfortable in unstructured situations. Unstructured situations are novel, unknown, surprising, different from usual. Uncertainty-avoiding cultures try to minimize the possibility of such situations by strict laws and rules, by safety and security measures, and, on the philosophical and religious levels, by a belief in absolute Truth. Uncertainty accepting cultures are more tolerant of opinions different from what they are used to. They try to have as few rules as possible, and on the philosophical and religious level they are relativist and allow many currents to flow side by side.
- *Long- vs. Short-Term Orientation*: can be said to deal with Virtue regardless of Truth. Values associated with long term orientation are thrift and perseverance; values associated with short term orientation are respect for tradition, fulfilling social obligations, and protecting one's "face".

Hofstede and his colleagues rated over 50 countries according to these dimensions. Although Hofstede's work received both praise and criticism, its influence cannot be denied. Several researchers in user interface and Web interface design are influenced or base their work on his theory. A few examples: Sungwoo and colleagues used Hofstede's theory to study cultural issues for mobile phone user interfaces, comparing Korean and US users [SJH+03]. Marcus and Baumgartner [MB04] collected opinions of over 50 experts about how cultural dimensions influence user interface design. Marcus and Gould [MG00] suggest guidelines to successfully localize Web sites based on Hofstede's theory. Dormann and Chisalita [DC02] conducted an empirical study to examine value differences between participants of "masculine" and "feminine" countries, and to determine to what extent value orientations are expressed in Web sites from such countries.

6.1.4 Web Design Methods and Localization/Internationalization

To effectively deliver localizated Web sites, internationalization and localization need to be taken into account throughout the development process of a Web application. Accordingly, some Web engineering methods have been extended to cope with the growing demand for localized Web applications. In the following, we describe two solutions that have been developed in the context of WSDM and WebML, respectively. As the reader will observe, the former provides localization support throughout the design process, while the latter mainly focuses on multi lingual support for Web applications.

Localization in WSDM

The approach to support internationalization and localization during the design of Web applications in WSDM is described in [TC04]. The approach acknowledges L10n and i18n as key issues to be taken into account throughout the design, starting from the requirements specification. A thorough overview of WSDM (without localization support) was given in Section 3.4.2. In the remainder of this section, we will shortly reiterate the WSDM design phases, and show for each phase where localization issues are taken into account throughout the design process.

Mission statement

The specification of the mission statement is the first phase of the WSDM design process. The intention is to clearly set the boundaries for the design by identifying the purpose of the Web site, the topics, and the target users. For localization purposes, the different targeted locales are also specified.

Audience modeling

During the audience modeling phase, the targeted visitors, who were informally identified in the mission statement, are classified into audience classes based on their requirements. Based on subclass relationships, an audience class hierarchy is obtained, where each subclass has additional requirements compared to its superclass. This sub-phase is called *audience classification*. During the *audience characterization* sub-phase, for each audience class, the characteristics and usability requirements of its members are formulated.

For localization purposes, requirements and characteristics specific to a locale are specified separately. This gives rise to two new sub phases: *locality specification* and *locality characterization*. Requirements and characteristics specific to a locale will typically be related to language, culture, habits or regulations. An examples of such a requirement is that state sales tax should be specified separately (for the US), and the address should include the state for the US. Examples of locale specific characteristics include Chinese-speaking (for China) and the Islamic religion (for Palestine).

Finally, the *locality mapping* sub phase specifies which locales are linked to which audience classes (i.e., some audience classes may not be relevant for certain locales). Figure 6.1 shows WSDM's updated audience modeling phase.

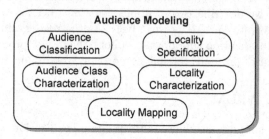

Fig. 6.1. The WSDM audience modeling phase updated for localization support

Conceptual design

During the conceptual design phase, the designer models the tasks that need to be performed by the different audience classes, the required content and functionality, and the conceptual navigation structure in an implementation-independent way. For each requirement defined during audience modeling, a task model is defined. A task model consists of a decomposition of a task needed to fulfill a requirement into elementary tasks, along with the temporal relations between them (e.g., sequential, order-independent). Subsequently, for each elementary task a so-called object chunk is created, which describes exactly what data and/or functionality is required to perform this task. Finally, the conceptual navigation structure, indicating how the different visitors will be able to navigate through the site, is built. The basic navigation structure can (but must not) be derived from the class hierarchy, leading to an audience-driven navigation structure consisting of so-called navigation tracks. The internal navigation structure in a navigation track is based on the task models, and consists of linked conceptual navigation nodes, to which (one or more) object chunks are connected.

To accommodate localization, WSDM requirements specified for each locale (during locality specification) need to be taken into account during task and information modeling. The locality requirements may give rise to a different task decomposition (i.e., additional or different steps) when constructing a task model. In this case, these divergent steps are labeled with their respective locales. In rather exceptional cases, a totally different task model may be required, in which case the complete task model is labeled with the respective locales. Similarly, if additional information and/or functionality is required for a certain locale, it is added to the respective object chunk and labeled with the respective locale. When creating an object chunk for an elementary task that is labeled with a locale, the complete object chunk is labeled with the locale. Also, when totally different information and/or functionality is required for different locales, different object chunks are created and labeled with their respective locales. Finally, in the navigation model, for each node and link it is specified for which locales the node is relevant. This can be easily done, since the navigation structure is (partly) derived from the task models, which are labeled with locales if appropriate.

Implementation design

During implementation design, the conceptual models are complemented with all necessary information details to prepare for the actual implementation, which can be generated automatically. During site structure design, the conceptual navigation structure is mapped onto pages. Several site structures are possible, depending on device, context, or platform (e.g., different screen sizes may give rise to different site structures). During the presentation design, the general look and feel for the Web site is defined. For each page, the designer decides upon concrete interface elements (e.g., a dropdown list or radio buttons to represent a single-choice list), their positioning, and the look and feel of the page in a page model. In the case of a data-intensive Web site, a database or CMS can be used to store the data. In this case, a mapping between the conceptual data model (i.e., the object chunks) and the actual data source is specified. This is done during the data design sub phase.

To support localization, WSDM allows creating different site structures for different locales, in case their tasks significantly differ. In this case, each site structure is labeled with the locales for which it is designed. In most cases, however, only one site structure will suffice for all locales. During presentation design, the localization characteristics specified during audience modeling need to be taken into account. As each page belongs to exactly one audience class, it is known for which locales each page is relevant. Therefore, for each locale, a different page model is specified for each page, taking into account the particularities of the locale. What exactly to take into account was elaborated earlier in this section. In the case of a data-intensive Web site, the data source needs to take into account different data for different locales. Therefore, the locale labeling of object chunks needs to be taken into account. [TC04] gives an intuition on how this can be done in the case where a relational database is used as the data source. In summary, for each locale-specific information, either a separate table is created or an attribute is added to an existing table indicating the relevance for a certain locale. Obviously, other solutions are possible.

Multilingual applications in WebML/WebRatio

WebML [CFB+02] and its accompanying CASE tool, WebRatio, provide mature support for the conceptual design and the implementation of multilingual Web applications, and thus natively partially cater for localization and internationalization [The07]. Developing multilingual applications requires:

- The design of a *data model* that enables the management of multilingual database content.
- The specification of proper *selection mechanisms* to enable users to choose a preferred locale.
- The translation of *static resources* of the application.
- The localization of *presentation style sheets* to align the look and feel of the application with the chosen locale.

While the modeling language WebML, upon which the WebRatio tool is built, provides the means to address the first two items of the previous list (i.e., data and hypertext design), the last two items of the list are supported by the WebRatio tool. As a pure modeling language of Web applications, WebML focuses on the conceptual modeling of data and hypertext and does not provide the means for the design of presentation properties; WebRatio complements WebML and also supports the design and implementation of the application's presentation layer on top of the WebML models.

In practice, developing multilingual Web applications with WebML and WebRatio requires the addition of a `Locale` entity to the application's data model, which needs to be connected to the other data entities in the application's data source that require localization; this connection may be specified through suitable relationships or through the addition of two attributes (`CountryISOCode` and `LanguageISOCode`), referencing the locale, to the affected entities. During hypertext design, the selection of contents to be published is then subject either to a selector condition that also takes into account the relationship between entities and locales, or to two additional selector conditions that query the additional attributes (e.g., `[CountryISOCode=US]` and `[LanguageISOCode=en]`). Locales may be explicitly set by the user; they may be extracted from his profile, or be derived from the Web browser's default locale; locales are then stored in suitable global parameters that can easily be accessed during query execution. WebRatio allows the translation and management of different display formats for date, time, currencies, and numbers, and of static labels and system/error messages, as well as the fine tuning of presentation properties. Finally, properly set up multilingual designs can automatically be translated into running applications by means of the WebRatio code generator.

6.2 Personalization, Adaptation, and Context-Awareness

With the advent of new and powerful mobile devices, the Web is addressing a continuously growing number of users and is more and more pervading our everyday lives. The need to improve the user's browsing experience, e.g., by adapting the application to user preferences or device characteristics, has become manifest. Localization/internationalization and personalization have already proved their benefits for both application providers and content or service consumers. To a similar degree, more advanced adaptation features are also gaining consensus. Typical application adaptations in Web applications are, for example, the adaptation of content or hyperlinks, the execution of operations or services, and the adaptation of presentation or style properties in charge of changing usage requirements.

Pioneering work in this area has mainly been done in adaptive hypermedia systems (see [Bru96, Bru01] for an overview of adaptive hypermedia, and [BHW99] for the well-known adaptive hypermedia reference model AHAM); but nowadays numerous works aim at enlarging the applicability of adaptive application features on the Web from adaptive hypermedia systems to adaptive and even context-aware Web applications [CDMF07, GGBH05, CWH07]. While the former typically are based on a user model that is dynamically updated based on the observation of the user's navigation actions, the latter may be based on a more complex context model and active, context-triggered application features.

Typical applications that leverage adaptive features can be found in domains such as e-learning, where the course is automatically personalized to the learner's knowledge or expertise derived from periodical tests; guide applications (e.g., tourist guides), navigation systems, where contents and advertisements are tailored to the user's position; and monitoring applications, where active support for the management of exceptional situations is of crucial importance.

6.2.1 Terminology

For a better comprehension of the following discussion and of the works referenced throughout this section, it is important to master the basic terminology used in this research area. As the following definitions will show, there are differences even between terms which, at the first glance, look very similar. To start we define *personalization* as the founding idea underlying the more advanced features of *adaptivity* and *context-awareness*.

Personalizing a Web page means adapting the Web page to an individual based on his identity and individual needs. By personalizing an application to individual users, it is possible to tailor to individual needs the usage experience of a user with an application. As a consequence, each user may have his individual view on application content and features. In the AI community, personalization is also called *customization* [PE97], where it is contrasted with *optimization*, i.e., adapting a Web site as a whole, improving its navigation structure for all users, based on the (browsing) behavior of all users. Others use the term personalization only in reference to changes that are applied based on *implicit* data, while customization is related to changes based on *explicit* data. For the purpose of this book, however, we do not think it is necessary to distinguish the two kinds of data.

What is interesting, instead, is that personalizing a Web page intrinsically means *adapting* the page. As we will see, adaptation is also the basis for adaptivity and context-awareness.

Adaptation of an application to determined requirements is the activity performed to fit the application to the specified requirements. The crucial part here is the term *requirements* as, based on the context in which an adaptation is performed, requirements are typically expressed differently. In the case of basic *personalization*, requirements at the basis of the adaptation action may for instance be expressed as explicitly provided *user inputs*, i.e., the user specifies his preferences over application contents and features. But there may be other data to which an application may be adapted; based on the different data underlying the adaptive application, we distinguish between three kinds of application adaptation and, hence, of nuances of personalization.

In adaptive hypermedia systems, two adaptation-specific terms have commonly been accepted [DHW99] (see also [MFM02]), *adaptability* and *adaptivity* (as well as their adjective counterparts *adaptable* and *adaptive*, used to characterize applications). Based on the definitions in [DHW99, DBH99, MFM02], we will use the following definitions in this book. Adaptability is the ability to adapt an application to device capabilities and/or user preferences prior to the execution of the application. Adaptivity is the ability of an application to adapt to the user's browsing history stored in a user model during the execution of the application.

A final form of adaptation we will consider is *context-awareness*. A recent approach is described in [CDMF07], where the definition of adaptivity is based on a more general, dynamic *context model*. Context-Awareness is the ability of an application to adapt to varying context conditions during the execution of the application, to use context data, or to do both.

Context-awareness is intended as the capability to take into account any properties or information that characterize the interaction with the application, i.e., the context, and to react to changes that such properties or information may experience during the use of the application. Reactions, i.e., application adaptations, are therefore no longer only based on user preferences, device characteristics, or user browsing behaviors, but in general on any property that characterizes the context of the interaction.

Summarizing, we can say that adaptability is a design-time property to be associated with the development method or the tools that are used to design the application and with the technologies that are adopted to implement the application, rather than with the application itself. Adaptivity and context-awareness, instead, refer to the application's capability to adapt during application execution (runtime), after the deployment of the application. Accordingly, adaptability is considered *static*, i.e., affected application properties are fixed at design or deployment time, while adaptivity and context-awareness are *dynamic*, i.e., affected application properties may change even after the deployment of the application. Dynamic adaptations are typically harder to design than static adaptations, because of their tight integration into the application's business logic.

6.2.2 Methods and Techniques

The previous definitions distinguish between different kinds of adaptation, based on the nature of the requirements to which an application is to be adapted, i.e., the distinction is based on the *to what?* question. In the following, we will have a more detailed look at *what* can be adapted, that is, we will discuss which part of a Web application may typically be subject to adaptation. For each part, we will slightly hint at *how* the respective adaptation is typically achieved.

In his review of adaptive hypermedia systems [Bru96, Bru01], Brusilovsky distinguished between two main facets of adaptation: *adaptive presentation* and *adaptive navigation* support. In Brusilovky's view, written in the context of adaptive hypermedia, adaptive presentation refers to text and multimedia presentations, and adaptive navigation support refers to guidance mechanisms and (adapting) hyperlink structures. The described parts are still valid objects of adaptation, but, as we are now talking about adaptive *Web applications* and no longer about adaptive *hypermedia systems*, we have to consider a slightly broader spectrum of application parts that may become the object of adaptation. In today's adaptive Web applications, we may thus find one or more of the following adaptive features:

- *Adaptation of contents*: contents (e.g., data items published on a page) are adapted in order to enhance the effectiveness of the content delivery. Contents may be adapted by selecting alternative data items, alternative representations of the same item (e.g., there may be a long and a short version of a text), different levels of detail, etc.
- *Automatic navigation actions*: instead of adapting the contents of an individual page, users are redirected to another page to enhance the effectiveness of the overall application (e.g., to allow a user to handle an exceptional situation).
- *Adaptation of navigation structure*: hyperlinks may be hidden or shown to deny or allow users access to specific pages or features of the application. This is typically achieved by associating suitable presentation conditions with links.
- *Adaptation of layout*: the layout (i.e., the arrangement of contents and graphical elements on the page) are adapted, typically to better suit different screen resolutions or browser window sizes. The layout may be adapted

by using alternative page templates or by suitably changing the CSS properties associated with the application.

- *Adaptation of style properties*: style or presentation properties are adapted in order to allow for fine-grained adjustments of the application's appearance (e.g., fonts or colors). Style properties are typically managed through CSS.
- *Adaptation of the hypertext structure*: the whole application structure (pages, layout, style properties) are adapted to support coarse-grained adaptation requirements, for example, to react to changes of the user's device, role, or activity in a multi-channel, mobile usage environment. There are different approaches to this kind of adaptation; the two main approaches are (i) providing alternative views of the same applications in advance, and (ii) computing alternative views on the fly, e.g., through suitable XSLT transformations.
- *Automatic execution of operations or external services*: the application decides autonomously to enact internal or external operations in order to leverage additional business logic. This typically implies the invocation of a function, a class method, an external Web service, or an external program.

There is one further question that is important in the design of adaptive Web applications: *when* should an adaptation be performed? The logical answer to this question would actually be "as soon as the need for adaptation is revealed," but due to the peculiarity of the Web, the situation is not that simple. The standard HTTP protocol underlying most of today's Web applications implements a strict pull paradigm, in which the actual Web application is "active" only when computing the response to a user-generated page request. Adaptations that need to be performed are thus typically delayed until the user takes a navigation action.

But there are application domains that demand for *active* behaviors and in which the typical *reactive* behavior does not suffice anymore (e.g., a geographical navigation system). In such cases, in the absence of dedicated server-side push mechanisms for delivering timely adapted pages, the HTML http-equiv META-option, or JavaScript, Java applets, or Flash scripts provide valuable client-side mechanisms to "simulate" the required active behavior by periodically polling the application. Periodically polling, unfortunately, typically implies periodically recomputing (i.e., refreshing) a viewed page, a behavior that could be perceived as annoying by users. In this regard, technologies like AJAX or Flash provide the right means to perform the polling transparently in the background, thus avoiding periodical refreshes and allowing the application to recompute a page only if an adaptation is really necessary.

6.2.3 Web Design Methods and Adaptation/Personalization

Several conceptual Web design methods and languages have been extended to also cope with adaptivity at the modeling level: *Hera* [VFHB03], *OOHDM*

[SRB96, SR98], *OO-H* [GCP00], *WSDM* [CTB03], *WebML* [CDMF07], *UWE* [KKH01], *OntoWebber* [JDW01], and *SiteLang* [TD01]. A common approach, stemming from the Adaptive Hypermedia research area, consists of annotating elements with conditions in the relevant design models. Based on the truth value of the evaluated condition, these particular elements are visible or omitted in the final Web application (e.g., [VFHB03]). Another common way is the use of Event-Condition-Action (ECA) rules to perform adaptation/personalization (e.g., [CTB03, GCG05, CDF06]. More recently, aspect-orientation has been applied (e.g. [BKKZ05, CWH07]).

It is not our intention to discuss each of the extended models; instead, we would like to provide the reader with an impression of how adaptivity and context-awareness can be taken into account during the modeling of an application. It is indeed important to understand that adaptation and context-awareness are not only implementation concerns, but first-class design issues. Therefore, in the following we will illustrate two interesting approaches: WSDM and WebML. While WSDM proposes an audience-driven approach to adaptivity, WebML proposes one of the first approaches to context-awareness in Web applications.

Adaptivity in WSDM

WSDM (*Web Site Design Method*) is an *audience-driven* Web Site Design Method[4]: from the very first phases of design, the method puts emphasis on the identification of the needs and characteristics of different classes of the target audience, called *audience classes* [DD00]. Subsequently, these audience classes lead the overall design, and in particular the navigation structure: for each audience class, a separate navigation track is constructed, containing all and only the information and functionality required for that audience class. As such, WSDM offers an approach which positions itself perfectly between a one-size-fits-all and a personalized navigation structure. For an overview of WSDM, we refer to Section 3.4.2.

WSDM offers an extension to allow design-time specification of adaptive behavior at runtime [CTB03, Cas05]. In contrast to most existing approaches, the adaptation is based on the browsing behavior of *all* users (i.e., optimization), as opposed to using the browsing information of one particular user (i.e., customization or personalization). It allows exploiting the audience-driven nature of WSDM, but it is not restricted to it.

To allow adaptation specification, WSDM proposes a high-level Event-Condition-Action (ECA) rule-based language, called the Adaptation Specification Language (ASL). ASL allows the designer to specify:

- *Which information to track*: the designer can specify exactly which information needs to be tracked, by attaching monitors to selected elements of the design (pages, navigation nodes, links, etc.). Once a monitor is installed

---

[4] Later re-baptized to Web Semantics Design Method

(in an adaptation policy, see later), it will react on certain user-generated events (e.g., clicking a link, accessing a page), and store this information in the storage facility.

- *How to adapt*: once the relevant monitors are installed, the information that is gathered can be exploited to specify adaptation. The actual adaptation specification, i.e., the required modifications to the navigation structure, is captured in an *adaptation strategy*. The basic ingredients offered by ASL to specify adaptation strategies include native operations (e.g., adding and removing a link, adding and removing pieces of information, re-locating information, etc), iterations, and conditional execution. At its core, ASL provides sets and set operations (to specify and manipulate elements used in the Web design, such as pages, links, etc.) and expressions (mainly used to calculate certain relevant values, e.g., thresholds).
- *When to adapt*: once monitors and adaptation strategies are defined, the designer needs to specify when these monitors should be installed, and when the strategies should come into action. This is specified by *adaptation policies*. Using adaptation policies, the designer can specify exactly when to install certain monitors (e.g., at deployment, at the start of a session, etc.), and when to perform certain adaptation strategies (e.g., after three months of monitoring, every week).

Using ASL, the designer wields a powerful tool to specify, at design time, which adaptation (possibly) needs to be performed at runtime. Given our space constraints, it is not possible for us to go into details of this approach. However, based on an example, we will give the reader the basic idea of how adaptation specification works using ASL. The example adaptation strategy we will consider here is promoting a page: the most popular page of a certain set of pages is moved (*promoted*) closer to the home page, increasing its visibility and descreasing the amount of clicks required to reach it.

A first step in promotion is specifying which navigation nodes need to be monitored. Using a generic script, this is done as follows:

```
(1)  script trackAmountOfAccesses(Set) :
(2)     forEach element in Set
(3)     begin
(4)       addTrackingVariable element.amountOfAccesses ;
(5)       monitor load on element do element.amountOfAccesses:=
(6)       element.amountOfAccesses + 1
(7)  end
```

Without going into details on the syntax, this script specifies that for each element of a certain set (line 2), a monitor is added (line 4), which monitors load-events on the element (line 5), and increments the relevant variable which stores this information (lines 5 and 6) in the storage facility.

The adaptation strategy performing the actual promotion is specified by the following script:

```
(1) script promoteNode(Set, promoteTo) :
(2) begin
(3)   let promoteNodeMaxAccesses be
(4)   max(Set [MAP on element: element.amountOfAccesses]);
(5)   forEach node in Set :
(6)   if node.amountOfAccesses = promoteNodeMaxAccesses
(7)   then addLink (promoteTo, node)
(8) end
```

In lines 3 and 4, the maximum amount of accesses is computed. Subsequently, the node with the maximum amount of accesses is promoted, in this case, by adding a link from a certain specified node (most likely, this will be the home page) to the node that was found to be most popular.

Finally, the adaptation policy that specifies when promotion should be performed could look as follows. In this example, we assume we are working with a research group Web site, and we will promote the most popular publication of a researcher (publications are specified in a node called PublicationNode) to the home page:

```
(1) when initialization do
(2)   call trackAmountOfAccesses(ALL PublicationNode);

(3) when 1 month from initialization do
(4) call promoteNode(ALL PublicationNode, root);
```

The example policy installs the monitors on all instances of PublicationNode (lines 1 and 2) at initialization of the Web application, and calls the promotion strategy after one month of monitoring (lines 3 and 4). Note that this is only a simple strategy, it would, for example, also be possible to periodically update the most popular publication (e.g., every month).

ASL allows the designer to anticipate and react to runtime behavior during the design, to automatically evaluate and select among design alternatives, to detect and correct design flaws, and to better tailor the Web application to satisfy business requirements. More information, and example strategies for all the aforementioned benefits, can be found in [Cas05].

Adaptivity and context-awareness in WebML

Recently, WebML has been extended to support the design of adaptive or, in general, context-aware Web applications [CDMF07, CDFM07]. According to the proposed extension (see Figure 6.2 for the architectural framework of the extension), an application may consist of context-aware (adaptive) and non adaptive parts. The former part is called adaptive hypertext and indicates those pages of a Web application that present some form of adaptive behavior, while the non adaptive hypertext collects those pages that do not present any adaptive behavior.

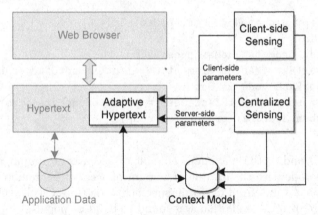

Fig. 6.2. Context data in context-aware Web applications. Gray shaded boxes correspond to conventional, non adaptive parts; white boxes correspond to extensions required to support context-awareness

As highlighted in Figure 6.2, the computation and the adaptation of context-aware pages are performed based on a context model, which is part of the application's data source and is dynamically updated during the execution of the application. Hence, to enable context-awareness, support for the following design tasks is provided:

- *Context model definition and representation* in an application-accessible format. Context properties that are required to support the application's adaptivity features need to be identified and modeled as application data. This activity fully reflects the data modeling conventions of WebML and, thus, is done by means of the Entity-Relationship model.
- *Context model management*, consisting of:
  - *Context data acquisition* by means of measures of real-world, physical context properties, characterizing the usage environment. This activity is highly application-dependent and requires the design of suitable sensing infrastructures, possibly on both the client and the server sides.
  - *Context data monitoring* to detect those variations in context data that trigger adaptivity. Any variation may cause a context-triggered, adaptive behavior of the Web application. This activity abstracts the dynamics of context data and specifies which variations of the data require an adaptation of the application. In [CDFM07] the authors describe a suitable background polling mechanism for the monitoring of context data.
- *Hypertext adaptation.* If context monitoring detects a situation demanding for adaptation, suitable adaptation operations need to be enacted in order to translate the detected context state into visible effects or operations that augment the effectiveness and usability of the application. The specification of adaptivity actions is directly performed in the WebML hy-

pertext modeling phase on top of the context model and the application data defined during the data modeling phase.

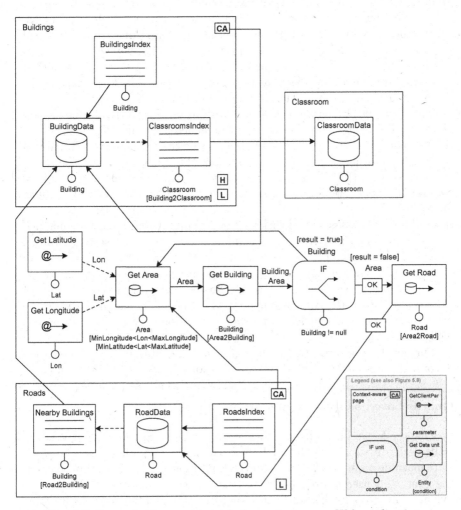

Fig. 6.3. Example hypertext model of a context-aware Web application

The modeling of context-aware pages leverages not only existing WebML operation units, but also a set of newly introduced, adaptivity-specific units: a GetClientParameter unit to access client-side-sensed context parameters, a GetData unit to access context data in the context model, and a ChangeSiteView unit and a ChangeStyle unit to switch site view and to change style properties, respectively. Pages, areas, and site views may be tagged as context-aware and associated with a chain of operations, representing the adaptivity logic associated with them and executed each time context monitoring (restricted to the currently viewed page) demands an adaptation.

Figure 6.3 shows a simplified WebML hypertext schema for an application producing location-aware information about buildings and roads. There are three pages (Buildings, Roads, and Classroom), two of which are context-aware (the ones tagged with the C-label). Page Buildings shows a list of buildings and the details of the selected building together with the list of its classrooms. By selecting a classroom, the user may view the details of the respective classroom. Page Roads shows a list of roads, the details of the selected road, and the list of the buildings located on the selected road.

The pages Buildings and Roads share the same adaptivity logic, represented by the operation chain that can be enacted through the link exiting the C-label of the two pages. The meaning of the schema is as follows: If context monitoring demands an adaptation, the application gets the user's current position (GPS parameters longitude and latitude) by means of two GetClientParameter units. It then retrieves (by means of two GetData units) first the geographical area the user is located in, and then – possibly – the building that is associated with that area (buildings and roads are mapped onto a set of contiguous areas). If a building is retrieved, the user is forwarded to page Buildings, and the content of the BuildingData unit is adapted. If no building can be retrieved, the application retrieves the road the user is located in and forwards the user to the Roads page, which shows details of the retrieved road. Hence, depending on which pages the user is viewing, the described adaptation logic leads to either adaptation of contents or automatic navigation actions.

Further details about the modeling of context data and the specification of context-aware and adaptive Web applications can be found in [Dan07].

Guards-based adaptivity in state machines

In Chapter 5, we have introduced state machine abstraction for navigation trails design used also in the ADRIA method. We have shown how to use a state machine approach for simple navigation trails design, taking into account the context a user is arriving from. State machines can be used for more dynamic adaptive navigation trail design. In this section, we will illustrate the use of UML state diagrams for adaptive navigation design according to [DN03].

There are three issues a designer needs to focus on when designing adaptive Web applications with UML Guide in addition to simple navigation trail design:

- *Context (User) Model*: a domain/data model for context/user data, in which observed runtime data about context parameters are maintained. The context/user model also features methods to access and update the data.

- *Observation Actions*: side-effect observation actions assigned to entry, internal, or exit actions on states and side-effect actions of transitions. The methods of the context/user model are used for enacting such actions.
- *Adaptation Rules*: guards on states or transitions that enable or disable certain transitions, change presentation behaviors of a state, or disallow rendering in certain navigation states. Queries over the states of a user model or data access methods are used in boolean conditions for this purpose.

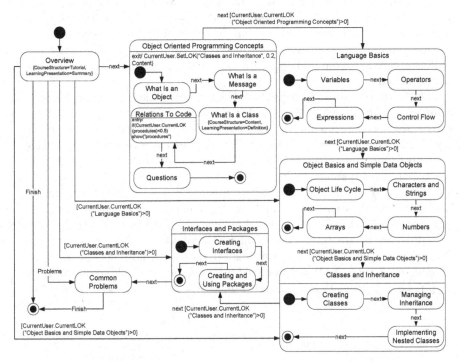

Fig. 6.4. Example of an adaptive navigation trail model according to the UML Guide for a Java tutorial [CDMN04]

The UML Guide state diagram of Figure 6.4 illustrates a personalized learning environment for teaching object-oriented programming in JAVA borrowed from a well-known Sun tutorial.[5] The chosen personalization example focuses on link adaptation; other adaptation aspects are covered in [DN03].

The tutorial starts with an overview of available lectures, as represented by the **Overview** state, which summarizes the available lectures in the tutorial, as represented by the **Summary** value in the **LearningPresentation** tagged value. It also presents the high-level tutorial steps (**Tutorial** value in the

---

[5] See http://java.sun.com/docs/books/tutorial/java/index.html.

`CourseStructure` tagged value). Links from the overview point not only to the first section of the tutorial, but also to the other main sections; all these links, except the first one, are associated with guard conditions that check whether the user has enough knowledge to jump directly to the respective lectures.

The next step from the `Overview` is a lecture on the `Object Oriented Programming Concepts`. This state is accessible without any prerequisite on background knowledge; it is a composite state, containing four steps, represented by four substates: `What is an Object`, `What is a Message`, `What is a Class`, and `Relations to Code`. The `Relations to Code` state also shows an `entry procedure` addressing *content-level adaptation*. The procedure applies to a learning step about building programs; it states that if the current user does not have sufficient knowledge on basic concepts about object-oriented programming procedures, then learning content on procedures will be added.

The next step from the `Object Oriented Programming Concepts` is the composite state `Language Basics`. The transition between the two states features a `next` event and a guard. The guard specifies a *link-level adaptation* rule, saying that the link is recommended when the current user level of knowledge is greater than zero. The other learning steps modeled in the state diagram can be interpreted similarly.

State diagrams in UML Guide are used as input for visualizing navigation maps, whose structure is made of documents (nodes), composite nodes (folders), links (arrows), and parallel regions (dashed boxes). State diagrams are edited by means of a commercial tool (Poseidon[6]); the navigation map is then generated through a transformation method, whose input is the state diagram encoded in XMI (as produced by Poseidon), and whose output is the map. The transformation is discussed in [DN03].

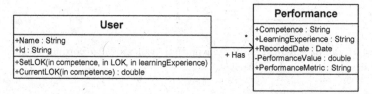

Fig. 6.5. A user model for the Java tutorial [CDMN04]

The personalization specification within state diagrams is based on the user model depicted in Figure 6.5. It is inspired by the LTSC IEEE 1484.2 Learner Model WG Standard proposal for public and private information

---

[6] http://www.gentleware.com/

(PAPI) for a learner.[7] The user model is composed of the classes User and Performance, plus an association expressing that a learner can have several performance records based on the acquired LearningExperience and Competence.

The Performance class stores the user's level of knowledge about the concepts described by the tutorial. This value is the one used for determining whether a transition into a new state is appropriate, and must be suggested to a given user. For example, the following condition:

[CurrentUser.CurrentLOK(''Classes and Inheritance'')>0]

is a guard that in the state diagram determines whether a link can be followed between the Classes and Inheritance state and the Interfaces and Packages state, based on current user's level of knowledge. The Performance class maintains as well the value of competence, recorded date, and metric used to measure the level of competence.

The User class provides operations to set and get the acquired level of knowledge or level of competence. These operations are used in guards and actions for adaptivity rules, and for updating the learner profile. For example, in the state diagram of Figure 6.4, the user level of knowledge about "Classes and Inheritance" can be acquired either in the Object Oriented Programming Concepts lecture or in the Classes and Inheritance lecture. Exit Procedures of these states contain similar update operations, such as the following one:

CurrentUser.SetLOK(''Classes and Inheritance'',0.2,Content).

More information on this approach, included examples illustrating different types of adaptation, can be found in [DN03, CDMN04].

6.3 Accessibility and Users with Disabilities

Historically, most of the current Web engineering approaches and development processes can be derived in large part from traditional software engineering practices, where functional and non functional requirements are typically well identified and stable. However, as we have seen throughout this book, the domain of the Web presents some distinguishing peculiarities that ask for proper adjustments of traditional software engineering techniques: In Chapter 3 we already discussed the typical, *fast* product life cycles and the highly *incremental* development approaches; in this section, we will discuss how modern Web development methods allow designers to take into account the *heterogeneous*

---

[7] http://ltsc.ieee.org/archive/harvested-2003-10/working_groups/wg2.zip

(and typically unpredictable) nature of the possible audience that may access a Web application. More precisely, in this section we will show how a careful and intelligent design may cater to impaired users, such as the deaf, the blind or visually impaired people, such as the colorblind, people with physical disabilities, and so on. In short, this section tackles the problem of content *accessibility*.

We refer to *Accessible Content* when it may be used by someone with a disability.[8] Accessibility, hence, guarantees that applications and content may be used by people with *disabilities*. While in general it is not an easy task to design a Web site for "normal" users, i.e., users who do not have any disability, it is an even harder task to develop a Web site that, to the same degree, conveys its content, for example, to blind people; they cannot see the actual Webpage and, hence, completely depend on proper assistive technologies, such as screen readers or braille[9] devices. In a slightly wider interpretation, accessibility also enables people with *temporary* disabilities (e.g., people who are involved in activities that do not allow the use of the hands, like driving a car) or users with outdated client browsers that do not support modern graphics and layout requirements (e.g., simple text browsers) to use a Web application or Web site.

6.3.1 Enabling Accessibility

Enabling accessibility to a Web application typically requires (i) proper assistive technologies, depending on the kind of disability that needs be addressed, and (ii) suitable coding and authoring techniques that allow Web designers to take into account the peculiarities of the different modes in which a user may navigate published content.

Assistive technologies may be required in addition to the actual Web browser (the standard client application to access Web content) to overcome disabilities that impede the use of a Web application via standard interaction mechanisms (mouse, keyboard, monitor). Some representative assistive technologies – both software and hardware – are:

- *Screen readers*: a software product that aims at interpreting text being displayed on a screen and at reading it out loud in order to assist visually impaired users. So-called *text-to-speech* technologies provide for the vocal output, while *automatic speech recognition* technologies provide for the interpretation of speech inputs and, thus, provide suitable means for navigating.
- *Screen magnifiers*: a software product that allows a user to enlarge portions of a computer's graphical output. The typical effect is that of a magnifying lens put between the screen and the observer.

---

[8] See the glossary of the W3C Web Content Accessibility Guidelines [CVJ99].
[9] The braille system enables blind people to "read": braille characters are made of up to six dots that can be felt with the fingers.

- *Braille displays and printers*: a hardware device that allows blind people to read displayed contents as sequence of braille characters. The dots of the braille characters can be raised or lowered dynamically, according to the text currently navigated.
- *Special keyboards and pointing devices*: physical disabilities oftentimes require proper, ad hoc hardware devices for the input of user data. Depending on the kind of disability, special joysticks (e.g. for the use with the mouth), keyboards (e.g., for use with the feet), or pointing devices (e.g., for the use with the eyes) may be necessary.

Whereas software technologies can easily and even automatically be added and installed on a client machine, this is not the case for special hardware devices, which generally require an explicit installation (hardware device, software drivers, device configuration) by the user himself. However, from a Web engineering perspective, it is in general not possible to distinguish users who use special hardware devices from users with conventional input devices. While Web engineering approaches can provide support for the (automatic) generation of Web sites specifically aimed for use with these special devices (an example of such an approach will be given in Section 9.1.3), an automatic adaptation of the application is usually not possible.

However, a Web engineering approach can enforce accessibility-enabling (HTML) *coding techniques* and, to a lesser degree, demand accessible *authoring styles*. The former aims at gearing an application to support possible assistive technologies (e.g., a screen reader) or at preventing non-accessible page layouts and styles (e.g., by taking into account the special needs of colorblind people); the following Section 6.3.2 will provide some more details in this regard. The latter aims at providing accessible content (both textual and graphical) and mainly impacts on the editorial style of content authors. For instance, bureaucratic regulations are typically hardly accessible (i.e., readable) to non expert readers; such kind of readers would greatly benefit from easier and audience-targeted writing styles. Accessibility-enabling coding techniques can be seen as functional requirements in the software development process; accessible editorial styles represent non functional requirements that need to be agreed on, but which are not part of the actual application engineering task.

6.3.2 The Web Content Accessibility Guidelines

To emphasize the importance that accessibility should assume in the design of Web content and to foster the diffusion and the standardization of proper accessibility-enabling coding techniques, the W3C founded a proper *Web Accessibility Initiative* (WAI[10]) in the late 1990s. The final goal of the WAI was (and still is) the definition of a set of guidelines and best practices that are

---

[10] http://www.w3.org/WAI/

able to support a wide range of user agent devices (e.g., Web browsers and screen readers). In 1999, the effort by the WAI produced the so-called *Web Content Accessibility Guidelines* (WCAG [CVJ99]), version 1.0, a W3C Recommendation that has still validity even ten years after its first publication. Soon after the publication of the WCAG 1.0, the WAI started working on version 2.0 of the WCAG, which, however, is still a W3C Working Draft, and not yet a Recommendation. We will discuss the two versions in the following.

It is worth noting that the WAI in the WCAG 1.0/2.0 concentrates on the accessibility of Web content from a Web engineering point of view. There are also other efforts by the W3C that aim at supporting accessibility, but from slightly different perspectives: the *User Agent Accessibility Guidelines 1.0*[11] provide guidelines for the design of accessible *user agents* (e.g., Web browsers), and the *Authoring Tool Accessibility Guidelines 1.0*[12] provide guidelines for the development of Web authoring tools (e.g., HTML editors). A discussion of these recommendations is, however, out of the scope of this book.

WCAG 1.0

The WCAG 1.0 Recommendation [CVJ99] focuses on two main themes of accessible design, namely the assurance of graceful transformations and the understandability and navigability of content. Web pages that transform gracefully remain accessible also to people with physical, sensory, and cognitive disabilities; key techniques in this regard are separation of concerns (content, structure, and presentation), text equivalents (e.g., for images), support for screen readers, and device independence. Making content understandable and navigable means using a clear and simple language and providing understandable means for navigating within and between pages.

The WCAG 1.0 includes 14 so-called *guidelines*, each equipped with its own set of *checkpoints*, which explain how the guidelines apply in typical scenarios. Each checkpoint has an associated *priority level*, which is based on the impact the checkpoint may have on accessibility: priority 1 means that the checkpoint *must* be satisfied, priority 2 means that the checkpoint *should* be satisfied, and priority 3 means that the checkpoint *may* be satisfied. Based on the satisfaction of the checkpoints, it is then possible to define a page's *conformance level*: level A means all priority 1 checkpoints are satisfied, level double-A means all priority 1 and 2 checkpoints are satisfied, and level triple-A means all priority 1, 2, and 3 checkpoints are satisfied.

But let us examine one of the guidelines concretely. In the following we provide an abbreviated citation of the guideline number 1 from the WCAG 1.0 Recommendation, May 5, 1999[13] (missing parts are indicated with "..."):

---

[11] http://www.w3.org/TR/UAAG10/

[12] http://www.w3.org/TR/WAI-AUTOOLS/

[13] http://www.w3.org/TR/WAI-WEBCONTENT/

Guideline 1. Provide equivalent alternatives to auditory and visual content.
Provide content that, when presented to the user, conveys essentially the same function or purpose as auditory or visual content.

...

Checkpoints:
1.1 Provide a text equivalent for every non-text element (e.g., via "alt", "longdesc", or in element content)... [Priority 1]...
1.2 Provide redundant text links for each active region of a server-side image map. [Priority 1]...
1.3 Until user agents can automatically read aloud the text equivalent of a visual track, provide an auditory description of the important information of the visual track of a multimedia presentation. [Priority 1]...
1.4 For any time-based multimedia presentation (e.g., a movie or animation), synchronize equivalent alternatives (e.g., captions or auditory descriptions of the visual track) with the presentation. [Priority 1]...
1.5 Until user agents render text equivalents for client-side image map links, provide redundant text links for each active region of a client-side image map. [Priority 3]...

The cited guideline requires auditory and visual content be equipped with equivalent text descriptions, which, in the case in which a user is not able to hear or see the content, provides a so-called *text alternative* that can be accessed. In the case of a deaf user, the text equivalent can be read, while in the case of a blind user, the text equivalent can be read aloud by a screen reader. The guideline has five checkpoints, four with priority level 1 and one with priority level 3, which provide some more details on how to achieve the different conformance levels.

A thorough discussion of this (and the other 13 guidelines) is out of the scope of this book; however, the described example suffices to provide the reader with some insight into the problems related to accessibility and into how the WCAG 1.0 Recommendation addresses them. The interested reader can find all the necessary details in [CVJ99].

WCAG 2.0

The WCAG 2.0 Working Draft [CCRV07] builds upon the work of WCAG 1.0 and aims at overcoming some of its shortcomings. Above all, more testable conditions of the satisfaction of the guidelines and a higher technology independence than in WCAG 1.0 are paramount in WCAG 2.0. While the version 1.0 guidelines are still highly technology-dependent (e.g., they explicitly refer to HTML and CSS), version 2.0 is meant to be technology-agnostic as much as possible, in order to be applicable to emerging and future technologies.

WCAG 2.0 provides a set of guidelines, which have been developed around four principles that Web content in general should satisfy [CCRV07]:

1. *Perceivable*: Information and user interface components must be perceivable by users.
2. *Operable*: User interface components must be operable by users.
3. *Understandable*: Information and operation of user interface must be understandable by users.
4. *Robust*: Content must be robust enough that it can be interpreted reliably by a wide variety of user agents, including assistive technologies.

The terminology used in the Working Draft slightly differs from the one used in the WCAG 1.0 Recommendation: There are 12 *guidelines* that are equipped with a set of *success criteria* (formerly "checkpoints"), which allow the easy assessment of the respective conformance levels. Indeed, success criteria are formulated in a way that they will be either true or false when specific Web content is tested against them. *Conformance* levels have new names: A means that all level A success criteria are satisfied, AA means that all level A and AA success criteria are satisfied, and AAA means that all A, AA, and AAA criteria are satisfied.

Let us consider guideline 1.1 of the WCAG 2.0 of the Working Draft as of May 17, 2007.[14] It roughly represents the new version of the previously discussed guideline 1 of WCAG 1.0, and shows how the terminology and the overall approach have changed:

Guideline 1.1 Provide text alternatives for any non-text content so that it can be changed into other forms people need, such as large print, braille, speech, symbols, or simpler language.
Success criteria:
1.1.1 Non-text Content: All non-text content has a text alternative that presents equivalent information, except for the situations listed below (Level A).

- *Controls-Input*: if non-text content is a control or accepts user input, then it has a name that describes its purpose.
- *Media, Test, Sensory*: if non-text content is multimedia, live audio-only or live video-only content, a test or exercise that must be presented in non-text format, or primarily intended to create a specific sensory experience, then text alternatives at least identify the non-text content with a descriptive text label.
- *CAPTCHA*[15]: if the purpose of non-text content is to confirm that content is being accessed by a person rather than a computer,

---

[14] http://www.w3.org/TR/WCAG20/

[15] A CAPTCHA is a so-called challenge-response test used to determine whether a user is human or not (e.g., a distorted, blurred image that needs to be interpreted). The acronym stands for *Completely Automated Public Turing test to tell Computers and Humans Apart*.

then text alternatives that identify and describe the purpose of the non-text content are provided, and alternative forms in different modalities are provided to accommodate different disabilities.

- *Decoration, Formatting, Invisible*: if non-text content is pure decoration, or used only for visual formatting, or if it is not presented to users, then it is implemented in such a way that it can be ignored by assistive technology.

The above guideline is very similar to the one discussed for WCAG 1.0, but the careful reader will have noticed how the language has changed: there are no direct references to coding scenarios, nor are there any special coding recommendations. The guideline is more general in nature. If we look at the (only) success criterion, we will notice that, in its current formulation, there are only two possible values it may assume: true or false. Assigning the conformance level A based on the given formulation of the success criterion is a straightforward task.

Although the WCAG 2.0 Working Draft seems to be going in the right direction, the current official standard for accessibility is still represented by the WCAG 1.0 Recommendation of 1999. As a matter of fact, in the last few years several governments have been working on their own, national accessibility regulations (think, for example, of *Section 508* in the United States or the so-called *Stanca Law* in Italy), especially to define proper rules for the public administration, but their common starting point is the W3C WCAG 1.0. As a consequence, such regulations typically reflect both strengths and weaknesses of the slightly outdated WCAG 1.0.

6.3.3 The Dante Approach

Unfortunately, accessibility guidelines are not well followed, or not taken into account at all by the majority of Web designers and implementers. The recent United Nations Global Audit of Web Accessibility (November 2006)[16] revealed 97% of Web sites do not obtain a Single-A WCAG 1.0 conformance level, which means that one or more user groups with disabilities will find it impossible to access information. The study covered 100 Web sites of five different sectors (travel, finance, media, politics, retail) in 20 countries, and used a combination of manual and automated techniques to check the Web Content Accessibility Guidelines (WCAG) 1.0.

The evolution of the simple HTML language to more advanced Web authoring languages and technologies, and the increasing visual focus of Web applications resulted in increasingly less accessible Web applications for visually impaired users. Screen readers may provide visually impaired users some relief. They allow line-based interaction, or simply read the entire page, from

---

[16] Available at the UN Web site, http://www.un.org/esa/socdev/enable/gawanomensa.htm (access date September 2007)

top to bottom and word by word. Screen readers work reasonably well as long as the page is properly (and linearly) laid out. Unfortunately, this is often not the case, and screen readers also have problems with Web pages that are highly visually oriented and/or not properly (and linearly) laid out. Where unimpaired users are intuitively able to detect the structure of a Web page, or the intended meaning of a page object, screen readers are not. No distinction between relevant and irrelevant information can be made. Consider the example of an image, such as a bullet, used purely for presentation purposes, versus an image conveying relevant information. Visual cues used by sighted users to identify the semantics of a page object are lost to screen readers. Menu structures, for example, can easily be recognized by an unimpaired user, while screen readers cannot make a distinction between a few (unrelated) links and an actual link menu. As a result, visually impaired users often find it very difficult or impossible to make sense of a Web page read aloud by a screen reader.

An approach to overcome this problem is the Dante approach [YHGS04]. In this approach, an ontology, called the Web Authoring for Accessibility (WAfA) ontology, was created to capture knowledge about structural and navigational properties of Web pages. The ontology is used to annotate (existing) Web pages, so that the intent and meaning of page objects relevant to support travel of a visually impaired user is made explicit. Travel, the virtual counterpart of travel in the physical world, comprises orientation and navigation, the environment, and the purpose of the journey. On the Web, these are provided by the page design and the browser [YSG03]. Relevant page objects thus include menus, check boxes, headings, title, logos, hyperlinks, etc. The annotations are done manually [YSG03], using COHSE [BGC+03] and the Dante RDF editor [Yes05].

As screen readers are not able to exploit these annotations directly, Dante proposes a transcoding approach. Exploiting the WAfA annotations, the original page is transcoded in a form that is more appropriate for visually impaired users. Useful examples of transcoding include elimination of doubles or fragmenting pages in smaller chunks and providing a linked index page to the fragments. The transcoded pages are constructed in such a way that they are very suitable for (existing) screen readers, and thus aid the visually impaired user in his Web travels.

6.3.4 Web Design Methods and Accessibility

Little emphasis on accessibility has been put in Web design methods. One of the rare exceptions is WSDM, which takes accessibility concerns into account during the design. In [PCY+05], the authors describe a method to generate WAfA annotations (see previous section) automatically as a side-product of the (regular) design process. The authors report being able to generate 70% of WAfA concepts, possibly extended to 85%, without any additional effort from the designer. In a nutshell, the approach consists of a set of mapping rules, which map WSDM design elements onto WAfA concepts. Based on these mapping rules, and a WSDM design, the WAfA annotations can be automatically generated, alongside the Web application. The approach is discussed in more detail in the next chapter, when discussing the Web design methods in relation to the Semantic Web, see Section 9.1.3.

6.4 Product Line Engineering and Feature Modeling

As we discussed earlier in this chapter, Web applications are accessed by users from different cultures and locations, and with different personal profiles and preferences, work contexts, and (dis)abilities. Therefore, an engineering team needs to handle and manage the variability imposed by different contexts as part of a Web product's engineering. On the other hand, it is also important to identify, manage, and reuse those Web product assets which are common across different contexts to make the engineering process less costly and more effective. This is directly related to the field of software product line engineering, where a family of software products is engineered based on the identification of a set of commonalities and variabilities. The focus here lies on the development of reusable and configurable software components, thereby reducing development time and cost for individual products. In this section, we'll shortly review the notion of software product line engineering, and show how the main principles can be applied to the engineering of adaptation in Web applications.

6.4.1 Software Product Line Engineering

The main motivation in software product line engineering is the reuse of modules in software development processes. The essential characteristic here is "engineering for reuse," while that of application engineering processes is "engineering with reuse." Emphasis thus lies on components designed for reuse, which are customizable for new software applications and extensible with new (custom) components developed for specific customers according to their specific requirements.

Figure 6.6 summarizes software development based on software product line engineering. There are two main phases in software product line engineering: *domain engineering* and *application engineering*.

Domain engineering

Domain engineering concentrates on providing reusable solutions for families of systems. There are several definitions for domain engineering. According to [MA02], product line engineering supports the systematic development of a set of similar software systems by understanding and controlling their common and distinguishing characteristics. It is driven by concepts from the real-world

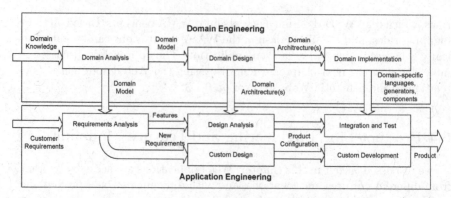

Fig. 6.6. Software development based on domain engineering according to [Wit94].

domain of the software products, in this way pursuing reuse. In this book, we have adopted a definition from [JGJ97, CE00], according to which domain engineering is a systematic way of identifying a domain model, commonality and variability, potentially reusable assets, and an architecture to enable their reuse.

The idea behind this approach is that the reuse of components between applications occurs in one or more application domains. As a result, the components that are created during the domain engineering activities are reused during the subsequent application system engineering phase. Several approaches to domain engineering for software systems have appeared, for example, the Model-Based System Engineering [Wit94] of SEI, which was later replaced by the Framework for Software Product Line Practice [Wit96].

According to [Wit94, CE00], domain engineering consists of three main activities:

- *Domain analysis*: defines a set of reusable requirements for the systems in the domain.
- *Domain design*: establishes a common architecture for the systems in the domain.
- *Domain implementation*: implements reusable components, domain-specific languages, generators, and a reuse infrastructure.

Domain analysis is a requirements engineering phase, sometimes described as "domain requirements engineering [PBvdL05]." In this way, the importance of requirements is stressed with respect to the further development of a product line. The result of domain analysis is a domain model. This model represents common and variable properties of the systems in the domain and relationships between them. Domain analysis starts with a selection of the domain being analyzed. Concepts from the domain and their mutual relationships are analyzed and modeled. The domain concepts in the model may represent a domain vocabulary. Each concept is then extended by its common and variable features and its dependencies with other concepts and is usually modeled by feature models. This is the key concept of domain engineering. Variable features determine the configuration space of the systems family. There have been several proposals for techniques to model variability and commonality in software systems. Feature-Oriented Domain Analysis (FODA) [KCHN90] employs a type of feature modeling where an AND/OR graph is used to denote variable features of domain concepts and variation points are used to depict dependencies between concepts. A Story Board is used to model variability in PuLSE [BFK+99]. The story boards reflect the basic ideas behind the PuLSE methodology where incremental development of architecture is guided by scenarios. The story boards model the scenarios with alternative paths. requirements, architecture, and There have been several extensions of UML for feature modeling (see, e.g., [GFdA98]). In [DN04, Dol08], feature modeling is employed and a metamodel in UML which closely accords with the FODA version is defined. We will use this approach later in this section in examples.

Domain design and domain implementation are closely related and are sometimes presented as one phase (e.g., product line infrastructure construction [BFK+99, MA02]). Domain realization is sometimes used to denote domain implementation (e.g., [PBvdL05]).

The domain design produces a generic abstract architecture for the family of systems according to commonly accepted architectural patterns (layered, model-view controller, etc.). Domain implementation implements the architecture by applying the appropriate technology or technologies in specific environments. Sometimes, domain implementation is followed by domain testing (see, e.g., [PBvdL05]). We see testing as an activity which cuts across all the activities of domain engineering; thus, it is an integral part of the activities.

In addition, several other domain engineering methods have been developed. These includes, for example, Organizational Domain Modeling [STA96], Domain Specific Software Architecture [TC92]. Refer to [PBvdL05] for more details on software product lines and domain engineering.

Application engineering

Application engineering is a sub process of software product line engineering in which the applications of the product line are built by reusing domain artifacts and exploiting product line variability. Application engineering follows traditional approaches to single software application engineering: requirements engineering, design and implementation, and integration and testing. In addition, it uses the product line infrastructure to select and instantiate reusable software assets which should be integrated with custom components.

According to [Wit94], application engineering develops software applications from software assets created by the domain engineering process.

6.4.2 Adaptive Web Applications and Software Product Lines

Let us now look at the adaptation defined in Section 6.2 from the software product line perspective. In this view, the basic principle of adaptation is to select appropriate variants of particular product features or a combination of product features (either by a human or a system) to satisfy user needs. Features which are adaptable are the ones which vary, and thus we consider these variable features of the application. The features which are not varying can be considered as common features of the application.

From the point of view of software product lines, the engineering of adaptive (Web) applications has the following point in common: the application should be ready for customization for different customers, but still retain some parts in common. However, the customization idea should be taken beyond the static customization done by a development team. True adaptive Web applications adapt to changed environments, user features, and other parameters on the fly (i.e. at runtime) according to knowledge gathered by their "sensors."

In the remainder of this section, we will study a software product line engineering method for adaptive Web applications as proposed in [DN04, Dol08]. This approach proposes a domain engineering framework for adaptive Web applications which adopts the software product line principles mentioned above. The framework incorporates established Web-based application modeling aspects into activities of domain engineering. Figure 6.7 depicts a framework for engineering adaptive Web-based information-intensive product lines [Dol08, Dol07].

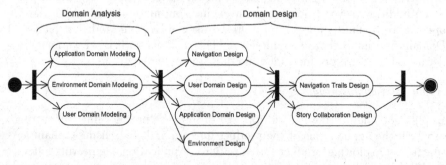

Fig. 6.7. Domain engineering approach for adaptive Web-based application [Dol08, Dol07].

Domain analysis for Web-based applications involves *application, environment, user domain conceptual* and *feature models* where:

- *Conceptual models*: are used to model concepts and their mutual relationships in a particular domain and serve as vocabularies for later feature models and domain designs.

- *Feature models*: are used to encode configuration knowledge, i.e., to maintain common and variable features of concepts and their dependencies, such as a company's stored experience. While the configuration specification is user-regulated in application and environment domains, it is regulated by adaptation requirements in user domains.

The purpose of the conceptual models is to document domain and environment vocabulary used in all other models. For example, the domain/content presented in a training suite of a Java lecture implies that the domain conceptual model will refer to concepts from the Java programming language. As the lecture is accessible in a course environment, the course structure and some other concepts will be depicted in the environment conceptual model.

Feature models are on the other hand used to document configuration relations between concepts from the conceptual models. This means that in Web applications they usually document which content concepts are used to articulate a particular concept in a presentation on a Web page, e.g., Java objects in case of a page on Java objects. The user domain feature models document configuration aspects according to the requirements of adaptation functionalities, i.e., which features and which combinations of features are required for certain adaptation strategies.

Domain design for Web-based applications involves *the navigation design, the user design, the application domain design*, and *the environment design.* The navigation domain design produces an architecture which enables the hypertext solution domain to generate HTML documents for particular environments with relevant content. The user domain design produces an architecture for user models to be used with applications in the domain. The application domain design produces an architecture to access content as an instance of application domain concepts and features. The architecture can be domain-specific, i.e., based on vocabulary defined in an application domain conceptual model from domain analysis, or it can be generic in order to access any content. The environment design defines an architecture for accessing and manipulating the environment.

Further refinements of domain design concentrate on content composition and navigation between content components. The domain design elements are used to bind the concerned domains together to produce reusable units of Web applications. The application and environment domains are bound together to create content. An environment called *story collaboration models* serves to create content components.

The domain design also incorporates mappings of the collaboration models to *navigation trails* which specify the sequences of content components to be presented to a user as presented in section on navigation behavior design (Section 5.4.2). The state diagram approach is adopted for this purpose. The access to content components and links between them are annotated by guards. The guards consist of constrains specified by conditions, functions updating user profiles, information presentation, and access environment appearance represented as side-effect actions.

Domain implementation includes construction of parameterized implementation components with their mutual dependencies. Parameterization of implementation components can be realized, for example, as HTML templates, active server templates, WAP templates, or components in other implementation languages. Domain implementation should also incorporate domain-specific languages such as query languages or languages for selecting and integrating components for a given application from the application family. All the mentioned models and their parameterizations are transformed into these implementation components.

Application engineering is the activity that follows the domain engineering activities, and defines a particular contract for an application. The Web-based application is built according to requirements specific to a particular application. Similarly to software systems, the requirements are split into those which

- can be satisfied by the components from the application family framework created during the domain engineering process.
- should be satisfied by a custom development.

The results of the framework generation and custom development are integrated into the final product.

6.4.3 Domain Analysis in Detail

In this section we focus on the domain analysis part of the method to explain how to employ variability modeling for adaptation management in a Web application family. The domain analysis is governed by conceptual and feature models. These models are used to manage the common and variable features of the applications. The conceptual and feature modeling is explained by use of examples. Note that the examples used in this section are descriptive and not prescriptive, i.e., they merely illustrate the introduced models for Web-based applications, and may be different in different contexts.

Features which can be denoted as adaptable are the ones which vary and are thus regarded as the variable features of the application. The features which stay unadapted are common and are thus regarded as the common features of the application. The commonalities and variabilities of software families are the main concerns in domain engineering methods.

The process of such information modeling can be summarized in the following steps [DN04]:

1. Define a concept model for the application, user, and environment (e.g., concepts used to teach the Java programming language in a course as for the application concept model, concepts for a learner's performance as for the user model, and concepts for course framework as for the environment model);

2. Define a feature model for all concepts from the application, user, and environment concept model;
3. Update concept and feature models of the domain, the user, and the environment if new concepts and/or features have been developed.

Concept modeling

Concept models represent abstracted knowledge of the real world. Entities of interests are mapped one-to-one to concepts in these conceptual models. Similarly, the relations of interest between the entities are mapped to associations (relations) in the conceptual models. In Web applications, as we have seen in the previous chapters, the conceptual models are usually concerned with the information (or its representation) being served, including information chunk representation and software artifacts which help to support access to information.

Information is usually comprised of one or more concepts from a domain where general conceptual models, taxonomies, or ontologies may already exist. For example, a Java tutorial serves information which belongs to the domain of computer science. There are several taxonomies which are used to classify computer science literature (ACM CCS[17]) or to describe a body of computing knowledge and curricula.[18] Companies also use their own conceptual models to communicate terminology used in their information systems. Information delivery environments can also feature different concepts which are related to each other.

In [DN04, Dol08] the Unified Modeling Language (UML) was used to model the application domain and environment domain models. A concept is modeled by a class, which is stereotyped by the Concept stereotype. Concepts can be connected by one of the relationship types, association, generalization/ specialization, or aggregation in order to support the known abstractions of model domains.

Furthermore, some domains provide information which is more of a "procedural knowledge" character. For those domains, we employed activity diagrams to model activity concepts with control flow relations between them.

Content concepts

Content concepts refer to an application domain as a domain of information (or content) which is to be served by a Web application. Conceptual modeling of an application domain models the domain in terms of concepts which are relevant to the content (or are described by the content) served by a Web application.

---

[17] http://www.acm.org/class/1998/
[18] http://www.computer.org/education/cc2001/

Figure 6.8 depicts an example of such an *application domain conceptual model*, showing a content of a page fragment in basic object-oriented programming (in JAVA). It is modeled by the UML class diagram with concepts annotated by the Concept stereotype and their mutual relationships. The figure expresses one possible view on relationships between Object, Class, and the object's State and Behaviour. Methods and Variables are used as additional concepts to describe the relationships, later realized by content fragments.

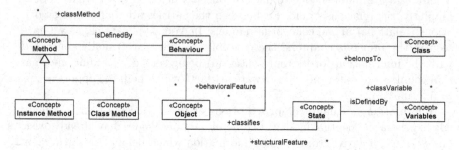

Fig. 6.8. An example of a conceptual application domain model which describes content with Java object-oriented programming

The process of application domain modeling differs from application to application and from organization to organization. It may well be that the conceptual models are created according to content which already exists in some applications (having already been supplied by a particular organization). In this case, the models are created for the purpose of reuse and customization, to document what has been already developed. But on the other hand it may well be that an organization foresees that its applications will be partially reused, and already uses models from the beginning of the development process.

The following are the main activities in application domain modeling:

- Collecting information sources on the application domain[19]
- Analyzing the information sources.
- Extracting instances of concepts of interests from the information sources.
- Classifying/categorizing the instances into concepts.
- Creating relationships of interests between the concepts.
- Refining the conceptual models.

Information environment concepts

This refers to an information or environment domain as a domain for representation and organization of information in the context of a delivery platform.

---

[19] This may involve the existing content or references to be used as a source for new content.

An example of an environment is a course with its lectures or modules. Another example is an e-book with its chapters. In a customer support domain, an environment can be a problem ticket with its subproblems, activities, contracts, and so on.

An Environment Domain Model is a set of models with concepts interconnected by association, aggregation, and generalization/specialization relationships. The concepts and the relationships originate from a domain which is used to organize the content for presentation, delivery, or management purposes in a Web application.

An example of an environment conceptual model in a training suite is depicted in Figure 6.9. As the training suite can be provided with several possible virtual environments, a development company team needs to communicate how the environments are structured. An example of such an environment suitable for a Java tutorial can be a virtual course. Concepts such as **Course**, **Lecture**, **Module**, **Learning Object**, and **Person** in various association roles such as **Lecturer**, **Garant**, and **Provider** would then appear in a similar UML class diagram for the *environment conceptual model*.

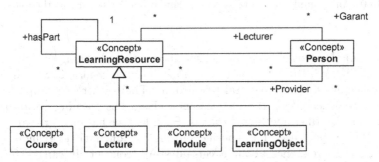

Fig. 6.9. An example of a conceptual environment/information model

A process of information/environment modeling generally consists of the following activities:

- Identifying existing and planned environments within a Web product portfolio.
- Analyzing organization patterns for such environments.
- Identifying typical instances of concepts for such environments.
- Classifying/categorizing the instances into concepts.
- Creating relationships between the concepts.
- Refining the environment conceptual models.

User concepts

In this approach, a user domain model is defined as a model which characterizes the users, their behavior and features, their knowledge, and so on. The concepts are selected according to whether they are used in current Web applications or will be used in future Web applications to parameterize adaptation processes. A user model is created in a similar way to the application domain and environment model. The main characteristic of a user model then concerns the concepts and features which will be used as parameters for adaptation.

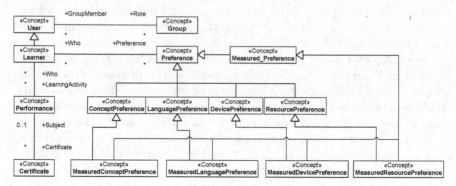

Fig. 6.10. An example of a user (learner) domain model specific to the e-learning domain.

An example of such a user model specific for the e-learning domain is depicted in Figure 6.10. A `Learner` is a subclass of the generic `User`. The user usually belongs to one of several role groups. The learner's learning performance is represented by the `Performance` class. The learning performance is sometimes certified by `Certificates`. Each learner has own `Preferences`. These can be specialized into specific subclasses. `ConceptPreference` refers to a learner's preference about a certain study concept. It can be further specialized to account for different learning style preferences with respect to different concepts. Similarly, `LanguagePreference` defines a user's preference for a particular language, `DevicePreference` records a user's preference for a particular device to be used for running a Web application or for implementing additional external features connected to the application. `ResourcePreference` records a preference for a specific information resource which might also be used for recommendations. Further specialization is catered for via the `MeasuredPreference` class which accommodates metrics used to measure preferences of all kinds.

Feature modeling

Adaptation components in adaptive Web applications usually recommend one of the options for links, content fragments in a content composition, or information items which are configurable in the Web application based on a user profile or the possibilities offered by a specific environment. This means that there are parts of the content, environment, and software components which are stable or common for any user or customer and parts which are variable depending on certain factors (mostly the values of user features).

To plan such an application, a designer should be able to think and reason about the common and variable parts. As pointed out in Section 6.4.2, there is a similarity between domain engineering approaches concentrating on reuse and adaptive application engineering. In domain engineering, feature modeling plays a prominent role. The main reason for employing feature modeling in current domain engineering approaches is to handle variability in and dependencies between concept features of a system family resulting from different requirements of stakeholders using the applications from the family.

In adaptive applications, the customization has an even broader scope; i.e., in addition to the customization based on the explicit requirements of stakeholders, there is still some variability which is left until runtime to be exploited according to an evolving user profile or other factors.

From the system point of view, variability has been studied in the context of the software configuration management community. In such cases, variability is handled at the systems component level by means of versions which contribute to different system releases. Version control in the document-oriented hypermedia domain has been studied in several works [Nel, SRS00]. All the works mentioned provide a model of versions and a model of configurations, which define how the versions contribute to the final configuration.

The variability considered in feature models has a broader sense when considered at the application level. At this level, it is taken into consideration in several modeling aspects of Web applications, and not just in the context of source code and changes to be made to the source code [DN04, DB02a].

Variability in product lines is defined as a measure of how members of a product family may differ from each other [WL99]. Variability can occur in all the significant aspects (products) of the Web application engineering process; i.e., in the application domain, in navigation, and in presentation.

In the application domain, different content can be used to communicate the same information to people with different backgrounds and characteristics. Moreover, the same content can be represented by different media and this content can evolve in time. The content can also be presented in different environments using different media, e.g., as a book, a lecture, or an article. Also overall access to the content can be managed through different patterns, such as a digital library, an e-course (virtual university), or online help.

Each user group may require a different information fragment to browse a different composition of the presented information (local navigation) and a different order of and interconnections between information chunks (global navigation). Also, different navigation styles can be determined according to the target environment where the information is served to a user.

Similarly, it may be appropriate to supply different user types with specific display designs, layouts, and organization of the information to be read. The target environment can also restrict presentation possibilities. Thus, it is important to take account of this kind of variability as well.

A feature model is a set of models which represent configuration aspects of concepts from domains analyzed in Web application engineering. Each feature model has one concept and its respective features. The concept and features are connected to each other by a composition relationship. Configuration relations between features and the concept are represented as variation points. The concepts and features in feature models are mapped onto the concepts and relationships from the conceptual model.

A *concept* in a feature model represents:

- *In an application domain model*: an information item which is part of the main purpose (main information goal) of the content which an author had when he authored that content.
- *In an environment/information model*: a main structural unit of content in a particular Web-based application (different representations are modeled by different concepts).
- *In a user domain model*: a main concept governing an adaptation process (e.g., user preference for recommendation of items, or learner performance to recommend the next step in a learning path).

A feature model has to be maintained for all concepts of a conceptual model which are going to be depicted as main information entities in a Web application environment. A feature is a prominent or distinctive user-visible aspect, quality, or characteristic of a software system [Her98]. A feature in a feature model represents [Dol08]:

- *In an application domain model*: information fragments which are needed to communicate a concept of a feature model effectively,
- *In an environment/information model*: supporting structural units of content in a particular Web-based application.
- *In a user domain model*: qualitative and quantitative features which are needed for decisions about a certain adaptation strategy within an adaptation process (e.g., a competence acquired within learner performance to decide whether a user is able to grasp a particular content item or exercise or metrics of the performance for finer recommendations relating to the next learning steps).

The fact that there are some features which are common to all configurations and that some vary is reflected by:

- *Mandatory features*: common or core features for all situations which are to be considered in our applications (application family).
- *Optional features*: variable features needed only within a specific context.

Sometimes some features need to be presented together with other information features to provide sufficient explanatory material to enable the user to understand the presented information. Some other information features cannot be presented together because they could confuse a learner. In some cases, the combination of features is not so relevant. To distinguish between these cases, *variability relationships* have been introduced between features and they are usually denoted as *variation points* [Wit94] or *variations* [GFdA98]. A variation point is a point or stage in design artifacts where a specific decision has been narrowed to several options but the option to be chosen for a particular system has been left open [Atk01]. The variation point can define:

- *Mutually exclusive variants (XOR).*
- *Mutually required features (AND).*
- *Mutually inclusive features (OR).*

The semantics of the variation point types defined in the literature is usually the same, but the labels used to denote them sometimes differ. For example, [BGdPL+03] defines several types of variation points but denotes them as *excludes* (XOR), *requires* (AND), and *ensures*. To achieve a consistent and unified framework for modeling, we maintain our feature models in UML. UML does not directly support feature models, so it requires us to provide a lightweight extension of the class diagrams of UML by using additional stereotypes. The `Concept` stereotype remains from the conceptual models. Features are annotated according to type by `MandatoryFeature` and `OptionalFeature` stereotypes. A variation point is annotated by `VariationPoint` and its kind (XOR, AND, OR). The concepts, features, and variation points are connected by directed edges, which stand for composition. The direction indicates the parts of the composition. In some cases, the whole configuration of features (variation point with all the connected features) may be considered optional. In that case, the whole configuration can be excluded from the Web application. If no stereotype is mentioned, then it is considered to be a mandatory configuration and the rules implied by using such a variation point have to be observed.

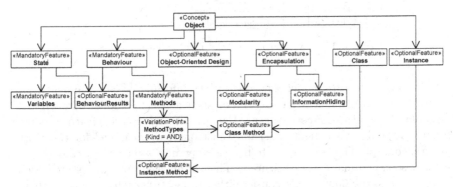

Fig. 6.11. An excerpt of the *Object* feature model

An example of a feature model is depicted in Figure 6.11. It is an excerpt of a feature model for the `Object` concept for the Java lecture. The `Object` concept is usually described with the help of the concept of its State and Behaviour. Both appear as concepts in the conceptual model in Figure 6.8.

The State and Behaviour are considered to be mandatory features. The Object-Oriented Design, Encapsulation, Class, and Instance) concepts are considered to be optional features, i.e., they do not have to appear in all applications.

Figure 6.11 depicts a variation point for the Methods mandatory feature. The model defines that the Methods also have to be described on the context of the Instance Method and Class Method.

All other concepts from the conceptual model (Fig. 6.8) usually have such feature models if they are communicated to learners as they become available in the application. Note also that the models depicted in our examples are not intended to determine the only possible solution, but just to illustrate how to create custom feature models which generate best practice guidance for information being served in Web-based applications.

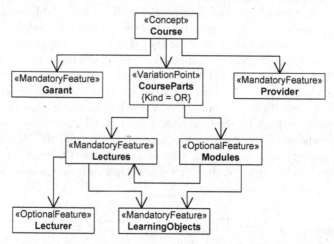

Fig. 6.12. An excerpt from the *Course* feature model

Similarly, a feature model is needed for the information/environment concepts. Figure 6.12 depicts an excerpt of such a feature model of a virtual environment for the Course concept. Usually, the information feature model for one virtual environment consists of just one feature model for the most general concept. The Course has to have a Provider and also a Garant (modeled by so-called mandatory features). Then, if another customer stated such requirements, the Course can consist either of Lectures where some of them can be encapsulated into thematic Modules, or just from Lectures alone (this is reflected by the OR variation point of the Course). The Lecture can be provided with a Lecturer who plays a role of a tutor when somebody needs

further information or support related to the lecture. Both `Lectures` and
`Modules` refer to learning objects.

A process of feature modeling generally consists of the following activities:

- Identifying the concepts from the conceptual models which are of the main
  information entities to be communicated by the Web application and mapping them to the concepts in the feature models.
- Identifying supporting concepts and relationships from conceptual models
  for each concept created for the feature models and mapping them to
  features in the feature models.
- Analyzing whether features are mandatory or optional in existing and
  planned applications.
- Specifying mandatory and optional features according to the previous step.
- Analyzing dependencies and composition relations between features of current and planned applications.
- Specifying variation points and their kinds based on the results of the
  previous steps.
- Specifying composition relations between the identified concepts, features,
  and variation points.
- Refining the feature models.

Similarly to the domain models described in the previous section, the user
model is refined to the feature models level as well in order to provide explicit
information on how it can be configured. Here, the variability dimension to be
considered is based on which adaptation strategies are involved in Web applications, which features are mandatory and optional, and what dependencies
exist between them.

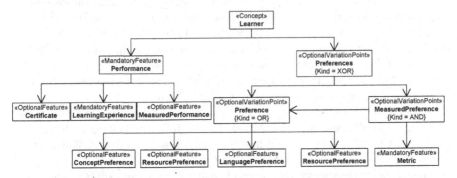

Fig. 6.13. An excerpt from a user (learner) feature model specific to the e-learning
domain

An example of a feature model excerpt for a learner is depicted in Figure 6.13. The example indicates that adaptation of an e-learning application
must at least be based on a learner's learning performance. The learning performance consists of a report on a learning experience, which is a mandatory

feature. The experience can be certified and measured (two optional features). In addition, the adaptation can be complemented by a strategy based on learner preferences (`Preferences` optional `XOR` variation point). The preferences can be simply stated in a user profile (`Preference` optional `OR` variation point) or can be measured, for example, by a degree of relevance for a learner. If the `Preference` variation point is chosen then one or more preference subtypes are chosen as well. On the other hand, when the `MeasuredPreference` `AND` variation point is chosen, both the `Metric` feature and the `Preference` variation point have to be selected.

The process of the user domain analysis and modeling is similar to that of the application domain or environment modeling. It is, however, worth mentioning that the user model can be useful only when it reflects real latent factors which might lead to the recommendations. Thus, creating a user model for a particular class of applications is very challenging and usually involves at least some research. The sources of factors suitable for adaptation, or, in other words, the sources of factors which differentiate people from each other, are sociological studies, demographic studies, or psychological studies.

6.5 Summary

In this chapter we have looked into some design concerns that are increasingly becoming mandatory features of modern Web applications, i.e., localization, internationalization, personalization and adaptation, and accessibility. These three concerns are peculiar characteristics of Web applications.

While in traditional software products, localization and internationalization mostly meant translating all the menu items, commands, information, help instruction, and so on into multiple languages, localization and international in Web engineering typically goes beyond the mere linguistic problems. For instance, big companies or associations that have affiliations in multiple countries and country-specific merchandising or assistance facilities (e.g., call· centers) need a corporate Web application that is not only translated in multiple languages, but that also takes into account country-specific information, regulations, laws and cultures. In this chapter, we described the problems leading to the demand for localization, the anthropological research underpinning localization support, and how localization is addressed in Web design methods.

Given the wide variety of potential visitors, and the different contexts Web applications can be used in, adaptation is a feature that is of growing importance. Adapting a Web page is the general process of changing it to fulfill a certain requirement. It comes in different forms. Personalization is the adaptation for the specific user, based on his identity, his characteristics and his individual needs. Adaptivity is the ability of the Web application to adapt according to the user's browsing history. Context-awareness is a form of adaptation that allows a Web application to adapt according to the changing context. All these adaptations occur at runtime, i.e., in the running Web application. In this chapter, we have discussed all these forms of adaptation and explained how Web design methods support them.

With a significant percentage of users exhibiting some kind of disability, taking into account these users increases the accessibility of the Web site for a wider audience. Recently, many countries have even imposed minimum accessibility levels to their Government or Public Administration Web sites, turning accessibility from an optional into a mandatory requirement. Web engineers are thus faced with the issue of adapting their Web sites so that users with disabilities may equally well access it. This might mean slight adjustments so that e.g., users with screen readers are able to interact with the Web site without problems, yet it might also involve a complete re-design of the Web site. In this chapter, we have discussed accessibility, enabling technologies, guidelines, and approaches.

Finally, we have introduced the reader to product line engineering as one of the techniques to implement the previous features, and to manage their complexity.

6.6 Further Readings

The latest research results, technologies, and practical approaches in localization and internationalization can be found, for instance, in the proceedings of the Internationalization and Unicode Conference series or on the Web site of W3C's Internationalization Activity (http://www.w3.org/International/).

Probably the main source for state-of-the-art research on adaptive hypermedia are the proceedings of the bi-annual Adaptive Hypermedia (AH) Conference series. Since 2009, the AH conference has been merged with the User Modeling conference to form the anual User Modeling, Adaptation and Personalization conference. For the latest information and results on (the engineering of) adaptive Web-based systems, authors typically publish their work in Web and Web Engineering conferences and their respective workshops. Two important sources are the World Wide Web (WWW) and the International Conference on Web Engineering (ICWE) conferences. Other conferences featuring Web and Web engineering tracks include but are not limited to the International Conference on Conceptual Modeling (ER), Web and Information Systems Engineering (WISE), Symposium on Applied Computing (SAC), Asian Pacific Web Conference (APWeb), and Hypertext conferences.

Accessibility issues are discussed and published in the proceedings of the International Cross-Disciplinary Conference on Web Accessibility. The W3C also maintains a large repository of technical material and tutorials along with the actual Web Content Accessibility Guidelines on the Web site of the Web Accessibility Initiative (http://www.w3.org/WAI/).

Furthermore, there are several journals targeting work on the Web and Web engineering. Examples include, but are not limited to: the WWW Journal (WWWJ), the Journal of Web Engineering (JWE), IEEE Internet Computing, and ACM Transactions of Internet Technologies (TOIT). In these journals, works on different aspects and from different angles on the Web and Web engineering are published; they thus provide an excellent source of information concerning the topics discussed in this chapter. Furthermore, special issues target particular specialization fields.

7

Implementation, Deployment, and Maintenance

During the design phase in the Web or software engineering process, the functional and non functional requirements that have been agreed upon by the customer and the developer are translated into a suitable software solution. Such a solution typically describes the conceptual decomposition of the overall Web application into a variety of constituent parts or modules, the arrangement of application data, the solutions adopted for communication purposes, and so on. The design phase, hence, produces as output a set of logical and conceptual solutions, architectural choices, and design patterns.

Such output is the input of the *implementation* phase where the elaborated, conceptual solutions are translated into proper application code. Implementing a design of a Web application typically requires the use of different technologies, programming languages, and code libraries; in Chapter 2, we introduced the most important technologies. The decision which technology to chose in a specific implementation situation does not always have an immediate answer. Typically, several (equivalent) implementation alternatives are possible. In this chapter we provide some insight into advanced implementation frameworks and tools (Section 7.2), as they represent best practices in industry and academia. For a better understanding of the frameworks and tools, we first discuss the adopted implementation practices for the presentation layer (Section 7.1).

Once an application has been implemented, its *deployment* requires some further decisions to be made. Going online with a Web application is not a difficult task, but there are a few issues that need to be addressed before the application can be accessed from the Web. For instance, typical decisions regard the selection of suitable Web server software, the physical location of the server, and the registration of the final domain name. Section 7.3 addresses these issues in more detail.

Finally, as the software life cycle is a continuous process, it requires proper *maintenance* and *evolution* efforts even after the final deployment of an application. Maintenance guarantees the continuous availability and functioning of the application; evolution regards the adaptation of the application to newly

S. Casteleyn et al., *Engineering Web Applications*, Data-Centric Systems and Applications, DOI: 10.1007/978-3-540-92201-8_7, © Springer-Verlag Berlin Heidelberg 2009

emerging or changing requirements. Maintenance and evolution are the subject of Section 7.4.

7.1 Implementing the Presentation Layer

Web applications in general have been evolving steadily since the emergence of the Web in both their technological and their functional aspects. From a strict presentation point of view, we identify the following three steps in the evolution of Web user interfaces that heavily impacted the way a Web application's interface is programmed:

- *Static HTML*: The first Web "applications" consisted of collections of static Web pages encoded in HTML and interlinked by means of embedded, static hyperlinks. Developing a static Web site was a daunting task, as each update of the site required the developer to manually maintain consistency in the collection of pages.
- *Dynamically generated HTML*: With the emergence of server-side scripting solutions, HTML pages could finally be assembled automatically, starting from a limited set of template documents. Especially, the maintenance of the typically large number of hyperlinks (think, for example, of today's data-intensive Web applications) benefited largely from dynamically computed URLs.
- *Dynamic HTML and RIAs*: Today's Web applications tend to augment their user interfaces with dynamic features also at the client side in order to minimize network traffic and to allow for highly responsive interfaces. In contrast to the server-side generation of HTML, the embedding of client-side logic also provides for fine-grained dynamic features, such as the update of single HTML elements.

We assume the reader is familiar with static HTML, and we hinted at dynamic HTML and RIAs in Chapter 2. The following discussion will thus focus on the dynamic generation of HTML markup on the Web server.

7.1.1 Template-Based Layout

The server-side generation of HTML markup is typically achieved by means of languages like JSP, PHP, and ASP.NET (cf. Chapter 2). A Web server that interprets a .jsp, a .php, or an .asp file intercepts the output sent by the program code to the standard output device and assembles it into the response (the page) that is sent to the user. Typically, the languages support not only the imperative, programmed specification of output, but also a hybrid approach, where HTML is interwoven with program code. Consider, for example, the PHP code of the `example.php` file in Figure 7.1. The code inside the `<?php ... ?>` instruction is the business logic of the page; the following lines are the HTML markup of the page. Note how the <H1> tag embeds an additional PHP instruction. The instruction refers to the variable $title that is set in the business logic part of the script and allows the runtime assignment of the title to the page. Of course, the example is intentionally kept simple; usually the business logic part performs more complex calculations, accesses local or remote data sources, and so on.

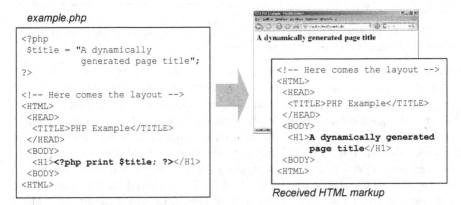

example.php

```php
<?php
  $title = "A dynamically
           generated page title";
?>

<!-- Here comes the layout -->
<HTML>
 <HEAD>
  <TITLE>PHP Example</TITLE>
 </HEAD>
 <BODY>
  <H1><?php print $title; ?></H1>
 <BODY>
<HTML>
```

Received HTML markup

```
<!-- Here comes the layout -->
<HTML>
 <HEAD>
  <TITLE>PHP Example</TITLE>
 </HEAD>
 <BODY>
  <H1>A dynamically generated
      page title</H1>
 <BODY>
<HTML>
```

Fig. 7.1. A simple PHP script (at the left) that dynamically assigns a title to the HTML page (at the right)

The example shows a very basic *templating* mechanism. An HTML markup template[1] is a "master page" that is used to produce HTML pages. A template contains so-called *placeholders* (or parameters), which are filled only during page computation and allow the generation of a multitude of different Web pages, starting from one template. The placeholder in Figure 7.1 is represented by the highlighted instruction <?php print $title; ?>, which binds the content of the placeholder to the variable $title.

While the described template logic looks quite intuitive, it still suffers one main drawback: it does not respect the separation of concern principle. More precisely, the PHP script in Figure 7.1 requires the application logic and the layout to be coded together. In general, this is not a good solution, as typically application logic is programmed by Web developers, and layout and style are designed by graphic designers. A better separation of the two concerns is needed, so as to enable developers and graphic designers to work independently and, possibly, in parallel. For this purpose, typically each of the prominent programming languages comes with one or more implementations of advanced *templage engines* that allow the separation of the program code from the HTML markup.

---

[1] In this book, we use the term *template* exclusively to refer to HTML markup templates; we do not consider programming templates, as in C++, nor document templates, as in word processing software.

tmpexample.php

```php
<?php
 include "PHPTAL.php";
 $template = new PHPTAL("tmp.html");

 $title = "A dynamically
          generated page title";

 $template->set("title", $title);
 ?>
```

tmp.html

```html
<HTML>
 <HEAD>
  <TITLE>Template Example</TITLE>
 </HEAD>
 <BODY>
  <H1 tal:content="title"></H1>
 <BODY>
<HTML>
```

Fig. 7.2. Templating with PHPTAL: business logic (`tmpexample.php`) and presentation logic (`tmp.html`) are cleanly separated

In Figure 7.2 we show, for instance, how to apply the PHPTAL[2] template engine to our example. One final Web page is now split into two distinct files, one for the page's business logic (`tmpexample.php`), and one for its layout (`tmp.html`). The two files can be created and modified independently. For the layout of the page, the graphic designer does not need any programming knowledge. The creation of the template only him requires to master a very limited set of HTML conform extensions (in the case of PHPTAL, such extensions consist of a set of additional attributes to be used inside the HTML tags), which allow the designer to specify how placeholders are filled with content. In Figure 7.2, the designer references the variable `title`. The Web developer, on the other hand, only focuses on the application logic and the setup of the template engine: the developer includes the template engine, instantiates the template, fills the variable `$var`, and defines a reference with name `title` to `$var`.

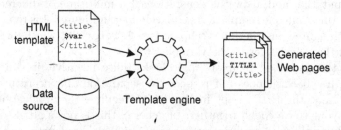

Fig. 7.3. Filling page templates with application data

The computation of the `tmpexample.php` script is graphically summarized in Figure 7.3. For each invocation of the script, the template engine takes as input the HTML template and the data that are used to fill the placeholders (in our example, the variable `$title`) and produces as output a filled Web page. Templating allows the generation of multiple similar Web pages starting

---

[2] PHP Template Attribute Language: `http://phptal.motion-twin.com/`

from one template and from data that is dynamically computed during the execution of the application. Pages that are generated from the same template, hence, differ in the content of their placeholders, while the static part of the template remains the same across all the pages.

7.1.2 XSLT at Runtime

If data are provided in form of XML documents instead of data structures in the programming environment, the XSLT [Cla99] approach may be used for the generation of Web pages. As introduced in Chapter 2, XSLT is a very powerful, XML-based templating language that is particularly well suited to document transformations. Proper template engines (so-called *XSLT processors*) are available for all common programming languages, and most of the recent releases of Web browsers internally support XSLT for document formatting. Conceptually, the logic expressed by Figure 7.3 also applies to XSLT, with the only difference that, in the case of XSLT, the data source consists of XML documents and, depending on whether an XSLT processor API or the browser's internal processor is used, the transformation is performed on either the server or the client.

Due to the nature of its source data, XSLT slightly differs in its approach to accessing data. XSLT is not intended to be used by graphic designers but by programmers. Therefore, some programming skills are required for writing XSLT transformations, i.e., templates. For instance, data access in XSLT requires intimate knowledge of XML and XPath [CD99], a non-XML language for addressing parts of an XML document. More precisely, XSLT leverages XPath for selecting elements, for processing conditions, and for generating text.

If XSLT is processed on the server in a programming environment, a suitable XSLT processor API[3] needs to be loaded. This solution allows the application logic to select or compose the XML input for the XSLT processor at runtime and to control the transformation process. Especially in multi-channel Web applications, the use of XSLT is a powerful means to provide suitable document formats for different delivery channels, starting from one and the same XML source.

The processing of XSLT on the client is typically achieved in two different ways: automatically by the *browser* or programmatically through *JavaScript*. The former solution is similar to the HTML/CSS approach and uses the XSLT template as a style sheet for the formatting of the XML document, as shown in the following code lines:

```
<?xml version="1.0"?>
<?xml-stylesheet type="text/xsl" href="template.xsl"?>
```

---

[3] There is a multitude of XSLT processors for each programming language. See, for example, *XT* (http://www.jclark.com/xml/xt.html), *Saxon* (http://saxon.sourceforge.net/), and *Xalan* (http://xml.apache.org/xalan-j/).

```
<ROOT>
...
<!-- Here goes the actual XML data to be formatted -->
...
</ROOT>
```

The second line of the above code shows how to instruct the browser to use an XSLT style sheet for the formatting of the XML content in the body of the XML document (in the example code above, the body is delimited by the `<ROOT>` element). Note the use of the mime type `text/xsl` for correctly referencing the style file.

Using JavaScript on the client for the formatting of XML documents requires accessing the browser's XSLT processor from the JavaScript code, loading the XML document to be formatted along with its XSLT file, and executing the respective transformation. The access to the browser's XSLT processor is provided by the browser in the form of a proper JavaScript object that can be instantiated. As this is a browser-specific task, the name of the object typically differs from browser to browser. In Firefox, for example, the `XSLTProcessor` object needs to be instantiated; in Internet Explorer the XSLT support is provided by the `MSXML` ActiveX object.

It is worth noting that XSLT processing on the fly for presentation purposes (on both the server and the client) is generally not an efficient solution. XSLT style sheets and XML documents in general are verbose, and their transformation requires a considerable amount of memory and processor time. For this reason, XSLT is typically used during the Web engineering process to perform model transformations or to generate HTML templates as described in the previous section and used less during the actual execution of an application.

7.1.3 Model-View-Controller Pattern

As outlined earlier in this chapter, the template-based approach to the implementation of the presentation layer provides an intuitive and efficient means for separating the concerns of Web developers and graphic designers. From a software engineering point of view, however, HTML templates like the ones in Figures 7.1 and 7.2 still suffer a few shortcomings [CFB+02]: For instance, the business logic part of a Web page is dispersed, in the sense that each single page contains its own logic, and changes or evolutions of the overall application logic typically impact several apparently independent templates. Page templates, in turn, have a tight coupling with data structures. In short, simple templating is not very scalable, in that each page is conceived in an isolated fashion, and reuse is not fostered.

These problems are not specific to Web applications only. They are general in nature and regard the modularization of applications. One of the most advanced answers by software engineering to this need for modularization is the so-called *Model-View-Controller* (MVC) design pattern, which is an architectural design pattern for the implementation of user interfaces that has particularly been conceived with scalability and separation of concerns in mind. Figure 7.4 exemplifies the MVC pattern adapted to Web applications:

- The *Model* contains the business logic of the application. Typically, the Model consists of a set of business actions that are designed for reuse and may be shared with other applications. The Model ignores how user requests are issued and how data are presented to the user.
- The *View* contains the user interface logic of the application (the HTML templates). An application may have multiple alternative Views to chose among. The View ignores the form of the user request and the source of the data.
- The *Controller* manages the user interactions and instantiates the Model and the View for the performed navigations or choices. The Controller completely ignores the nature of the business actions in the Model and the logic with which the View composes the presentation of the results.

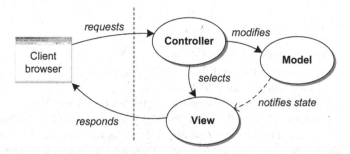

Fig. 7.4. The Model-View-Controller pattern adapted to Web applications

If a user issues a page request to the Web application, the request is intercepted by the Controller, which is in charge of deciding which business operation needs to be performed. The Controller, hence, invokes the respective component in the Model, which contains the necessary logic to execute the requested action, to update the state of the application, and to assemble the data to be presented to the user. The change of the application state activates the View, which fills the presentation template with the data computed by the Model. Finally, the so-constructed HTML response is sent to the client browser.

In the following Section 7.2.1, our overview of Web application frameworks will provide some more insights into the MVC design pattern in practice by discussing the Apache *Struts* framework, which is based on a Java implementation of the MVC pattern.

7.2 Web Application Frameworks and Engineering Tools

Implementing a Web application from scratch is a time-consuming and error-prone process. Typically, a developer will not start from scratch, but try to benefit from existing tools and frameworks to ease his job. In this section, we will examine two solutions from which a Web application developer may benifit: Web application frameworks and Web engineering tools. The former offer the developer additional abstractions, tools, and libraries to handle typical Web application issues (e.g., session management, templates libraries) and thus speed up the development process. The latter provide code generation starting from a design made by one of the Web engineering methods.

7.2.1 Web Application Frameworks

In this section, we shortly discuss Web application frameworks. Many of them exist, and discussing and comparing all of them would lead us much too far here. Therefore, we will discuss two illustrative and popular examples of current Web application frameworks: Apache Struts 2 and Ruby on Rails.

Apache Struts 2

Apache Struts is a Java-EE-based open-source Web application framework. It builds upon Java Servlets and JavaServer Pages (see Chapter 2), Sun Microsystems's server-side solution technologies.

Like many Web application frameworks, it applies the Model-View-Controller (MVC) (see Section 7.1.3) architectural design pattern to achieve a clean separation of concerns. The key purpose of the MVC is to separate the data (the model) from its presentation (the view). This allows changes to the model without required changes to the view, and vice versa. Communication and coordination between the model and the view is handled by the controller. Applied to Apache Struts, the model represents the underlying data, the view is the actual rendered page, and the controller handles HTTP requests, selects and invokes application logic, and performs page selection (i.e., handles navigation logic). For the controller, Apache Struts relies on servlet technology and provides a default servlet implementation for this purpose, while it suggests the use of JavaServer Pages for a template-based approach to the view (although other technology may be used). In addition to the view technology of choice, Apache Struts provides its own tag library providing additional expressibility. The code for the model itself is left to the developer. Some developers critique this lack; others embrace it, as it gives them complete freedom when implementing the model (which includes the use of existing frameworks).

Generally, requests by the user are handled in the following way:

1. Request: the user sends a request to the Web server. The controller intercepts the request, and invokes the action associated with the particular request.
2. Action: The action communicates with the model and performs the required functionality, or forwards the request to a specific handler. Apache Struts supports many default actions (e.g., file download), but also allows the developer to implement a particular required action. Actions may be chained in order to support a given logical sequence of actions or to implement a workflow. Before and after an action execution, one or more so-called interceptors may apply some additional logic on the request or result (e.g., validation of input or output).
3. Result: After an action completes, a result is responsible for communicating the outcome of the action to the user. Apache Struts provides many default result actions (e.g., redirection, HTTP header control, data streaming) and allows the developer to develop custom result actions. In a typical case, the result will cause a JSP file to be rendered.

Apache Struts furthermore provides support for various technologies, such as AJAX, SOAP, JavaScript, Velocity, XML and XSLT. Finally, we mention that Apache Struts is very flexible and extensible. It rigorously utilizes interfaces throughout the framework, allowing easy replacement of particular functionality or application logic by subclassing or replacing the existing classes. In the same vein, any missing functionality can be added to the framework.

Ruby on Rails

Ruby on Rails[4] is another popular open-source Web application framework. It is a combination of the compact yet expressive object-oriented programming language Ruby and the Web application framework Rails, suited to build Web Applications supported by a database back-end. Like Apache Struts, Ruby on Rails applies the Model-View-Controller architectural design pattern to obtain a clean separation of concerns. The view consists of simple templates which allow inserting separately prepared and/or computed data. The model consists of persistent domain objects made possible by an object-relational mapping framework (see Section 2.5.4). This framework handles reading from and writing to the database, while allowing the Web developer to handle and manipulate data in the form of higher-level domain objects, and implement business logic upon them. Finally, controller classes handle the user requests. Ruby on Rails thrives on simplicity and straight forward support for the Web developer. One technique made popular by Ruby on Rails is *scaffolding*, the practice of code generation for interfacing with a database. With a simple command and given a model element, it will generate all the necessary application code to create, read, update, and delete (so-called CRUD operations) entries

---

[4] http://www.rubyonrails.org/

in a particular database table (which adheres to the model element). Ruby on Rails also provides many helper scripts which allow the Web developer to generate most of the skeleton code for his Web application automatically. By using simple programming and naming conventions, Ruby on Rails prevents complex configuration files. Ruby on Rails is particularly appreciated for its extreme ease of use and its ability to quickly generate a running Web application. It furthermore supports advanced concepts and technologies, such as Web services, SOAP, AJAX, JavaScript, and many more through plug-ins and extensions (e.g., SWORD[5], a Ruby on Rails extension for the Semantic Web).

7.2.2 Web Engineering Tools

Most of the Web engineering methods described in this book rely on the Model-Driven Engineering paradigm, and thus provide some support to obtain a (partial) implementation from the instantiated models. This section describes two of the most mature Computer-Aided Web Engineering (CAWE) tools, namely WebRatio [Web07b] and VisualWade [Góm04], respectively supporting WebML and OO-H, and mentions some of the other approaches.

WebRatio Site Development Studio

Throughout Chapter 5 we described the visual modeling language for the development of data-intensive Web applications proposed by the Web Modeling Language (WebML) [SRB96]). The methodology and the modeling language are accompanied by a CAWE tool, called WebRatio Site Development Studio [Web07b], one of the most advanced tools in the area of Web engineering. With respect to the WebML development process introduced in Section 3.4.1, WebRatio covers the phases of data design and hypertext design, and supports the implementation by automating the production of the relational database and of the application page templates. More precisely, WebRatio provides support for five main development concerns:

- *Data design*: supports the design of Entity-Relationship data schemas with a graphical user interface for drawing and specifying the properties of entities, relationships, attributes, and generalization hierarchies.
- *Hypertext design*: it assists the design of site views, providing functions for drawing and specifying the properties of areas, pages, units, and links.
- *Data mapping*: permits declaring the set of data sources to which the conceptual data schema has to be mapped, and automatically translates Entity-Relationship diagrams and OCL expressions into relational databases and views.

---

[5] https://launchpad.net/sword

- *Presentation design*: offers functionality for defining the presentation style of the application, allowing the designer to create XSL style sheets and associate them with pages, and organize page layout by arranging the relative position of content units in the page.
- *Code generation*: automatically translates site views into running Web applications built on top of the Java2EE Struts platform.

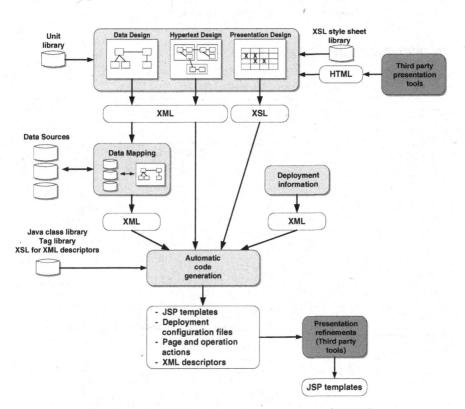

Fig. 7.5. The WebRatio development process [SRB96].

Figure 7.5 graphically summarizes the design flow of WebRatio, highlighting the design phases together with their inputs and outputs. Data design and hypertext design are encoded by means of a suitable XML representation; presentation design is encoded by means of XSL transformations, which are derived from a library of XSL style sheets and from application-specific HTML templates. Figure 7.6 shows a screen shot of WebRatio's graphical hypertext modeling environment, highlighting the consistent implementation of the WebML language; data and presentation design are performed in a similar, visual fashion. So-designed data schemas are automatically translated into suitable tables and views inside the data sources specified in the modeling environment for the data mapping. The specification of the necessary deployment settings finally allows the automatic generation of the running application, starting from the XML and XSL inputs, WebML's class library, a JSP tag library, and XSL transformations for the generation of XML descriptors. The descriptors allow the runtime instantiation of the individual WebML constructs (e.g., pages, units, links) based on the parameterized class library. Optionally, the generated JSP templates may be further refined for a fine-grained adjustment of presentation properties.

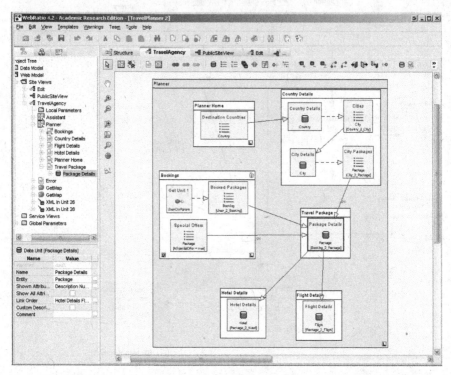

Fig. 7.6. WebML hypertext modeling in WebRatio Site Development Studio

Thanks to the automatic code generation feature, WebRatio can be used for fast prototyping, thus shortening the requirements validation cycle. Differently from traditional prototyping tools, which generate application mockups, the WebRatio code generator produces application modules running on a state-of-the-art architecture, and can be used for implementation, maintenance, and evolution. Code generation starts from the outputs of conceptual design and therefore implementation and maintenance benefit from the presence of a conceptual specification of the application.

WebRatio internally uses XML and XSL as the formats for encoding both the specifications and the code generators. XML and XSL are also the foundation for advanced CAWE features such as validity checking and automatic project documentation. The extensive use of XML and XSL facilitates custom extensions, which apply both to the WebML language, which can be extended with user-defined units and operations, and to the tool functions, which can be enriched with custom consistency checkers, documentation and code generators, and presentation rules.

VisualWade

OO-H is a Web engineering method and notation based on the object-oriented programming paradigm. The OO-H method has been applied in several small and large real-life cases in various application domains, and is accompanied by a CAWE tool called VisualWade[6] [Góm04].

The OO-H approach prescribes an iterative design process that consists of three phases:

- *Domain Modeling*: captures the domain of the target Web application. OO-H allows the reuse of an existing OO-based specification (i.e., a UML class diagram) of the domain, thereby facilitating providing a Web interface for an existing software system.
- *Navigation Modeling*: enhances the domain model with navigational and interaction aspects, which are captured in the so-called Navigation Access Diagram (NAD). Restrictions on navigation and information may be specified using the Object Constraint Language (OCL).
- *Presentation Modeling*: adds the necessary details for presentation, which are captured in the XML-based Abstract Presentation Diagram (APD). Older sources (and the VisualWade documentation) also mention the Composite Layout Diagram (CLD) to specify additional presentation details; but this model seems to have become obsolete.

VisualWade supports each of these design phases, providing a graphical user interface which allows the designer to construct each corresponding design diagram with all its particularities. More precisely, VisualWade provides the Web developer with the following functionality:

- *Domain Modeling*: VisualWade allows the creation of UML class diagrams in a point-and-click fashion. Basic class diagram ingredients (e.g., classes and attributes, relations, composition, inheritance, multiplicity) can be specified and combined in an intuitive manner to form a class diagram.
- *Navigation Modeling*: VisualWade allows the creation of NAD diagrams. All NAD ingredients may be specified, along with their properties. OCL constraints are supported through an integrated OCL parser which allows for validation of the given OCL formula. See also Figure 7.7 for a screenshot of a NAD diagram in VisualWade.

---

[6] See http://www.visualwade.com/

- *Presentation Modeling*: After compiling the NAD diagram, a set of XML pages is obtained corresponding to the modeled Web application. They contain a primitive user interface, which can be refined by the Web developer using VisualWade. Visual aspects such as location of elements, style, and color may be changed by the designer.
- *Code generation*: VisualWade applies a code generation approach to generate the actual Web Application, based on a (correct) design provided by the Web developer. VisualWade generates ready-to-be-deployed PHP code along with the necessary database scripts (SQL-code), and supports a variety of relational databases (e.g., MySQL, PostgreSQL, ORACLE).

VisualWade offers the Web developer usual editing and usability support, such as copy/paste, undo, and search facilities. Furthermore, the tool provides integrated Python support and some debugging and tracing facilities. Figure 7.7 shows a screenshot of the VisualWade CAWE tool, illustrating a NAD diagram.

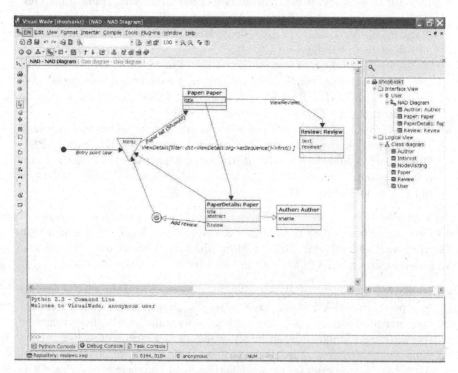

Fig. 7.7. VisualWade screenshot

Other Tools

Other less elaborated tools and code generation approaches have been described in the literature. We will shortly discuss them here.

Hera Presentation Generator

The Hera Presentation Generator (HPG) [FHB06] is an integrated development environment that supports model building and presentation generation for the Hera design methodology. It consists of model builders, supporting the creation of the main Hera models and two flavors of a presentation generation engine. HPG provides the Web designer with four different model builders in the form of Microsoft Visio stencils. Visio typically shows the available modeling elements on the left side of the screen, from where they can be dragged and dropped on the drawing area on the right. The Hera model builders are:

- *Conceptual Model (CM) builder*: allows the designer to model the data (or domain) of the Web application. In Hera, this is done in RDF(S); and subsequently the CM builder offers a graphical means to model RDF(S) data and their relevant properties.
- *Application Model (AM) builder*: allows the designer to model, using data from the CM, the actual application, i.e., how the information is grouped together and what the navigation is. Hera prescribes a custom-made graphical notation based on slices (for grouping), rounded rectangles (concepts), ellipses (attributes), and arrows (links).
- *Presentation Model (PM) builder*: allows the designer to model basic presentation by means of regions on top of the Application Model.
- *User Profile (UP) builder*: is a dedicated application (i.e., not a Visio stencil) that allows the definition and instantiation of a Composite Capability/Preference Profile (CC/PP) user profile.

Next to the model builders, the HPG provides two presentation generation engines. The most primitive presentation engine, HPG-XSLT, is XSLT-based. It takes as input a Conceptual Model, an Application Model, a Presentation Model, and a User Profile, and some input data (conforming to the CM) in the form of a CMI file. By means of a series of XSLT transformations and starting from the CM and the actual data, the models are step by step transformed to the (complete) final presentation in a suitable format (e.g., HTML, SMIL). Note that the Web application is thus generated as a whole. The second presentation generation engine, HPG-Java, is a more advanced engine based on Java. It is based on Java servlets (see Section 2.5.2) technology and uses transformations based on Jena[7] and RDF querying based on Sesame[8]. HPG-Java better exploits the RDF(S) semantics, allows the generation of a single page "on demand" and provides form support (all of these are lacking in

---

[7] http://jena.sourceforge.net/

[8] http://www.openrdf.org/

HPG-XSLT). For more information on all aspects of the Hera Presentation Generator, the interested reader is referred to [FHB06].

HyperDE

HyperDE [NS06] is an environment supporting the SHDM [LS03] design method. It is an extension of the Ruby on Rails framework[9], combined with the Sesame framework[10], which focuses on rapid prototyping and domain-specific language support in a model driven (Web) engineering approach. As most approaches, SHDM distinguishes a conceptual model (i.e. in the case of SHDM, this may be an existing ontology), a navigational view (defining the navigation through the hypermedia structure) and an interface specification. HyperDE stores all these models as RDF data, and supports editing of the models through Web-based interfaces. HyperDE allows to exploit the expressive power of SeRQL, Sesame's query language, to specify complex queries to retrieve particular data. However, the approach also offers the designer a simple domain specific language, which allows him to specify simple data access queries in a simplified way. When specifying an SHDM in this way, HyperDE benefits from Ruby on Rails' usual prototyping abilities to obtain a running Web application. For more details, the interested reader is referred to [NS06].

ArgoUWE

ArgoUWE[11] is a CAWE tool developed to support the UML-based Web engineering (UWE) methodology. UWE is defined as an extension of the UML meta-model, using UML's extension mechanisms in the form of a UML profile to define Web-specific modeling elements if needed. By adhering to UML, UWE allows the use of existing UML CASE-tools. ArgoUWE is defined as an extension of ArgoUML,[12] an open-source UML modeling tool supporting all UML diagrams. ArgoUWE provides modeling support for its main models: process, navigation, presentation, and adaptation models. It furthermore allows us to partly derive one model from another model (more on model transformations in Section 7.2.3). ArgoUWE does not support code generation; yet it is part of the OpenUWE environment, which does include a code generation tool called UWEXML. This tool provides semi automatic code generation for deployment in the Cocoon publishing framework. Interested readers are referred to [KKZH04, KKZ05] for more details on ArgoUWE and UWEXML.

7.2.3 Model-driven Engineering and Model Transformation

All Web engineering methods described in this book, and most found in literature, rely to a large extend on the model-driven paradigm. In model-driven

---

[9] http://www.rubyonrails.org/

[10] http://www.openrdf.org/

[11] http://www.pst.informatik.uni-muenchen.de/projekte/uwe/argouwe.shtml

[12] http://argouml.tigris.org/

engineering, model transformations are of particular importance, as they allow to (partly) automatically transform one model into another, thus assisting the Web engineer in obtaining (part of) design models to be designed out of existing models. In the ideal case, these transformations are fully automated, requiring no additional effort from the Web engineer. Examples of such transformations include the code generation transformation pipelines described in in WSDM [PCY+05] or in Hera-XSLT (see Section 7.2.2). However, in many cases, a fully automatic transformation is not possible. They require human decisions during the transformation (e.g., to select one alternative in case of a non-deterministic mapping), and in worst case need to be performed completely manually. In some cases, model transformations produce only a partial target model. These are useful when generating skeleton models or code, which subsequently need to be completed by the designer. Examples of such incompletely generated models are the derivation of the skeleton navigational model starting from the audience classification (see Section 3.4.2), or the implementation skeleton generation in the OOH4RIA approach [MGPD08].

To implement the transformation, different possibilities exist. First of all, the transformations may be written in an ad hoc manner, using any scripting or programming language (Java, C++, PHP, etc) and thus wielding their full power. However, the transformation logic needs to be fully implemented by the programmer and the transformations are not re-usable. Another possibility is the use of a transformation language (e.g., XSLT), which is specifically designed to transform a (formal) input to a target output, or model transformation languages and tools (e.g., ATLAS Transformation Language ATL, Query/View/Transformation), specifically designed to perform model transformations. Transformation languages and model transformation languages give the designer explicit support for specifying the transformations, thus allowing him to focus on the transformations at hand as opposed to implementing the transformation logic itself.

As in Section 5.8, we illustrate the transformational aspect of model-driven engineering in the context of OMG's Model-Driven Architecture using UWE, a Web design method strictly adhering to OMG's MDA proposal. As a short recap, UWE defines different CIM, PIM and PSM level models: Web requirements models to describe the requirements (CIM level), process models to describe the processes or functionality, content models to describe the content, navigation models to describe navigation, presentation models to describe presentational aspects, and architecture models to describe architectural details (PIM level). The latter models are commonly called functional models. A big picture model integrates the different functional models, and the integrated model integrates the big picture model and the architectural models (both PIM level models). Finally, from these models, the PSM models, containing an actual implementation, can be derived. See Section 5.8 for details.

Transformations in UWE are classified into three categories [Koc06, Koc07]:

1. *Transformations generating the functional models*: map the requirements captured in the WebRE compatible requirements model (CIM level) to the UWE functional models (PIM level). To do so, CIM-to-PIM model transformations are defined between the WebRE meta-model and the UWE meta-model [CK06]. Several such transformations are needed (i.e. targeting content, navigation, architecture, presentation). Furthermore, PIM-to-PIM refinement transformations are defined between content and navigation models, navigation and presentation models and between presentation and presentation models. The latter indicates the fact that these models cannot be obtained in a single pass.

2. *Transformations generating the big picture and integrated models*: in order to facilitate the subsequent transformations, a PIM-to-PIM graph-transformation is defined to integrate the different functional models into the big picture model. It also allows model checking taking into account the different aspects of the Web application. To obtain the integrated model, UWE defines transformation rules between the MOF compliant WebSA and UWE meta-models [MKK05].

3. *Transformations generating the final implementation(s)*: literature describes two main approaches to generate the final implementation(s) [Koc07]. One consists of transforming the functional model to the target implementation (PIM-to-PSM), encoding the architectural details in the transformations. The second consists of transforming the integrated model, containing architectural details, to a final implementation (PIM-to-PSM).

UWE's rigorous use of OMG standards, UML and MOF, allows it to also use OMG standards for model transformations: QVT. Nevertheless, most of the above transformations are implemented using a general purpose programming language (Java), graph transformations and model transformation languages and tools (ATL). Some of these transformations need human intervention (e.g., in the content model, content elements need to be "marked" for their navigational relevance before transformation to a navigational model is possible), and some are performed manually (e.g., adding architectural details).

7.3 Deployment and Installation

After the design and the implementation of a Web application (which is typically done on a proper test Web server), there are still some decisions that need to be made in order to go online with the developed Web application. For instance, the most important decisions regard the selection of a suitable Web server (in terms of software), on which the application will be running, and the selection of a suitable configuration for the operation of the chosen Web server (in terms of hardware, connectivity, and cost).

Depending on choices that need to be made during the implementation phase (e.g., the adopted programming language, Web application framework, or Web engineering tool), their degrees of freedom typically differ: Web engineering tools, for instance, may make choices on behalf of their users regarding the programming language, the implementation architecture, and/or the Web server, thus limiting developers in freely choosing their own configurations; free, unassisted implementations, on the other hand, leave all doors open, and developers may choose their preferred deployment architecture without any restrictions. The following discussion will concentrate on the latter case, where the developer is required to autonomously exercise the final choices.

7.3.1 Choosing a Web Server

Generally, the term *Web server* has two different flavors: on the one hand, we can use the term to refer to the *hardware* device (i.e., the physical computer) on which a Web application runs and, on the other hand, we can use the term to refer to the *software* product that is responsible for accepting and serving HTTP requests. In this subsection, we concentrate on the software aspect of the term *Web server* and only slightly hint at some hardware aspects in the next subsection.

Why do we need to choose between different Web server products? The answer to this question is actually quite straight forward: because there are different products on the market which differ in the features they support, the operating systems they rely on, their cost, etc. Fortunately, however, choosing a suitable Web server is not a difficult task, because the market of Web server products is dominated by only a few big players, as shown in Figure 7.8.

The figure shows Netcraft's[13] February 2009 overview of the market shares of Web servers: According to the survey, the currently most used Web server software on the Web is *Apache*,[14] followed by Microsoft's *Internet Information Services* (IIS[15]); then, there are the *Google Web Server*, which has been steadily gaining market shares over the last years, the *Sun* Web servers, and the recently emerged *nginx* (pronounced "engine X"), an open-source Web server that is designed and optimized for high performance. The NCSA HTTPd Web server, also depicted in Figure 7.8, was one of the earliest Web servers that followed Tim Berners-Lee's ideas; the project, however, was suspended in 1998, and is reported in the figure for historical reasons. Under the label *Others* the figure summarizes the market shares of several dozens of Web server products with minor support.

---

[13] Netcraft is a UK-based Internet service company that, among other services, provides monthly free surveys about several aspects of the Internet. The cited Web server survey can be found at `http://news.netcraft.com/archives/web_server_survey.html`.

[14] `http://www.apache.org/`

[15] `http://www.microsoft.com/WindowsServer2003/iis/default.mspx`

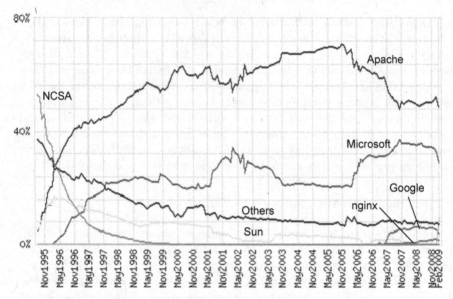

Fig. 7.8. Web server survey by Netcraft Ltd. The diagram reflects the Web server usage shares as of February 2009 [Net09].

The selection of a suitable Web server software for a Web application is driven by two major choices: the *programming language* that is being used for the implementation of the dynamic features of the application and the privileged *operating system*. While the former represents a hard requirement, the choice of the operating system has been losing importance over the last few years: if only a few years ago Unix/Linux machines were the preferred choice of most Web developers – the choice was mainly based on security and efficiency considerations – today Microsoft's Windows systems are being equally considered.

The programming language represents a hard requirement, as it is typically chosen at the beginning of the implementation phase and has implications on other design decisions such as communication styles or software architectures. Typically, no Web server provides native support for more than one (server side) programming language. Hence, the Web server needs to be chosen for the adopted programming language. For instance, Apache-Tomcat[16] provides native support for JSP and Java servlets, and IIS provides native support for ASP.NET. If an application is programmed in one of these languages, one of the mentioned Web servers may already be the right choice.

But increasingly Web applications are also programmed in languages like PHP, Perl, and Python for which there is typically no built-in support available. In such cases, the Web servers' *extension mechanisms* need to be taken into account when selecting a Web server. PHP and Perl, for example, can

---

[16] http://tomcat.apache.org/

easily be integrated into Apache by enabling suitable modules and by setting proper configuration parameters. If no predefined extension mechanisms for individual languages are provided, then a developer needs to look for the support of *CGI/FastCGI* provided by the Web servers and to check whether his preferred programming language can be supported in this way. CGI/FastCGI allow the Web server to pass incoming requests to an external application (i.e., the interpreter of the scripting or programming language) in a very flexible fashion. Although the performance of CGI/FastCGI is typically lower than that of built-in language support, oftentimes it represents the only feasible solution to enable the interpretation of the chosen language.

For more details on the Web server products on the market, the interested reader can consult the entry "Comparison of Web server software" in Wikipedia,[17] which provides a comprehensive overview of Web server software currently in use and, for each of the products, also shows which of the main features are supported.

7.3.2 Hosting, Housing, or Own Web Server?

Once a suitable Web server software has been chosen, a decision regarding the operation of the physical Web server needs to be taken. As in several other business situations, a Web server may be operated *in-house*, meaning that the operation and maintenance of the physical server and its connection to the Web is done internally, or the server may be *outsourced*, meaning that an external service provider is entrusted with the management of the server. The outsourced management of a Web server (i.e., the agreement or service contract between the customer and the service provider) may be of two kinds, i.e., hosting and housing, which leads us to the distinction of the following three ways of operation of a Web server:

- *Hosting:* Hosting a Web application means that the service provider who operates the physical Web server provides the customer with an agreed-upon combination of disk space, computing power, connectivity quality, and Web server software on a server that is shared among several customers. The consideration behind this form of contract is that there are Web applications that do not require high bandwidth or high computing power and that one Web server can easily be shared by several Web applications running on the same server without significant slowdowns. Hosting is typically a cost-effective solution. It does not require any specific server operation knowledge from the customer, and it is usually the preferred solution for smaller Web applications, such as personal home pages or smaller business applications.
- *Housing:* Housing is very similar to hosting, but the main difference is that in the case of a housing contract the customer has at his disposal a

---

[17] http://en.wikipedia.org/wiki/Comparison_of_web_server_software

whole server on his/her own. The service provider is in charge of operating and maintaining the physical server and of guaranteeing the agreed on connectivity quality. Depending on the provider, either a customer rents one of the provider's servers, or the customer may also be allowed to connect an own server to the provider's network infrastructure. Usually, both housing and hosting contracts also include periodical backups of the contracted Web space.

Housing, of course, implies higher costs than hosting, as the provider is no longer able to share the housed Web server among different customers. Again, there is no special knowledge required from customers, as long as the customer does not explicitly ask for managing the server on his own. This form of contract is suited to the case of bigger Web applications with a high number of accesses or high requirements in terms of computation power required for the execution of the application.

- *Own Web server:* Finally, there is always the possibility to operate the physical Web server in-house. In this case, the whole control of the Web server is kept in the company or institution that wants to run the Web application. This solution guarantees the highest control over the server to developers and administrators, but also requires the availability of personnel with the necessary expertise.

  Hence, the cost-effectiveness of operating an own in-house Web server depends on the expertise available. Own Web servers are typically adopted in those situations where the Web application must handle highly sensitive or confidential data and outsourcing may be dangerous for the business of the company or institution, or in situations where the Web application is seamlessly integrated with the company's or institution's information system to feed and fetch operative data.

7.3.3 Registering a Domain Name

From the moment a Web server is physically connected to the Web and a Web server software is running on the server, resources published on the server are immediately available for access through suitable HTTP client devices, such as a Web browser. In order to access resources on the server, however, the user still needs to know the exact IP address of the Web server, because we did not register a suitable *domain name* for our server.

For instance, if we would like to load the home page of the Politecnico di Milano into our preferred Web browser, we would have to use the IP address 131.175.12.34. Hence, the URL to be used would be `http://131.175.12.34`. If, instead, we want to use a more expressive (and typically human-understandable) URL, we have to register the respective domain name with a so-called DNS *registry*, which associates domain names with physical IP addresses for easier retrieval. Only now we can access the Politecnico di Milano home page via the address `http://www.polimi.it`.

The registration of a domain name is usually done by contacting a so-called *registrar*, which is an institution or a company that acts as mediator between the actual *registry* and the *registrant* or *domain holder*. Depending on the kind of top-level domain (e.g., country code top-level domains such as .it or .be, or generic top-level domains such as .gov or .com), different registries are in charge of managing the respective entries. Hence, to check whether the preferred URL for our Web application is still available – domain names are assigned with a first-come-first-served policy –, we can check the respective registry.[18] If the chosen domain name (e.g., myserver.org) is still available, it can be "acquired" by paying an annual fee to the registrar, which is in charge of publishing the new domain name. Typically, after 24 to 48 hours our Web server is accessible online through the new name.

7.3.4 Deploying a Web Application

In order for a developed Web application to be accessible over the Web, it needs to be *deployed*, that is, the application needs to be installed (i.e., copied and properly configured) on an online Web server.

Independently of whether the operation of the Web server is outsourced or not, the deployment of a Web site or application is usually done via (S)FTP upload of the actual program and HTML files and, possibly, through proper administration panels, e.g., for the configuration of the database. For this purpose, when setting up the HTTP server software, the server is typically also equipped with an (S)FTP server (e.g., reachable via ftp.myserver.org), and suitable access rights are granted to the application developers and administrators in form of (S)FTP access credentials. By means of those credentials, developers and administrators are enabled to upload the Web application, to set access rights over individual directories, and to configure some application-specific Web server configuration parameters. The Web application is online.

The deployment of the application may be performed by means of dedicated (S)FTP clients. However, modern Web design instruments (e.g., Macromedia/Adobe's Dreamweaver) can be configured with the necessary access information so as to support the easy deployment of single files or of the whole application via its (user-friendly) graphical user interface. Typically, such instruments also support advanced synchronization mechanisms that relieve developers from tracking which files need updating and which do not.

7.4 Maintenance and Evolution

Only with the deployment of the final application does the life of a Web application start. It is important to note that, during its life, a Web application,

---

[18] Domain name registries are also called *Network Information Centers* (NICs); they are typically accessible to the public through their Web sites.

like any other application, is not just a static piece of code and that its operation typically requires further maintenance and evolution. Indeed, after deployment, Web applications often undergo some form of *change*. In a study published in 2000 [CGM00], around 720.000 pages of 270 popular Web sites (including http://www.yahoo.com/ and http://www.microsoft.com/) were crawled daily for a bit more than four months. In this study, Cho et al. found that over 20% of all pages changed at least once daily. For some domains, such as the .com domain, more than 40% of the pages changed at least once daily. In a follow-up experiment, Fetterly et al. [FMNW04] studied over 150.000.000 Web pages weekly for 11 weeks. Their observations show that 34.8% of all pages that remained reachable over these 11 weeks underwent one or more changes (over 11 weeks).

These results clearly show that Web application maintenance and evolution are important aspects to consider in Web engineering. Maintenance and evolution do not have a universally accepted definition (see [CHK⁺01] for several definitions and a discussion), and sometimes they are even used as synonyms. Ghezzi et al. [GJM02], for instance, only talk about corrective, adaptive, and perfective maintenance. In this book, we interpret *maintenance* as the modification or change activity that is necessary to correctly operate an existing (Web) application without altering its characteristics. *Evolution* on the other hand is the (continuous) change process a (Web) application undergoes, from deployment to dismissal, which may include altering the characteristics of the application (e.g., by adding new features). The exact borders between the two activities cannot always be clearly identified. Often, evolution is caused by maintenance activities, but it can also be caused by other factors, as we will see further on.

As can be observed from the previous definitions, the common factor between maintenance and evolution is *change*. In this section, we therefore discuss the main reasons for change required in Web applications, discuss how maintenance and evolution address such demands, and discuss the role of Web engineering methods and industry solutions in the context of change.

7.4.1 Maintenance of Web Applications

The focus of Web applications, as opposed to regular software applications, lies primarily on content and navigation (and to a lesser extent, presentation).

A Web application is typically highly *content-intensive*, where content is often delivered by a different person or instance than the actual development team deploying the Web application. Content providers may be external entities (e.g., a news feed), individuals (e.g., a researcher providing his home page within the Web site of a university), or, in the case of Web 2.0, the *user* himself. In most cases, a generic Web application is deployed by a development team, with the possibility for individual users to provide some content. In some cases, Web applications are even deployed without any a priori content (e.g., think of Wikipedia). These individual content providers are often not skilled programmers or experts and, as such, are liable to introduce errors, both in content (e.g., inappropriate, incorrect, or repeated content), navigation (e.g., invalid links), and presentation (e.g., conflicting style).

An important part of the maintenance activity for Web applications is thus spent on these particular issues. As an answer to the aforementioned problems that might arise, the role of the so-called *webmaster* has emerged. The webmaster is responsible for taking care of the described deficiencies and of assuring that the contents are always accessible and available, that navigation is correct, and that consistent presentation is preserved, i.e., the webmaster maintains the Web application. In particular, the following maintenance activities are the responsibility of the webmaster:

- Users who want to contribute their own content or update or change formerly published content oftentimes do not fully respect (or even know about) an application's *style* and *formatting guidelines* (e.g., in the case of blogs and wiki's). An alignment with the application's conventions is thus necessary.
- Users may introduce inappropriate content (e.g., spam, malicious code), not desirable by the intended users of the Web application. Manual editing might be necessary to avoid such inappropriate content.
- One of the fundamental characteristics of the Web is its ability to easily link resources distributed over the network, without the need for any control over the link by the linked resources. *Links* are what make the text on the Web hypertext. The lack of a proper control of hyperlinks, especially in user-provided content, oftentimes results in what are commonly called "broken" links, i.e., links whose destinations do not exist any longer or which are simply mistyped. Maintaining an application's hyperlink navigation structure (e.g., repairing incorrect linking and connecting unreachable pages) is fundamental for the functionality of Web applications.
- The described lack of control over the resources pointed at by a link also implies that if linked contents change, it is not guaranteed that their meaning is still consistent with the reason to add the link to a page in the first place. Guaranteeing *consistency* with changing external sources (e.g., a referenced ontology or a linked newspaper) is important for the overall correctness of the contents published by an application.

Besides maintenance activities resulting from the particular content- and navigation-based nature of Web applications, and the special role for individual users as content providers for the application, maintenance activities similar to those for regular software applications also need to be performed. This mainly comprises fixing bugs, such as invalid HTML code or programming bugs in scripts. Web applications are particularly more vulnerable to code becoming invalid, due to their dependence on third-party software. Web applications run on a Web server, which might be updated, possibly causing problems for the Web applications (e.g., by deprecating certain functionality). Any updated extensions or libraries for the Web server may cause similar problems. Also, software updates on the client side may cause problems. In particular, new or updated browser software may cause various problems (e.g., different page rendering, changed support for scripting languages). In all of these cases the Web application requires maintenance to compensate for these changed conditions.

7.4.2 Evolution of Web Applications

While the maintenance activity mostly focuses on the minor changes and updates of a Web application due to various reasons, evolution refers to all kinds of changes the application may undergo over time. As already mentioned, this includes maintenance changes, but may go beyond these smaller changes. Major Web application updates, such as those adding new application features or changing and improving existing application logic, are also part of evolution.[19] In many cases, the already existing, underlying contents are not touched, but rather the Web application as a whole is updated. In this section, we will focus on this kind of evolution.

Evolving an application means taking into account new requirements posed by the user and/or new wishes by any of the application's stakeholders. The required changes are realized by starting anew a part of or the complete development process in order to design, implement, test, and evaluate the evolved application. This corresponds to what we called the "evolution cycle" when discussing the online evolution model in Chapter 3. Note that the whole development process does not necessarily need to be undertaken. For example, when the stakeholder decides a new look and feel might be desirable, it might be sufficient to only iterate the presentation design, keeping the rest of the design intact.

We have discussed that in the case of Web applications we have a special role, the Webmaster, responsible for the daily maintenance of the application. There is no such role for evolution. Evolution is done by *developers* who understand the code of an existing application and are able to implement the required new solutions consistently with the existing application.

Typical reasons for new or changing requirements, giving rise to evolution, include:

- *Inadequacy of developed solutions*: only with the real use of an application does it become clear whether the initially collected requirements have been met by the implementation of the application and whether the collected requirements really expressed the actual needs of the users. Often, only the

---

[19] As already mentioned, standard definitions for maintenance and evolution are missing. It is worth noting that in literature, some authors consider only these major application updates as evolution. This is not the view taken in this book.

real use of the application raises the need to change implemented solutions and allows developers to counterbalance such kinds of shortcomings.

- *Change of business practices*: the business practices of the audience of an application may change over time, e.g., due to new knowledge, practices, business processes, management approaches, and so on. Adequately taking into account such changes typically also demands a restructuring of the application in order for the application not to become obsolete.
- *Adoption of new technologies*: the Web is a continuously evolving and changing environment, where new trends and technologies may drive user interests and, hence, the market (think of the current trend toward Web 2.0 technologies; in Chapter 9 we provide a few respective details). Adapting an application to new technologies is generally not an easy task and typically also demands for a restructuring of the application's source code.
- *Refurbishing* the Web application for business or commercial reasons: often, a Web application's look and feel is updated simply because the stakeholders demand so. This could be due to commercial reasons (e.g., adhere to a more fashionable design) or imposed by the overall organization policy (e.g., a new company style guide needs to be followed). Such refurbishment is often restricted to purely presentational issues, but in principle could also include structural and navigational updates.
- *Improving the source code*: in order to facilitate the implementation of future changes or to assure the future scalability of an application, it is good to apply preventive measures that aim at augmenting the readability and maintainability of the source code. A typical situation is the reimplementation of an application from its initial prototype to a running production system.
- *Interoperability*: the integration of a Web application with external applications, providing new or alternative application features and augmenting one's own application's productivity, is becoming more and more important on the modern Web. As an example, think about the integration of the applications used by the different actors in a typical supply chain scenario, where a supplier may be interested in interoperating with a customer's application in order to establish a privileged communication channel and to access up-to-date order data.

Of course, there are a multitude of other reasons that result in new or changing application requirements, but the above list provides an overview of the most common situations that demand evolution in Web engineering. Very likely, the above list will also be subject to evolution over time.

7.5 The Role of Model-Driven Design and Industry Solutions

In the previous chapter we have seen that all of the most prominent model-driven Web engineering methods (see [GCG05, BKKZ05, VFHB03, CTB03,

CDF06]) come with mature design support for change in Web applications. However, change as a design concern addresses features like personalization, adaptation, and context-awareness; it does not address change in the sense of maintenance or evolution. So what role do model-driven development practices play when it comes to maintenance and evolution?

There are very few scientific investigations of the effective impact of model-driven development techniques on the two activities [ABB+07, GRD07]. However, among the arguments most commonly brought forward in favor of model-driven design techniques are "ease of maintenance", and "fast evolution cycles." The commonly accepted claim is that the adoption of model-driven design techniques in the development of a Web application implicitly also enhances the maintainability and evolvability of the application.

Let us consider what it means to evolve an existing model-driven Web application. Since in the most advanced model-driven Web engineering methods the actual application code is generated from the application's conceptual design models, coping with change of any kind is done directly on the models themselves (where possible). Subsequently, once the necessary changes have been applied to the design models, the complete Web application is regenerated and deployed for use. As already hinted at earlier in this section, the described process starts again from requirements analysis, passes then on to the design, implementation, and test and validation phases, and finally releases the evolved application to the public. Ideally, everything is done at the model or conceptual level.

Figure 7.9 describes the maintenance and evolution performance that has been obtained with the WebRatio CAWE tool for WebML in the development of a real enterprise-class eBusiness solution, the European Web site of Acer EMEA, the fourth branded PC vendor worldwide [ABB+07]. In the time interval from 2001 to 2005, the number of applications maintained with the help of the WebRatio tool has been growing from 17 to 31 applications, eventually serving 56 different countries and over ten million visits per month. But what is more interesting is the number of developers involved in the maintenance and evolution of such applications: initially four, then five. After an initial training period of about four to six months, developers have proved to reach their full productivity and to be able to master more then ten fully operational, complex, and distributed Web applications each. If we consider that within conventional Web development methods more than 60% of the total life cycle cost of an application can be ascribed to maintenance and evolution ([ABB+07]), model-driven development proves to be a viable and cost-effective means.

These data describe an impressive performance of a model-driven development method. However, in general, little attention has been paid to coping specifically with maintenance and evolution issues in existing Web engineering methods. At the time of writing, this is definitely an area for future research, and we are convinced that there is still room for improvement.

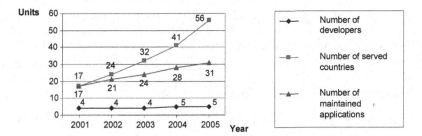

Fig. 7.9. Evolution of manpower versus number of maintained applications and served countries in the Acer EMEA WebRatio project [ABB+07].

It is worth noting that, regarding evolution in particular, in general it is good practice in both conventional and model-driven development practices to rely on dedicated versioning systems for the consistent maintenance of a typically shared code or model base. Such systems provide teams of developers with automated support for the storing and retrieval of the latest versions of development artifacts, the ability to split the code/model base into parallel branches, and to track the history of applied changes in order to support undo or compensation operations.

7.6 Summary

In this chapter, we discussed the further stages in Web development process once the application has been designed: implementation, deployment, maintenance and evolution.

First, we elaborated on the possibilities to realize a Web application, starting from a design as described in the previous chapters of this book. We discussed how the technologies discussed in Chapter 2 can be applied to implement the presentation layer of a Web application. Three important mechanisms were highlighted:

- *Template-based layout*: the Web developer designs templates which are run server-side in response of a client-side request. Templates typically combine static HTML code with application code, which dynamically computes part of the result page. Both parts may be interwoven, or separated depending on the technology of choice.
- *XSLT at runtime*: in case the data is available in XML format, the Web developer may choose the XSLT approach, transforming the XML data source in an appropriate output format. This approach is conceptually similar to the template-based approach, with the main different that the XSLT transformations can be run on the server or on the client.
- *Model-View-Controller*: in this approach, stemming from software engineering, the programming logic on server-side is separated in three components: the model, the view and the controller. Client requests are captured

by a controller. Depending on the particular request, (part of) the model is updated and an appropriate view is selected. The view is responsible for generating the presentation and communicating it to the client in the form of a Web page. The Model-View-Controller approach is more scalable than then previous approaches, and advocates a separation of concerns typically lacking in the previous two approaches.

Next, we focused on the different framework and tools available to Web developers. We discussed Web application frameworks, which provide the developer with support for recurring Web application functionality and typically apply the Model-View-Controller paradigm. We continued by discussing the most popular Web engineering tools. These tools provide dedicated support to transform a Web design made in one particular Web engineering method into a final implementation. We covered the tools supporting the WebML, OO-H, Hera, SHDM methods. Due to its particular popularity in Web engineering, we also elaborated on transformation-based approaches, typical for model-driven approaches. This was illustrated using the UWE method.

Continuing our coverage of the final stages of the Web development process, we pointed out different issues to be taken into account when deploying the Web application: choice of Web server, hosting and registering a domain name.

Finally, in the last section of this chapter we discussed maintenance and evolution, two aspect of Web applications where change plays a central role. If we recall the design for change discussed in Chapter 6, we can identify the following four types of change along with their main actors:

- *Personalization*: typically, the *user* is enabled to tailor an application to his own needs and to customize specific aspects of an application, such as graphical skins or the arrangement of content on his home page.
- *Adaptation*: the *application* itself autonomously enacts adaptations in order to proactively adapt the application, e.g., to changing context conditions of device properties.
- *Maintenance*: the *Webmaster* performs corrective changes, striving to provide a bug-free implementation and guaranteeing consistency of content, navigation and presentation.
- *Evolution*: denotes the overall process of change, from deployment to retirement, performed on the Web application. Typically, evolution includes smaller changes (caused by maintenance) and more fundamental changes made to the application in order to support new or changing application, user, or stakeholder requirements.

The first two (personalization and adaptation) are concerns that are limited to the design activity; the latter two (maintenance and evolution) are continuous activities that aim at assuring the long-term success and survival of an application.

7.7 Further Readings

Most Web application frameworks provide online documentation, reference guides, API's and tutorials. See for example the documentation sections on `http://www.rubyonrails.org/` (for Ruby on Rails) and `http://struts.apache.org/` for Apache Struts. Additionally, there are many books that explain how to work with any particular Web application framework. Recent editions that received excellent user reviews include [THB+06] for Ruby on Rails and [BDS08] for Apache Struts 2.

Unfortunately, there is few additional information on the existing Web engineering tools besides the work that was already referenced in their relative sections. We advise authors to look for up-to-date information on the Web sites of the respective Web engineering methods.

The ultimate source of relevant information on the Model Driven Architecture is OMG's dedicated site `http://www.omg.org/mda/`. It contains a FAQ, presentations, papers and specifications. Over recent years, several books have been dedicated on the subject as well (e.g., [MB02]), yet none of them specifically targets the model-driven development of Web applications.

Good sources for recent work on software maintenance in general are the European Conference on Software Maintenance and Re-engineering (CSMR) and the IEEE International Conference on Software Maintenance (ICSM) proceedings. Although both conferences are targeting software maintenance in general, they have also published work that is relevant for the Web. The authors are not aware of any books specifically targeting Web site evolution. A good source of recent information however is the IEEE International Symposium on Web Site Evolution (WSE).

8

Quality Assessment

Quality is a relevant factor for the success of Web applications. In the last few years, it has received great attention, being recognized as a fundamental property for acceptability by users of Web applications. Defining methods for assessing quality is therefore one of the goals of Web engineering research. Also, much attention to quality is paid by the industry: some studies and best practices have in fact demonstrated that adopting methods for quality assessment during the whole development process enables cost saving, with a high cost-benefit ratio, since they reduce the need for changes after application delivery [Mad99, NL93, JBR99, Con02, LC02].

In order to achieve high-quality applications, it is necessary to address quality issues explicitly, by adopting appropriate techniques spanning the entire application life cycle [JBR99, Con02]. The practice of adopting quality assessment methods at any stage of the development process, by evaluating quality of incremental design artifacts, as well as of the final product, is therefore increasingly receiving consensus. This has resulted in the proposal of the so-called *iterative design* [Som96, Con02]. With respect to more traditional models suggesting a top-down, analytic approach (as, for example, the traditional waterfall model), iterative design proposes the development process be complemented by a bottom-up, synthetic approach, in which the requirements, the design, and the product gradually evolve, becoming well defined step by step. The essence of iterative design is that the only way to ensure the effectiveness of some design decisions is to build and evaluate them, through the use of application prototypes. The application design can be then modified to correct any false assumptions detected during evaluation, or to accommodate newly emerged requirements; the cycle of design, evaluation, and redesign must be repeated as often as necessary.

Quality assessment is central in this model, relevant at all the stages in the life cycle, not only at the end of product development. All the aspects of application development, related to both functional and non-functional requirements, are in fact subject to constant assessment involving both expert evaluators and users.

S. Casteleyn et al., *Engineering Web Applications*, Data-Centric Systems and Applications,
DOI: 10.1007/978-3-540-92201-8_8, © Springer-Verlag Berlin Heidelberg 2009

It is possible to recognize two main classes of activities aimed at assessing different quality dimensions:

- *Testing*: has the goal of discovering code and architectural *failures*, by running the Web application using several combinations of inputs and states. Failures may be related to application behavior (i.e., functionality), as well as to application response in some specific workload conditions (i.e., performance). This chapter will discuss *functional testing* and *performance testing*, two relevant and largely adopted testing activities.
- *Usability evaluation*: intended as an extension of testing, is carried out to verify the application design against user needs and requirements. Since Web applications have a highly interactive nature, and their success greatly depends on users' satisfaction, usability is gaining large consensus. This chapter will therefore illustrate the notion of usability and its related evaluation methods.

This chapter will discuss the quality of Web applications, starting from the assumption that quality can be effectively achieved only if (i) a *quality model* identifying the entities of the evaluation and (ii) a set of *techniques* to measure such entities are identified [FP97]. The chapter will therefore start by introducing the dimensions that commonly characterize the quality of Web applications (i.e., candidate entities of evaluation) as a guide to the selection of quality attributes that can be the object of quality assessment. It will then illustrate the most largely adopted techniques for assessing such dimensions. Automatic tools supporting quality assessment activities will be also shortly illustrated.

8.1 The Need for Quality Models

A relevant contribution to the definition of quality comes from some ISO/IEC standards, focusing on the quality of software systems as well as on the evaluation process supporting quality assessment.

The standard ISO 8402-86 [ISO86] defines quality as the "totality of features and characteristics of a software product that relate to its ability to satisfy stated or implied needs." More concretely, the standard ISO/IEC 9126-1 [ISO01] defines quality as the combination of six characteristics that represent the attributes of a software product by which its quality can be described and evaluated:

- *Functionality*: focusing on the provision of correct and adequate functions.
- *Reliability*: referring to the application's capability of ensuring a given level of performance.
- *Usability*: related to the ease of use by end users.
- *Efficiency*: related to the ratio of the performance achieved by the system to the number of used resources.

- *Maintainability*: focusing on the ease of modification of the software, even after its deployment in the usage environment.
- *Portability*: related to those properties that enable an application to be correctly run in different execution environments.

Table 8.1 reports the definition of the six attributes as proposed by the standard. With the goal of facilitating quality assessment, and making it more systematic and less subjective, for each characteristic the standard also specifies a set of finer-grained sub-characteristics (see Figure 8.1). Finally, the standard proposes some *quality metrics*, i.e., quantitative scales and assessment methods, that can be used to quantify each sub characteristic [ISO02a, ISO02b, ISO02c].

Table 8.1. Quality characteristic definitions in the ISO/IEC 9126 standard [ISO01]

Characteristic	Definition
Functionality	A set of attributes that bear on the existence of a set of functions and their specified properties. The functions are those that satisfy stated or implied needs.
Reliability	A set of attributes related to the capability of the software system to maintain its level of performance under stated conditions for a stated period of time.
Usability	A set of attributes that bear on the effort needed for use, and on the individual assessment of such use, by a stated or implied set of users.
Efficiency	A set of attributes related to the relationship between the level of performance of the software system and the amount of resources used, under stated conditions.
Maintainability	A set of attributes related to the effort needed to make specified modifications. Modifications may include corrections, improvements, or adaptation of software to changes in environment and in requirements and functional specifications.
Portability	A set of attributes related to the ability of the software system to be transferred from one environment to another.

Given the pool of characteristics and sub characteristics that can influence software quality, a *quality model* consists of a selection of some quality characteristics which are considered relevant for a given software application. In general, the quality characteristics suggested by the ISO/IEC 9126 standard are not all addressed during the development of a given software application. The choice of which characteristics to consider, and the extent to which they must be satisfied, largely depends on the specific requirements characterizing the specific context of use (the hardware infrastructure, the users, the supported processes, etc.).

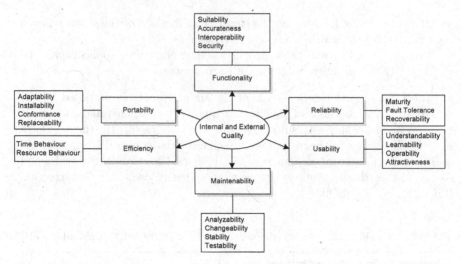

Fig. 8.1. Refinement of quality characteristics into sub characteristics, as defined by ISO/IEC 9126 [ISO01]

Quality models can be used during application design as benchmarks for ensuring a given level of quality since the initial development phases. Quality models are, however, largely used to guide the evaluation process, occurring during the overall application life cycle. In order to be effective, any evaluation technique must be based on the identification of some quality criteria to focus on. Evaluation methods relying on well-defined quality models have indeed the merit of establishing systematic frameworks, where the different dimensions relevant for the assessment are identified in advance, precisely decomposed into quantifiable attributes, and then measured through appropriate techniques [FP97].

8.1.1 Quality Perspectives

According to ISO/IEC 9126, three different perspectives contribute to the overall quality of a software product:

- *Internal quality*: reflects a *white-box* model, which considers some intrinsic properties of the software functionalities, independent of the usage environment and the user interaction, to be measured directly on the the source code and its control flow. Internal quality mainly focuses on the product functionality and is assessed by means of *functional testing* techniques.
- *External quality*: relates to the technical behavior of the software product in a given running environment (enabling hardware, people, business processes, etc.). It reflects a *black-box* model, which typically focuses on architectural factors such as product performance and reliability, and is assessed through *performance testing techniques*.

- *Quality in use*: refers to the effectiveness and efficiency with which the software product satisfies user needs. This concept is related to the perception of quality that the users gain while interacting with the application in the real usage environment. It is therefore related to usability factors and is assessed through *usability evaluation* methods.

Quality in use is in particular represented by the following four characteristics, which add new quality attributes to those previously introduced:

- *Effectiveness*: the capability of a software product to support users, in given contexts of use, in reaching their goals with accurateness and completeness.
- *Productivity*: the capability of a software product to support users by spending an appropriate amount of resources in relation to the effectiveness to be achieved.
- *Safety*: the capability of a software product to achieve, in a given context of use, acceptable levels of risk for the users, the usage environment, and the users' activities.
- *Satisfaction*: the capability of a software product to satisfy the user in a given context of use.

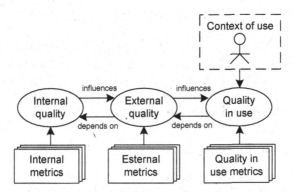

Fig. 8.2. Mutual influences occurring among different quality perspectives [ISO01, ISO02a]

The quality of software applications can be therefore evaluated by measuring internal attributes (i.e., "static" measures on the code of the final or intermediate products), external attributes (i.e., "dynamic" measures related to the behavior of the code when executed), and quality-in-use attributes. It is worth noting that, as illustrated in Figure 8.2, the three perspectives mutually influence each other, because it is impossible to achieve quality in use if the product does not show an adequate level of internal and external quality. Also, some cross-relationships occur among the characteristics (and sub characteristics) representing each perspective [OCR06]. For example, it typically happens that problems related to the efficiency of a product (for example, low response times) reduce the capability of a system to support users achieve their goals, thus impacting the product's usability.

In general, the quality of a software application, as perceived by the final user, is progressively determined through the whole development process, and also strongly depends on the quality of the adopted process. The objective is for the product to have the required effects in a particular context of use. To ensure that these effects are produced, adequate development strategies (such as the model-based methodologies described in the previous chapters), and in particular effective evaluation techniques have to be adopted during the whole application life cycle.

8.1.2 Quality Factors Characterizing Web Applications

A huge number of software and hardware technologies for Web applications are currently available. Such diversity enables the construction of very heterogeneous Web applications and services, which differ in terms of the provided functionality, their performance, and their usability [ACL06]. In such a context, it is difficult to identify the best solution for engineering a high-quality Web application. However, testing architectural and functional requirements, and evaluating the quality in use in terms of usability, still remain key factors for the success of Web applications [SG00, ACL06, LF06].

In line with the general framework proposed by the ISO/IEC 9126 standard, and taking into account the Web scenario, several works have so far promoted different sets of characteristics as key drivers for the evaluation of Web application quality. In particular, according to [Off02, CFB$^+$02], Web practitioners consider *functionality*, *performance*, and *usability* the most relevant factors for the Web domain.

Web Application Functionality

Given the hypertext nature of the Web application front end, the correctness and adequateness of Web application functions largely depends on the *correctness* and *adequateness* of navigation mechanisms. Some ad hoc activities must be therefore conducted to evaluate hypertext properties such as *link integrity*.

Content correctness and *adequacy*, especially for dynamically generated pages, also play a relevant role. They require the use of dynamic validation techniques, able to reproduce the application behavior when generating pages, in order to discover possible failures related both to content extraction from the application data source and visualization on the Web pages. Also, the heterogeneous execution environments, spanning a variety of hardware components, network connections, operating systems, Web servers, and Web browsers, demand for compatibility testing issues to check the correct behavior of the Web application using different configurations. As discussed in Section 8.2.1, *functional testing* aims at assessing such issues.

Performance

In the Web context, the most critical resource is time, and performance is measured in terms of throughput (the number of requests that can be served per unit of time) and response time (the time employed to serve a request). Performance must be evaluated both in average and peak conditions. Average refers to the normal operational conditions in which the application is used, whereas peaks are special situations in which high volumes of requests are concentrated in short intervals. Given the huge number of concurrent accesses by geographically distributed users, testing must be conducted in a scenario where *workload models* must emulate the number of expected user requests. Workload models may depend on the mix of Web resources (e.g., static pages, dynamic pages, secured services, multimedia contents, etc.) that characterize Web applications. Section 8.2.2 will discuss such issues and illustrate some techniques generally adopted for *performance testing*.

Usability

Although several quality factors play a relevant role in determining the quality of a Web application, given the large base of users accessing the Web, the majority of work on quality assessment has so far focused on usability. According to a survey of Web metrics [CRP04], out of 326 metrics defined in literature 53% were indeed about usability.

Usability focuses on the quality of products and systems from the point of view of the users who use them. Part 11 of the ISO 9241 standard (Ergonomic Requirements for Office Work with Visual Display Terminals) defines usability as "the extent to which a product can be used by specified users to achieve specified goals with effectiveness, efficiency and satisfaction in a specified context of use". In this definition, effectiveness means "the accuracy and completeness with which users achieve specified goals", efficiency refers to "the resources expended in relation to the accuracy and completeness with which users achieve goals", and satisfaction is described as "the comfort and acceptability of use".

In the context of the Web, usability is particularly affected by the hypertext nature of Web interfaces [Nie95, Nie00, MRC06]. Usable Web applications must provide users with easy-to-use navigation mechanisms, able to support them to quickly reach relevant contents and operations without getting lost. To enhance this capability, each page in the hypertext front end should be composed in a way so that contents are easy to understand and navigation mechanisms are easy to identify. Thanks to the comprehensibility of available contents and the easy identification of navigation commands, users should feel that they are in control of the hypertext/application.

Recently, the concept of usability has been extended to cover *accessibility*, thus focusing on those application features that support universal access by any class of users and technology [Shn00, Shn93]. In particular, the W3C

Web Accessibility Initiative (WAI) [Con07] defines accessibility as the set of properties of the markup code of a Web application that make page contents "readable" by technologies assisting impaired users, proposing a set of guidelines to be followed when coding Web pages. A number of works in the literature however assign to this concept a broader meaning, defining it as the ability of an application to support any users identifying, retrieving, and navigating its contents [TR03, Hul04, CMRD07].

Usability evaluation is traditionally conducted by observing users, or having usability experts simulating the users' behavior while checking for usability violations. Section 8.3 will discuss the *usability evaluation* methods commonly adopted for assessing the previous issues.

8.2 Testing Web Applications

The main goal of testing is to discover functional or architectural defects by running the application using combinations of inputs and states, and evaluating results against an expected output. Some testing activities focus on the application to discover lacks related to functional requirements; some others address the running environment to assess architectural issues that can cause failures related to non functional requirements, such as performance.

The aim of testing is therefore to discover *failures*, i.e., any lack of a system or one of its components in performing the required functions while fulfilling some specified performance requirements. The set of conditions or variables under which it is possible to determine if a given requirement is fulfilled is a *test case*.

As with any other class of software application, testing activities for Web applications can be conducted according to some well-known strategies for test case design:

- *White-box testing*: identifies the set of test cases on the basis of a representation of the internal structure of the application. *Models* must be adopted to represent the application structure in terms of its components, and *coverage criteria* taking into account structural features must be defined, e.g., to specify the acceptable set of components to be addressed by the testing in order for the test to be "reliable". For example, a coverage criteria can establish that all the blocks of scripting code included in the pages of a Web application must be tested at least once.
- *Black-box testing*: assumes an external view of the application. Test cases focus on specific functions to be tested, and are designed by selecting valid and invalid input to observe the corresponding application behavior and determine whether a correct output is produced. The knowledge of the internal structure of the application and its components is not required.
- *Gray-box testing* : has come into common usage in recent years to denote a combination of the two previous strategies. It is aimed at testing

the external behavior of the application based on the knowledge of its internal components. This entails setting up or manipulating the testing environment, for example, by seeding a database, or viewing the state of a component after its execution, such as performing an SQL query on the database to verify the correctness of contents displayed on a dynamic Web page.

Web application testing can be then broken down into the classical activities of unit testing, integration testing, and system testing:

- *Unit testing*: is performed first to determine the correctness of single components. White-box strategies are used to exercise all component functions, as well as relevant sequences and possible decision branches. According to representation models, such as those presented in [Con02, LF06, RT05], the basic components of a Web application to be addressed by unit testing are Web pages. The different nature of pages (static vs. dynamic pages, pages enriched with client-side scripting, server pages implementing forms of business logic) must be also taken into account. The analysis is based on white-box testing, which helps scan Web pages and detect possible failures.
- *Integration testing*: aims at assessing the correct behavior of groups of components, combined according to some integration criteria. Gray-box approaches are used for integration testing.
- *System testing*: finally focuses on discovering failures related to the whole application by adopting black-box approaches especially focusing on external quality factors.

Despite the similarities with traditional software testing, there are some key features of Web applications that demand ad-hoc testing [LF06]. In the rest of this section, we will discuss functional and performance testing by highlighting the peculiar aspects of Web applications.

8.2.1 Functional Testing

Functional testing aims at assessing the functional correctness and adequateness of an application, to verify whether it works as expected with respect to the functional requirements collected and specified during the requirements analysis phase. Examples of Web application anomalies that can be detected by means of functional testing are *ghost pages* due to links referring to nonexistent pages, and *unreachable pages*, i.e., pages stored in the Web server file system that are not accessible due to the absence of links or paths leading to them [RT05].

In functional testing, typical usage scenarios are reproduced, and the application behavior, namely the produced output, is verified against some target functional requirements previously identified. Possible failures or mismatches may reveal the need for modifications to the application code. Non-functional requirements, such as performance or usability, are not considered in this phase.

Functional testing is generally based on the availability of models, which describe the structure of the application in terms of its components. In the context of the Web, such models can represent the application at a high level, describing pages and navigation links, or at a low level, considering the execution flow occurring at the server and client sides. Based on the nature of the adopted models, two main testing techniques can be adopted: *model-based testing*, especially addressing the definition of navigation in the application hypertext, and *data flow testing*, focusing on the code level.

Model-based testing

Model-based testing is based on the availability of some models specifying the structure or the behavior of the Web application, which guide the definition of test cases. Model-based testing can support the detection of anomalies related to the hypertext structure, such as wrong definitions of URLs, duplication of links, and also errors in the generation of error pages [RT05].

For example, in [RT01, LF06], test coverage criteria (i.e., the pages and links to be addressed by the testing activity) are identified on the basis of a structural model that represents the different pages and components composing the Web application (e.g., static and dynamic pages, forms, and any other kind of Web objects enriching the Web pages at the client side or executed at the server side), and the relationships occurring among them (e.g., links connecting pages).

Figure 8.3 shows a simplified UML-based representation of the meta-model proposed in [RT01] to describe the Web application structure – the model of a given Web application is then an instantiation of such a meta-model. The central entity is the Web page, which can contain contents and links and can include forms. Pages can be static or dynamic. Since in dynamic pages the publication of links and forms may depend on the input provided by users, the class `ConditionalEdge` represents a boolean condition, which is a function of the user's input and represents conditions for instantiating the association between a Web page and its constituent components. Given such a representation, test cases are defined as sequences of visited pages together with the input values determining the page computation.

Other approaches to model-based testing use behavioral models, describing the functions of a Web application without considering their implementation, which are more appropriate for black-box testing. For example, in [AOA05] a Finite State Machine is used to represent the navigation model; test cases are then generated as subsequences of states.

Some interesting exploitations of conceptual models as structural and behavioral models supporting Web application testing have been recently proposed. In Section 8.4 we will illustrate the most prominent approaches and

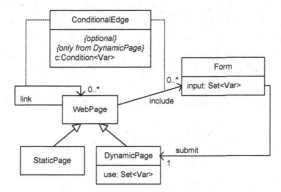

Fig. 8.3. The structural model supporting Web application testing proposed in [RT01]

show how the existence of systematic methods for Web application design can offer several advantages also when assessing the application quality.

Data flow testing

Data flow testing is a white-box testing technique used to identify invalid uses of data values due to coding errors. The test focuses on verifying the application control flow by establishing and analyzing the associations between the value assignment of a variable (i.e., *definition*) and its potential value fetch (i.e., *use*).

Some approaches extend traditional data flow testing to Web applications. They adopt flow graphs to represent the application control flow. For example, in [LKHH01] different kinds of flow graphs are used to discover and analyze *definition-use chains* occurring in the client side scripting code of Web pages, in server components, in sequences of different pages, and in sequences of function invocations depending on user actions. A typical problem that can be identified through such technique is the incorrect setting of cookie values [RT06].

A similar technique is also presented in [RT05]. As illustrated in Figure 8.4, nodes of the control flow model of a given Web application represent statements executed by the Web server or by the client, while edges represent the control transfer. The figure shows the control flow model for a dynamic page. In particular, boxes denote HTML code portions, while ellipses denote scripting language statements. Starting from such a model, several coverage criteria can be defined, such as:

- *Path Coverage*: all paths defined in the model are traversed by the defined test cases.
- *Branch Coverage*: all the edges in the model are traversed by the defined test cases.

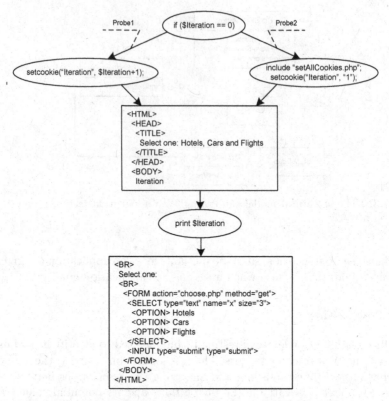

Fig. 8.4. Control flow model as proposed in [RT05]

- *Node Coverage*: all the nodes in the model are traversed by the defined test cases.

Such coverage criteria ensure that all the components of a Web application, or at least all the most relevant components, are executed at least once during the test. To determine the level of coverage of a testing session, based on the defined criteria, the application code must be augmented so that the branches in the control flow that are traversed during the test execution can be traced.

Statistical testing

The huge set of possible usage scenarios that characterize Web applications, mainly deriving from the variability of both the users and the combinations of navigation paths they can follow, makes it hard to apply exhaustive coverage-based testing to Web applications. Some priority schemes can help the selection of test cases.

Statistical testing [HM06] can be adopted as a technique to automatically select the paths to be analyzed. A *usage model* is defined to characterize all the possible usage scenarios in a specific usage environment for a specific user group. Such a model is constructed starting, for example, from the usage log of a Web application. The result is a directed graph whose nodes represent the states of the usage model (for example, the access to a given page), while the arcs are transitions between states (corresponding to link traversals or the invocation of an operation). A probability distribution reflecting the actual use of the application – as recorded in the usage log – is applied to the arcs. For example, arcs denoting link traversal are weighted by means of the frequency of the links' selection. Such a probability model then drives the selection of test cases, ensuring that they will address the most frequent operations.

Since statistical testing is based on statistical models, the detected anomalies are the basis for estimating application reliability, i.e., the probability of failure-free operations. For this reason, unlike other functional testing techniques, statistical testing cannot be considered a debugging method.

8.2.2 Performance testing

Functional testing focuses on the application code and aims at identifying failures related to the adequacy and correctness of the application's functions. Several additional factors to be tested to assess the quality of a Web application refer to the architectural layer. In particular, a relevant issue to be considered concerns the application performance [CFB+02]. Performance is critical for Web applications: Web users expect that the application is available and that they do not have to wait long time for getting a response to their request.

In the rest of this section we will focus on the main activities for performance testing. For more details on further testing activities related to assessing other factors influencing the quality of the architectural design of a Web application, the reader is referred to [LF06].

Estimating the workload

The starting point for verifying the performance of a Web application architecture is the definition of *workload models*, characterizing the Web application's access by its users [ACL06]. Therefore, performance requirements must be identified, typically, predicting the number and type of page requests that clients will make, and the response time needed to answer to these requests acceptably. Estimating the workload based on such requirements is not an exact discipline, and the margin of error greatly increases when moving from B2B and Intranet applications to B2C applications offered to the huge audience of Internet users.

For B2B or enterprise applications, the number of users can be determined with a good approximation, and the usage scenarios identified during requirements analysis should permit one to turn these numbers into a sensible guess of the page requests to expect. Conversely, B2C applications are far less predictable because the number of hits greatly depends on the success of the application – a factor hard to estimate beforehand. In any case, the workload should be characterized by means of a spectrum of parameters that then are candidates to becoming the object of testing:

- *Number of page requests*: the average and peak number of requests emitted by clients, expressed, for instance, in pages per second. This parameter expresses the throughput of the application as perceived by the client.
- *Number of concurrent users*: this number differs from the number of page requests because it expresses the prediction of the average and maximum number of users that will access the application simultaneously. The number of concurrent users impacts especially the application back end, where queues may occur in the business and data tier.
- *Response time*: the maximum number of seconds that the client should wait for the response. Ideally, the response time should not exceed the user's thinking time (three seconds), and should be relatively stable in peak conditions. Response time could be further distinguished as:
  - *Time To First Byte* (TTFB): it gives an indication of the performance of the back-end processing because it ignores any network latency due to the transmission of the entire page.
  - *Time To Last Byte* (TTLB): it is more significant for the client because it measures the time needed to receive the complete response.
- *Request mix*: given that an application is made of many different pages and services with different complexity, the number of requests per second is insufficient to characterize the load. To make performance testing more trustable, it is necessary to estimate the user's behavior, and then generate a workload model that matches real situations. A request mix can be therefore used to associate with each application page and service a "weight," which denotes the probability that the user accesses the page or the service in an average interactive session. Page probabilities can be used during test sessions to construct realistic workloads.

For more details on the workload model representation the reader is referred to [ACL06].

Setting up the test environment

Performance testing should be done on the actual hardware, software, and network infrastructure, using the real application. The real application, of course, is available only at the end of implementation. However, deferring performance assessment to such a late time is dangerous, because it delays the verification of the architecture to the very end of the development process.

To anticipate performance analysis, it may be possible to build an application prototype and make it available during the architecture design phase. The prototype may implement only a subset of the application pages, corresponding to the most critical use cases, and should reproduce as faithfully as possible the data access and update queries of the real application.

Also, to minimize hardware and licensing costs, the real hardware and software are usually provisioned only at the end of the implementation. In this case, analysis can start from a preliminary test configuration, pragmatically selected based on past experiences and economical and organizational constraints (for example, based on existing hardware and infrastructure), and then proceed by trial and error, following experimental cycles such as the one based on bottleneck identification and removal.

The results obtained with the preliminary architecture could then be projected on the real configuration to gain confidence that the ultimate architecture will meet the identified performance requirements. However, performance must be re-evaluated prior to the application deployment, on the real software and hardware.

Verifying performance

Once a configuration is in place, it must be stress-tested in order to determine performance. Performance evaluation entails:

1. Defining the test sessions and testing tools;
2. Running the experiments;
3. Collecting and analyzing test data.

Testing a Web application requires simulating the clicking behavior of clients by generating a suitable number of requests for the application pages. This task is supported by specialized testing tools, which offer functions for:

- *Defining the mix of page requests* that simulate a usage session. For each usage session, it is possible to specify a set of pages to call, and the percentage of requests that should be addressed to each page in the mix.
- *Defining the maximum number of concurrent clients* that send requests to the application and fine-tuning the clicking behavior of each client, for example, by setting a thinking time between consecutive requests or by simulating different bandwidths of the client connections (for instance, ISDN, ADSL, or fast connections).
- *Scheduling and running the test sessions.*
- *Collecting reports about various performance parameters.* Typically, Web stress tools chart parameters such as the number of pages per second, the total duration of the test session, the number of communication and server errors, and so on.

Identifying bottlenecks

In a complex Web application, performance is determined by the slowest component, which is the so-called *bottleneck*. Bottlenecks may hide in any of the architectural elements, including the Web server, the scripting programs and page templates, the business components, and the database, or in the connections between the various components and tiers. In a well-designed architecture, the workload should be proportionally distributed across the different tiers and components, so that there is no single bottleneck, and each component should work at a reasonable fraction of its maximum capacity, so that some extra power is available to accommodate exceptional events such as the anomalous increase of the workload or the failure of some components.

Tuning performance involves a cyclic process comprising the tasks shown in Figure 8.5: the process consists in defining a configuration, verifying that it satisfies the performance requirements previously established, and, in the negative case, identifying and removing bottlenecks.

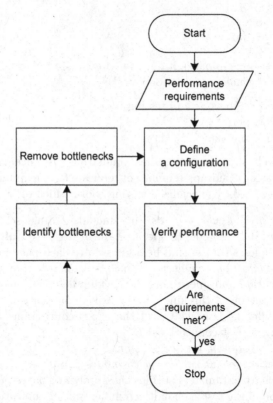

Fig. 8.5. The process for performance tuning [CFB$^+$02]

A pragmatic approach to identifying performance problems is to progressively stress the system until one of the components reaches a saturation point and manifests itself as the performance bottleneck. Saturation can be discovered by running a set of experiments in which the stress level, for example, the number of simulated concurrent users, is increased, and by monitoring the system throughput. The occurrence of a bottleneck typically shows in the *performance/load diagram* , presenting a curve like the one in Figure 8.6. According to the curve, the throughput (i.e., the number of requests served per second) increases almost linearly with the traffic volume (the number of users' requests) until one of the components "breaks" and then either remains constant or even decreases, revealing a situation of overstress.

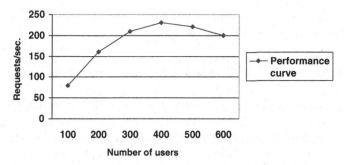

Fig. 8.6. A performance curve, highlighting saturation

When saturation is encountered, the next step is to identify the saturating component. An indication may come from the analysis of performance indicators on the different physical machines. For instance, any component that in the stress tests runs constantly at a high level of CPU utilization (say, above 75%) is a candidate bottleneck. The most frequently encountered situations include:

- The Web server being unable to serve the incoming requests.
- The server-side scripting interpreter being overloaded due to the execution of complex programs or page templates.
- The business components used by the server-side scripts or page templates being overloaded.
- The database connection being slowed down by too many concurrent requests.
- The database processor taking too much time to execute a complex query.

If the tested configuration is such that each machine hosts a single component, then the machine where the overstress has occurred clearly points to the component to revise. If the overstressed machine hosts multiple components, for example, the Web server and the database, then separating the components on different machines and running further tests may permit us to make the diagnosis. Sometimes, isolating components is not feasible, but still some insight may be acquired with more detailed measurements. For example, if the machine that hosts the Web server and the scripting engine saturates, it is possible to verify what is slowing down the system by looking at the request queue of the Web server; if the number of requests waiting in queue increases with the slowdown, it is likely that the scripting programs or page templates are forced to wait, because the business object to which they address requests are overloaded.

When the bottleneck is identified, there are different applicable strategies to solve the problem:

- Acting on the application code to fix problems and optimize execution time.
- Adding more resources to the configuration, thus introducing replication.
- Introducing caching or pooling mechanisms.

In principle, intervening on the application code is the most appropriate solution, as there should be no bottlenecks due to the ill design of application components. Optimization is particularly relevant in the data tier, where well-established database tuning techniques are available, which may yield substantial reductions in the execution times of database queries. However, optimizing the implementation code is a complex task, and a sensible compromise must be reached between achieving 100% implementation efficiency, which is an ideal goal, and the effort spent in code optimization.

When the application code is reasonably efficient, further performance improvement can be gained by upgrading the hardware resources, for example when some forms of saturation are observed, or increasing their number through replication.

Further improvements consist of introducing pooling and/or caching mechanisms. *Resource pooling* consists of generating multiple software resources, independently of their use, and grouping them in *pools* so that they are immediately available when requests must be served. When released, such resources are not destroyed and return to be part of the original pool. *Caching*, which consists of temporarily storing resources in a fast access location for later retrieval, is a very consolidated practice which allows developers to obtain low-cost and low-impact performance improvements.

8.3 Usability Evaluation

Applying principles for the design of usable applications is not sufficient for ensuring the usability of the final product. Even though accurate design techniques are used, it is still necessary to check the intermediate results, and to test the final application for verifying whether it actually has the expected features and meets user requirements. The role of *usability evaluation* is to help verify such issues.

The main goals of usability evaluation are to assess the application functionality to verify the effect of its interface on the user and to identify any specific problem with the application, such as features that show unexpected effects when used in their intended context [DFAB98]. Evaluating the usability of Web applications in particular requires verifying whether the application design allows users to easily retrieve and browse contents, and invoke available services and operations. It also addresses the pleasantness of the provided interaction mechanisms, and the satisfaction of users that use them. This implies not only having adequate and correct content and services available in the application (as addressed by functional testing), but also making them easily reachable by users through appropriate and pleasant hypertext front ends.

Different usability evaluation methods can be used at different stages of product development. The most commonly adopted are *user testing*, where real users are studied, and *usability inspection*, which is conducted by specialists. Recently, *Web usage analysis* has also emerged as a method for studying user behavior through the computation of access statistics and the reconstruction of user navigation on the basis of Web access logs.

The rest of this section is devoted to illustrating the main features of these three classes of evaluation methods, highlighting their advantages and drawbacks.

8.3.1 User Testing

User testing deals with real behavior, observed from some representative of real users [Nie93]. It requires that users perform a set of tasks through physical artifacts, prototypes or final systems, while the experimenter observes their behaviors and collects empirical data about the way they execute the assigned tasks [DFAB98, PRS+94]. Typical data collected during user testing are user execution time, number of errors, and user satisfaction. After the test's completion, the collected data are interpreted and used to ameliorate the level of application usability.

Usability testing is explicitly devoted to analyzing in detail how users interact with the application for accomplishing well-defined tasks. This feature determines the difference between usability testing and beta testing, largely applied in industry. Beta testing is conducted on the final product: after the application release the end users are contacted and interviewed about their satisfaction. Conversely, usability testing is conducted by observing a sample of users that perform specific tasks while interacting with the application. The test is usually video-recorded. The list of detected problems is reported together with specific redesign suggestions.

In order to avoid any inconvenience related to the reliability of results, the design of the test and its execution have to be carefully planned and managed. Good usability testing could be therefore articulated as follows:

1. *Defining the goals of the test.* The objectives of the evaluation can be generic, as, for example, the improvement of end user satisfaction and the design of a product easy to use; or they can be specific, as, for example, the evaluation of the effectiveness of a navigation bar for user orientation; the readability of labels, etc.

2. *Defining the sample of users that will participate in the test.* The sample of subjects for the test has to be representative of the entire end user population. Possible criteria that can be used to define the test sample are: user experience (experts vs. novices), age, frequency of use of the application, and experience with similar applications. The number of participants can vary, depending on the objectives of the test. Nielsen and Molich [NM90] affirm that the 50% of the most important usability problems can be identified with three users. Other authors claim that the involvement of five users enables discovering 90% of usability problems [Vir92, Nie94, BBC+03].

3. *Selecting tasks and scenarios.* The tasks submitted to users during the test have to be real; in other words, they have to represent the activities that people would perform on the application. Scenarios can be selected from the results obtained during requirements elicitation; in addition, they can be purposely prepared to test unexpected situations.

4. *Establishing how to measure the level of usability of the system.* Before conducting usability testing, it is necessary to define the parameters that will be used to measure the results. The type of measures can vary from the subjective ones, such as *user satisfaction* and the *difficulty of use*, to the most objective and quantitative ones, such as *task completion time*, *number and the typology of errors, number of successfully accomplished tasks*, and *number of times users invoke help* (verbal, online, manual). The participants will be anonymous and be informed about the results. Besides observation, the experimenter may use other techniques for gathering data about task execution: *think aloud*, in which the subject is required to tell explicitly all the actions he is taking, the reasons for his actions, and his expectations; *co-discovery* (or collaborative approach), in which two participants execute the tasks together, helping each other; *active intervention*, in which the experimenter stimulates participants to reflect on the events of the test session. It is worth noting that such techniques do not provide ways for collecting data about user satisfaction. Such a kind of subjective measure can be instead obtained through *survey techniques*, based on the use of questionnaires and interviews [Shn93], submitted to users after the execution of the testing tasks.

5. *Preparing the needed material and the experimental environment.* The experimental environment has to be organized by equipping it with a computer and a video camera for recording user activities, establishing the roles of the experimental team members, and preparing any supporting material (manuals, pencils and paper, etc.). Executing the test in a laboratory is not mandatory. Prior to the testing session, a pilot trial is necessary for checking and possibly refining all the test procedures.

User testing provides reliable evaluations because it involves samples of real users. It allows evaluators to overcome the lack of precision manifested in predictive models when the application domain is not supported by a strong and detailed theory. Such a method, however, has a number of drawbacks. It is difficult to select a proper sample of the user community: an incorrect sample may lead to wrong perceptions about user needs and preferences. It is difficult, in a limited amount of time, to train users to master the most sophisticated and advanced features of a Web application; users not well trained may produce "superficial" conclusions, related only to the most immediate features of the application. Furthermore, it is difficult, in a limited amount of time, to reproduce actual situations of usage, which require setting up the environment where the application is going to be used, and the motivations and goals that users may have in real-life situations. Failure to reproduce such a context may lead to "artificial" conclusions rather than to realistic results.

Finally, user observation gives little information about the cause of the problem, because it primarily deals with the symptoms [DRSS97]. Not understanding the underlying cause has implications for redesign. In fact, the new design can remove the original symptom, but if the underlying cause remains, a different symptom can be triggered. The previous reasons have led to the definition of alternative evaluation methods. In particular, usability inspection methods have been proposed as "discount usability methods," providing developers with easy-to-use techniques to predict usability problems. Web usage analysis techniques have been recently defined to analyze the real behavior of Web users, as recorded in Web server logs.

8.3.2 Inspection Methods

Usability inspection refers to a set of evaluation techniques that are an evolution of prior function and code inspection methods used in software engineering for debugging and improving code. According to such methods, evaluators examine usability-related aspects of an application, trying to detect violations of established usability principles [NM94], and then provide feedback to designers about possible design improvements. The inspectors can be usability specialists, or designers and engineers with special expertise (e.g., knowledge of specific domains or standards). In any case, the application of such methods relies on a good understanding of the usability principles and on how they apply to the specific application being analyzed, and on the particular ability of the evaluators to discover critical situations where principle violations occur.

Usability inspection methods were proposed when the issue of cost effectiveness started guiding methodological work on usability evaluation [MB94]. The cost of user studies and laboratory experiments became a central issue. Therefore, many proposals were made for usability evaluation techniques based on the involvement of specialists to supplement or even replace direct user testing [NM94, NM90].

Different methods can be used for inspecting an application [NM94]. Among them, the most commonly used are *heuristic evaluation* [Nie93, NM94], in which usability specialists judge whether the application properties conform to established usability principles, and *cognitive walkthrough*

[WRLP94], which uses detailed procedures for simulating users' problem-solving processes, to verify whether the functions provided by the application are efficient for users and lead them to the next correct actions. In the sequel of this section we will describe heuristic evaluation, the most largely adopted inspection method. For a detailed description of other inspection techniques the reader is referred to [Nie93, NM94].

Table 8.2. An example of a table for reporting heuristic violations

Problem	Heuristic	Severity	Suggested improvement
Download time is not indicated	Feedback	High	Use a scrolling bar for representing the time left till the end of download

Heuristic evaluation

Heuristic evaluation is the most informal of inspection methods. It prescribes having a small set of experts analyzing the application against a list of recognized usability principles, the *heuristics*. This technique is part of the so-called discount usability methods. In fact, some researches have shown that it is a very efficient usability engineering method [JD92], with a high benefit-cost ratio [Nie94].

During the evaluation session, each evaluator goes individually through the system interface at least twice. The first step is to get a feel of the flow of the interaction and the general scope of the application; the second is to focus on specific objects and functionality, evaluating their design and implementation against a list of heuristics. The output of a heuristic evaluation session is a list of usability problems with reference to the violated heuristics (see Table 8.2 for an example). Reporting problems in relation to heuristics enables the easy generation of a revised design, in accordance with what is prescribed by the guidelines underlying the violated principles. Once the evaluation has been completed, the findings of the different evaluators are compared.

Heuristic evaluation is especially valuable when time and resources are short, because skilled evaluators, without needing the involvement of representative users, can produce high-quality results in a limited amount of time [KR97]. In principle, heuristic evaluation can be conducted by only one evaluator. However, in an analysis of six studies, it has been assessed that single evaluators are able to find only 35% of the total number of the existing usability problems [NL93], and that different evaluators tend to find different problems. Therefore, the more the number of experts involved in the evaluation, the more is the number of problems possible to find. Figure 8.7 shows the percentage of usability problems found by having different numbers of

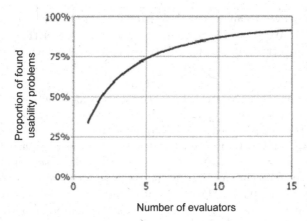

Fig. 8.7. The percentage of usability problems found by heuristic evaluation when using different numbers of evaluators [NL93]

evaluators, as reflected by a mathematical model defined in [NL93]. From the curve it is evident that reasonable results can be obtained by having only five evaluators, and certainly not less than three.

Heuristic evaluation and, in general, inspection methods, have a number of drawbacks. As highlighted in [DRSS97, JMWU91, KR97], a major drawback is the high dependence upon the skills and the experiences of the evaluators. Nielsen states that novice evaluators with no usability expertise are poor evaluators, usability experts are 1.8 times as good, and application domain and usability experts (the double experts) are 2.7 time as good [Nie02, Nie93]. This means that the specific experience with the specific category of applications really improves the evaluators' performance.

To overcome such a drawback, some works have been proposed in literature to make usability inspection more systematic. For example, in [MCGP02] authors propose an inspection method that exploits the specification of some recurrent "evaluation patterns" for Hypermedia and Web applications to precisely guide inspectors in their evaluation activities. The presented approach has also the advantage of being based on a model-based representation of the application under evaluation, expressed in terms of the conceptual primitives of the Hypermedia Design Model (HDM) [GPS91, BGP01]. This makes systematic the identification of the relevant application entities to be evaluated and the usability criteria guiding the evaluation.

8.3.3 Web Usage Analysis

A relatively new direction in the evaluation of Web applications deals with Web usage analysis [IH01], performed on the record of user accesses to the application pages, collected in a Web server log [SCDT00] in one of the available standard formats [Con]. After Web applications are deployed, Web usage analysis can be employed to analyze how users exploit and browse the information provided by the Web site. For instance, it can help discover those navigation patterns which correspond to high Web usage or those which correspond to early leaving.

Very often, Web logs are analyzed with the aim of calculating *traffic statistics*. Such a type of analysis can help identify the most accessed pages and content, and may therefore highlight some user preferences, not detected at design time, that might need to be accommodated by restructuring the hypertext. Traffic analysis is not able to detect users' navigation behavior. To allow deeper insight into users' navigation paths, the research community has been studying techniques to reconstruct user navigation from log files [Coo03, SCDT00, EV03, FLMM04]. Most of them are based on extensions of Web logging mechanisms for recording additional semantic information about content displayed in the accessed pages, to make sense of the observed frequent paths and of pages on these paths [BHS02]. Such extensions exploit Semantic Web techniques, such as RDF annotations for mapping URLs onto a set of ontological entities. Also, as it will be discussed in Section 8.4.3, some recent works [FLMM04, PKZ01] have proposed conceptual enrichment of Web logs, through the integration of information about the actual contents displayed by pages at runtime, and the hypertext structure deriving from the application conceptual specifications. The reconstruction of user navigation can be then incorporated into automatic tools providing designers and evaluators with statistics about the identified navigation paths, which can be useful for evaluating and improving the application organization with respect to actual application usage.

User navigation paths can also be analyzed by means of *Web Usage Mining* techniques, which consist of applying data mining techniques over Web logs for identifying interesting associations among visited pages and contents [Coo03, EV03]. With respect to the simple reconstruction of user navigation, Web Usage Mining can discover unexpected user behavior, not foreseen by the application designers, which can be the symptom of design lacks, not necessarily errors. The aim is to identify possible amendments for accommodating such user needs.

Different techniques can be used to mine Web logs. Mining of association rules is probably the one most used. Association rules are implications of the form $X \Rightarrow Y$, stating that in a given session where the X log element (e.g., a page) is found, the Y log element is also very likely to be found. Methods for discovering association rules can also be extended to the problem of discovering *sequential patterns*. These are extensions of association rules to the case where the relation among rule items specifies a temporal pattern. The sequential pattern of the form $X.html \Rightarrow Y.html$ states that users who in a session visit page $X.html$ are also likely to visit page $Y.html$ later in the same session [NSER02].

The discovery of association rules and sequential patterns is interesting from the Web usage perspective because the results produced can evidence content or pages that frequently appear in association. If the discovered behavior is not supported by appropriate navigation structures connecting such content and pages, this can suggest possible changes for improving the ease of content browsing.

Web server log analysis seems to solve a series of problems in the field of the usability evaluation, since it might reduce the need for usability testing involving samples of real, physical users. Also, with respect to experimental settings, it offers the possibility of analyzing the behavior of a high number of users, thus increasing the number of evaluated variables and the reliability of the detected errors.

However, log files are not without problems. The most severe one is about the meaning of the information collected and how much it describes the real behavior. In fact, even when they are effective in finding patterns in the users' navigation sessions, such techniques do not solve the problem of how to infer users' goals and expectations, central information for usability evaluation.

A further drawback of Web usage mining techniques is that they require a substantial amount of preprocessing [Coo03, SCDT00] to clean the logs, extract user navigation sessions containing consistent information, and format data in a way suitable for analysis. In particular, user session identification can be very demanding [CMS99]. Requests for pages tracked into the Web logs must be grouped in order to identify the navigation paths of single users; but this phase may suffer problems mainly due to proxy servers, which do not allow the unique identification of users, generally based on IP addresses. Some solutions for circumventing this problem are illustrated in [CMS99].

8.4 Web Design Methods and Quality Assessment

The conceptual models adopted for Web application design, already discussed in Chapter 5, can be also exploited as structural and behavioral models supporting quality assessment at different stages in the development process.

8.4.1 Early Assessment of Navigation Models

The specification of conceptual models, representing the navigation semantics, is one of the first activities conducted when designing a Web application. The existence of such models, even in the development phases where prototypes are not available yet, can facilitate the early assessment of the application quality. This is a notable advantage: improving the quality of the early design artifacts can indeed strongly influence the quality of the final application. It also drastically reduces the need for changes during the implementation activity, thus enhancing the overall development process.

Early assessment on navigation models is generally conducted by computing metrics that quantify in which measure the defined conceptual models fulfil some quality requirements. For example, in [ACFOP03] the authors define metrics for analyzing navigation schemas defined with the OO-H method [PGIP01], which address two relevant navigation aspects, namely:

- *Design of navigation maps*: metrics in this set relate to the morphological characteristics of the navigation model that have impact on the navigation complexity in the final application, such as the *size* of the navigation model (i.e., the number of navigation nodes), its *depth* (i.e., the distance from a root navigation context to a leaf context), its *breadth* (i.e., the number of alternative navigation paths), its *compactness* (i.e., the degree of node interconnectivity).
- *Design of navigation contexts*: metrics in this set relate to the quality of navigation nodes, and in particular to issues such as the *coupling* of nodes (i.e., the number of link exiting and entering a specific node), and the *intrinsic complexity* of nodes, such as the number of attributes and methods used for the definition and computation of the navigation node.

A similar analysis technique has been defined for the analysis of WebML-based hypertext schemas [CMM02, FMM02]. The technique is also supported by a tool, the *WebML Quality Analyzer (WQA)*, that automatically inspects an XML-based representation of WebML schemas [FMM02], to discover pitfalls that can be observed on the hypertext structure, and that negatively impact the quality of the final application.

The WQA analysis focuses on *correctness* and *usability*. The correctness of a conceptual schema can be approached from two different perspectives:

- *Syntactic correctness*: a conceptual schema is syntactically correct if all the constructs used in the model are correct and consistent with respect to a given syntax. Syntactic correctness verification is quite straightforward, and consists in checking syntactic properties of the model primitives used in the hypertext schema.
- *Semantic correctness*: a conceptual schema is semantically correct if the corresponding Web application runs correctly, according to the semantics associated with each single page unit and navigation link. This quality dimension addresses conceptual errors, such as *non-determinism* (i.e., starting from a given state in the Web application, two different states can be reached, and no priorities can be implicitly assigned to them), *racing conditions* (i.e., different, but legal, execution orders in computing a set of units provide different results), *deadlocks* (i.e., two or more units cannot be computed, because they depend from each other, and each of them is waiting for the other to be computed), and so on [CF01].

Usability focuses on structural properties of the hypertext schema that are related to the definition of navigation mechanisms, page content composition, and invocation of functions and external services. The analysis therefore concentrates on the following usability attributes:

- *Consistency*: it refers to the coherent use throughout the application of patterns for page composition, navigation, and function invocation. Consistency must be privileged, because it helps users identify reliable expectations about the overall application structure, and easily recognize the way information can be accessed and functions activated.

- *Ease of navigation*: It refers to the availability of links for supporting users while exploring the Web application. The minimum set of links expected in a Web application is the one directly induced by the relationships defined among entities in the data schema. However, having only these links may be too limiting for users, and a richer set of links is recommended for efficiency purposes. For example, navigation can be improved at least providing each page in the hypertext with persistent links to the Home Page. A recurrent problem is indeed the presence of *dead-ends*, pages reachable through different navigation paths that however prevent the users to navigate further, thus making navigation difficult. Also, if a hypertext consists of different areas, then entry points to such areas must be provided in each page.

- *Low page density*: It refers to the number of content units and function invocations within single hypertext nodes. A high page density may indeed affect the users understandability of the provided contents and functions. It also greatly affects the complexity of page computation, thus the application response time, because unit population translates into a high number of queries over data sources.

The analysis of the previous structural properties is based on the identification within the WebML hypertext schemas of configurations, the so called *analysis patterns*, that represent potential sources of problems. A pattern consists of a chain of pages, units, and links serving a typical application purpose, for example the access to the application contents via one or more access paths, or the invocation of content management functions. Each quality attribute is associated with a *pattern description*, specifying the WebML compositions that need to be retrieved within the hypertext schema and checked against the quality attribute, and with an *analysis procedure*, defining the inspection steps over the retrieved patterns. The analysis procedure may consists in a *metric computation*, generating aggregated numerical values that quantify the level in which the analyzed attribute is satisfied, or in a *condition checking*, generating warnings that highlight potential problems. An example of metric computation function is the variance with which alternative patterns implementing the same function (e.g., the modification of content items) occur in the global navigation schema. An example of condition checking rule may be the generation of warnings when too many variants of the same hypertext pattern are used for solving the same problem – this design solution may indeed disorient users.

Let us now consider an example of consistency analysis, to show how this analysis technique works. For the purpose of consistency analysis, an analy-

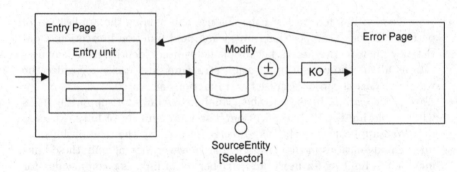

Fig. 8.8. Core specification of the Modify analysis pattern [CMM02]

sis pattern is decomposed into a *core specification*, representing an invariant WebML unit composition that characterizes the pattern, and a number of pattern variants, which extend the core specification with all the valid modalities in which the pattern can start (*starting variants*) or terminate (*termination variants*). Starting variants describe which units can be used for passing the context to the core pattern composition. Termination variants describe instead how the context generated by the core pattern composition is passed to successive compositions in the hypertext.

Figure 8.8 illustrates the core specification of the *Modify analysis pattern*. It consists of a hypertext chain, centered on the WebML Modify unit, used to specify the invocation of an operation for modifying an entity instance. This pattern is used whenever the modification of some data has to be specified. An example is the change of the quantity of an ordered item in a shopping cart. The core specification of the pattern consists of an entry unit, providing a form for inputting the new data, and a modify operation unit. If the operation fails (as represented by the KO link), an error page is displayed. A link to the initial page is also provided.

As illustrated in Figure 8.9, the Modify pattern can have two termination variants, *Same Page* and *Different Page*, that after the operation completion respectively lead the users back to the same page where the operation has started, or in a different page. The two variants are both valid configurations: the former allows users to further modify the same entity instance; in the latter, a further modification of the same entity instance, or of a different one, would require one or more additional navigation steps for going back to the initial page. It is important, however, to coherently adopt one of the two solutions throughout the whole application, whenever the same design problem (a data modification) must be addressed.

Given this pattern decomposition, consistency analysis can therefore consist in verifying whether the same pattern, characterized by the same core specification, is applied with the same termination variant. The analysis procedure corresponds to identifying all the modify operations, and computing a metric, for example based on the statistical variance, which quantifies the con-

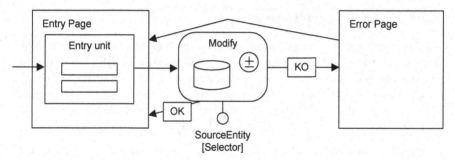

a) Same Page termination variant

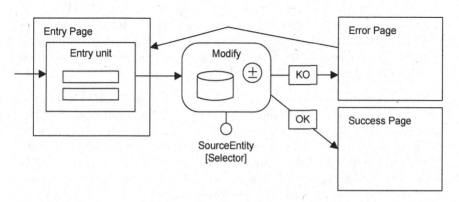

b) Different Page termination variant

Fig. 8.9. Two termination variants for the Modify pattern illustrated in Figure 8.8 [CMM02]

sistency of the adopted solutions with respect to the two different termination variants.

The WQA tool, supporting this analysis technique, employs XSL rules to express the analysis procedures (both the retrieval of patterns into the schema, and the computation of metrics over the retrieved patterns) to be performed over the XML-based specification of the WebML hypertext schema. This rule-based approach makes the framework very flexible and extensible: new measures can be easily specified by means of XSL rules, and added to the WQA repositories, giving to each design team the possibility to address further quality criteria and measures by writing XSL code, an extensively used W3C standard.

8.4.2 Web Application Testing

An interesting exploitation of conceptual models as structural and behavioral models supporting Web application testing is illustrated in [BFTM05], where authors investigate the relationship between the adoption of the WebML conceptual model for application design, and Web application testing. In particular, authors highlight that in the context of model-driven development, the activity of testing a Web application can be split into two subtasks:

- *Schema Validation*: it assesses whether the application conceptual schema is correct with respect to the application requirements, and adheres to the syntax and semantics of the chosen Web modeling language.
- *Code Generator Validation*: it aims at evaluating whether the code generator maps all correct conceptual schemas to correct implementations on all platforms. Indeed, since in conceptual modeling, and in particular in the context of the WebML methodology, automatic code generation substitutes manual coding, the focus of testing shifts from verifying individual Web applications to testing the Web code generator.

While the former activity must be performed for every individual application, the latter can be done only once for each deployment platform. The validation of the code generator is the novel and original problem addressed by this approach: if one could ensure that the code generator produces a correct implementation for all legal and meaningful conceptual schemas (i.e., combinations of modeling constructs), then testing Web applications would reduce to the more treatable problem of schema validation.

Such a testing approach was applied on the WebML code generator, to validate the generation of Web applications for the J2EE platform. A blackbox paradigm was adopted, with a test set consisting of a sample of WebML schemas, including cases developed to verify both the core features of WebML, and some advanced features of the tool or of the language. The verification of bugs also introduced a number of ad-hoc test cases.

To verify the output (a J2EE Web application) produced by the generator, an oracle program was used to run an input script, reproducing a sensible user navigation on the generated application, and to check whether the displayed pages published the expected content. This check was performed by evaluating logical expressions (expressed in XPath) on the HTML code of page. Testing confidence was then expressed by a notion of syntactic coverage, addressing issues such as the percentage of the WebML grammar rules, and the percentage of legal combinations of WebML constructs covered by the tested WebML schemas.

8.4.3 Web Usage Analysis

As already discussed in Section 8.3.3, in order to be effective, Web usage mining requires some extra activities, such as the tagging of Web pages for the purpose of logging meta-data about the page semantics. In the context of the WebML methodology, it has been proved that, if a model-driven approach is adopted for the development of the Web applications, the need for such additional activities can be reduced[FLMM04].

In the WebML method, the availability of the application conceptual model is exploited to enrich common Web logs with additional information useful to the Web mining process [FLMM04]. The enrichment consists of data extracted from the application hypertext schema, such as the content units composing Web pages, the data entities Web pages deal with, and the inclusion of pages within specific hypertext areas. The additional data also refer to the identifier of the user crawling session, and to the specific data instances that are published within dynamic pages. The resulting log data are called *conceptual logs*, because the enrichment is operated especially through the integration of elements deriving from the application conceptual schema. They are specified in XML, and are generated thanks to some extensions of the WebRatio framework, that at runtime are responsible for extracting and integrating logs from the application server, the application runtime, and the application hypertext schema. The XML-dump of the application data source is also used for deriving detailed information about data accessed within pages. Therefore, no extra effort is needed during or after the application development, to reconstruct exactly the semantics of user navigation and the actual data accessed within the visited pages.

Figure 8.11 illustrates a simplified example of a conceptual log for the access to the **Author Page** depicted in Figure 8.10. This page recalls the online magazine case study illustrated in Chapter 5. As represented in Figure 8.10a, the page publishes data about an author and his stories published in the online magazine. The page is composed of a data unit, publishing some author data (e.g., the name and the short bio), and an index of the author's stories. Figure 8.10b illustrates the XML-based specification of this visual schema, which specifies additional detailed properties (not conveniently expressed by the visual notation), such as the entity attributes displayed by each single unit (**DISPLAYATTRIBUTE** element), and the entity attribute determining the sorting of the content items in an index (**SORTATTRIBUTE** element).

The XML representation is used as source for the conceptual log enrichments. As can be seen in Figure 8.11, each page request recorded by the Web server logging mechanism is extended with elements of the hypertext schema, and with the identifiers of the data instances that populate the page at runtime, as produced and logged by the application runtime engine. For example, the log in Figure 8.11 includes:

- The identifiers of the units composing the page, delimited by the tag `<Unit>`.

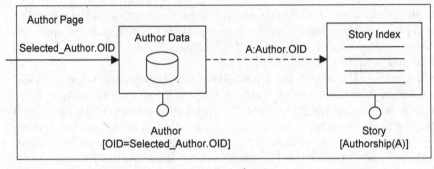

a)

```
<PAGE id="page3" name="Author Page">
  <CONTENTUNITS>
    <DATAUNIT id="dau84" name="Author Data"
      entity="ent4" entity_name="Author">
      <DISPLAYATTRIBUTE attribute="att51" name="Author Name"/>
      <DISPLAYATTRIBUTE attribute="att57" name="Author Bio/>
      <SELECTOR>
        <SELECTORCONDITION attributes="att58" att_name="OID"
             id="cond90" sel_name="Author Selection"
             predicate="eq" value="Selected_Author.OID"/>
      </SELECTOR>
      <LINK id="ln42" name="To_StoryIndex" newWindow="no"
          to="inu9" type="transport" parameter="Author.OID"/>
    </DATAUNIT>
    <INDEXUNIT id="inu9" name="Story Index"
      entity="ent19" entity_name="Story" >
      <SORTATTRIBUTE attribute="att60" name="Story Title"
             order="ascending"/>
      <DISPLAYATTRIBUTE attribute="att60" name="Story Title"/>
      <SELECTOR>
        <SELECTORCONDITION relationship="rel7"
                 id="cond40" sel_name="Story_Selection"
                 rel_name="Authorship" predicate="in"/>
      </SELECTOR>
    </INDEXUNIT>
    ... ...
</PAGE>
```

b)

Fig. 8.10. A WebML schema for a page of an online magazine (a) and its simplified XML-based representation (b)

- The OIDs of the data instances populating such units at runtime, delimited by the `<Data_Oid>` tag.[1]

The `SchemaRef` attributes, defined for pages and units, represent reference to pages and units within the application conceptual schema. They support

---

[1] Since the conceptual logs just include the OIDs of data items, the XML-dump of the application data source is used to retrieve the actual data accessed within pages.

```
<Request Request_Id="3178">
    <LocalTime>
        <DD>29</DD> <Month>Mar</Month> <YY>2009</YY>
        <hh>03</hh><mm>03</mm><ss>34</ss>
        <Timestamp>+0100</Timestamp>
    </LocalTime>
    <User>
        <IPaddress>XXX.XXX.XXX.XXX</IPaddress>
            <jSessionID>acbTwnzgkSz6</jSessionID>
            <Browser>MSIE</Browser>
        <Version>6.0</Version>
        <Platform>compatible</Platform>
        <OS>Windows NT 5.0</OS>
            <CountryName/>
    </User>
    <Page SchemaRef="page3">
    <PageContent>
        <Unit SchemaRef="dau84">
            <Data_Oid>4</Data_Oid>
        </Unit>
            <Unit SchemaRef="inu9">
            <Data_Oid>15</Data_Oid>
                <Data_Oid>24</Data_Oid>
            <Data_Oid>10</Data_Oid>
            </Unit>
    </PageContent>
    </Page>
</Request>
```

Fig. 8.11. An extract from a *conceptual log* that records the access to the Author page specified in Fig. 8.10

the retrieval of additional properties, not traced by the runtime logging mechanism, but represented in the conceptual schema, and their integration in the conceptual log, if needed. For example, for the analysis of the user navigation behavior, it could be useful to represent the complete set of links (not only the one selected by users) that can be navigated from one page.

Requests in the conceptual log are grouped by user session. With respect to the conventional Web logs, the identification of the user session is indeed simplified, thanks to availability of the session identifier (JSESSIONID), used by the application server to manage users sessions, and recorded into the application server log.

Conceptual logs offer multiple advantages. In addition to calculating basic traffic statistics (e.g., the number of requests per page), they enable the computation of advanced statistics, especially related to the access to database entities and their instances, and to hypertext elements of any granularity (site views, areas, pages, content units). Logging such data, especially the access to data items published within pages, is not trivial for dynamic Web pages. In the majority of other approaches such kinds of analysis are not supported and, if provided,[2] they require extra-efforts for the inclusion of some scripts,

---

[2] See, for example the approach adopted by Fireclick (http://www.fireclick.com/).

buried in the page code, to monitor and log the contents generated when the page is requested. Differently from such approaches, the production of conceptual logs does not require any additional activity. Thanks to the model-based approach, at runtime the application engine instantiates elements of the conceptual schema, and therefore is able to "naturally" log execution data that reflect the defined conceptual schema.

Conceptual logs also introduce a number of advantages with respect to Web usage mining. Several data mining projects have demonstrated the usefulness of a representation of the structure and content organization of a Web application [Coo03, SCDT00, EV03]. As affirmed in [Coo03], "the description of the application structure is considered a critical input to the pre-processing algorithms that can be used as filter before and after pattern discovery algorithms, and can provide information about expected user behaviors". However, Web usage mining approaches require additional, sometimes complex, computations for reconstructing the application schema. Conceptual logs alleviate this tasks. They can be easily tailored on specific Web usage mining algorithms, with the great advantage of eliminating the typical preprocessing phase completely. In fact, the identification of user sessions is done by the WebML runtime, and the post-mining retrieval of content and structure information is unnecessary since this information is available from the WebML hypertext schema, and is also integrated into the final conceptual logs.

8.5 Automatic Tools

Automatic tools can be adopted for the assessment of quality, covering both testing and usability evaluation activities. Generally, such tools are based on a set of rules dictating how to examine the application model or code to identify features that can cause failures.

The adoption of automatic tools can improve the reliability of the quality assessment process. As reported in [Bra04], automatic tools can address some of the issues that prevent developers from adopting testing and evaluation methods. In particular, tools are systematic, fast, and reliable, and can be effectively adopted for tackling repetitive and time-consuming evaluation tasks. Also, tools might allow developers to easily code and execute procedures for the verification of in-house guidelines to make them easily enforced.

8.5.1 Testing Tools

Several tools are available for testing Web sites (see [How07, web07a] for an exhaustive guide). The majority of them, especially those freely available, provide support for *link and page testing*, checking for browser compatibility, load time, navigability of the application hypertext (e.g., identifying ghost pages), accessibility, and so on. Some tools (see, for example, [Rat09, HTT07]) also support functional testing, providing *capture-replay* facilities for recording

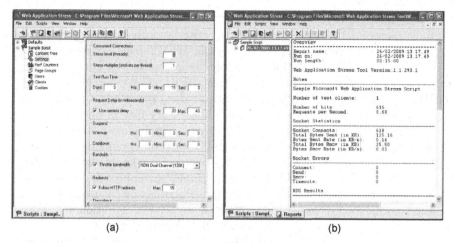

Fig. 8.12. Two windows of the WAS testing tool: a) the window to set test session parameters and b)the window to report test results [Mic07]

details of user interactions with the Web application and repeating them while checking for errors. Such tools are able to simulate the interaction with forms: they allow test designers to specify some values that are then used as input data for the form during the test execution.

Performance tools automatically execute stress and load tests to assess the server speed as well as its reliability. As a concrete example, Figure 8.12 shows the interface of the WAS (Web Application Stress) testing tool by Microsoft [Mic07]. Figure 8.12(a) shows the WAS window for setting the parameters of the test session, while Figure 8.12(b) displays the report produced after executing the test.

8.5.2 Usability Evaluation Tools

Even though the cost (in terms of time and effort) of inspection methods and user testing is not particularly high, and their effectiveness has been so far largely proved for augmenting the quality of Web applications, very often it happens that evaluation is not systematically performed on the whole application and at each development step. In particular, claims about the number of evaluators that are enough to detect usability breakdown, as well as the nature of the qualitative data per se (which does not allow conducting systematic verifications and comparison) are advocating for automatic tools able to efficiently treat the most repetitive evaluation tasks, without requiring much time and skill from human resources.

There are three main categories of Web evaluation tools [Bra04], which cover a large set of tests for usability and accessibility:

- *Tools for accessibility analysis*, such as webXACT (http://webxact. watchfire.com/), A-Prompt (http://aprompt.snow.utoronto.ca/), and

LIFT (http://www.usablenet.com). The metrics implemented by these tools correspond to official accessibility criteria (such as those prescribed by W3C), and refer to properties of the HTML page coding, such as browser compatibility, use of safe colors, appropriate color contrast, etc.

- *Tools for usability analysis*, such as CWW [BPKL02], WebTango [IH01],and WebCriteria SiteProfile (http://www.coremetrics.com), that analyze site design for verifying usability guidelines. They mostly operate at the presentation layer, with the aim of discovering problems such as the consistency of presentation of contents and navigation commands (e.g., link labels, color, etc.). Very often, they neglect structural and navigation problems. Some recent proposals (see, for example, the approach described in Section 8.4.1[FLMM04]) try to address such issues by focusing more on the identification of structural lacks in the hypertext definition.

- *Tools for Web usage analysis*, which allow calculating statistics on site activities and mining data on user behavior. The majority of the commercial tools (see, for example, AWSD-WebLog [http://awsd.com/scripts/weblog/index.shtml] and Analog [http://www.analog.cx.]) are traffic analyzers, producing site traffic reports referring to number of visits, server errors and pages not found, search engines accessing the application, or user and browser statistics. Only few academic researches address the analysis of user navigation paths and for Web usage mining [BS00,.Coo03, MLME04].

While the adoption of automatic tools for Web log analysis is mandatory, an important observation must be made about the first two categories of tools. Such tools constitute a valuable support for reducing the effort required by evaluators for analyzing "by hand" the whole application with respect to all the possible usability lacks. However, they are not able to exhaustively verify usability issues. In particular, they cannot assess all those properties that require judgements by human specialists (e.g., usage of natural and concise language). Also, automatic tools cannot provide answers about the nature of a discovered problem and the design revision that can solve it.

Automatic tools are therefore very useful when their use complements the activity of human specialists, since they can execute repetitive evaluation tasks for inspecting the application and highlighting critical features that are worth being later inspected by evaluators.

8.6 Summary

The ever-increasing spread of Web applications among non expert users, the abundance of content and the complexity of hypertext interfaces, as well as the increased use of Web applications for activities that range from everyday tasks to mission-critical action, represent a context in which quality is a relevant factor for the success of such applications. The Web modeling techniques so far proposed have brought many benefits; but even though applying design principles is now widely accepted, the problem of poor application design is still significant.

Web engineering provides designers with a collection of tools and languages; tools speed up the development process, while formal specification languages enforce some sort of syntactic rigor and allow for (semi- or complete) automatic code generation. Syntactic correctness prevents the designer from delivering an application containing flaws, resulting in bugged code generation, but a quality application is much more than a bug-free piece of code. Applications that incorporate quality assurance into their development process will be better able to comply with quality requirements. In particular, as reported in [Low03b]:

1. Evaluation is the key for assuring quality: the effort put into evaluation directly determines the quality of the final applications.
2. In order to be effective the evaluation must rely on the establishment of suitable quality attributes to be verified.

This chapter has illustrated the most acknowledged methods currently adopted for testing and usability evaluation of Web applications, together with the most relevant factors characterizing the quality models on which quality assessment of Web applications can be grounded.

Independently of the advantages offered by the adoption of a given method, it is worth noting that professionals and researchers suggest that a correct research plan for quality assessment should usually cover the application of multiple testing and evaluation techniques. The idea is that the characteristics of each method determine its effectiveness in discovering a specific class of failure. Therefore, different methods can be used in a complementary manner, so as to ensure a major completeness of the assessment results.

The adoption of automatic tools can also improve the reliability of the assessment process. However, tools can help verify structural properties while they fail to assess all those properties that require judgements by human specialists, especially as far as usability is concerned, as well as provide answers about the nature of a discovered problem and suggestions about the needed design revisions. Automatic tools are therefore very useful when their use complements the activity of human specialists.

8.7 Further Readings

An interesting starting point for investigating the concepts of Quality and Quality Assessment are the different standards defined by the ISO organization. In particular, the standards ISO 8402-86 [ISO86] and 9126-1 provide a definition of quality, also outlining the different attributes of a software product by which its quality can be described and evaluated.

A comprehensive guide to functional testing is provided in [Bei95, MBST04]. Performance analysis and planning is discussed in [MA98]. Usability evaluation is largely discussed in some classical Human-Computer Interaction books [PRS+94, DFAB98, Nie00].

A contribution to make quality assurance more systematic is given in the Fenton and Pfleeger's book [FP97]. The book indeed describes a rigorous framework for software measurement, outlining the different factors affecting software quality and providing the motivations for a rigorous and systematic assessment based on the definition of quality models.

9

Semantic Web and Web 2.0

In this final chapter, we provide the reader with a peek at the two main directions the Web has been heading in recent years: the Semantic Web and Web 2.0.

- *The Semantic Web*: So far, the Web has mainly been used as a communication medium of content and services for human consumers. Since the first emergence of the idea of the Semantic Web, there has been a trend toward accompanying content with machine-interpretable metadata to allow computers to "understand" the meaning of that content and, thus, to facilitate the access, retrieval, and exchange of whatever data that is on the Web. Huge funding and effort have been invested in this research area, and we will illustrate the principles, technologies, and main applications of the Semantic Web.
- *Web 2.0*: Since its first usage of the Web as a mere one-way communication medium, where there was a clear distinction between content providers and content consumers, things have radically changed. Currently, we see a clear trend of users acting not only as content consumers, but also as content providers. Social networks, wikis, blogs, and folksonomies, equipped with newer and more powerful technologies like AJAX, Flash, or RSS, represent what is commonly called Web 2.0. In addition, while the potential and possibilities of Web 2.0 are far from exhausted, the term Web 3.0 has already been coined. We will attempt to clarify the concepts behind these terms, and give the reader a view of what they are all about.

Semantic Web and Web 2.0 are currently hot research topics, both in academia and industry. Given their relative novelty, their results are not yet as stable as those of the topics discussed so far in this book, and their application is less widespread. Nevertheless, in this final chapter we will provide the reader with some insight into these topics, and point out how existing Web engineering methods have been adapted to cope with the additional requirements that came along.

S. Casteleyn et al., *Engineering Web Applications*, Data-Centric Systems and Applications,   293
DOI: 10.1007/978-3-540-92201-8_9, © Springer-Verlag Berlin Heidelberg 2009

9.1 The Semantic Web

A book on Web engineering would not be complete without a discussion on the Semantic Web. The Semantic Web is an extension to the current Web, and started out as a vision of one of its creators, Tim Berners-Lee. He realized that one of the major shortcomings of the traditional Web is the fact that its information is mostly *human-interpretable*, not *machine-interpretable*. To fully grasp this problem, consider the example of figure 9.1, showing two very simple Web pages, each representing a "mouse." You, the reader, will immediately notice that on the left Web page an animal is shown, and on the right page a computer accessory is shown. You do so by interpreting the image and using this knowledge to attach the correct interpretation to the word "mouse" in the sentence "This is a mouse." In other words, the *meaning* or *semantics* of the word "mouse" is provided by you, the human reader, using contextual information (in this case, the accompanying image). For a machine, however, it is impossible to grasp what is on each page. In fact, a machine only detects two pages, each containing an image and a string. It does not know what is represented in the image; it cannot interpret the sentence, nor can it correctly distinguish and interpret the two occurrences of the word "mouse." For a computer, the information contained in the page is *readable*, but not *interpretable*.

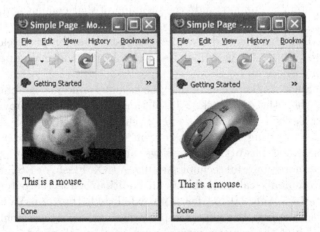

Fig. 9.1. Two different meanings for "mouse"

This problem is illustrated by the fact that all major search engines are mainly restricted to syntax-based search queries, as they are not able to grasp the semantics of the information on the Web. Also, for automated agents crawling the Web searching for relevant information, the lack of semantics is problematic. Imagine a shopping agent that searches for the cheapest 17-inch screen available. It will run into all kinds of problems related to the lack of semantics: when is something a (computer) screen, when are "monitors" also screens, how different currencies are handled, what about promotions? The automated agent will fail miserably.

To overcome this problem of lack of semantics on the Web, Tim Berners-Lee envisioned the Semantic Web. He defined it as an extension of the current Web in which information is given a well-defined meaning, better enabling computers and people to work in cooperation [BLHL01].

The Semantic Web is thus considered as an additional layer on top of the current Web. To give information a well-defined meaning, the Semantic Web relies on the use of ontologies. Intuitively, we can describe an ontology as the terminology used for concepts of a certain domain (e.g. "mouse," "cat," "animal," "reptile"), and the relations that exist between these concepts (e.g., "is a," "eats"). Our enhanced example page, representing a "mouse" with an ontology, is (schematically) depicted in Figure 9.2.

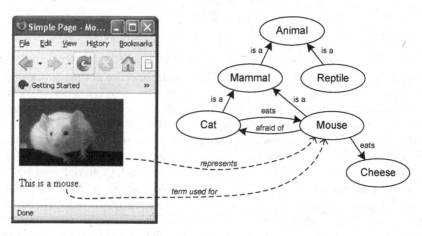

Fig. 9.2. Schematic representation of a simple ontology annotating a Web page

More formally, the term ontology is defined as *a formal, explicit specification of a shared conceptualization of a domain of interest* [Gru93]. In other words, ontologies form a formal and explicit representation of concepts and the relations between these concepts that can be distinguished in a particular domain. This explicit and formal specification allows machines to *understand* and *interpret* the information captured by an ontology, thus allowing automated processes to use this information (e.g. for reasoning, for crawling the Web, for performing search based on content).

9.1.1 Semantic Web Technologies

To realize the Semantic Web, the W3C has defined a number of languages, each fulfilling a particular role and implementing a layer of the Semantic Web. The different layers can be found in Figure 9.3 (taken from [Hyv02]).

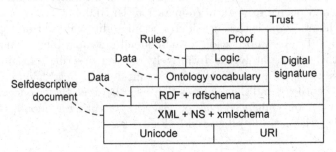

Fig. 9.3. Semantic Web layers [Hyv02]

The layers of the lower part of the stack, Unicode, URI, XML + namespaces (NS) + XML schema, RDF + RDF Schema, and the Ontology vocabulary layer (which consists of OWL), are largely in place. OWL has been a W3C Recommendation since February 2004. Research on the remaining top layers, Logic, Proof and Trust, has not yet resulted in W3C Recommendations.

The Unicode layer ensures that all languages on top make use of international character sets, while the URI layer provides means for identifying resources on the Semantic Web (i.e., any resource can be referred to using a URI). All languages (including RDF(S) and OWL) adopt XML (eXtensible Markup Language) as syntax as they are built on top of the XML + NS + XML Schema layer. XML allows users to add (a tree) structure to their documents by using a self-defined set of tags. XML Schema is used to define the allowed structure and vocabulary of an XML document. Note that such an XML schema does not define the semantics of the tags introduced.

There are a lot of XML-related technologies. The most notable example is XSL,[1] combining the XML transformation language XSLT,[2] the XML path language XPath,[3] and an XML vocabulary for specifying formatting semantics XSL-FO. There are also many software packages available to work with and handle XML, easing the job of programmers using XML. Two notable examples are the Xerces software project, an XML parser implementing the major APIs (e.g., SAX, DOM), and Xalan, an open-source software library implementing XSLT and XPath. Both are available in major programming languages (e.g., Java, C++).

---

[1] http://www.w3.org/Style/XSL/
[2] http://www.w3.org/TR/xslt
[3] http://www.w3.org/TR/xpath

RDF stands for *Resource Description Framework* and allows users to add structured metadata to the Web. The main modeling primitives of RDF are Resources, Properties, and Statements. A Resource can be anything one can refer to by means of a URI, and Properties describe relations between either Resources or characteristics of Resources (attributes). An RDF description consists of a number of Statements or triples of the form: subject (a Resource), predicate (a Property), and object (a Resource or Literal, e.g., string, number, date, etc.). Furthermore, RDF also introduces Containers and Collections which provide a way to group Resources. Although both Containers and Collections describe a group of Resources, their semantics are somewhat different. The semantics of a Collection specify that the listed Resources are all members and the only members of a particular Collection (i.e., no other members exist), while Containers do not impose this restriction. Three types of Containers exist: a Bag (an unordered Container), a Sequence (an ordered Container), and an Alternative (a list of alternative options). It is noteworthy that RDF allows the reification of Statements, i.e., treating Statements as if they were real data (intertwining the meta-data and data levels).

RDFS[4] is a vocabulary description language for RDF which allows us to define a domain-specific vocabulary. RDFS provides modeling primitives to describe Classes and Properties. Classes correspond to the generic concept of Type or Category, and are similar to classes in object-oriented programming languages. RDFS also allows to define subclass relations between two classes. To describe Properties, RDFS provides the means to describe both the domain and the range of a property and to define property hierarchies (subproperty statements). Furthermore, resources can be defined as being an instance of a particular Class. Note that the semantics that can be expressed by RDFS are rather limited. For example, no cardinality constraints can be expressed. In the situation where one desires to express more complex semantics, ontologies come into play.

There are several extensions to RDF, in the form of RDF vocabularies (we will discuss one such vocabulary in the next section). SPARQL[5] is the W3C recommendation for the query language for RDF. Two major frameworks to handle RDF data are open-source Java frameworks: Jena[6] and Sesame.[7] Jena provides an API to read RDF data, provides serialization possibilities to different data sources, supports SPARQL, and has reasoning support. Sesame provides somehow similar facilities. At the time of this writing, probably the main differences are the fact that Sesame implements a custom query language, SeRQL, and does not fully support SPARQL. In addition, Jena provides OWL support, which is lacking in Sesame.

---

[4] http://www.w3.org/TR/rdf-schema/

[5] http://www.w3.org/TR/rdf-sparql-query/

[6] http://jena.sourceforge.net/

[7] http://www.openrdf.org/

OWL[8] stands for Web Ontology Language, and it further extends RDF(S) to provide additional machine-processable semantics for resources on the Web. It provides the following added capabilities compared to RDF(S):

- Cardinality constraints on Properties (e.g., a person has exactly one name);
- Value constraints on Properties using all-values and some-values constructs (e.g., for a SoccerTeam, all values of the hasPlayer Property must be an instance of SoccerPlayer);
- Transitive, symmetric, and inverse Properties;
- Equivalence between Classes, Properties, or Instances (e.g., the Classes Aircraft and Plane are equivalent);
- Constructs to combine Classes (i.e., define Classes as unions, intersections, or complements of other Classes; define Classes to be disjoint from other Classes);
- Constraints on domain and range of specific Class-Property combinations (e.g., a Property hasPlayer has 11 values for a Class SoccerTeam, while it has only five values for a Class BasketballTeam).

OWL provides three increasingly expressive sublanguages (i.e., OWL Lite, OWL DL, and OWL Full), targeted at different types of users:

- OWL Lite supports those users primarily needing a classification hierarchy and simple constraints (e.g., OWL Lite permits only cardinality constraints of values 0 or 1).
- OWL DL supports users who want the maximum expressiveness while retaining computational completeness and decidability. The abbreviation DL refers to its formal foundation on Description Logics. The characteristics of computational completeness and decidability of course also apply to OWL Lite as it is a subset of OWL DL. Note that OWL DL (and OWL Lite) add a number of restrictions to the syntax of RDF(S). Most importantly, individuals and classes are clearly separated.
- OWL Full is meant for users who want maximum expressiveness and the syntactic freedom of RDF(S). The drawback is that no computational guarantees can be assured. Note that OWL Full allows Classes to be simultaneously a collection of individuals and an individual in its own right. This means that, in contrast to OWL DL and OWL Lite, OWL Full facilitates meta-modeling as found in RDFS.

The most popular tool to date for creating and editing OWL ontologies is Protege,[9] an open-source ontology editor. Protege offers the possibility for programmers to write plug-ins, thus providing extra functionalities (e.g., several visualization plug-ins are currently available).

---

[8] http://www.w3.org/2004/OWL/
[9] http://protege.stanford.edu/

9.1.2 The Friend Of A Friend Project

One popular example of the Semantic Web in action is the Friend Of A Friend (short: FOAF) project,[10] initiated by Libby Miller and Dan Brickley in 2000. FOAF is an RDF vocubulary[11] to describe people, their relations, and their properties. A FOAF profile is often informally described as a machine-readable version of a traditional home page: it describes a person, some facts of this person (e.g., interests, ongoing projects), and connections to other persons (people "known" by this person) in a semantically well-defined and machine-readable way.

The FOAF vocabulary can be broadly categorized into five categories:[12]

- *FOAF basics*: basic FOAF classes and properties describing persons and their basic properties. Examples include foaf:Person, foaf:name, foaf:homepage, etc.
- *Personal info*: FOAF classes and properties describing personal information about a person. Examples include foaf:knows, foaf:publications, foaf:weblog, etc.
- *Online account/IM*: FOAF classes and properties describing information about the online accounts a person possesses. Most of these are not yet stable. Examples include foaf:OnlineChatAccount, foaf:holdsAccount, foaf:msnChatID, etc.
- *Projects and groups*: FOAF classes and properties describing information about projects and their members. Examples include foaf:Project, foaf:member, foaf:fundedBy, etc.
- *Documents and images*: FOAF classes and properties describing information about documents and images. Examples include foaf:Document, foaf:Image, foaf:topic, etc.

A simple FOAF profile for one of the authors of this book, described in XML syntax, is given in Figure 9.4. It is quite self-explanatory, except maybe for the foaf:mbox_sha1sum property, which denotes the sha1 sum of the email address of the person being described.

The FOAF vocabulary should be considered a basic set of terms for describing persons, their activities and their connections. Like any RDF vocabulary, FOAF is extensible (e.g., by defining subclasses or properties, extending existing FOAF classes and properties) and may easily be combined with other RDF vocabularies. In fact, the FOAF specification itself uses other, more detailed vocabularies where possible. For example, a FOAF person is described as a subclass of a geo-spatial thing, a class defined in the Basic Geo vocab-

---

[10] http://www.foaf-project.org/
[11] The FOAF vocabulary specification can be found at http://xmlns.com/foaf/spec/.
[12] See http://xmlns.com/foaf/spec/.

```
<rdf:RDF xmlns:rdf="http://www.w3.org/1999/02/22-rdf-syntax-ns"
         xmlns:rdfs="http://www.w3.org/2000/01/rdf-schema"
         xmlns:foaf="http://xmlns.com/foaf/0.1/">

<foaf:Person rdf:ID="me">
 <foaf:name>Sven Casteleyn</foaf:name>
 <foaf:givenname>Sven</foaf:givenname>
 <foaf:family_name>Casteleyn</foaf:family_name>
 <foaf:title>Dr.</foaf:title>
 <foaf:gender>male</foaf:gender>
 <foaf:mbox_sha1sum>
    84db5efb9a3ecebeda27be3957df13c171c4b9e2
 </foaf:mbox_sha1sum>
 <foaf:homepage rdf:resource="http://wise.vub.ac.be/members/sven/"/>
 <foaf:workplaceHomepage rdf:resource="http://wise.vub.ac.be/"/>
 <foaf:img rdf:resource="http://wise.vub.ac.be/images/people/sven.jpg"/>
 <foaf:publications
rdf:resource="http://wise.vub.ac.be/members/sven/research/publications.bib"/>
 <foaf:knows>
  <foaf:Person>
   <foaf:name>Florian Daniel</foaf:name>
   <rdfs:seeAlso rdf:resource="http://www.floriandaniel.it/foaf.rdf"/>
  </foaf:Person>
 </foaf:knows>
</foaf:Person>
</rdf:RDF>
```

Fig. 9.4. A simple FOAF profile

ulary.[13] Furthermore, FOAF profiles are easily harvested and are integrable, as is any RDF data.

Over the years, many tools have been developed for FOAF. Notable examples include FOAF-a-Matic,[14] a Javascript application allowing users to create their own FOAF profile using a form-based Web page, and FOAF Explorer,[15] a FOAF browser which presents a FOAF profile in a human-readable format, by transforming the FOAF profile to an XHTML Web page. This allows users to easily explore and browse the depicted FOAF neighborhood. Eventually, generic RDF(S) and OWL tools can be used to harvest, process, query, and reason over FOAF profiles.

9.1.3 Web Design Methods and the Semantic Web

The Web engineering community has not been blind to the emergence of the Semantic Web. In the literature, we discern two different ways in which the Semantic Web plays a key role in current Web engineering approaches: one is by the creation of Web applications starting from semantically described data, and the second is by the generation of semantic annotations from the Web engineering process. We will discuss both cases in the following subsections.

---

[13] http://www.w3.org/2003/01/geo/

[14] http://www.ldodds.com/foaf/foaf-a-matic.html

[15] http://xml.mfd-consult.dk/foaf/explorer/

Hera: Engineering Web applications from semantic data

Hera [VFHB03] [FHB06] is a model-driven methodology for designing and developing Web Information Systems using Semantic Web technologies. The Hera methodology consists of three main design phases, resembling the classical phases of most existing Web engineering methods as described earlier in this book. Hera calls these phases the conceptual design, the application design, and the presentation design. The focus of Hera is on offering a classical hypermedia view on top of an existing Semantic Web data source (i.e., in the form of RDF(S) data).[16] Hera also uses RDF(S) to describe its own (meta-)models. Let us have a closer look at the role RDF(S) plays throughout Hera.

During conceptual design, the conceptual model is built, which describes the domain of the data for the application to be built. Furthermore, Hera specifies a *Media Model*, which associates attributes with media types. Both the conceptual model and the media model are described in RDF(S). During the application design, the application model is built, which describes the concepts and attributes presented to the user and grouped together on a page (in Hera called a *slice*). The application model is described in RDF(S). Finally, the presentation model, also described in RDF(S), specifies the layout and rendering.

The literature on Hera describes a toolkit, called HPG (Hera Presentation Generator), which is capable of generating an actual Web application from the Hera design models [FHB06].

A detailed description of HPG has been treated in Chapter 7, Section 7.2.2), but for the sake of this section we will recall the issues directly related to the Semantic Web and Semantic Web technology. HPG comes in two flavors: an XSLT-based engine and a Java-based engine. The first engine is a transformation-based pipeline, gradually transforming the different models into the actual Web application. Hereby, Hera uses existing XML and RDF(S) tools to perform the transformations. XSLT is used to perform the transformations, while RQL is used to query the RDF data. The Java-based HPG engine eliminates some shortcomings of the XSLT-based engine. Most notably, HPG-XSLT generates the full Web presentation at once, while HPG-Java generates a page upon request. Furthermore, XSLT is an XML-based transformation language, not capable of exploiting the full semantics of the RDF data models. Finally, HPG-Java provides form support, which is lacking in the HPG-XSLT version. HPG-Java is based on Java servlet technology, and uses Jena[17] to (programmatically) handle RDF data and check constraints upon the data, and Sesame,[18] an open-source RDF-based repository and querying facility, with its query language SeRQL to query and update RDF data.

---

[16] Another focus of Hera is adaptation, but since this is not the focus of this section we will not discuss it here.

[17] http://jena.sourceforge.net/

[18] http://www.openrdf.org/

Hera mentions the following as advantages from the use of RDF(S) data application: interoperability, direct availability of Semantic Web data (which may be published next to the traditional Web site), reuse of existing RDF vocabularies (e.g., the CC/PP vocabulary[19]), and extensibility of the existing models [FHB06]. Furthermore, Hera is able to benefit from the broad range of available RDF(S) tools, as was illustrated above.

WSDM: Generating structural and content-related semantic annotations from the Web design process

While Hera focuses on generating a presentation starting from RDF data, other methods focus on the generation of semantic annotations. In the context of WSDM (see Chapter 3), extensive work has been done to (semi-) automatically generate semantic annotations along with the actual Web application. WSDM distinguishes two different kinds of semantic annotations: content-related and structural semantic annotations. Content-related semantic annotations make the contents of the Web site explicit, by describing them in a Semantic Web format (OWL in case of WSDM). Structural semantic annotations describe some structural properties of the Web application, and make the semantics of the different structural elements (e.g., a navigation menu, a logo, a sidebar) explicit. Typically, dedicated ontologies are used to structurally annotate a Web page (e.g., the WAfA ontology [YHGS04] is used to denote the structural properties of a Web site specifically suited to assist visually impaired users when browsing it).

It is important to notice the use of OWL internally in WSDM, which facilitates the generation of both kinds of semantic annotations. In particular, OWL was used to formally define (the semantics of) the different design models. All these models together form an ontology, called the WSDM ontology. It can be considered a meta-model for WSDM. When designing a Web application with WSDM, the WSDM ontology is thus populated, and contains the instantiated WSDM design models. The semantics of the WSDM ontology is exploited to generate structural semantic annotations. Second, OWL is also used as a modeling language for the content and functionality of the Web application during conceptual design. This modeling is exploited to generate content-related semantic annotations.

We will now discuss both types of annotations in more detail and elaborate on how they are generated from a WSDM design.

Content-related semantic annotations

Content-related semantic annotations are generated based on the set of all object chunks, which are tiny conceptual models describing the pieces of content or functionality required by the visitors of the Web application. The combined object chunks are called the reference ontology. It may be newly constructed,

---

[19] http://www.w3.org/TR/CCPP-struct-vocab/

in case no suitable domain ontology was available, or an existing ontology may be reused, in which case the object chunks re-use the existing concepts and relations of this ontology.[20] WSDM allows object chunks to slightly differ from the relevant part of the reference ontology to which they map, allowing the designer to model the actual information needed from a visitor's point of view. For example, the designer might use a **hasAddress** property, while in the reference ontology the address is stored more fine-grainedly, i.e., by the **hasStreet**, **hasCity**, and **hasCountry** properties. The mapping between the object chunks, representing the particular needs of the visitors, and the reference ontology, describing the domain, is called object chunk mapping (OCM).

As part of the data design sub-phase of the implementation design, WSDM describes a data source mapping (DSM), which describes exactly how the reference ontology maps to the actual data source. If a relational database is used, the data source mapping describes which concepts and attributes map to which tables and attributes in the database. Using this mapping, the actual data is retrieved from the data source when generating the Web application, but it can also be used to generate the content-related semantic annotations, along with the data. As an example, consider Figure 9.5, which describes how a simple object chunk, representing the address of a man, results in the generation of the actual data as well as the content-related annotations.

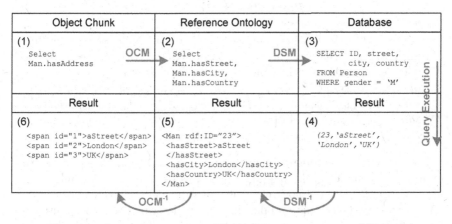

Fig. 9.5. Generating content-related semantic annotations [CPT06]

Finally, the generated output and the annotations are linked together, using an XPointer expression. For the example of Figure 9.5, the XPointer expression links the street (aStreet) and the annotation together:

```
page.html\#xpointer(id("1"))<=>
```

---

[20] WSDM also allows reusing multiple domain ontologies, each describing a part of domain of the Web application. For clarity, we do not consider this case here. Interested readers are referred to [CPT06]

```
refOnt\#xpointer(id("23")/hasStreet)
```

Note that it is important to link the data on the Web page and the annotation together in order to allow agents processing the Web page to exploit the semantics of the content and present a human with the result on the (regular) Web site. We will also see in the next section why linking the regular Web page and its annotations might be preferable to offering the semantic data independently.

Structural Semantic Annotations

To generate structural semantic annotations, WSDM exploits the semantics of the different modeling elements captured in the WSDM ontology. This is done by defining a mapping between these WSDM elements and the concepts of an external ontology, specialized for a certain use. As an example, WSDM describes how to generate structural semantic annotations using the WAfA ontology [PCY$^+$05], which is tailored to assist visually impaired users browsing a Web application [YHGS04]. The mapping rules were described both in first-order predicate logic and the Semantic Web Rule Language (SWRL[21]). As an example, consider the following two rules, taken from [PCY$^+$05]:

- *travel:Figure*: An image illustrating textual material.
  $Rule : \forall i \in L : wsdm : Figure(i) \rightarrow travel : Figure(i)$
- *travel:DropDownLinkMenu*: A DropDownLinkMenu is a menu that appears below an item when the user clicks on it. This corresponds to a `wsdm:Menu` represented as a `wsdm:List` in WSDM, with an associated behavior of "dropDown" when the event "onClick" occurs.
  $Rule : \forall i \in I, \exists x, y \in I : wsdm : Menu(i) \land wsdm : representedBy(i, x) \land$
  $wsdm : List(x) \land wsdm : hasBehavior(x, y) \land wsdm : Behavior(y) \land$
  $wsdm : onEvent(y,' onClick') \land wsdm : doAction(y,' dropDown') \rightarrow$
  $travel : DropDownLinkMenu(i)$

Note that some mapping rules are simply one-to-one mappings, while others are more complex. The mapping rules thus describe which combination of (occurring) WSDM ontology elements corresponds to which concept in the WAfA ontology. Once this mapping has been described, it can be used to generate the structural annotation for all Web applications developed with WSDM.

In the implementation generation, an extra transformation is defined to generate these structural annotations, based on the mapping rules. WSDM detects occurrences of the left side of a mapping rule in the instantiated WSDM models, generates the relevant annotations (found on the right side of a mapping rule), and finally links them together using an XPointer expression. The XPointer expressions use the unique IDs of the WSDM ontology instances to point to a certain element. As these unique IDs are also used for their

---

[21] http://www.w3.org/Submission/SWRL/

corresponding elements in the actual implementation (e.g., the HTML page), the XPointer expressions point to the correct (HTML) elements, although the detection was performed on the (semantically richer) WSDM ontology instantiations.

Such Web pages, which are semantically annotated with the WAfA ontology, can subsequently be transcoded to a form that is better suited for screen readers, typically used by visually impaired users (see [YHGS04]). Note that this again illustrates the usefulness of annotating (regular) Web pages with semantic annotations.

More information on the generation of both content-related and structural semantic annotations can be found in [PCY$^+$05, CPT06].

9.2 Web 2.0/3.0

One of today's most appealing but, at the same time, controversial terms in the field of Web engineering is *Web 2.0*: some time after the implosion of the so-called dot-com bubble in the fall of 2001, the Web community started analyzing the stories and peculiarities of those companies (i.e., Web sites) that successfully survived the burst of the bubble. After a joint brainstorming session, O'Reilly Media and MediaLive International found that the surviving companies indeed had some things in common [O'R05], which, if properly identified and leveraged on, would form a solid foundation for the success of new Internet businesses. They introduced the term *Web 2.0* to start discussions about the differences between Web 1.0 (the pre-bubble Web) and Web 2.0 to identify the success factors for the Web 2.0 applications to come.

Several years have gone by, but there is still no common agreement on what *Web 2.0* actually means. There are researchers and practitioners who refer to it in terms of business models; others think in terms of new technologies (especially new powerful client-side technologies like AJAX or Flash); still others think of user-provided content (e.g., blogs) and social (networking) Web sites; and, finally, there are people who say there is no such thing as "Web 2.0." As these positions show, economic, technological and social aspects are intertwined in most definitions and, interestingly, nobody has yet come up with a commonly agreed on definition of what should really be intended with "Web 2.0."

Among the numerous aspects that have been mentioned to describe Web 2.0, one of the main driving forces in today's Web applications is, in our view, the blurring of the initially well-defined distinction between content providers and content consumers. More and more content consumers are also becoming content providers: they maintain their own blogs, write contributions for WIKIs (probably the most striking example is Wikipedia[22]), they contribute to (commercial) Web sites through feedback and reviews (think of Web sites

---

[22] http://en.wikipedia.org

like eBay or Amazon), they publish photos and videos, and tag them with suitable keywords (e.g., Flickr[23]). In short, the Web is becoming more and more "open content," in addition to "open-source."

The described evolution of Web sites and applications leverages on different ingredients, of which two seem of particular importance: *social involvement* or participation and *new technologies*. Joining forces through social involvement of users (*networking*) means integrating users into the application and the content creation process. Typical Web users, however, are not skilled programmers or experts, and therefore need to be assisted in the content creation process through highly usable and rich Web interfaces. But even in the case of users with programming skills, they need to be helped in the integration of Web content and services in order to succeed. These two considerations demand rich client technologies and lightweight programming models.

9.2.1 Social Involvement/Participation

In [O'R05], the author argues that "the value of the software is proportional to the scale and dynamism of the data it helps to manage." Therefore, the more the number of users involved in an application, the more they contribute with their own data and knowledge and the more they add value to the application. Wikipedia, for example, would have reached neither its current dimensions nor the popularity it enjoys without its exemplary user participation and joint, collaborative editing mechanism. Data sharing applications like Flickr for photo sharing or professional social networks like LinkedIn[24] also completely rely on user participation for their success.

In the following subsections we will shortly describe the most prominent forms of applications that build on high user participation and that rely on content consumers also taking on the role of content providers.

Wikis

According to Wikipedia (probably the best-known wiki on the Web), "a wiki is a collaborative Web site which can be directly edited by anyone with access to it." "Wiki" is a shorter form of "wiki wiki," a Hawaiian word for *fast*; the name was first used by Ward Cunningham in 1994 for his first wiki called *WikiWikiWeb*.

A wiki can be seen as a database for creating, browsing and searching for information. The *creation* of a document, i.e., a wiki page, proceeds collaboratively: each user is allowed to create or modify a page through a proper markup language or WYSIWYG[25] editor. Edited contents are immediately

---

[23] http://en.wikipedia.org

[24] http://www.linkedin.com/

[25] What You See Is What You Get: The acronym WYSIWYG stands for the characteristic of applications in which a document appears on-screen exactly as it will appear when printed.

available online and may be subject to correction or modification by other users. Wikis usually also allow users to revert to a previous version of a page, undoing the latest changes. The *browsing* of the documents is performed via the actual wiki, which consists of the set of documents along with their internal and external links. The *search* function allows for fast, keyword-based search in the collection of documents stored in the wiki.

Typically, wikis are open to the public and do not require any registration; however, restricted areas or private wikis are possible as well; they require explicit user registration prior to any creation or update of content, occasionally also for the inspection of content. Also, there are multiple implementations of wiki systems, most of them open-source.[26]

Blogs

A blog is a Web site where entries are written by the blog owner in chronological order and commonly displayed in reverse chronological order. Blogs allow the publication in real time of news, information, opinions, stories, etc., and readers are able to comment on each entry, thereby starting a possible discussion for an entry. The term "blog" is a fusion of the term "Web log," which hints at the chronological registration of contributions and comments. Today, blogs often replace personal Web sites, as they provide more dynamic content management features and built-in collaborative discussions; but online newspapers also oftentimes use blogs to enable topic-specific discussions with their readers.

Folksonomies

A folksonomy is a collaborative, social approach to creating, maintaining, and evolving classification data (metadata). The term "folksonomy" is a contraction of "folk" (people) and "taxonomy" (classification). Folksonomies are typically adopted to allow users to tag (classify by means of freely chosen keywords) contents of a Web site or a Web application (e.g., text, photos, videos, etc.) in order to facilitate the search and browsing of the contents. Like wikis, folksonomies leverage user expertise and participation to grow collaboratively. A good example of a successful folksonomy on the Web is flickr,[27] an online photo sharing Web site with high user participation.

Social networking

A social network, in general, consists of a group of persons that are connected through diverse social relationships, which may range from simple acquaintanceship or family relationships to professional contacts. Since the emergence

---

[26] One of the best known implementations is MediaWiki: http://www.mediawiki.org/wiki/MediaWiki

[27] http://www.flickr.com/

of the World Wide Web, the Web has always been a platform enabling contact
between people, but especially in recent years this role has been made explicit,
and proper Web-based social networks were born. Social software typically
enables the creation of so-called *virtual communities*, which use the Web to
maintain contacts, to exchange opinions and experiences. Recently there has
been a trend toward the online maintenance of business connections, through
Web sites like LinkedIn and XING[28].

9.2.2 Technologies for Web 2.0

Users and developers in the Web 2.0 era expect participation through simplicity; that is, the easier to use and the more efficient a user interface, the
higher their tendency to participate. This principle is valid for normal users
who, for example, would like to comment on an entry in a blog, and also for
skilled programmers who, for example, would like to integrate news messages
updated in real time into their own Web applications.

In this regard, the Web 2.0 movement has mainly produced technological
answers and, more precisely, effective client-side technologies to enhance the
user's browsing experience. Most of these client-side approaches are actually
not really radically new inventions (e.g., the ingredients for AJAX have been
around for several years already). Their sudden success can be traced back
to the growing availability of high-speed Internet connections, which provided
for the necessary ease and speed when application code needs to be downloaded for execution, of growing browser support for JavaScript and DOM,[29]
and of availability of browser extensions through plug-ins. Thanks to these
improvements the new client-side technologies enjoy high acceptance among
users, which is the final and most important hurdle a new technology needs
to clear in order to succeed.

AJAX, Adobe Flash, JavaFX, and MS Silverlight

One of the most prominent representatives of Web 2.0 technologies is AJAX,
which is actually not a single technology, but rather a collection of technologies
accompanied by a "distributed" programming technique that leverages on
application logic being executed at the client side (i.e., in the client browser).

In the context of Web 2.0, AJAX has gained importance as an enabling
technology or paradigm for the development of highly usable and responsive
Web interfaces. In short, AJAX enables the development of Rich Internet
Applications (RIAs [All02]) through dynamic HTML (see Section 5.7 for a
discussion of how the design of RIA applications can be assisted via conceptual
modeling techniques). Dynamic HTML is based on a static markup language

---

[28] http://www.xing.com/

[29] The *Document Object Model* is a platform- and language-independent object
model for representing HTML or XML documents and related formats.

(HTML), on client-side scripting (JavaScript), on the use of Cascaded Style Sheets (CSS), and on DOM. The scripting language allows an application to access the structure of a document (the Web page) through the DOM and to *dynamically* set markup and style properties, thus yielding an interactive and animated Web site. AJAX adds to the dynamic HTML approach the capability of asynchronous communication between the client and the server.

As further discussed in Section 2.4.4, Adobe Flash,[30] JavaFX,[31] and Microsoft Silverlight[32] follow an alternative approach to the development of RIA applications, which is not based on dynamic HTML. Those approaches provide full-fledged, lightweight application development platforms that run inside the client browser. As such, all the three approaches require the installation of a dedicated browser plug-in (i.e., Flash Player, Java Virtual Machine, or Silverlight runtime), which enables the browser to parse programming scripts and to render content and user interface widgets. Applications developed with these techniques are typically characterized by highly interactive user interfaces featuring desktop-like user experiences. Overcoming the limitations posed by the traditional HTML/browser paradigm to the design of effective user interfaces is indeed the driving force that led to the development of such plug-in application platforms.

RSS and Atom

RSS (an acronym of *Really Simple Syndication* [Har03]) is an XML-based syndication protocol for the simple distribution of content over the Web. Its most widespread use is probably in distributing news headlines on the Web, in addition to events listings, news stories, project updates, or excerpts from discussion forums. Unlike Web services, RSS provides a fixed set of mandatory and optional elements and attributes to be included in a feed, which makes it relatively easy to integrate RSS contents into other applications; all feeds simply comply with the same XML structure. This simplicity led to a broad adoption of RSS by content providers, and the trend is growing.

Figure 9.6 shows a piece of an RSS feed (version 2.0 – see the header of the feed) by the New York Times. An RSS file contains a so-called *channel*, which can be seen as a container of an arbitrary number of items of a similar type. The feed starts with the channel context, i.e., with the definition of title, link, description, language, and some other metadata of the channel. Then, there is the definition of one item (for simplicity, other items have been omitted), which in the case of Europe News contains title, link, description, author, unique identifier (<guid> element), and publication date of the related news message. As can be seen in the figure, the feed only provides a headline of the news message and a link to the newspaper's Web site that can be accessed if the user is interested in reading the whole news article.

---

[30] http://www.adobe.com/products/flash/

[31] http://sun.com/javafx

[32] http://silverlight.net/

```
<?xml version="1.0" encoding="UTF-8"?>
<rss version="2.0">
<channel>

 <title>NYT > Europe</title>
 <link>http://www.nytimes.com/pages/world/europe/index.html?partner=rssnyt
 </link>
 <description></description>
 <language>en-us</language>
 <copyright>Copyright 2007 The New York Times Company</copyright>
 <lastBuildDate>Fri, 10 Aug 2007 08:05:01 GMT</lastBuildDate>
 <image>
  <title>NYT > Europe</title>
  <url>http://graphics.nytimes.com/images/section/NytSectionHeader.gif</url>
  <link>
  http://www.nytimes.com/pages/world/europe/index.html
  </link>
 </image>

 <item>
  <title>
  British Farmers Hopeful Cattle Disease Is Under Control
  </title>
  <link>http://www.nytimes.com/2007/08/10/world/europe/
  10britain.html?ex=1344398400&amp;en=785aaaba44b8b42d&amp;
  ei=5088&amp;partner=rssnyt&amp;emc=rss</link>
  <description>The British government&#8217;s relaxation of the
  ban on the movement of livestock was a first sign that the
  spread of foot-and-mouth disease was coming under control.
  </description>
  <author>JANE PERLEZ</author>
  <guid isPermaLink="false">http://www.nytimes.com/2007/08/10/
  world/europe/10britain.html</guid>
  <pubDate>Fri, 10 Aug 2007 07:04:31 GMT</pubDate>
 </item>
 ...
</channel>
</rss>
```

Fig. 9.6. An example RSS fragment taken from the New York Times Europe News RSS feed (August 10, 2007)

RSS feeds are not only for integration into existing applications; there are also proper RSS *readers* (many of them open-source) which allow for the easy access and the automatic update of RSS feeds. Also, there are currently three main versions of RSS sometimes used with sightly different names: RSS 0.91 and RSS 1.0 are commonly called *Rich Site Summary* or *RDF Site Summary*, RSS 2.0 is commonly called *Really Simple Syndication*.

Another syndication format like RSS is Atom [NS05], which provides very similar features and is now close to becoming a recognized Internet standard (RFC - emphRequest for Comments).

9.2.3 New Technologies and Accessibility

While technologies like AJAX and Flash provide very effective means to empower Web interfaces and to enhance the user's browsing experience, unfortunately such technologies represent a serious threat to accessibility if users have disabilities (mainly visual disabilities). Common screen readers are made for parsing and reading out loud traditional HTML markup pages, which lead to problems with the two technologies mentioned:

- *AJAX*: The programming style pushed forward by the AJAX approach is based on the partial update and reload of a viewed Web page. This means, that maybe only the content of a specific `<div>` element gets updated, and the remaining parts of the page do not. This behavior is critical because, having a sequential logic, the screen reader is not able to recognize content that has suddenly been updated. To be aware of the new content, the user is thus required to start over and to listen again to the whole page, which, of course, is very annoying, especially if no update happened.
- *Flash*: Flash movies or scripts are typically embedded in the HTML markup by means of the `<object>` tag. Therefore, contents inside the Flash object are not immediately available to the screen reader, and the only solution to provide some information about the object to visually impaired users is to provide suitable textual alternatives. In the case of embedded games or highly interactive applications, textual alternatives, of course, are not a satisfactory solution. Fortunately, Macromedia has demonstrated awareness of this issue and has developed suitable accessibility features for Flash [Reg05], but regrettably not all Web developers are capable of designing accessible Flash objects, or they simply are not willing to bear the additional burden of doing so.

However, as accessibility is more and more becoming a key factor for the acceptance of modern Web applications (especially in the case of public administrations), solutions for the above problems are expected to arise.

9.2.4 Web Design Methods and Web 2.0

As for the engineering of effective and high-quality Web 2.0 applications, the availability of new and powerful technologies alone does not suffice. To assist content creators through highly usable user interfaces, research in human-computer interaction (HCI) needs to be advanced, and efficient design patterns need to be identified. To assist Web developers in reusing and integrating Web content and services, some more work at the conceptual level needs to be done: there are new technologies, but there really are not new programming paradigms yet with the potential to radically change how Web applications are developed.

The design of rich user interfaces for Web applications typically demands more application logic at the client side. In traditional Web applications, the whole application logic is located at the server side, and the client browser only renders HTML markup; oftentimes, JavaScript is used to empower HTML presentation features, but in traditional Web applications there is generally no or very little real application logic at the client side. Supporting rich interfaces and asynchronous data transfers between the client and the server thus implies a rethinking of the allocation of the business logic of the application as a whole: the logic needs to be distributed over client and server, and roles need to be redefined accordingly. Little research has been done so far in this context [BCFT06, Tof07], but work is ongoing.

The reuse and the integration of Web content and services from third-party providers is already a reality, despite the lack of proper programming models and abstractions. The phenomenon is commonly known by the name of *Web mashups* [Mer06], which are Web sites or applications that are developed by integrating user interfaces, application logic, and content (data) that can be accessed over the Web and, for example, are provided by third parties as Web sites or services. The first mashups could not rely on APIs as programmable interfaces, as the actual content providers did not even realise that their Web sites were wrapped into other applications. The first mashups with Google Maps, for example, predate the official release of the Google Maps API.[33] The API is Google's answer to the growing number of hacked map integrations, where people read the application's AJAX code and autonomously derived the required functionalities.

Publicly available APIs for mashups are rare but still growing. Integration is performed in an ad hoc fashion by leveraging whatever programming language supported by the content source, on either client side (e.g., AJAX) or server side (e.g., PHP, Java, ASP.NET). Content is typically provided as markup code and integrated by wrapping the respective Web site. Since such kinds of "component interfaces" are typically not very stable (remember that the content provider may not know that his application is being wrapped), most effort in the development of mashups goes into manual testing and maintenance. Due to the lack of proper framework support, code isolation is not guaranteed (i.e., there may be code collision between two JavaScript source codes), and conflicts among UI components may occur. Building Web mashups thus remains an ad hoc time-consuming and challenging task, and the need for suitable lightweight programming models is manifest [DYB+07].

There are some attempts that aim at providing users with simple means to compose their own mashups; for instance, there is *Yahoo! Pipes* [34] or *Microsoft Popfly* [35]. Pipes is a Web application with which users can build their own applications through a user-friendly, graphical user interface by dragging and dropping RSS sources, defining filters over the feeds, and connecting outputs and inputs. RSS feeds from the Web are interconnected by applying the idea

---

[33] http://www.google.com/apis/maps/

[34] http://pipes.yahoo.com/pipes/

[35] http://www.popfly.ms/

of pipes, as known from the Unix operating system, to the feeds. The result
can then be executed through the Pipes Web application. Popfly too is a
Web application that enables the development of one's own applications in a
drag-and-drop fashion. Building blocks may have own HTML interfaces and
application logics that are not restricted to RSS feeds. Both sites, Pipes and
Popfly, however, act as platforms for their compositions only, and applications
can be executed only through their engines.

In [YBC+07, YBSP+07], authors provide an interesting approach to the
component-based development of Web applications at the user interface layer,
i.e., a framework for the integration of standalone modules or applications,
where integration occurs at the presentation layer. The design of the proposed framework is inspired by lessons learned from application integration,
appropriately modified to account for the specificity of the UI integration
problem. The approach leverages on an abstract component model to specify characteristics and behaviors of presentation components and proposes an
event-based composition model to specify the composition logic. Components
are abstractly described by means of a simple description language, the *UI
Service Description Language* (UISDL); compositions are specified by means
of an XML-based language, the *eXtensible Presention Integration Language*
(XPIL), which is interpreted by runtime middleware for the execution of the
resulting composite application. The two languages are similar in function
and logic to WSDL and BPEL for Web services. So far, two different runtime
frameworks have been developed, one in JavaScript for execution in the client
browser, and one in Java for execution on the Web server; each framework is
able to parse and execute XPIL compositions.

In line with the idea of a lightweight programming model, one of the
main contributions of the described approach is that it promotes a simple
yet powerful composition model for Web applications, based on a declarative
composition language and equipped with a graphical editor for drag-and-drop
application composition (cf. Figure 9.7). The final vision of the approach is
that, in addition to providing Web services interfaces, one day content and
service providers will also equip their content and services with suitable UI
components that can easily be integrated into other applications, without
requiring intimate knowledge of the component's internal logic.

9.2.5 Web 3.0

If there is still quite some uncertainty and discussion regarding the meaning
of the term "Web 2.0," then it is not surprising that the meaning of "Web
3.0" is even more blurred. The term is increasingly being used by researchers
and practitioners in the Web community to denote the Web after the current
Web 2.0 era. As a tentative definition of this future version of the Web, we
cite what Tim Berners-Lee said regarding Web 3.0 [Sha06]:

> "I think maybe when you've got an overlay of scalable vector
> graphics – everything rippling and folding and looking misty – on

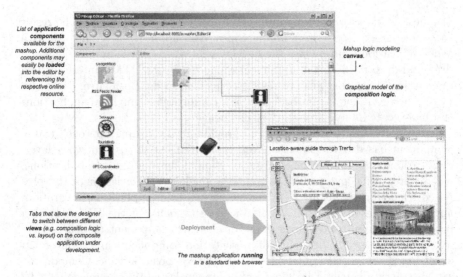

Fig. 9.7. The Mixup editor for visually composing the integration logic of a composite Web application starting from abstract UI component descriptions [YBC+07]: components are connected by means of so-called *listeners*, which bind an event of one component to an operation of another component

> Web 2.0 and access to a Semantic Web integrated across a huge space of data, you'll have access to an unbelievable data resource."

In short (and intentionally oversimplified), we can thus say that Web 3.0 is the vision of the merger of Web 2.0 and the Semantic Web. While the typical Web 2.0 technologies are nowadays regarded as quite stable, research on technologies for Web 3.0 is ongoing, RDF(S)[36] and SPARQL[37] being the most prominent representatives [LH07]. In [AKTV07] the authors discuss an interesting scenario that goes into the direction of Web 3.0.

9.3 Summary

The Web is constantly, if not increasingly, changing and evolving. New applications, trends, technologies and practices are emerging at a fast pace. In this book, we provided insight into the current practices in Web engineering, and we tried to look at the problem of developing good Web applications from a conceptual point of view, so as to smooth out technological biases and implementation-specific issues that, as hinted at above, may change rapidly

---

[36] *Resource Description Framework (Schema)* [RDF07]
[37] SPARQL is a recursive acronym standing for *SPARQL Protocol and RDF Query Language* [PS07].

over time. In this chapter, we looked at two of the recent trends in Web engineering: the Semantic Web and Web 2.0. The former puts the semantics, i.e., the meaning of Web content and applications, into the center; the latter focuses on the involvement of the end users into the content creation and application development processes. We also elaborated on how Web design methods target or make use of these recent evolutions.

In some sense, the two trends are diverging, in that on one hand the Semantic Web aims at enriching existing (purely syntactic) resources and content with annotations that provide information about their meaning, e.g., by linking them to a domain ontology. On the other hand, the characteristic of the Web 2.0 is to strip down complexity as much as possible from current applications and development practices, so as to enable even (unskilled) Web users to publish contents and create applications on the Web.

However, we also recognize that both trends aim at a similar goal: easing the usage of the Web and empowering users with novel features. Very likely, the two approaches will merge sooner or later (and indeed already do) and combine the power of both into a flexible and powerful platform for intuitive end user programming. There is still a lot of research to be done in order to achieve this goal, and we anticipate that the area of Web engineering will evolve accordingly.

9.4 Further Readings

A major resource for Web standards in general, and Semantic Web technologies in particular, is the Web site of the World Wide Web Consortium (W3C; see http://www.w3c.org/). The reader can find all W3C (candidate) recommendations, activities, and working groups on this Web site. Another major resource to stay up to date with the latest Semantic Web technologies and evolutions is the proceedings of the International Semantic Web Conference and the European Semantic Web Conferences.

In the field of Web engineering, interesting research has been performed in in WebML in the context of the Semantic Web and Semantic Web technologies. For instance, regarding the creation of Web applications starting from semantically described data, in [BF07] the authors describe an approach to the development of Semantic Web portals accessing different distributed or local ontological data sources; also, advanced query reasoning mechanisms are supported (a collection of related works can be found under the *Research* section of http://www.webml.org). Regarding the generation of semantic annotations from conceptual models during the Web engineering process research has mainly focused on Semantic Web services in the context of the *Web Service Modeling Ontology* (WSMO [FLP+06]): In particular, the authors show that business processes and Web engineering models have sufficient expressive power to support the semiautomatic extraction of semantic descriptions (i.e.,

WSMO ontologies, goals, Web services, and mediators), thus partially hiding the complexity of dealing with semantics [BCC⁺06, BCF⁺08].

Web 2.0 is attracting a large body of people from both academia and industry. As a consequence, there is a multitude of Web-2.0-related events, such as conferences, workshops, symposia, tutorials, and tech talks. As for Web 2.0 in Web engineering in particular, the reader can refer to the traditional conferences on Web research and technologies, such as the International World Wide Web Conference, the International Conference on Web Engineering, the Asian Pacific Web Conference, or the International Conference on Web Information Systems Engineering. Also journals like IEEE Internet Computing, the ACM Transactions on Internet Technology, the ACM Transactions on the Web, the Journal of Web Engineering (Rinton Press), or the World Wide Web Journal (Springer) publish valuable contributions to Web 2.0/3.0.

As for Web mashups in particular, one of the most renowned resources is the Web site by Programmable Web (http://www.programmableweb.com/). The site is particularly valuable for the interested mashup developer, as it represents the most extensive collection of Web APIs, which are the cornerstones for the successful development of mashup applications.

References

[ABB+07]   Roberto Acerbis, Aldo Bongio, Marco Brambilla, Massimo Tisi, Ste-
            fano Ceri, and Emanuele Tosetti. Developing eBusiness Solutions with
            a Model Driven Approach: The Case of Acer EMEA. In *Proceedings
            of the 7th International Conference on Web Engineering, Como, Italy*,
            pages 539–544. Springer Verlag, July 2007.

[ACFOP03]   Silvia Mara Abrahão, Nelly Condori-Fernández, Luis Olsina, and Oscar
            Pastor. Defining and Validating Metrics for Navigational Models. In
            *Proceedings of 9th IEEE International Software Metrics Symposium
            (METRICS 2003), Sydney, Australia*, pages 200–210. IEEE Computer
            Society, September 2003.

[ACKM03]   Gustavo Alonso, Fabio Casati, Harumi Kuno, and Vijay Machiraju.
            Web Services: Concepts, Architectures, and Applications. Springer-
            Verlag, 2003.

[ACL06]   Mauro Andreolini, Michele Colajanni, and Riccardo Lancelotti. Web
            System Reliability and Performance. In Mendes and Mosley [MM06],
            chapter 6, pages 181–218.

[AKTV07]   Anupriya Ankolekar, Markus Krtzsch, Thanh Tran, and Denny Vran-
            decic. The Two Cultures: Mashing up Web 2.0 and the Semantic
            Web. In *Proceedings of the International World Wide Web Conference
            (WWW'07), Banff, Alberta, Canada*, pages 825–834. ACM Press, May
            2007.

[All02]   Jeremy Allaire. Macromedia Flash MXA next-generation rich client.
            Macromedia White Paper, March 2002.

[AOA05]   Anneliese Amschler Andrews, Jeff Offutt, and Roger T. Alexander.
            Testing Web applications by modeling with FSMs. *Software and Sys-
            tem Modeling*, 4(3):326–345, 2005.

[Atk01]   Colin Atkinson. *Component-Based Product Line Engineering with
            UML.* The Component Software Series. Addison Wesley, November
            2001.

[BBC+03]   Nigel Bevan, Carol Barnum, Gilbert Cockton, Jakob Nielsen, Jared
            Spool, and Dennis Wixon. The "Magic Number" 5: Is It Enough For
            Web Testing? In *Proceedings of 2003 Conference on Human Factors
            in Computing Systems (CHI 2003), extended abstracts, Ft. Lauderdale,
            Florida, USA*, pages 698–699, New York, NY, USA, 2003. ACM Press.

[BCC⁺03]   Marco Brambilla, Stefano Ceri, Sara Comai, Piero Fraternali, and Ioana Manolescu. Specification and Design of Workflow-Driven Hypertexts. *Journal of Web Engineering*, 1(2):1–100, April 2003.

[BCC⁺06]   Marco Brambilla, Irene Celino, Stefano Ceri, Dario Cerizza, Emanuele Della Valle, and Federico Michele Facca. A Software Engineering Approach to Design and Development of Semantic Web Service Applications. In *Proceedings of the 5th International Semantic Web Conference (ISWC 2006), Athens, Greece*, volume 4273 of *Lecture Notes in Computer Science*, pages 172–186. Springer, November 2006.

[BCF⁺08]   Marco Brambilla, Stefano Ceri, Federico Michele Facca, Irene Celino, Dario Cerizza, and Emanuele Della Valle. Model-driven design and development of semantic web service applications. *Transactions on Internet Technology*, 8(1), 2008.

[BCFC06]   Alessandro Bozzon, Sara Comai, Piero Fraternali, and Giovanni Toffetti Carughi. Conceptual modeling and code generation for rich internet applications. In David Wolber, Neil Calder, Christopher H. Brooks, and Athula Ginige, editors, *Proceedings of the 6th International Conference on Web Engineering (ICWE 2006), Palo Alto, California, USA*, pages 353–360. ACM, July 2006.

[BCFM06]   Marco Brambilla, Stefano Ceri, Piero Fraternali, and Ioana Manolescu. Process modeling in web applications. *ACM Transactions of Software Engineering and Methodology*, 15(4):360–409, 2006.

[BCFT06]   Alessandro Bozzon, Sara Comai, Piero Fraternali, and Giovanni Toffetti Carughi. Conceptual modeling and code generation for rich internet applications. In *Proceedings of the 6th International Conference on Web Engineering (ICWE 2006), Palo Alto, California, USA*, pages 353–360. ACM, July 2006.

[BDS08]   Don Brown, Chad Davis, and Scott Stanlick. *Struts 2 in Action*. Manning Publications, 2008.

[Bec00]   Kent Beck. *Extreme Programming Explained: Embarace Change*. Addison-Wesley, 2000.

[Bei95]   Boris Beizer. *Black-Box Testing: Techniques for Functional Testing of Software and Systems*. John Wiley & Sons, New York, 1995.

[BEK⁺07]   Don Box, David Ehnebuske, Gopal Kakivaya, Andrew Layman, Noah Mendelsohn, Henrik Frystyk Nielsen, Satish Thatte, and Dave Winer. SOAP Version 1.2. W3c recommendation, W3C, April 2007. http://www.w3.org/TR/soap/.

[BF07]   Marco Brambilla and Federico Michele Facca. Building semantic web portals with webml. In *Proceedings of the 7th International Conference on Web Engineering (ICWE 2007), Como, Italy*, July 2007.

[BFK⁺99]   Joachim Bayer, Oliver Flege, Peter Knauber, Roland Laqua, Dirk Muthig, Klaus Schmid, Tanya Widen, and Jean-Marc DeBaud. Pulse: A methodology to develop software product lines. In *Proceedings of the 1999 symposium on Software reusability (SSR), Los Angeles, USA*, pages 122–131, 1999.

[BFTM05]   Luciano Baresi, Piero Fraternali, Massimo Tisi, and Sandro Morasca. Towards Model-Driven Testing of a Web Application Generator. In David Lowe and Martin Gaedke, editors, *Proceedings of the 5th International Conference on Web Engineering (ICWE 2005), Sydney,*

Australia, volume 3579 of *Lecture Notes in Computer Science*, pages 75–86. Springer, 2005.

[BGC⁺03] Sean Bechhofer, Carole Goble, Leslie Carr, Simon Kampa, Wendy Hall, and Dave De Roure. Cohse: Conceptual open hypermedia service. *Frontiers in Artifical Intelligence and Applications*, 96, 2003.

[BGdPL⁺03] Felix Bachmann, Michael Goedicke, Julio Cesar Sampaio do Prado Leite, Robert L. Nord, Klaus Pohl, Balasubramaniam Ramesh, and Alexander Vilbig. A meta-model for representing variability in product family development. In Frank van der Linden, editor, *Proceedings of the 5th International Workshop on Software Product-Family Engineering (PFE 2003), Siena, Italy*, volume 3014 of *Lecture Notes in Computer Science*, pages 66–80. Springer, November 2003.

[BGP01] Luciano Baresi, Franca Garzotto, and Paolo Paolini. Extending UML for Modeling Web Applications. In *Proceedings of the Hawaii International Conference on System Sciences (HICSS 2001), Maui, Hawaii, USA*. IEEE Press, January 2001.

[BHS02] Bettina Berendt, Andreas Hotho, and Gerd Stumme. Towards Semantic Web Mining. In Ian Horrocks and James A. Hendler, editors, *Proceedings of the first International Semantic Web Conference (ISWC 2002), Sardinia, Italy*, volume 2342 of *Lecture Notes in Computer Science*, pages 264–278. Springer, October 2002.

[BHW99] Paul De Bra, Geert-Jan Houben, and Hongjing Wu. Aham: A dexter-based reference model for adaptive hypermedia. In K. Tochtermann, J. Westbomke, U.K. Wiil, and J. Leggett, editors, *Proceedings of the 10th ACM Conference on Hypertext and Hypermedia: Returning to Our Diverse Roots (HYPERTEXT '99), Darmstadt, Germany*, pages 147–156. ACM, February 1999.

[BKKZ05] Hubert Baumeister, Alexander Knapp, Nora Koch, and Gefei Zhang. Modelling adaptivity with aspects. In David Lowe and Martin Gaedke, editors, *Proceedings of the 5th International Conference on Web Engineering (ICWE 2005), Sydney, Australia*, pages 406–416, 2005.

[BKM99] Hubert Baumeister, Nora Koch, and Luis Mandel. Towards a uml extension for hypermedia design. In Robert B. France and Bernhard Rumpe, editors, *Proceedings of The Unified Modeling Language - Beyond the Standard, 2nd International Conference (UML'99), Fort Collins, USA*, volume 1723 of *Lecture Notes in Computer Science*, pages 614–629, October 1999.

[BLC95] Tim Berners-Lee and Dan Connolly. Hypertext Transfer Protocol – HTTP/1.0. Technical report, MIT/W3C, September 1995. `http://www.w3.org/MarkUp/html-spec/html-spec\_toc.html`.

[BLFF96] Tim Berners-Lee, Roy Fielding, and Henrik Frystyk. Hypertext Transfer Protocol – HTTP/1.0. Request for Comment 1945, IETF, May 1996. `http://www.ietf.org/rfc/rfc1945.txt`.

[BLHL01] Tim Berners-Lee, Jim Hendler, and Ora Lassila. The semantic web. *Scientific American*, pages 34–43, May 2001.

[Boe88] Barry W. Boehm. A spiral model of software development and enhancement. *IEEE Computer*, 21(5):61–72, June 1988.

[BP04]   Davide Bolchini and Paolo Paolini. Goal-driven requirements analysis for hypermedia-intensive web applications. *Requirements Engineering*, 9(2):85–103, 2004.

[BPKL02]   Marilyn Hughes Blackmon, Peter G. Polson, Muneo Kitajima, and Clayton Lewis. Cognitive Walkthrough for the Web. In *Proceedings of CHI 2002 Conference on Human Factors in Computing Systems, Minneapolis, Minnesota, USA*, pages 463–470, April 2002.

[BPSM⁺08]   Tim Bray, Jean Paoli, C. M. Sperberg-McQueen, Eve Maler, and Franois Yergeau. Extensible Markup Language (XML) 1.0. Recommendation, W3C, November 2008. http://www.w3.org/TR/REC-xml.

[Bra04]   Giorgio Brajnik. Using Automatic Tools in Accessibility and Usability Assurance Processes. In Christian Stary and Constantine Stephanidis, editors, *Proceedings of the 8th ERCIM Workshop on User Interfaces for All, Vienna, Austria*, volume 3196 of *Lecture Notes in Computer Science*, pages 219–234. Springer, June 2004.

[Bru96]   Peter Brusilovsky. Methods and Techniques of Adaptive Hypermedia. *User Model and User-Adapted Interaction*, 6(2-3):87–129, 1996.

[Bru01]   Peter Brusilovsky. Adaptive hypermedia. *User Model. User-Adapt. Interact.*, 11(1-2):87–110, 2001.

[BS00]   Bettina Berendt and Myra Spiliopoulou. Analysis of Navigation Behaviour in Web Sites Integrating Multiple Information Systems. *VLDB Journal*, 9(1):56–75, 2000.

[BVGH00]   Vesna Bosilj-Vuksic, George M. Giaglis, and Vlatka Hlupic. Idef diagrams and petri nets for business process modelling: Suitability, efficacy, and complementary use. In *Proceedings of the 2nd International Conference on Enterprise Information Systems (ICEIS 2000), Setubal, Portugal*, pages 242–247, July 2000.

[Car]   Charles Carroll. ASP.net Tutorials. http://www.aspng.com.

[Cas05]   Sven Casteleyn. *Designer Specified Self Re-organizing Websites*. Ph.d. dissertation, Vrije Universiteit Brussel, 2005.

[CCMW01]   Erik Christensen, Francisco Curbera, Greg Meredith, and Sanjiva Weerawarana. Web Services Description Language (WSDL) 1.1. W3c note, W3C, March 2001. http://www.w3.org/TR/wsdl.

[CCRV07]   Ben Caldwell, Michael Cooper, Loretta Guarino Reid, and Gregg Vanderheiden. Web Content Accessibility Guidelines 2.0. W3C Working Draft, W3C, May 2007. http://www.w3.org/TR/WCAG20/.

[CD99]   James Clark and Steve DeRose. XML Path Language (XPath) - Version 1.0. W3C Recommendation, W3C, November 1999.

[CDF06]   Stefano Ceri, Florian Daniel, and Federico Michele Facca. Modeling web applications reacting to user behaviors. *Computer Networks*, 50(10):1533–1546, 2006.

[CDFM07]   Stefano Ceri, Florian Daniel, Federico M. Facca, and Maristella Matera. Model-Driven Engineering of Active Context-Awareness. *World Wide Web Journal*, 10(4):387–413, December 2007.

[CdL95]   Donald D. Cowan and Carlos José Pereira de Lucena. Abstract data views: An interface specification concept to enhance design for reuse. *IEEE Transactions on Software Engineering*, 21(3):229–243, 1995.

[CDMF07]   Stefano Ceri, Florian Daniel, Maristella Matera, and Federico M. Facca. Model-driven Development of Context-Aware Web Applications. *ACM Transactions on Internet Technology*, 7(1), February 2007.

[CDMN04]   Stefano Ceri, Peter Dolog, Maristella Matera, and Wolfgang Nejdl. Model-driven design of web applications with client-side adaptation. In Nora Koch, Piero Fraternali, and Martin Wirsing, editors, *Proceedings of the International Conference on Web Engineering (ICWE 2004), Munich, Germany*, volume 3140 of *Lecture Notes in Computer Science*, pages 201–214. Springer, July 2004.

[CE00]   Krysztof Czarnecki and Ulrich Eisenecker. *Generative Programing: Principles, Techniques, and Tools*. Addison Wesley, 2000.

[CF01]   Sara Comai and Piero Fraternali. A semantic model for specifying data-intensive web applications using webml. In *Proceeding of Semantic Web Workshop, Stanford, USA*, July 2001.

[CFB00a]   Stefano Ceri, Piero Fraternali, and Aldo Bongio. Web Modeling Language (WebML): a modeling language for designing web sites. *Computer Networks and ISDN Systems*, 33(1–6):137–157, June 2000.

[CFB00b]   Stefano Ceri, Piero Fraternali, and Aldo Bongio. Web Modeling Language (WebML): a modeling language for designing web sites. In *Proceedings of 9th International World Wide Web Conference (WWW 2000), Amsterdam, the Netherlands*, May 2000.

[CFB+02]   Stefano Ceri, Piero Fraternali, Aldo Bongio, Marco Brambilla, Sara Comai, and Maristella Matera. *Designing Data-Intensive Web Applications*. Morgan Kauffmann, 2002.

[CFM02]   Stefano Ceri, Piero Fraternali, and Maristella Matera. Conceptual modeling of data-intensive web applications. *IEEE Internet Computing*, 6(4), August 2002.

[CG88]   B. Campbell and J. M. Goodman. Ham: A general purpose hypertext abstract machine. *Communications of the ACM*, 31(7):856–860, July 1988.

[CGM00]   Junghoo Cho and Hector Garcia-Molina. The evolution of the web and implications for an incremental crawler. In Amr El Abbadi, Michael L. Brodie, Sharma Chakravarthy, Umeshwar Dayal, Nabil Kamel, Gunter Schlageter, and Kyu-Young Whang, editors, *Proceedings of the 26th International Conference on Very Large Data Bases (VLDB 2000), Cairo, Egypt*, pages 200–209. Morgan Kaufmann, September 2000.

[CHK+01]   Ned Chapin, Joanne E. Hale, Khaled Md. Khan, Juan F. Ramil, and Wui-Gee Tan. Types of software evolution and software maintenance. *Journal of Software Maintenance and Evolution: Research and Practice*, 13(1):3–30, 2001.

[CK04]   María José Escalona Cuaresma and Nora Koch. Requirements engineering for web applications - a comparative study. *Journal of Web Engineering*, 2(3):193–212, 2004.

[CK06]   Mara Jose Escalona Cuaresma and Nora Koch. Metamodeling the requirements of web systems. In Joaquim Filipe, José Cordeiro, and Vitor Pedrosa, editors, *Proceedings of the International Conference on Web Information Systems and Technologies (Selected Papers), Setubal, Portugal*, volume 1 of *Lecture Notes in Business Information Processing*, pages 267–280. Springer, 2006.

[CK07]   María José Escalona Cuaresma and Nora Koch. Metamodeling the requirements of web systems. In Joaquim Filipe, José Cordeiro, and Vitor Pedrosa, editors, *Proceedings of the International Conferences on*

Web Information Systems and Technologies WEBIST 2005 and WE-BIST 2006 (Selected Papers), Setubal, Portugal, volume 1 of Lecture Notes in Business Information Processing, pages 267–280. Springer, April 2007.

[Cla99]   James Clark. XSL Transformations (XSLT) - Version 1.0. W3C Recommendation, W3C, November 1999.

[CMM02]   Sara Comai, Maristella Matera, and Andrea Maurino. A Model and an XSL Framework for Analyzing the Quality of WebML Conceptual Schemas. In Proceeding of the International Workshop on Conceptual Modeling Quality (IWCMQ 2002), Tampere, Finland, Lecture Notes in Computer Science. Springer Verlag, October 2002.

[CMRD07] Stefano Ceri, Maristella Matera, Francesca Rizzo, and Vera Demaldé. Designing Data-Intensive Web Applications for Content Accessibility Using Web Marts. Communication of ACM, 50(4):55–61, 2007.

[CMS99]   Robert Cooley, Bamshad Mobasher, and Jaideep Srivastava. Data Preparation for Mining World Wide Web Browsing Patterns. Knowledge and Information Systems, 1(1):5–32, 1999.

[Con]   W3C Consortium. Extended Common Log File format. Technical report.

[Con99]   Jim Conallen. Modeling Web application architectures with UML. Communications of the ACM, 42(10):63–70, 1999.

[Con00]   Jim Conallen. Building Web Applications with UML. Addison Wesley, 2000.

[Con02]   J. Conallen. Building Web Applications with UML. Object Technology Series. Addison Wesley, 2002.

[Con07]   W3C Consortium. Wai guidelines and techniques. Technical report, http://www.w3.org/WAI/guid-tech.html, 2007.

[Coo03]   Robert Cooley. The Use of Web Structures and Content to Identify Subjectively Interesting Web Usage Patterns. ACM Transaction On Internet Technologies, 3(2), May 2003.

[CPT06]   Sven Casteleyn, Peter Plessers, and Olga De Troyer. On generating content and structural annotated websites using conceptual modeling. In David W. Embley, Antoni Olivé, and Sudha Ram, editors, Proceedings of the 25th International Conference on Conceptual Modeling (ER 2006), Tucson, USA, volume 4215 of Lecture Notes in Computer Science, pages 267–280, July 2006.

[CRP04]   Coral Calero, Julián Ruiz, and Mario Piattini. A Web Metrics Survey Using WQM. In Nora Koch, Piero Fraternali, and Martin Wirsing, editors, Proceedings of 4th International Conference on Web Engineering (ICWE 2004), Munich, Germany, volume 3140 of Lecture Notes in Computer Science, pages 147–160. Springer, July 2004.

[CT01]   Sven Casteleyn and Olga De Troyer. Structuring web sites using audience class hierarchies. In Hiroshi Arisawa, Yahiko Kambayashi, Vijay Kumar, Heinrich C. Mayr, and Ingrid Hun, editors, Conceptual Modeling for New Information Systems Technologies, ER 2001 Workshops, HUMACS, DASWIS, ECOMO, and DAMA, Yokohama, Japan, number 2465 in Lecture Notes in Computer Science, pages 198–211. Springer Verlag, November 2001.

[CTB03]   Sven Casteleyn, Olga De Troyer, and Saar Brockmans. Design time support for adaptive behavior in web sites. In Proceedings of the

2003 ACM Symposium on Applied Computing (SAC 2003), Melbourne, Florida, USA, pages 1222–1228, 2003.

[CVJ99]   Wendy Chisholm, Gregg Vanderheiden, and Ian Jacobs. Web Content Accessibility Guidelines 1.0. W3C Recommendation, W3C, May 1999. http://www.w3.org/TR/WAI-WEBCONTENT/.

[CWH07]   Sven Casteleyn, William Van Woensel, and Geert-Jan Houben. Adaptation engineering: A semantics-based aspect-oriented approach. In Simon Harper, Helen Ashman, Mark Bernstein, Alexandra I. Cristea, Hugh C. Davis, Paul De Bra, Vicki L. Hanson, and David E. Millard, editors, Proceedings of the eighteenth ACM Conference on Hypertext and Hypermedia (HYPERTEXT 2007), Manchester, UK, pages 189–198, 2007.

[Dan07]   Florian Daniel. Model-Driven Design of Context-Aware Web Applications. Ph.d. dissertation, Politecnico di Milano, 2007.

[DB02a]   Peter Dolog and Mária Bieliková. Hypermedia modelling using UML. In Petr Hanáček, editor, Proceedings of Information Systems Modelling Conference (ISM'2002), Rožnov pod Radhoštěm, Czech Republic, pages 79–86, April 2002.

[DB02b]   Peter Dolog and Mária Bieliková. Hypermedia systems modelling framework. Computing and Informatics, 21(3):221–239, December 2002.

[DBH99]   Paul De Bra, Peter Brusilovsky, and Geert-Jan Houben. Adaptive hypermedia: from systems to framework. ACM Computing Surveys, 31(4es):12, 1999.

[DC02]   Claire Dormann and Cristina Chisalita. Cultural Values in Web Site Design. In Proceedings of the 11th European Conference on Cognitive Ergonomics, Catania, Italy, September 2002.

[DD00]   Olga De Troyer and Tom Decruyenaere. Conceptual modelling of web sites for end-users. World Wide Web Journal, 3(1):27–42, 2000.

[Dei00]   Wolfgang Deiters. Information gathering and process modeling in a petri net based approach. In Wil M. P. van der Aalst, Jörg Desel, and Andreas Oberweis, editors, Business Process Management, Models, Techniques, and Empirical Studies, volume 1806 of Lecture Notes in Computer Science, pages 274–288. Springer, 2000.

[DFAB98]   A. Dix, J. Finlay, G. Abowd, and R. Beale. Human-Computer Interaction, volume 1. Prentice Hall, 2nd edition, 1998.

[DFHS04]   Anke Dittmar, Peter Forbrig, Simone Heftberger, and Christian Stary. Support for task modeling - a "constructive" exploration. In Rémi Bastide, Philippe A. Palanque, and Jörg Roth, editors, Proceedings of the Joint Working Conferences on Engineering Human Computer Interaction and Interactive Systems (EHCI-DSVIS 2004), Hamburg, Germany, volume 3425 of Lecture Notes in Computer Science, pages 59–76. Springer, July 2004.

[DHW99]   Paul De Bra, Geert-Jan Houben, and Hongjing Wu. AHAM: a Dexter-based reference model for adaptive hypermedia. In Proceedings of the 10th ACM Conference on Hypertext and hypermedia (HYPERTEXT '99): returning to our diverse roots, Darmstadt, Germany, pages 147–156, 1999.

[DLWZ03]   Reiner Dumke, Mathias Lother, Cornelius Wille, and Fritz Zbrog. Web Engineering. Pearson Education, 2003.

[dMS04]   Sabrina Silva de Moura and Daniel Schwabe. Interface development for hypermedia applications in the semantic web. In *Joint Conference 10th Brazilian Symposium on Multimedia and the Web & 2nd Latin American Web Congress, (WebMedia & LA-Web 2004), Ribeirao, Brazil*, pages 106–113. IEEE Computer Society, 2004.

[DN03]   Peter Dolog and Wolfgang Nejdl. Using UML and XMI for generating adaptive navigation sequences in web-based systems. In Perdita Stevens, Jon Whittle, and Grady Booch, editors, *Proceedings of the 6th International Conference on The Unified Modeling Language. Model Languages and Applications (UML 2003), San Francisco, CA, USA*, volume 2863 of *Lecture Notes in Computer Science*, pages 205–219. Springer, October 2003.

[DN04]   Peter Dolog and Wolfgang Nejdl. Using UML-based feature models and UML collaboration diagrams to information modelling for web-based applications. In Thomas Baar, Alfred Strohmeier, Ana Moreira, and Stephen J. Mellor, editors, *Proceedings of 7th International Conference on The Unified Modeling Language. Model Languages and Applications (UML 2004), Lisbon, Portugal*, volume 3273 of *Lecture Notes in Computer Science*, pages 425–439. Springer, October 2004.

[Dol07]   Peter Dolog. Engineering adaptive web applications. *KI - Zeitschrift Künstliche Intelligenz*, 7(4), 2007.

[Dol08]   Peter Dolog. *Engineering Adaptive Web Applications: A Domain Engineering Framework*. VDM Verlag Dr. Mller, 2008. http://www.vdm-publishing.com/.

[DRSS97]   Ann Doubleday, Michele Ryan, Mark V. Springett, and Alistair G. Sutcliffe. A Comparison of Usability Techniques for Evaluating Design. In *Proceedings of the Symposium on Designing Interactive Systems, Amsterdam, the Netherlands*, pages 101–110, 1997.

[DS07]   Peter Dolog and Jan Stage. Designing interaction spaces for rich internet applications with uml. In Piero Fraternali, Luciano Baresi, and Geert-Jan Houben, editors, *Proceedings of the 7th International Conference on Web Engineering (ICWE 2007), Como, Italy*, volume 4607 of *Lecture Notes in Computer Science*, pages 358–363. Springer, July 2007.

[dTC03]   Olga de Troyer and Sven Casteleyn. Modeling complex processes for web applications using wsdm. In *3rd International Workshop on Web-Oriented Software Technologies at ICWE2003 (IWWOST2003), Oviedo, Spain*, July 2003.

[DW98]   Desmond F. D'Souza and Alan Cameron Wills. *Objects, Components, and Frameworks with UML: The Catalysis Approach*. Addison-Wesley, 1998.

[DYB+07]   Florian Daniel, Jin Yu, Boualem Benatallah, Fabio Casati, Maristella Matera, and Regis Saint-Paul. Understanding UI Integration: A survey of problems, technologies. *IEEE Internet Computing*, 11(3):59–66, may/jun 2007.

[EG96]   Khaled El Emam and Dennis R. Goldenson. An empirical evaluation of the prospective international spice standard. *Software Process Improvement and Practice Journal*, 2(2):123–148, 1996.

[EV03]   Magdalini Eirinaki and Michalis Vazirgiannis. Web Mining for Web Personalization. *ACM Transactions on Internet Technology*, 3(1):1–27, 2003.

[FC99]   William A. Florac and Anita D. Carleton. *Measuring the Software Process*. Addison-Wesley, 1999.

[FGM⁺98]   Roy Fielding, Jim Gettys, Jeffery C. Mogul, Henry Frystyk, Larry Masinter, Paul Leach, and Tim Berners-Lee. Hypertext Transfer Protocol – HTTP/1.1. Technical report, W3C, November 1998. http://www.w3.org/Protocols/rfc2616/rfc2616.html.

[FHB06]   Flavius Frasincar, Geert-Jan Houben, and Peter Barna. HPG: the Hera Presentation Generator. *Journal of Web Engineering*, 5(2):175–200, 2006.

[Fie07]   Roy Fielding. *Architectural Styles and the Design of Network-based Software Architectures*. Ph.d. dissertation, University of California, Irvine, 2007.

[FLM98]   Daniela Florescu, Alon Y. Levy, and Alberto O. Mendelzon. Database techniques for the world-wide web: A survey. *SIGMOD Record*, 27(3):59–74, 1998.

[FLMM04]   Piero Fraternali, Pier Luca Lanzi, Maristella Matera, and Andrea Maurino. Model-Driven Web Usage Analysis for the Evaluation of Web Application Quality. *Journal of Web Engineering*, 3(2):124–152, 2004.

[FLP⁺06]   Dieter Fensel, Holger Lausen, Axel Polleres, Jos de Bruijn, Michael Stollberg, Dumitru Roman, and John Domingue. *Enabling Semantic Web Services: The Web Service Modeling Ontology*. Springer-Verlag, Secaucus, NJ, USA, 2006.

[FMM02]   Piero Fraternali, Maristella Matera, and Andrea Maurino. WQA: an XSL Framework for Analyzing the Quality of Web Applications. In *Proceedings of the International Workshop of Web and Software Technologies (IWWOST'02), Malaga, Spain*, June 2002.

[FMM03]   Piero Fraternali, Maristella Matera, and Andrea Maurino. Conceptual-Level Log Analysis for the Evaluation of Web Application Quality. In *Proceedings of the 1st Latin American Web Congress (LA-Web 2003), Santiago, Chile*. IEEE Computer Society, November 2003.

[FMNW04]   Dennis Fetterly, Mark Manasse, Marc Najork, and Janet L. Wiener. A large-scale study of the evolution of web pages. *Software: Practice and Experience - Special Issue: Web Technologies*, 34(2):213–237, 2004.

[FP97]   Norman E. Fenton and Shari L. Pfleeger. *Software Metrics: A Rigorous and Practical Approach*. PWS Publishing, Boston, MA, USA, 1997.

[FS94]   Richard Furuta and P. David Stotts. A formally-defined hypertextual basis for integrating task and information, 1994. Tech. Report TAMU-HRL 94-007.

[GA01]   Jaap Gordijn and J.M. Akkermans. Designing and evaluating e-business models. *IEEE Intelligent Systems*, 16(4):11–17, 2001.

[GA03]   Jaap Gordijn and J. M. Akkermans. Value-based requirements engineering: exploring innovative e-commerce ideas. *Requirements Engineering*, 8(2):114–134, 2003.

[GCG05]   Irene Garrigós, Sven Casteleyn, and Jaime Gómez. A structured approach to personalize websites using the oo-h personalization framework. In Yanchun Zhang, Katsumi Tanaka, Jeffrey Xu Yu, Shan Wang, and Minglu Li, editors, *Web Technologies Research and Development - APWeb 2005, Shanghai, China*, Lecture Notes in Computer Science 3399, pages 695–706, March 2005.

[GCP00] Jaime Gómez, Cristina Cachero, and Oscar Pastor. Extending a Conceptual Modelling Approach to Web Application Design. In *Proceedings of the 12th International Conference on Advanced Information Systems Engineering (CAiSE'00), London, UK*, pages 79–93. Springer-Verlag, 2000.

[GCP01] Jaime Gómez, Cristina Cachero, and Oscar Pastor. Conceptual modeling of device-independent web applications. *IEEE MultiMedia*, 8(2):26–39, 2001.

[GFdA98] Martin L. Griss, John Favaro, and Massimo d' Alessandro. Integrating feature modeling with the RSEB. In P. Devanbu and J. Poulin, editors, *Proceedings of 5th International Conference on Software Reuse, Victoria, Canada*, pages 76–85. IEEE Computer Society Press, June 1998.

[GG99] Hans-Werner Gellersen and Martin Gaedke. Object-oriented web application development. *IEEE Internet Computing*, 3(1):60–68, 1999.

[GGBH05] Irene Garrigós, Jaime Gómez, Peter Barna, and Geert-Jan Houben. A Reusable Personalization Model in Web Application Design. In *Proceedings of The ICWE 2005 Workshop on Web Information Systems Modelling (WISM'05), Sydney, Australia*, pages 40–49. University of Wollongong, School of IT and Computer Science, July 2005.

[GJM02] Carlo Ghezzi, Mehdi Jazayeri, and Dino Mandrioli. *Fundamentals of Software Engineering*. Prentice Hall PTR, Upper Saddle River, NJ, USA, 2002.

[Góm04] Jaime Gómez. Model-driven web development with visualwade. In Nora Koch, Piero Fraternali, and Martin Wirsing, editors, *Proceedings of the 4th International Conference on Web Engineering (ICWE 2004), Munich, Germany*, volume 3140 of *Lecture Notes in Computer Science*, pages 611–612. Springer, 2004.

[GP93] Franca Garzotto and Paolo Paolini. HDM — a model-based approach to hypertext application design. *ACM Transactions on Information Systems*, 11(1):1–26, January 1993.

[GPS91] Franca Garzotto, Paolo Paolini, and Daniel Schwabe. HDM, a Model for the Design of Hypertext Applications. In *Proceedings of ACM Hypertext Conference (HT 1991), San Antonio, Texas, USA*, pages 313–328, 1991.

[GRD07] Alejandra Garrido, Gustavo Rossi, and Damiano Distante. Model Refactoring in Web Applications. In *Proceedings of the 9th IEEE International Workshop on Web Site Evolution (WSE'07), Paris, France*, pages 89–96. IEEE Press, October 2007.

[Gro] The Web Design Group. HTML 4.0 Reference. http://www.htmlhelp.com/reference/html40/.

[Gro00] Object Management Group. OMG unified modelling language specification, version 1.3, March 2000. Available at http://www.omg.org/.

[Gro06] Object Management Group. Business process modeling notation specification. Technical report, Object Management Group, 2006. Available at: http://www.bpmn.org.

[Gru93]   Thomas R. Gruber. A translation approach to portable ontology spec-
             ifications. *Knowledge Acquisition*, 5(2):199–220, 1993.

[GYvdR06]   Jaap Gordijn, Eric Yu, and Bas van der Raadt. E-service design using
             i* and e³value modeling. *IEEE Software*, 23(3):26–33, 2006.

[Hal01]   Alon Y. Halevy. Answering queries using views: A survey. *VLDB
             Journal*, 10(4), 2001.

[Har01]   Elliotte Rusty Harold. *XML Bible*. Hungry Minds Inc., 2001.

[Har03]   Harvard University. RSS 2.0 Specification. `http://cyber.law.
             harvard.edu/rss/rss.html`, July 2003.

[HBFV03]   Geert-Jan Houben, Peter Barna, Flavius Frasincar, and Richard Vdov-
             jak. Hera: Development of semantic web information systems. In
             Juan Manuel Cueva Lovelle, Bernardo Martin Gonzalez Rodriguez,
             Luis Joyanes Aguilar, Jose Emilio Labra Gayo, and Maria del Puerto
             Paule Ruiz, editors, *Proceedings of the 3rd International Conference on
             Web Engineering (ICWE 2003), Oviedo, Spain*, number 2722 in Lec-
             ture Notes in Computer Science, pages 529–538. Springer Verlag, July
             2003.

[HBvR94]   Lynda Hardman, Dick C. A. Bulterman, and Guido van Rossum. The
             amsterdam hypermedia model: adding time and context to the dexter
             model. *Communications of the ACM*, 37(2):50–62, 1994.

[HCH⁺08]   Jinpeng Huai, Robin Chen, Hsiao-Wuen Hon, Yunhao Liu, Wei-Ying
             Ma, Andrew Tomkins, and Xiaodong Zhang, editors. *Proceeding of
             the 17th international conference on World Wide Web (WWW 2008)*,
             Beijing, China, New York, NY, USA, April 2008. ACM.

[Her98]   American Heritage. The american heritage dictionary. Houghton Mif-
             flin, Boston, MA, 1998.

[HH04]   Geert Hofstede and Gert Jan Hofstede. *Cultures and Organizations:
             Software of the Mind (second edition)*. McGraw-Hill, New York, 2004.

[HK00]   Rolf Hennicker and Nora Koch. A UML-based methodology for hyper-
             media design. In Andy Evans, Stuart Kent, and Bran Selic, editors,
             *Proceedings of The 3rd International Conference on the Unified Model-
             ing Language: Advancing the Standard (UML2000), York, UK*, volume
             1939 of *Lecture Notes in Computer Science*, pages 410–424. Springer,
             October 2000.

[HM06]   Jianhua Hao and Emilia Mendes. Usage-based Statistical Testing of
             Web Applications. In David Wolber, Neil Calder, Christopher H.
             Brooks, and Athula Ginige, editors, *Proceedings of the 6th Interna-
             tional Conference on Web Engineering (ICWE 2006), Palo Alto, Cal-
             ifornia, USA*, pages 17–24. ACM, July 2006.

[How07]   Rick Hower. Web Site Test Tools and Site Management Tools. `http:
             //www.softwareqatest.com/qatweb1.html`, 2007.

[HS94]   Frank G. Halasz and Meyer Schwartz. The Dexter Hypertext Reference
             Model. *Comunications of the ACM*, 37(2):30–39, February 1994.

[HTT07]   HTTPUnit. `http://httpunit.sourceforge.net/`, 2007.

[Hul04]   Larry Hull. Accessibility: it's not just for disabilities any more. *ACM
             Interactions*, 11(2):36–41, 2004.

[Hum89]   Watts S. Humphrey. *Managing the Software Process*. Addison-Wesley,
             1989.

[Hyv02]   Eero Hyvonen. *Semantic Web kick-off in Finland - Vision, technolo-gies, research, and applications*, volume 2002-001 of *HIIT Publications*. Helsinki Institute for Information Technology, 2002.

[IH01]   Melody Y. Ivory and Marti A. Hearst. The State of the Art in Au-tomating Usability Evaluation of User Interfaces. *ACM Computing Surveys*, 33(4):470–516, 2001.

[IPW⁺95]   Carnegie Mellon Univ. Software Engineering Inst., Mark C. Paulk, Charles V. Weber, Bill Curtis, and Mary Beth Chrissis. *The Capa-bility Maturity Model: Guidelines for Improving the Software Process*. Addison-Wesley, 1995.

[ISB95]   Tomás Isakowitz, Edward A. Stohr, and P. Balasubramanian. RMM: A methodology for structured hypermedia design. *Communications of the ACM*, 38(8):34–44, 1995.

[ISO86]   ISO. *ISO 8402:1994. Quality Management and Quality Assurance - Vocabulary*, 1986.

[ISO01]   ISO/IEC. *ISO/IEC 9126-1 Software Engineering. Product Quality - Part 1: Quality model*, 2001.

[ISO02a]   ISO/IEC. *ISO/IEC 9126-2 Software Engineering. Product Quality - Part 2: External metrics*, 2002.

[ISO02b]   ISO/IEC. *ISO/IEC 9126-3 Software Engineering. Product Quality - Part 3: Internal metrics*, 2002.

[ISO02c]   ISO/IEC. *ISO/IEC 9126-4 Software Engineering. Product Quality - Part 4: Quality in use*, 2002.

[JBC⁺07]   Eric Jendrock, Jennifer Ball, Debbie Carson, Ian Evans, Scott Fordin, and Kim Haase. The Java EE 5 Tutorial. Technical report, Sun Mi-crosystems, 2007. http://java.sun.com/javaee/5/docs/tutorial/doc/.

[JBR99]   Ivar Jacobson, Grady Booch, and James Rumbaugh. *The Unified Soft-ware Development Process*. Addison Wesley, 1999.

[JD92]   Robin Jeffries and Heather Desurvire. Usability Testing vs. Heuristic Evaluation: Was There a Contest? *ACM SIGCHI Bulletin*, 24(4):39–41, 1992.

[JDW01]   Yuhui Jin, Stefan Decker, and Gio Wiederhold. OntoWebber: Model-Driven Ontology-Based Web Site Management. In *Proceedings of the 1st International Semantic Web Working Symposium (SWWS'01), Stanford University, California, USA*. Springer Verlag, jul/aug 2001.

[JE07]   Diane Jordan and John Evdemon. Web Services Business Pro-cess Execution Language Version 2.0. Oasis standard, OASIS, April 2007. http://docs.oasis-open.org/wsbpel/2.0/OS/wsbpel-v2.0-OS.html.

[JGJ97]   Ivar Jacobson, Martin Griss, and Patrik Jonsson. *Software Reuse: Architecture, Process and Organization for Business Success*. ACM Press, 1997.

[JMWU91]   Robin Jeffries, James R. Miller, Cathleen Wharton, and Kathy Uyeda. User Interface Evaluation in the Real World: A Comparison of Four Techniques. In *Proceedings of the SIGCHI conference on Human Fac-tors in Computing Systems (CHI'91), New Orleans, Louisiana, USA*, pages 119–124, New York, NY, USA, 1991. ACM Press.

[JSR02]   Mark D. Jacyntho, Daniel Schwabe, and Gustavo Rossi. A software architecture for structuring complex web applications. *Journal of Web Engineering*, 1(1):37–60, 2002.

[KBHM00]   Nora Koch, Hubert Baumeister, Rolf Hennicker, and Luis Mandel. Extending UML for modeling navigation and presentation in web applications. In Geri Winters and Jason Winters, editors, *Proceedings of Modeling Web Applications in the UML Workshop at UML 2000 conference, York, UK*, October 2000.

[KBR⁺04]   Nickolas Kavantzas, David Burdett, Gregory Ritzinger, Tony Fletcher, and Yves Lafon. Web Services Choreography Description Language Version 1.0. W3C Working Draft, W3C, December 2004. http://www.w3.org/TR/ws-cdl-10/.

[KCHN90]   Kyo C. Kang, Sholom G. Cohen, James A. Hess, and William E. Novak. Feature-oriented domain analysis (foda) feasibility study. Technical Report CMU/SEI-90-TR-21, ESD-90-TR-222, Software Engineering Institute, Carnegie Mellon University, Pittsburgh, Pennsylvania 15213, 1990.

[KGT04]   Vera Kartseva, Jaap Gordijn, and Yao-Hua Tan. Analysing preventative and detective control mechanisms in international trade using value modelling. In Marijn Janssen, Henk G. Sol, and René W. Wagenaar, editors, *Proceedings of the 6th International Conference on Electronic Commerce (ICEC 2004), Delft, The Netherlands*, volume 60 of *ACM International Conference Proceeding Series*, pages 51–58. ACM, October 2004.

[KKH01]   Nora Koch, Andreas Kraus, and Rolf Hennicker. The Authoring Process of the UML-based Web Engineering Approach. In Daniel Schwabe, editor, *First International Workshop on Web-oriented Software Technology (IWWOST'01), Valencia, Spain*, 2001.

[KKZ05]   Alexander Knapp, Nora Koch, and Gefei Zhang. Modelling the behaviour of web applications with argouwe. In David Lowe and Martin Gaedke, editors, *Proceedings of the 5th International Conference on Web Engineering (ICWE 2005), Sydney, Australia*, volume 3579 of *Lecture Notes in Computer Science*, pages 624–626. Springer, 2005.

[KKZB07]   Nora Koch, Alexander Knapp, Gefei Zhang, and Hubert Baumeister. *Web Engineering: Modelling and Implementing Web Applications*, chapter UML-Based Web Engineering, An Approach Based on Standards, pages 157–192. Human-Computer Interaction Series. Springer Verlag, 2007.

[KKZH04]   Alexander Knapp, Nora Koch, Gefei Zhang, and Hanns-Martin Hassler. Modeling business processes in web applications with argouwe. In Thomas Baar, Alfred Strohmeier, Ana M. D. Moreira, and Stephen J. Mellor, editors, *Proceedings of the 7th International Conference on the Unified Modelling Language: Modelling Languages and Applications (UML 2004), Lisbon, Portugal*, volume 3273 of *Lecture Notes in Computer Science*, pages 69–83. Springer, October 2004.

[Koc98]   Nora Koch. Towards a methodology for adaptive hypermedia systems development. In Timm and Marc Rssel, editors, *Proceedings of Workshop Adaptivitat und Benutzermodellierung in interaktiven Softwaresystemen (ABIS-98)*, October 1998.

[Koc06]   Nora Koch. Transformation techniques in the model-driven development process of uwe. In Luis Olsina Nora Koch, editor, *Workshop Proceedings of the 6th International Conference on Web Engineering, Palo Alto, USA*, volume 155 of *ACM International Conference Proceeding Series*, page 3. ACM, 2006.

[Koc07]   Nora Koch. Classification of model transformation techniques used in uml-based web engineering. *Software, IET*, 1(3):98–111, 2007.

[KPRR03]   Gerti Kappel, Birgit Prll, Siegfried Reich, and Werner Retschitzegger. *Web Engineering: Systematic Development of Web Applications*. dpunkt.verlag, 2003.

[KR97]   Laurie Kantner and Stephanie Rosenbaum. Usability Studies of WWW Sites: Heuristic Evaluation vs. Laboratory Testing. In *Proceedings of the 15th Annual International Conference on Computer Documentation (SIGDOC'97), Salt Lake City, Utah, USA*, pages 153–160, New York, NY, USA, 1997. ACM Press.

[Lar03]   Craig Larman. *Agile and Iterative Development. A Manager's Guide*. Addison-Wesley, 2003.

[Lau01]   Simon. St. Laurent. *XML: A Primer*. Hungry Minds Inc., 2001.

[LBW99]   David B. Lowe, Andrew J. Bucknell, and Richard G. Webby. Improving hypermedia development: a reference model-based process assessment method. In *Proceedings of the ACM International Conference on Hypertext and Hypermedia (Hypertext '99), Darmstadt, Germany*, pages 139–146. ACM, February 1999.

[LC02]   Grant Larsen and Jim Conallen. Engineering web-based systems with uml assets. *Annals of Software Engineering*, 13(1–4):203–230, June 2002.

[LF06]   Gisueppe A. Di Lucca and Anna R. Fasolino. Web application testing. In Mendes and Mosley [MM06], chapter 7, pages 219–260.

[LH07]   Ora Lassila and James Hendler. Embracing "Web 3.0". *IEEE Internet Computing*, 11(3):90–93, may/jun 2007.

[LKHH01]   Chien-Hung Liu, David Chenho Kung, Pei Hsia, and Chih-Tung Hsu. An Object-based Data Flow Testing Approach for Web Applications. *International Journal of Software Engineering and Knowledge Engineering*, 11(2):157–179, 2001.

[LLY99]   Heeseok Lee, Choongseok Lee, and Cheonsoo Yoo. A scenario-based object-oriented hypermedia design methodology. *Information and Management*, 36(3):121–138, September 1999.

[LMM04]   Pier Luca Lanzi, Maristella Matera, and Andrea Maurino. A Framework for Exploiting Conceptual Modeling in the Evaluation of Web Application Quality. In Nora Koch, Piero Fraternali, and Martin Wirsing, editors, *Proceedings of the 4th International Conference on Web Engineering (ICWE 2004), Munich, Germany*, volume 3140 of *Lecture Notes in Computer Science*, pages 50–54. Springer, July 2004.

[Low03a]   David Lowe. Emergent knowledge in web development. In Aybke Aurum, Ross Jeffery, Claes Wohlin, and Meliha Handzic, editors, *Managing Software Engineering Knowledge*, pages 157–176. Springer, Berlin, Germany, 2003.

[Low03b]   David Lowe. Web System Requirements: an Overview. *Requirement Engineering*, 8(2):102–113, 2003.

[LS03]   Fernanda Lima and Daniel Schwabe. Application modeling for the
            semantic web. In *Proceedings of 1st Latin American Web Congress
            (LA-Web 2003), Santiago, Chile*, pages 93–102. IEEE Computer Soci-
            ety, November 2003.

[MA98]   Daniel Menasce and Virgilio A. F. Almeida. *Capacity Planning for Web
            Performance: Metrics, Models, and Methods*. Prentice Hall, 1998.

[MA02]   Dirk Muthig and Colin Atkinson. Model-driven product line architec-
            tures. In Gary J. Chastek, editor, *Proceedings of 2nd International
            Conference on Software Product Lines (SPLC 2), San Diego, USA*,
            volume 2379 of *Lecture Notes in Computer Science*, pages 110–129.
            Springer, August 2002.

[Mad99]   K.H. Madsen. Special Issue on "The Diversity of Usability Practices".
            Communication of ACM, 42(5), 1999.

[MB94]   Deborah J. Mayhew and Randolph G. Bias, editors. *Cost-Justifying
            Usability*. Academic Press, Boston, MA, USA, 1994.

[MB02]   Stephen J. Mellor and Marc J. Balcer, editors. *Executable UML: A
            Foundation for Model-Driven Architecture*. Addison-Wesley Profes-
            sional, 2002.

[MB04]   Aaron Marcus and Valentina-Johanna Baumgartner. A practical set of
            culture dimensions for global user-interface development. In Masood
            Masoodian, Steve Jones, and Bill Rogers, editors, *Proceedings of the
            6th Asia Pacific Conference on Computer Human Interaction (APCHI
            2004), Rotorua, New Zealand*, Lecture Notes in Computer Science,
            pages 252–261. Springer, 2004.

[MBC⁺05]   Ioana Manolescu, Marco Brambilla, Stefano Ceri, Sara Comai, and
            Piero Fraternali. Model-Driven Design and Deployment of Service-
            Enabled Web Applications. *ACM TOIT*, 5(3):In print, August 2005.

[MBST04]   Glenford J. Myers, Tom Badgett, Corey Sandler, and Todd M.
            Thomas. *The Art of Software Testing (second edition)*. John Wiley &
            Sons, New York, 2004.

[MCF03]   Stephen J. Mellor, Anthony N. Clark, and Takao Futagami. Guest
            editors' introduction: Model-driven development. *IEEE Software*,
            20(5):14–18, 2003.

[MCGP02]   Maristella Matera, Maria Francesca Costabile, Franca Garzotto, and
            Paolo Paolini. Sue inspection: an effective method for systematic us-
            ability evaluation of hypermedia. *IEEE Transactions on Systems, Man,
            and Cybernetics, Part A*, 32(1):93–103, 2002.

[MCMO79]   Desmond Morris, Peter Collett, Peter Marsh, and Marie
            O'Shaughnessy. *Gestures, their origins and distribution*. Jonathan
            Cape, 1979.

[MD01]   San Murugesan and Yogesh Deshpande, editors. *Web Engineering
            2000*, number 2016 in Lecture Notes in Computer Science. Springer,
            2001.

[Mer06]   Duane Merrill.   Mashups: The new breed of Web app.
            http://www-128.ibm.com/developerworks/library/x-mashups.
            html?ca=dgr-lnxw16MashupChallenges, August 2006.

[MESP02]   Alicia Martínez, Hugo Estrada, Juan Sánchez, and Oscar Pastor. From
            early requirements to user interface prototyping: A methodological ap-
            proach. In *Proceedings of the 17th IEEE International Conference*

on Automated Software Engineering (ASE 2002), Edinburgh, Scotland, UK, pages 257–260. IEEE Computer Society, September 2002.

[MFM02]   David Mérida, Ramón Fabregat, and José L. Marzo. Shaad: Adaptable, adaptive and dynamic hypermedia system for content delivery. In Proceedings of the Workshop on Adaptive Systems for Web Based Education (WASWE2002), Malaga, Spain, May 2002.

[MG00]   Aaron Marcus and Emilie Gould. Crosscurrents: Cultural dimensions and global web user-interface. ACM Interactions, 2(4):32–46, 2000.

[MG06]   Santiago Meliá and Jaime Gómez. The websa approach: Applying model driven engineering to web applications. Journal of Web Engineering, 5(2):121–149, 2006.

[MGPD08]   Santiago Meliá, Jaime Gómez, Sandy Pérez, and Oscar Díaz. A model-driven development for gwt-based rich internet applications with ooh4ria. In Daniel Schwabe, Francisco Curbera, and Paul Dantzig, editors, Proceedings of the 8th International Conference on Web Engineering (ICWE 2008), Yorktown Heights, New York, USA, pages 13–23. IEEE, July 2008.

[Mic07]   Microsoft Co. MS Web Application Stress Tutorial. http://www.microsoft.com/downloads/details.aspx?familyid=e2c0585a-062a-439e-a67d-75a89aa36495&displaylang=en, 2007.

[Mic09a]   Sun Microsystems. Java Server Pages Technology, January 2009. http://java.sun.com/products/jsp/index.html.

[Mic09b]   Sun Microsystems. Java Servlet Technology, January 2009. http://java.sun.com/products/servlet/index.html.

[MKK05]   Santiago Meliá, Andreas Kraus, and Nora Koch. Mda transformations applied to web application development. In David Lowe and Martin Gaedke, editors, Proceedings of the 5th International Conference on Web Engineering (ICWE 2005), Sydney, Australia, volume 3579 of Lecture Notes in Computer Science, pages 465–471, 2005.

[MLME04]   Rosa Meo, Pier Luca Lanzi, Maristella Matera, and Roberto Esposito. Integrating Web Conceptual Modeling and Web Usage Mining. In Bamshad Mobasher, Olfa Nasraoui, Bing Liu, and Brij M. Masand, editors, Advances in Web Mining and Web Usage Analysis - Proceedings of the 6th International Workshop on Knowledge Discovery on the Web (WebKDD 2004), Revised Selected Papers, Seattle, WA, USA, volume 3932 of Lecture Notes in Computer Science, pages 135–148. Springer, August 2004.

[MM03]   J. Miller and J. Mukerji. MDA Guide Version 1..0.1. Technical report, Object Management Group (OMG), June 2003.

[MM06]   Emilia Mendes and Nile Mosley, editors. Web Engineering. Springer, 2006.

[MRC06]   Maristella Matera, Francesca Rizzo, and Giovanni Toffetti Carughi. Web usability: Principles and evaluation methods. In Mendes and Mosley [MM06], chapter 5, pages 143–180.

[MS01]   Donny Mack and Doug Seven. Programming Data Driven Web Applications with ASP.NET. Sams, 2001.

[MS04]   David Martin and Ian Sommerville. Patterns of cooperative interaction: Linking ethnomethodology and design. ACM Transactions on Computer-Human Interacteraction, 11(1):59–89, 2004.

[NeC00]   Nuno Jardim Nunes and João Falcão e Cunha. Towards a uml profile for interaction design: the wisdom approach. In Andy Evans, Stuart Kent, and Bran Selic, editors, *UML 2000: 3rd International Conference on the Unified Modeling Language: Advancing the Standard, York, UK*, volume 1939 of *Lecture Notes in Computer Science*, pages 101–116. Springer, October 2000.

[Nel]   Theodor Holm Nelson. Xanalogical Structure, Needed Now More than Ever: Parallel Documents, Deep Links to Content, Deep Versioning and Deep Re-Use . Available at: http://www.sfc.keio.ac.jp/ ted/XUsurvey/xuDation.html. Accessed on March 1, 2002.

[Net09]   Netcraft Ltd. February 2009 Web Server Survey. `http://news.netcraft.com/archives/2009/02/18/february_2009_web_server_survey.html`, February 2009.

[Nie93]   Jakob Nielsen. *Usability Engineering*. Academic Press, 1993.

[Nie94]   Jakob Nielsen. Guerrilla HCI: Using Discount Usability Engineering to Penetrate the Intimidation Barrier. In *Cost-justifying usability*, pages 245–272. Academic Press, Inc., Orlando, FL, USA, 1994.

[Nie95]   Jakob Nielsen. *Multimedia and Hypertext: Internet and Beyond*. Academic Press, London, 1995.

[Nie00]   Jakob Nielsen. *Web Usability*. New Riders, 2000.

[Nie02]   Jakob Nielsen. The Usability Engineering Lifecycle. *IEEE Computer*, 25(3):12–22, 2002.

[NL93]   Jakob Nielsen and Thomas K. Landauer. A Mathematical Model of the Finding of Usability Problems. In *Proceedings of the ACM International Conference on Human Factors in Computing Systems (INTER-CHI'93), Amsterdam, The Netherlands*, pages 296–213. ACM Press, apr 1993.

[NM90]   Jakob Nielsen and Rolf Molich. Heuristic evaluation of user interface. In *Proceedings of the ACM International Conference on Human Factors in Computing Systems (INTERCHI'90), Seattle, USA*, pages 249–256. ACM Press, apr 1990.

[NM94]   Jakob Nielsen and Robert L. Mack, editors. *Usability Inspection Methods*. Wiley and Sons, New York, 1994.

[NN95]   Jocelyne Nanard and Marc Nanard. Hypertext design environments and the hypertext design process. *Communications of the ACM*, 38(8):49–56, August 1995.

[NN99]   Jocelyne Nanard and Marc Nanard. Toward an hypermedia design patterns space. In *Proceedings of 2nd Workshop in Hypermedia Development: Design Patterns in Hypermedia, Darmstadt, Germany*, February 1999.

[NOP+06]   Christian Monrad Nielsen, Michael Overgaard, Michael Bach Pedersen, Jan Stage, and Sigge Stenild. Exploring interaction space as abstraction mechanism for task-based user interface design. In Karin Coninx, Kris Luyten, and Kevin A. Schneider, editors, *Proceedings of Task Models and Diagrams for Users Interface Design, 5th International Workshop, (TAMODIA 2006), Hasselt, Belgium*, volume 4385 of *Lecture Notes in Computer Science*, pages 202–216. Springer, October 2006.

[NS05]   M. Nottingham and R. Sayre. The Atom Syndication Format. http://
            www.ietf.org/rfc/rfc4287.txt, December 2005. Network Working
            Group RFC 4287.

[NS06]   Demetrius Arraes Nunes and Daniel Schwabe. Rapid prototyping
            of web applications combining domain specific languages and model
            driven design. In David Wolber, Neil Calder, Christopher H. Brooks,
            and Athula Ginige, editors, *Proceedings of the 6th International Con-*
            ference on Web Engineering (ICWE 2006), Palo Alto, USA, pages
            153–160. ACM, 2006.

[NSER02]   Nan Niu, Eleni Stroulia, and Mohammad El-Ramly. Understanding
            Web Usage for Dynamic Web-Site Adaptation: A Case Study. In *4th*
            International Workshop on Web Site Evolution (WSE 2002), Montreal,
            Canada, pages 53–62. IEEE Computer Society, October 2002.

[OCR06]   Luis Olsina, Guillermo Covella, and Gustavo Rossi. Web Quality. In
            Mendes and Mosley [MM06], chapter 4, pages 109–142.

[Off02]   Jef Offutt. Quality Attributes of Web Software Applications. *IEEE*
            Software, pages 25–32, mar/apr 2002.

[OHM+88]   William T. Olle, Jacques Hagelstein, Ian G. Macdonald, Colette Rol-
            land, Henk G. Sol, Frans J. M. Assche, and Alexander A. Verrijn-
            Stuart. *Information Systems Methodologies : A Framework for Under-*
            standing. Addison Wesley, 1988.

[OMG09]   OMG.   Business process modeling notation (bpmn) 1.2.
            http://www.omg.org/docs/formal/09-01-03.pdf,   January   2009.
            available at http://www.omg.org/docs/formal/09-01-03.pdf.

[O'R05]   Tim O'Reilly. What Is Web 2.0: Design Patterns and Business Models
            for the Next Generation of Software.   http://www.oreillynet.
            com/pub/a/oreilly/tim/news/2005/09/30/what-is-web-20.html,
            September 2005.

[Ove00]   Scott P. Overmyer. What's different about requirements engineering
            for web sites? *Requirements Engineering*, 5(1):62–65, 2000.

[Pap08]   Michael P. Papazoglou. *Web Services: Principles and Technology*.
            Pearson Education Limited, Harlow, UK, 2008.

[Pat00]   Fabio Paterno. *Model-Based Design and Evaluation of Interactive Ap-*
            plications. Springer-Verlag, 2000.

[PBvdL05]   Klaus Pohl, Gnter Bckle, and Frank J. van der Linden. *Software*
            Product Line Engineering Foundations, Principles and Techniques.
            Springer Verlag, 2005.

[PCCW93]   Mark C. Paulk, Bill Curtis, Mary Beth Chrissis, and Charles V. Weber.
            Capability Maturity Model, version 1.1. *IEEE Software*, 10:18–27, July
            1993.

[PCY+05]   Peter Plessers, Sven Casteleyn, Yeliz Yesilada, Olga De Troyer, Robert
            Stevens, Simon Harper, and Carole Goble. Accessibility: A web engi-
            neering approach. In Allan Ellis and Tatsuya Hagino, editors, *Pro-*
            ceedings of the fourteenth International World Wide Web Conference
            (WWW 2005), Chiba, Japan, pages 353–362, 2005.

[PE97]   Mike Perkowitz and Oren Etzioni. Adaptive web sites: an AI chal-
            lenge. In *Proceedings of the 15th International Joint Conference on*
            Artificial Intelligence, Nagoya, Japan, volume 1, pages 16–23. Morgan
            Kaufmann, 1997.

[PGIP01]   Oscar Pastor, Jaime Gómez, Emilio Insfrán, and Vicente Pelechano. The OO-Method Approach for Information Systems Modeling: from Object-Oriented Conceptual Modeling to Automated Programming. *Information Systems*, 26(7):507–534, 2001.

[PJC98]   Thomas A. Powell, David L. Jones, and Dominique C. Cutts. *Web Site Engineering: Beyond Web Page Design*. Prentice Hall, 1998.

[PKZ01]   John R. Punin, Mukkai S. Krishnamoorthy, and Mohammed Javeed Zaki. LOGML: Log Markup Language for Web Usage Mining. In Ron Kohavi, Brij M. Masand, Myra Spiliopoulou, and Jaideep Srivastava, editors, *3rd International Workshop on Mining Web Log Data Across All Customers Touch Points (WEBKDD 2001), Revised Papers, San Francisco, CA, USA*, volume 2356 of *Lecture Notes in Computer Science*, pages 88–112. Springer, August 2001.

[PMM97]   Fabio Paterno, Cristiano Mancini, and Silvia Meniconi:. Engineering task models. In *Proceedings of the 3rd IEEE International Conference on Engineering of Complex Computer Systems (ICECCS'97), Como, Italy*, page 69, Washington, DC, USA, 1997. IEEE Computer Society.

[Pre05]   Roger S. Pressman. *Software Engineering: a practitioner's approach - 6th ed.* McGraw-Hill, 2005.

[PRS+94]   Jennifer Preece, Yvonne Rogers, Helen Sharp, David Benyon, Simon Holland, and Tom Carey, editors. *Human-Computer Interaction: Concepts and Design*. Addison Wesley, 1994.

[PS07]   Eric Prud'hommeaux and Andy Seaborne. SPARQL Query Language for RDF. W3C Candidate Recommendation, W3C, June 2007. http://www.w3.org/TR/rdf-sparql-query/.

[PTdOM98]   Fabiano Borges Paulo, Marcelo Augusto Santos Turine, Maria Cristina Ferreira de Oliviera, and Paulo Cesar Maseiro. Xhmbs: A formal model to support hypermedia specification. In *Proceedings of the 9th ACM Conference on Hypertext and Hypermedia: Links, Objects, Time and Space—Structure in Hypermedia Systems (Hypertext 98), Pittsburg, USA*, pages 161–170, June 1998.

[PTMC+08]   Juan Carlos Preciado, Marino Linaje Trigueros, Rober Morales-Chaparro, Fernando Sánchez-Figueroa, Gefei Zhang, Christian Kroiss, and Nora Koch. Designing rich internet applications combining uwe and rux-method. In Daniel Schwabe, Francisco Curbera, and Paul Dantzig, editors, *Proceedings of the 8th International Conference on Web Engineering (ICWE 2008), Yorktown Heights, New York, USA*, pages 148–154. IEEE, July 2008.

[Rag97]   Dave Raggett. HTML 3.2 Reference Specification. W3c recommendation, W3C, January 1997. http://www.w3.org/TR/REC-html32.html.

[Rag98]   Dave Raggett. Adding a Touch of Style, August 1998. http://www.w3.org/MarkUp/Guide/style.html.

[Rat09]   RationalRobot. http://www-306.ibm.com/software/awdtools/tester/robot/, 2009.

[RDF07]   RDF Core Working Group. Resource Description Framework (RDF). Technical report, W3C, 2007. http://www.w3.org/RDF/.

[Reg05]   Bob Regan. Best Practices for Accessible Flash Design. Technical report, Macromedia Inc., August 2005. http://www.adobe.com/resources/accessibility/best_practices/bp_fp.html.

[RHJ99]   Dave Raggett, Arnaud Le Hors, and Ian Jacobs. HTML 4.1 Specification. W3c recommendation, W3C, December 1999. http://www.w3.
org/TR/REC-html40/.

[Rol98]   Colette Rolland. A comprehensive view of process engineering. In Bar-
bara Pernici and Costantino Thanos, editors, *Proceedings of the 10th
International Conference on Advanced Information Systems Engineering (CAiSE'98), Pisa, Italy*, volume 1413 of *Lecture Notes in Computer
Science*, pages 1–24. Springer, June 1998.

[Roy87]   Winston W. Royce. Managing the development of large software systems: concepts and techniques. In *Proceedings of the 9th international conference on Software Engineering (ICSE'87), Los Alamitos,
CA, USA*, pages 328–338. IEEE Computer Society Press, 1987.

[RPSO08]   Gustavo Rossi, Oscar Pastor, Daniel Schwabe, and Luis Olsina. *Web
Engineering: Modelling and Implementing Web Applications*. Human-
Computer Interaction Series. Springer, 2008.

[RT01]   Filippo Ricca and Paolo Tonella. Analysis and Testing of Web Applications. In *Proceedings of the 23rd International Conference on
Software Engineering (ICSE 2001), Toronto, Ontario, Canada*, pages
25–34. IEEE Computer Society, May 2001.

[RT05]   Filippo Ricca and Paolo Tonella. Web Testing: a Roadmap for the
Empirical Research. In *7th IEEE International Workshop on Web
Site Evolution (WSE 2005), Budapest, Hungary*, pages 63–70. IEEE
Computer Society, September 2005.

[RT06]   Filippo Ricca and Paolo Tonella. Detecting Anomaly and Failure in
Web Applications. *IEEE MultiMedia*, 13(2):44–51, 2006.

[SCD08]   Daniel Schwabe, Francisco Curbera, and Paul Dantzig, editors. *Proceedings of 8th International Conference Web Engineering (ICWE
2008), Yorktown Heights, New York, USA*. IEE Computer Society, July
2008.

[SCDT00]   Jaideep Srivastava, Robert Cooley, Mukund Deshpande, and Pang-
Ning Tan. Web Usage Mining: Discovery and Applications of Usage
Patterns from Web Data. *SIGKDD Explorations*, 1(2):12–23, 2000.

[Sch]   W3 Schools. HTML tutorial. http://www.w3schools.com/html/
default.asp.

[SdAPM99]   Daniel Schwabe, Rita de Almeida Pontes, and Isabela Moura.
OOHDM-Web: An environment for implementation of hypermedia applications in the WWW. *SIGWEB Newsletter*, 8(2), June 1999.

[SF89]   P. David Stotts and Richard Furuta. Petri-net-based hypertext: Document structure with browsing semantics. *ACM Transactions on Information Systems*, 7(1):3–29, January 1989.

[SG00]   Harry M. Sneed and Siegfried Göschl. Testing software for Internet
Applications. *Software Focus*, 1(1):15–22, 2000.

[Sha06]   Victoria Shannon. A 'more revolutionary' Web. *International Herald
Tribune*, May 24 2006.

[Shn93]   Ben Shneiderman. *Designing the User Interface: Strategies for Effective Human-Computer Interaction (fourth edition)*. Addison Wesley,
Reading, MA, USA, 1993.

[Shn00]   Ben Shneiderman. Universal Usability. *Communication of ACM*,
43(5):84–91, 2000.

[SJH⁺03]   Kim Sungwoo, Kim Mi Jeong, Choo Heejeong, Kim Sang-Hwan, and
            Kang Hyun Joo. Cultural Issues in Handheld Usability: Are Cultural
            Models Effective for Interpreting Unique Use Patterns of Korean Mo-
            bile Phone Users? In *Usability Professionals' Association Conference*,
            2003.

[Som96]   Ian Sommerville. Software Process Models. *ACM Computing Surveys*,
            28(1):269–271, 1996.

[Som04]   Ian Sommerville. *Software Engineering, 7th Edition*. Addison-Wesley,
            2004.

[SR95]   Daniel Schwabe and Gustavo Rossi. The object-oriented hypermedia
            design model. *Communications of the ACM*, 38(8):45–46, August 1995.

[SR98]   Daniel Schwabe and Gustavo Rossi. An object-oriented approach to
            web-based application design. *Theory and Practise of Object Systems
            (TAPOS), Special Issue on the Internet*, 4(4):207–225, October 1998.

[SRB96]   Daniel Schwabe, Gustavo Rossi, and Simone Diniz Junqueira Barbosa.
            Systematic hypermedia application design with oohdm. In *Proceeding
            of The 7th ACM Conference on Hypertext (Hypertext '96), Washington
            DC, USA*, pages 116–128. ACM, March 1996.

[SRS00]   Luiz Fernando G. Soares, Rogrio F. Rodrigues, and Dbora
            C. Muchaluat Saade. Modeling, authoring and formatting hyperme-
            dia documents in the HyperProp system. *ACM Multimedia System
            Journal*, 8(2):118–134, March 2000.

[STA96]   Unisys STARS. Software technology for adaptable reliable systems. or-
            ganization domain modeling (ODM) guidebook, version 2.0. Technical
            Report STARS-VC-A025/001/00, Unisys STARS, 1996.

[TC92]   W. Tracz and L. Coglianese. Domian-specific software architecture
            engineering process guidelines. Technical Report ADAGE-IBM-92-02,
            Loral Federal Systems, 1992.

[TC03]   Olga De Troyer and Sven Casteleyn. Modeling complex processes for
            web applications using wsdm. In Daniel Schwabe, Oscar Pastor, Gus-
            tavo Rossi, and Luis Olsina, editors, *Proceedings of the 3rd Interna-
            tional Workshop on Web-Oriented Software Technologies (IWWOST
            2003), Malaga, Spain*, 2003.

[TC04]   Olga De Troyer and Sven Casteleyn. Designing localized web sites. In
            X. Zhou, S. Su, M.P. Papazoglou, M.E. Orlowska, and K.G. Jeffery,
            editors, *Proceedings of the 5th International Conference on Web Infor-
            mation Systems Engineering (WISE 2004), Brisbane, Australia*, pages
            547–558, 2004.

[TCP05]   Olga De Troyer, Sven Casteleyn, and Peter Plessers. Using orm to
            model web systems. In Robert Meersman, Zahir Tari, Pilar Herrero,
            Gonzalo Méndez, Lawrence Cavedon, David Martin, Annika Hinze,
            George Buchanan, María S. Pérez, Víctor Robles, Jan Humble, An-
            tonia Albani, Jan L. G. Dietz, Hervé Panetto, Monica Scannapieco,
            Terry A. Halpin, Peter Spyns, Johannes Maria Zaha, Esteban Zimányi,
            Emmanuel Stefanakis, Tharam S. Dillon, Ling Feng, Mustafa Jarrar,
            Jos Lehmann, Aldo de Moor, Erik Duval, and Lora Aroyo, editors,
            *On the Move to Meaningful Internet Systems 2005: OTM 2005 Work-
            shops, International Workshop on Object-Role Modeling (ORM 2005),
            Agia Napa, Cyprus*, pages 700–709, 2005.

338   References

[TD96]   Klaus Tochtermann and Gisbert Dittrich. The dortmund family of
           hypermedia models—concepts and their applications. *Journal of Uni-
           versal Computer Science*, 2(1):34–56, 1996.
[TD01]   Bernhard Thalheim and Antje Düsterhöft. SiteLang: Conceptual Mod-
           eling of Internet Sites. In *Proceedings of the 20th International Con-
           ference on Conceptual Modeling (ER'01), London, UK*, pages 179–192.
           Springer-Verlag, 2001.
[TF08]   Tetsuo Tamai and Xavier Franch, editors. *Proceedings of IEEE Inter-
           national Requirements Engineering Conference (RE 2008), Barcelona,
           Catalunya, Spain*. IEEE Computer Society, September 2008.
[THB+06]   Dave Thomas, David Hansson, Leon Breedt, Mike Clark, James Dun-
           can Davidson, Justin Gehtland, and Andreas Schwarz. *Agile Web De-
           velopment with Rails, 2nd Edition*. Pragmatic Bookshelf, 2006.
[The07]   TheWebRatio team. Advanced Features Tutorial - WebRatio 4.3.
           Technical report, Web Models S.r.l, November 2007.
[THT97]   Fons Trompenaars and Charles Hampden-Turner. *Riding the waves of
           culture, Understanding Diversity in Global Business (second edition)*.
           McGraw-Hill, 1997.
[TL98]   Olga De Troyer and Kees Leune. Wsdm: A user centered design method
           for web sites. *Computer Networks*, 30(1-7):85–94, 1998.
[TL03]   Rachatrin Tongrungrojana and David Lowe. Webml+: a web modeling
           language for forming a bridge between business modeling and informa-
           tion modeling. In *Proceedings of the Fifteenth International Conference
           on Software Engineering & Knowledge Engineering (SEKE'2003), San
           Francisco Bay, CA, USA*, pages 17–24, July 2003.
[Tof07]   Giovanni Toffetti Carughi. Modeling data-intensive Rich Internet Ap-
           plications with server push support. In *Workshop proceedings of the
           7th International Conference on Web Engineering (MDWE'07), Como,
           Italy*. Politecnico di Milano, July 2007.
[Tom89]   Frank WM. Tompa. A data model for flexible hypertext database sys-
           tems. *ACM Transactions on Information Systems*, 7(1):85–100, Jan-
           uary 1989.
[TPSF07]   Marino Linaje Trigueros, Juan Carlos Preciado, and Fernando
           Sánchez-Figueroa. Engineering rich internet application user inter-
           faces over legacy web models. *IEEE Internet Computing*, 11(6):53–59,
           2007.
[TR03]   Mary Frances Theofanos and Janice Redish. Bridging the Gap between
           Accessibility and Usability. *ACM Interactions*, 10(6):36–51, 2003.
[Ull88]   J. D. Ullman. *Principles of Database and Knowledge-Base Systems*.
           Computer Science Press, 1988.
[vdAvH02] Wil van der Aalst and Kees van Hee. *Workflow management: models,
           methods, and systems*. MIT Press, 2002.
[vdRGY05] Bas van der Raadt, Jaap Gordijn, and Eric Yu. Exploring web services
           from a business value perspective. In *Proceedings of 13th IEEE Inter-
           national Conference on Requirements Engineering (RE 2005), Paris,
           France*, pages 53–62. IEEE Computer Society, September 2005.
[VFHB03]   Richard Vdovjak, Flavius Frasincar, Geert-Jan Houben, and Peter
           Barna. Engineering Semantic Web Information Systems in Hera. *Jour-
           nal of Web Engineering*, 2(1-2):3–26, 2003.

[VH05]   Richard Vdovjak and Geert-Jan Houben. A model-driven approach
            for designing distributed web information systems. In *Proceedings of
            the 5th International Conference on Web Engineering (ICWE 2005),
            Sydney, Australia,* volume 3579 of *Lecture Notes in Computer Science.*
            Springer, July 2005.

[Vic97]   David A. Victor. *International Business Communication.* Prentice
            Hall, New York, 1997.

[Vir92]   Robert A. Virzi. Refining the Test Phase of Usability Evaluation:
            How Many Subjects Is Enough?. *ACM Transactions on Information
            Systems,* 34(34):457–468, 1992.

[VSdS00]   Patricia Vilain, Daniel Schwabe, and Clarisse Sieckenius de Souza. A
            diagrammatic tool for representing user interaction in uml. In Andy
            Evans, Stuart Kent, and Bran Selic, editors, *Proceedings of The 3rd
            International Conference on the Unified Modeling Language: Advanc-
            ing the Standard (UML2000), York, UK,* volume 1939 of *Lecture Notes
            in Computer Science,* pages 133–147. Springer, October 2000.

[W3Ca]   W3C Consortium. XML Query (XQuery). Technical report. http:
            //www.w3.org/XML/Query/.

[W3Cb]   W3C Consortium. XML Schema. Technical report. http://www.w3.
            org/XML/Schema.

[W3C98]   W3C Consortium. Extensible Style Language (XSL), 1998. http:
            //www.w3.org/TR/1998/WD-xsl.

[W3C09]   W3C. Document Object Model (DOM), March 2009. http://www.w3.
            org/DOM/.

[web07a]   Web Test Tools Directory. http://www.webtesttools.com, 2007.

[Web07b]   WebModels s.r.l. WebRatio Site Development Studio. http://www.
            webratio.com, 2007.

[Wit94]   James V. Withey. Implementing model based software engineer-
            ing in your organization: An approach to domain engineering, 1994.
            CMU/SEI-94-TR-01, see also http://www.sei.cmu.edu/mbse/index.
            html.

[Wit96]   James V. Withey. Investment analysis of software assets for product
            lines, 1996. CMU/SEI-96-TR-010.

[WL99]   David M. Weiss and Chi Tau Robert Lai. *Software Product-Line En-
            gineering: A Family-Based Software Development Process.* Addison
            Wesley, August 1999.

[Wri55]   Quincy Wright. *The Study of International Relations.* Appleton-
            Century-Crofts, New York, 1955.

[WRLP94]   Cathleen Wharton, John Rieman, Clayton Lewis, and Peter Polson.
            The Cognitive Walkthrough Method: A Practitioner's Guide. In
            Nielsen and Mack [NM94], chapter 5, pages 105–140.

[YB00]   Joonhee Yoo and Michael Bieber. Towards a relationship navigation
            analysis. In *Proceedings of 33rd Annual Hawaii International Confer-
            ence on System Sciences (HICSS'33), Maui, Hawaii.* IEEE Computer
            Society, January 2000.

[YBC+07]   Jin Yu, Boualem Benatallah, Fabio Casati, Florian Daniel, Maristella
            Matera, and Regis Saint-Paul. Mixup: a Development and Runtime
            Environment for Integration at the Presentation Layer. In *Proceedings
            of the 7th International Conference on Web Engineering (ICWE 2007),
            Como, Italy,* pages 479–484. Springer Verlag, July 2007.

[YBSP+07]   Jin Yu, Boualem Benatallah, Regis Saint-Paul, Fabio Casati, Florian Daniel, and Maristella Matera. A Framework for Rapid Integration of Presentation Components. In *Proceedings of the 16th International Conference on World Wide Web (WWW'07), Banff, Alberta, Canada*, pages 923–932. ACM Press, May 2007.

[Yes05]   Yeliz Yesilada. *Annotation and Transformation of Web Pages to Improve Mobility for Visually Impaired Users*. Ph.d. dissertation, The University of Manchester, 2005.

[YHGS04]   Yeliz Yesilada, Simon Harper, Carole A. Goble, and Robert Stevens. Screen readers cannot see: Ontology based semantic annotation for visually impaired web travellers. In Nora Koch, Piero Fraternali, and Martin Wirsing, editors, *Proceedings of the 4th International Conference on Web Engineering (ICWE 2004), Munich, Germany*, volume 3140 of *Lecture Notes in Computer Science*, pages 445–458, 2004.

[YSG03]   Yeliz Yesilada, Robert Stevens, and Carole A. Goble. A foundation for tool based mobility support for visually impaired web users. In *Proceedings of the 12th International World Wide Web Conference (WWW 2003), Budapest, Hungary*, pages 422–430, May 2003.

[Yu97]   Eric Yu. Towards modelling and reasoning support for early-phase requirements engineering. In *Proceedings of the 3rd IEEE International Symposium on Requirements Engineering (RE 1997), Annapolis, MD, USA*, pages 226–235. IEEE Press, January 1997.

Index

Nomenclature

ADO	Active Data Objects
ADRIA	Abstract Design of Rich Internet Applications
AJAX	Asynchronous JavaScript and XML
Ajax	Asynchronous JavaScript and XML
AMF	Action Message Format
APD	Abstract Presentation Diagram
ASL	Adaptation Specification Language
ATL	Atlas Transformation Language
B2B	Business to Business
B2C	Business to Consumer
BPMN	Business Process Modeling Notation
CAWE	Computer-Aided Web Engineering
CC/PP	Composite Capability/Preference Profile
CGI	Common Gateway Interface
CIM	Computational-independent Model
CLD	Composite Layout Diagram
CM	Conceptual Model
CRUD	Create, Read, Update, Delete
CSS	Cascading Style Sheets
DBI	DataBase Interface
DBMS	Database Management System
DOM	Document Object Model
DTD	Document Type Definition
e^3-value	Early Requirements Engineering Method for eCommerce Systems Focusing on Economic Value Exchange between Actors
ECA	Event-Condition-Action
GUI	Graphical User Interface
GWT	Google Web Toolkit
HPG	Hera Presentation Generator
HTML	HyperText Markup Language

HTTP	Hypertext Transfer Protocol
i*	Goals (Intentions) Modeling Requirements Engineering Method
i18n	Internationalization
IDEF	Integrated Definition Methods
IDEF0	IDEF - Function Modeling Method
IP	Internet Protocol
JDBC	Java Database Connectivity
JSP	JavaServer Pages
L10n	Localization
MDA	Model Driven Architecture
MOF	Meta Object Facility
NAD	Navigation Access Diagram
OCL	Object Constraint Language
ODBC	Open Database Connectivity
OLE	Object Linking and Embedding
OMG	Object Management Group
OOHDM	Object-Oriented Hypermedia Design Method
ORM	Object-Relational Mapping
ORM	Object-Role Modeling
OWL	Ontology Web Language
PDA	Personal Digital Assistant
PIM	Platform-independent Model
PM	Presentation Model
PSM	Platform-specific Model
QVT	Query/View/Transformation
RDF	Resource Description Format
REST	Representational State Transfer
RIA	Rich Internet Applications
RMM	Relationship Management Methodology
RNA	Relationship Navigation Analysis
SGML	Standard Generalized Markup Language
SHDM	Semantic Hypermedia Design Method
SOA	Service-Oriented Architecture
SOAP	Simple Object Access Protocol
TCP	Transmission Control Protocol
UDDI	Universal Description, Discovery and Integration
UI	User Interface
UML	Unified Modeling Language
UP	User Profile
URL	Uniform Resource Locator
UWE	UML-based Web Engineering
W3C	World Wide Web Consortium
WAP	Wireless Application Protocol
WCAG	Web Content Accessibility Guidelines

WebML	Web Modeling Language
WebML+	WebML Extended with Business Information Flow Analysis
WML	Wireless Markup Language
WSDL	Web Service Description Language
WSDM	Web Semantics Design Method
XML	Extensible Markup Language
XSD	XML Schema Definition
XSL	eXtensible Stylesheet Language
XSLT	Extensible Stylesheet Language Transformations